Catherine M. Dunn

9.00

D0820968

Paradise Lost
AND THE
GENESIS TRADITION

821.47
Ev15

Paradise Lost
AND THE
GENESIS TRADITION

❧

J. M. EVANS

WITHDRAWN

OXFORD
AT THE CLARENDON PRESS
1968

LIBRARY ST. MARY'S COLLEGE

Oxford University Press, Ely House, London W. 1

GLASGOW NEW YORK TORONTO MELBOURNE WELLINGTON
CAPE TOWN SALISBURY IBADAN NAIROBI LUSAKA ADDIS ABABA
BOMBAY CALCUTTA MADRAS KARACHI LAHORE DACCA
KUALA LUMPUR HONG KONG TOKYO

© OXFORD UNIVERSITY PRESS 1968

PRINTED IN GREAT BRITAIN

TO MY
MOTHER AND FATHER

ACKNOWLEDGEMENTS

THIS book is a revised version of a thesis submitted for the degree of Doctor of Philosophy at the University of Oxford in 1963. During the course of its preparation I incurred many obligations which, though I can never hope adequately to discharge them, I should like to acknowledge. The nature of my subject inevitably involved me in a considerable amount of work beyond the scope of my immediate academic training, and this part of my research would have been all but impossible without the very generous assistance I received from scholars in fields other than my own. In particular, I owe a deep debt of gratitude to Professor David Daube and Professor Henry Chadwick, who guided me through the rabbinic and patristic writings on the Fall; to Professor R. C. Zaehner, who advised me on the Gnostic and Manichaean interpretations of the story; to Mr. Colin Hardie, Mr. Peter Llewellyn, Dr. Barri Jones, Dr. John Percival, Mr. Albert Schachter, Mr. B. W. T. Williams, Mr. Harry Lewis, Mr. J. Durden-Smith, and Mr. Peter Hughes who all made many helpful contributions to, and corrections of, my translations of Latin sources; and to Miss Beryl Smalley, who advised me on the medieval exegesis of the story. Any errors that remain in these early chapters are not there for want of their vigilance.

No less generous was the help and advice I was given by scholars of the English Faculty. Miss Celia Sisam, Professor Nevill Coghill, and Professor Norman Davis gave unstintingly of their time and attention to read and criticize various sections of my drafts for the last seven chapters; while Dr. George Rigg spent many hours subsidizing my depleted funds of medieval Latin and Old English. My greatest single debt, however, is to my former supervisor, Dr. Helen Gardner, whose wide learning and unfailing kindness were a constant source of stimulation and encouragement. To have been a student of hers is to be aware that scholarship and criticism are complementary rather than competing disciplines.

Since leaving Oxford I have enjoyed the additional benefit of the advice of my colleagues in the English Department at Stanford University, California. Dr. V. A. Kolve, Dr. Ronald A. Rebholz,

Professor Lawrence V. Ryan, and Professor George A. Sensabaugh have contributed many constructive suggestions which I have incorporated in the course of my revision, and Dr. Murray Roston very kindly read and commented on several chapters while he was a Visiting Professor at Stanford. Professor Merrit Y. Hughes and Professor Frederick J. Cassidy of Wisconsin University rectified several omissions in my bibliography.

Finally, I should like to record my gratitude to Mr. J. B. Bamborough for permission to use in Chapter V material which had appeared in an earlier form in my article 'Genesis B and its Background', *R.E.S.*, N.S. xiv (1963), 1–16, 113–23; to the Warden and Fellows of Merton College, Oxford, where my final two years of doctoral research were supported by a Harmsworth Scholarship; to Stanford University, in particular to Professor Thomas C. Moser and Professor Virgil K. Whitaker, who made available the time and the money to pursue this study to a conclusion; and to my wife, co-partner in this pleasant labour 'which were it toilsom, yet with thee were sweet'.

J. M. EVANS

Stanford University
1967

CONTENTS

PART THREE

Paradise Lost *and the Tradition*

ABBREVIATIONS

JEWISH SOURCES

Ab. Z.	*'Abodah Zarah (B.T.).*
Apoc. Mos.	*Apocalypsis Mosis.*
A.R.N.	*Aboth of Rabbi Nathan.*
B.B.	*Baba Bathra (B.T.).*
Ber.	*Berakoth (B.T.).*
B.T.	*Babylonian Talmud.*
De Op. Mun.	*De Opificio Mundi* (Philo).
Deut. Rab.	*Deuteronomy Rabba (M.R.).*
Ecc. Rab.	*Ecclesiastes Rabba (M.R.).*
Er.	*'Erubin (B.T.).*
Es. Rab.	*Esther Rabba (M.R.).*
Ex. Rab.	*Exodus Rabba (M.R.).*
Gen. Rab.	*Genesis Rabba (M.R.).*
Hag.	*Hagigah (B.T.).*
Hull.	*Hullin (B.T.) .*
Jer.	*Chronicles of Jerahmeel.*
Leg. All.	*Legum Allegoria* (Philo).
Lev. Rab.	*Leviticus Rabba (M.R.).*
M.R.	*Midrash Rabba.*
Nid.	*Niddah (B.T.).*
Num. Rab.	*Numbers Rabba (M.R.).*
Pes.	*Pesahim (B.T.).*
P.R.E.	*Pirkê de Rabbi Eliezer.*
Q.A.	*Questions and Answers on Genesis* (Philo).
Sanh.	*Sanhedrin (B.T.).*
Shabb.	*Shabbath (B.T.).*
Sot.	*Sotah (B.T.).*
S.S.Rab.	*Song of Songs Rabba (M.R.).*
Targ. Jon.	*Targum of Jonathan ben Uzziel.*
Yeb.	*Yebamoth (B.T.).*

PATRISTIC AND RELATED SOURCES

Ad Autol.	*The Three Books of Theophilus to Autolycus.*
Adv. Haer.	*Against the Heresies* (Irenaeus).
Adv. Omn. Haer.	*Against All the Heresies* (Pseudo-Tertullian).
Cat.	*The Catechetical Lectures* (Cyril of Jerusalem).
Clem. Hom.	*The Clementine Homilies.*
Coll.	*Conferences* (Cassian).
Comm. in Gen.	*Commentary on Genesis* (Raban Maur).

Con. Cels.	*Against Celsus* (Origen).
Con. Gent.	*Against the Heathen* (Athanasius).
De An.	*A Treatise on the Soul* (Tertullian).
De Bapt. Chr.	*On the Baptism of Christ* (Gregory of Nyssa).
De Bon. Pat.	*On the Good of Patience* (Cyprian).
De Civ. Dei	*On the City of God* (Augustine).
De Doct. Christ.	*On Christian Doctrine* (Augustine).
De Gen. ad Litt.	*Genesis according to the Letter* (Augustine).
De Gen. con. Man.	*Genesis against the Manichees* (Augustine).
De Grat.	*On the Grace of Christ and Original Sin* (Augustine).
De Hom. Op.	*On the Making of Man* (Gregory of Nyssa).
De Init. Creat.	*On the Beginning of the Creation* (Ælfric).
De Nat.	*On Nature and Grace* (Augustine).
De Nupt.	*On Marriage and Concupiscence* (Augustine).
De Par.	*On Paradise* (Ambrose).
De Pat.	*Of Patience* (Tertullian).
De Pecc. Mer.	*On the Merits and Forgiveness of Sins* (Augustine).
De Praescr.	*Prescription against Heretics* (Tertullian).
De Princ.	*On Principles* (Origen).
De Resurr.	*From the Discourse on the Resurrection* (Methodius of Olympus).
Dem.	*The Demonstration of the Apostolic Teaching* (Irenaeus).
Dial.	*Dialogue of Justin with Trypho* (Justin Martyr).
Div. Inst.	*Divine Institutes* (Lactantius).
Ench.	*Faith, Hope, and Charity* (Augustine).
Ep.	*Letters* (Ambrose).
Epist.	*Letters* (Jerome).
Expos. in Pent.	*Expositions on the Pentateuch* (Bruno Astensis).
Frag.	*Fragments* (Justin Martyr).
Hex.	*Hexaemeron* (Basil).
Hexaem.	*Hexaemeron* (Bede).
Hist. Ecc.	*Ecclesiastical History* (Bede).
Hist. Schol.	*Historia Scholastica* (Comestor).
Homil. in Gen.	*Homilies on Genesis* (Origen).
Hom. in Gen.	*Homilies on Genesis* (Chrysostom).
Hom. in Joh.	*Homilies on John* (Chrysostom).
Hom. in Ps.	*Homilies on the Psalms* (Hilary of Poitiers).
Hom. in Tim.	*Homilies on Timothy* (Chrysostom).
In Pent. Comm.	*Commentaries on the Pentateuch* (Pseudo-Bede).
Interr.	*Questions and Answers on Genesis* (Alcuin).
Mor.	*Morals on the Book of Job* (Gregory the Great).
Myst. Ex. Sac.	*Expositions of the Mystic Sacraments* (Isidore of Seville).
Orat.	*Orations* (Gregory of Nazianzus).
Orat. Cat.	*The Great Catechism* (Gregory of Nyssa).
Orat. con. Graec.	*Address to the Greeks* (Tatian).
Orth. Fid.	*Expositions of the Orthodox Faith* (John of Damascus).
Quaest. in Vet. Test.	*Questions on the Old Testament* (Ambrosiaster).
Quod Deus.	*That God is not the Author of Evil* (Basil).

Resp.   An Answer to the Jews (Tertullian).
Strom.   Miscellanies (Clement of Alexandria).
Tract. Theol.   Theological Treatise (Hildebert).

CHRISTIAN-LATIN AND RELATED SOURCES

De Mos. Hist.   Poematum de Mosaicae Historiae Gestis Libri Quinque.
De Rer. Nat.   De Rerum Natura.
De Vir. Illust.   De Viris Illustribus.
Ec.   Ecloga.
Hept.   Heptateuchos.
Metam.   Metamorphoses.
Met. in Gen.   Metrum in Genesim.

MISCELLANEOUS

A.C.W.   Ancient Christian Writers.
A.J.A.   American Journal of Archeology.
A.N.C.L.   Ante-Nicene Christian Library.
B.A.P.   Bibliothek der Angelsachsischen Prosa.
C.C.   Corpus Christianorum.
C.M.H.   Cambridge Medieval History.
C.S.E.L.   Corpus Scriptorum Ecclesiasticorum Latinorum.
E.E.T.S.   Early English Text Society.
E.E.T.S., E.S.   Early English Text Society, Extra Series.
E.L.H.   Journal of English Literary History.
E.S.   Essays and Studies.
H.U.C.A.   Hebrew Union College Annual.
J.E.   Jewish Encyclopedia.
J.E.G.P.   Journal of English and Germanic Philology.
J.E.H.   Journal of Ecclesiastical History.
J.Q.R.   Jewish Quarterly Review.
J.T.S.   Journal of Theological Studies.
L.A.R.   Library Association Record.
L.C.C.   Library of Christian Classics.
L.F.   Library of Fathers.
Lud. Cov.   Ludus Coventriae.
M.L.N.   Modern Language Notes.
M.L.Q.   Modern Language Quarterly.
M.P.   Modern Philology.
M.P.G.   Migne's Patrologia Graeca.
M.P.L.   Migne's Patrologia Latina.
Neophil.   Neophilologus.
O.D.C.C.   Oxford Dictionary of the Christian Church.
P.L.   Paradise Lost.
P.M.L.A.   Publications of the Modern Language Association of America.
P.Q.   Philological Quarterly.
R.E.S.   Review of English Studies.

R.S.S.C.W.	*Research Studies of the State College of Washington.*
S.A.	*Samson Agonistes.*
S.B.T.	*Studies in Biblical Theology.*
S.L.N.P.N.F.	Select Library of Nicene and Post-Nicene Fathers.
S.P.	*Studies in Philology.*
U.T.Q.	*University of Toronto Quarterly.*

INTRODUCTION

THE STUDY OF A TRADITION

'THERE seems to me to be a division, in Milton, between the philosopher or theologian and the poet.' T. S. Eliot's judgement, pronounced in 1935,[1] might be the motto of the last half-century of commentary on *Paradise Lost*. For there is in this body of criticism, if not in its subject, a remarkably clear division between the theological and the poetical, between, that is to say, those studies which explore the work's intellectual background and those which confine their attention to purely literary appraisal. The former have generally displayed a curious reluctance to bring the evidence they have assembled to bear on the text they purport to be annotating, while the latter have taken little or no account of that evidence in their assessment of Milton's achievement. In the no-man's-land separating them has been left the question: what does an inquiry into the history of the Fall story have to contribute to our understanding of *Paradise Lost* as a poem? This book is an attempt to answer it.

The desirability of even asking such a question has, however, been challenged by at least one influential critic, on the grounds that a concern with earlier treatments of the myth serves only to contaminate our response to Milton's version of it. In his *Paradise Lost and its Critics* A. J. A. Waldock claims that C. S. Lewis, one of the few commentators who has tried to reunite the two schools, was betrayed by his knowledge of the standard theological exegesis of Genesis into superimposing Augustine's conception of Adam upon the very different figure we encounter in Books IV–VIII. To avoid this kind of mistake, he goes on to argue, we must attend exclusively to the words Milton actually wrote; what matters is the thing itself, and no amount of scholarly erudition should ever persuade us to stray from the poetic facts in front of us.[2]

Undoubtedly the danger that Waldock emphasizes cannot be lightly dismissed. It is only too easy to distort the meaning of any

---

[1] 'A Note on the Verse of John Milton', *E.S.* xxi (1935), 38.
[2] *Paradise Lost and its Critics*, 1947, ch. ii.

given character, episode, or situation to make it conform to a similar one in some putative source, and as I shall suggest later Lewis is not entirely blameless in this regard. But it does not follow that an investigation of the Fall tradition is necessarily misleading. On the contrary, it can be one of the most efficient ways of finding out what the real 'facts' of *Paradise Lost* are. The poem, after all, was not conceived in a complete vacuum, and the critic who insists on removing it from its environment, both historical and contemporary, in order to analyse it in clinical isolation is likely to learn rather less about it than if he had left it where it was. He may, for instance, take to be original, and therefore especially significant, a feature which is in fact perfectly commonplace. Worse still, he may neglect the genuine innovations altogether. Unless, in short, a work is studied in its context, which in this particular case comprehends most previous writings on the Fall of Man, it is difficult if not impossible to see it for what it truly is. Its uniqueness can be measured and defined only in terms of its relationship to the landscape out of which it grew.

The shortcomings of the pseudo-scientific method advocated by Waldock and practised by many of his successors are clearly illustrated in his opening chapter. The description of Man's first disobedience given in Genesis is, he remarks, 'lined with difficulties of the gravest order'. God's behaviour, for example, appears to be malicious, and Adam's inexplicable. But whereas a twentieth-century reader is well equipped to foresee these difficulties thanks to his acquaintance with the novel, the unfortunate seventeenth-century poet was not, 'because he had not the technique for assessing such complications that we (quite involuntarily) possess'. Waldock might have been less impressed by our credentials had he known that every one of the problems he found in the Biblical account, together with several others he passed over, had been noted, debated, and more often than not solved during the two thousand years preceding the composition of *Paradise Lost*, and that its author had at his disposal an extensive corpus of theoretical and practical interpretations of every aspect of his theme.

The gradual emergence of these interpretations, which I have categorized as the exegetical and literary traditions respectively, will form the subject of the following two sections; the use to which Milton put them will be considered in the third. In thus tracing the development of the Fall story from its source in Genesis up to its most elaborate and satisfying treatment in *Paradise Lost* I shall, in the initial stages, be covering a certain amount of ground that is already familiar through recent source studies of the latter, but with one important difference: I shall be travelling in the opposite direction. For many years the accepted procedure in such studies has been to begin with the poem, to focus on those points at which it diverges from the Scriptural version, and then to work backwards in search of precedents. The present inquiry is written in the belief that there is much to be said for reversing the process and beginning at the beginning. Milton's epic will be my destination, not my point of departure.

As a result, this survey will differ fundamentally from those which have examined the specific question of the sources of *Paradise Lost*. The researches of scholars like E. C. Baldwin, Sister M. I. Corcoran, H. F. Fletcher, G. McColley, G. C. Taylor, and A. Williams have taught us a good deal about its background, and my debt to them will be only too apparent. Nevertheless, they are all, to a greater or lesser degree, limited by the range of their interests; each claims for the particular part of the Fall tradition it deals with a priority which a wider view might suggest it does not have. By attempting to put the whole tradition in perspective I hope to avoid over-emphasizing any one facet of it at the expense of the others.

I hope, too, that by pursuing the story along the path it followed I shall be able to circumnavigate some of the pitfalls that await those who proceed backwards. Of these the most common is the assumption that similarity proves dependence. For the simple fact is too often ignored that if a great number of writers choose to retell the same story, any two or more of them might easily hit upon the same variation of it quite independently. To take a concrete example, Genesis tells us nothing of the means Eve used to persuade Adam to eat the forbidden fruit with her, so any subsequent amplification of the incident must provide a strategy for her. Given that she was a woman and her victim a man, it would indeed be surprising if a large proportion of poets and dramatists did not infer that she had recourse to some form of female blandishment. Before a feature in one adaptation of the myth is stated to be the source of a similar feature in another, therefore, the most stringent criteria should be satisfied. The author in question must be shown to have had access to the earlier version, to have been likely to read it, and to have been unable to find the same feature anywhere else. In the case of a tradition as rich and as complex as that of the Fall the profusion of analogues makes this last point hard to establish. Source for the goose is not always source for the gander.

My major concern, then, will be with the evolution of the Fall story, of which the parallels singled out by some of the scholars I have mentioned are often the natural result, rather than with the precise connexions between the parallels themselves. As a student of literature I have necessarily concentrated more on the literary than on the doctrinal issues involved, though of course this can be no more than a matter of emphasis; narrative developments frequently depend on dogmatic developments and vice versa. The existence of N. P. Williams's monumental work, *The Ideas of the Fall and of Original Sin*, has enabled me to consider their interdependence without venturing too far into fields beyond my competence.

Yet even when these reservations have been made, the scope of this project remains extremely wide, and the problem arises of how best to present such a large and varied quantity of material. I considered two ways of doing so: either to examine each treatment or group of treatments in its entirety and in historical order, or to divide the story up into its basic constituents and discuss each of them separately. Both systems have their drawbacks. The first tends to obscure the links between the various interpretations of individual episodes and characters, while the second ignores the relationship between these elements within the framework of the treatment in which they appeared. As I remarked in a recent review,[1] a story of any length is a complex narrative organism with its own internal logic; when a new component is introduced or an old one modified, the whole intricate pattern has to be adjusted to accommodate the change. Thus the portrayal of the temptation is determined to a large extent by the characterization of Adam and Eve, and this in turn affects their reactions after the Fall and the nature of their condemnation. To understand a part we have to understand the whole.

In the light of these considerations I decided to combine the two methods, adopting the first in my survey of the exegetical and literary traditions, and the second in my analysis of *Paradise Lost*. By building up the argument in horizontal layers, as it were, and then drawing the vertical conclusions, I hoped to reveal the characteristics of the successive re-creations of the myth, and at the same time to clarify their relevance both to each other and to the intellectual

[1] *Medium Ævum*, xxxiv (1965), 85–88

temper of the ages that produced them. The result, I am aware, is a tiresome amount of cross-reference, notably in the final chapters, but the consequent demands on the reader's patience seemed to me justified by the compensating advantages. I make no apology, on the other hand, for the amount of quotation I have permitted myself. If the book was to fulfil its purpose I thought it right that wherever possible the evidence should be presented at first hand rather than in paraphrase. I have used existing translations of apocryphal, rabbinic, and patristic material, but cited the literary texts, whose exact wording and phraseology might be significant, in their original languages.[1]

---

[1] In preparing the prose translations that appear in the footnotes I have leaned heavily upon the advice of my friends and colleagues listed in the Acknowledgements, and upon the following works:

Gordon, R. K., *Anglo-Saxon Poetry*, reprint of 1959;
Innes, M. M., *The 'Metamorphoses' of Ovid*, reprint of 1961;
Kirkconnell, W., *The Celestial Cycle*, Toronto, 1952;
Kuhnmuench, O. J., *Early Christian Latin Poets*, Chicago, 1929;
Latham, R. E., *Lucretius' 'On the Nature of the Universe'*, reprint of 1955;
Rieu, E. V., *Virgil: 'The Pastoral Poems'*, reprint of 1961;
Stone, E. M., *Adam*, University of Washington Publications in Language and Literature, vol. iv, Seattle, 1926.

PART ONE

The Exegetical Tradition

I

THE TEXT

FEW stories have worked so powerfully or so continuously on the imagination of Western Man as that of the Fall of Adam and Eve. It has been one of the dominant themes of our theology, literature, and art for nearly two thousand years, the subject of commentaries by every major Christian and Jewish thinker from Philo to Dietrich Bonhoeffer, of poems and plays by writers from Prudentius to Bernard Shaw, and of pictures by artists from the anonymous painter who decorated the crypt of San Gennaro in Naples to Marc Chagall. The reasons for its enduring vitality are many, but perhaps the most potent of them is to be found in its nature as a myth. For it is a myth not only in the strictly anthropological sense of that term, but also in the vaguer poetic sense, defined by C. S. Lewis as a narrative sequence having 'a value in itself—a value independent of its embodiment in any literary work'. In the presence of such a story, he suggests, we are aware of a certain numinous quality; although the characters may be remote and the events preternatural, we feel 'as if something of great moment had been communicated to us'.[1] It is the urge to formulate this 'something' in the myth of the Fall of Man that has prompted each new generation of readers to reinterpret the first three chapters of Genesis in terms of its own particular values and experience.

For a story which inspired some of the world's greatest masterpieces it had surprisingly humble origins. Modern Biblical scholars[2] are generally agreed that it began as a straightforward aetiological myth, designed to explain why a man cleaves to his wife and why he is the senior partner in the union, why he has to labour in the fields and she in childbirth, why we wear clothes, why we dislike snakes, and why they crawl on their bellies. During the early centuries of our era, however, this simple narrative came to acquire a significance

---

[1] *An Experiment in Criticism*, 1961, pp. 41 and 44.

[2] The factual information in this chapter is drawn from several critical commentaries, ranging from A. Dillmann's *Genesis* (trans. W. B. Stevenson), 1897, to U. Cassuto's *A Commentary on the Book of Genesis* (trans. I. Abrahams), Jerusalem, 1961. For a complete list see Bibliography, p. 294.

far beyond that intended by its Hebrew authors, as a result of
St. Paul's assertion that Adam's transgression was the cause of
Christ's mission: 'For as by one man's disobedience many were
made sinners, so by the obedience of one shall many be made
righteous.'[1] In the Pauline Epistles the actions of Adam and Eve
were set directly opposite those of Christ and His Church, and the
Fall was established as the primal disaster which made necessary
the Redemption. From the first century on, therefore, the myth was
expected to provide the answer to questions rather more profound
than those of reptilian locomotion and domestic authority. It
revealed the ultimate source of human misery. If asked to account
for the apparent contradiction between the benevolence and omnipotence of God on the one hand and the imperfection of Nature
on the other, a well-educated Christian living at any time in the
sixteen hundred years that separate Milton from St. Paul would
have pointed to the third chapter of Genesis.

Given this unique position in the structure of Christian dogma,
the Fall story inevitably became the focus of intense doctrinal
scrutiny both by the Church and by its adversaries. Under such
immense pressure it might well have been expected to harden and
contract into an unyielding core, but in fact, far from being com-
pressed, it expanded in every conceivable direction, undergoing
almost as many transformations as it had interpreters. Two factors
were responsible for its flexibility. The first was external: although
Adam's failure to abstain from the tree of knowledge was regarded
as the explanation of the existence of evil, each successive culture
conceived of evil in a different way, each had different questions to
ask, and in eliciting the answers they sometimes modified the story's
whole form and meaning. The second lay within the narrative
itself: various causes combined to make certain of its features
extremely puzzling; it posed almost as many questions as it answered,
and in attempting to resolve them commentators and poets alike
were compelled to introduce increasingly far-reaching innovations
into the original Biblical text. Thus there developed the vast and
complex series of elaborations which finally went to the making of
Paradise Lost. In the chapters following I shall try to unravel the
most important of them. In this I propose to study the problems out
of which they grew.

[1] Rom. v. 19. Unless otherwise stated all quotations from the Bible are from the
Authorized Version.

The description of the Creation and Fall that occupies the first
three chapters of Genesis is not the work of one author. It consists,
rather, of a combination of two quite distinct documents, designated
by common consent as P and J respectively. P, or the Priestly
document, which extends from the beginning of the first chapter
to the fourth verse of the second,[1] was written in the fifth or sixth
century B.C. It contains what became the standard Jewish and
Christian account of the work of the six days:

And God said, Let us make man in our image, after our likeness: and
let them have dominion over the fish of the sea, and over the fowl of the
air, and over the cattle, and over all the earth, and over every creeping
thing that creepeth upon the earth.
So God created man in his own image, in the image of God created
he him; male and female created he them.
And God blessed them, and God said unto them, Be fruitful, and
multiply, and replenish the earth, and subdue it: and have dominion over
the fish of the sea, and over the fowl of the air, and over every living thing
that moveth upon the earth.[2]

Several features set it apart from J, or the Jahwist document. The
most obvious of them is lost in the English translation, that is, the
use of the generic term *Elohim* (the Lord) rather than the proper
name *Jahweh* (Jehovah) for God. In P the Deity is a concept, in
J a person, and this basic difference is symptomatic of the more
general characteristics that have enabled practitioners of 'higher
criticism' to distinguish between the two versions. Where J, as we
shall see, is vivid and pictorial, P is precise, repetitive, and largely
abstract, and its austere description of the Creation seems prosaic
beside J's striking anthropomorphisms. This stylistic contrast
reflects in turn the divergent standpoints from which the two narratives are written: in P we seem to be looking down from some
remote position in space, witnessing the Creation from the Creator's
point of view, whereas in J we are firmly rooted to the earth,
observing the beginning of things from the creaturely level.

The theology implicit in P is correspondingly elevated, notably
its very sophisticated conception of the Deity. He alone is the author
of the universe,[3] which He creates not with His hands but merely

[1] These remarks, of course, pertain only to the first three chapters of Genesis. Both
the Priestly and the Jahwist documents continue further than the end of the third
chapter.   [2] Gen. i. 26–28.
[3] The use of the plural in the verses describing the creation of Man has led some
commentators to suppose that there lies behind the Priestly account a polytheistic

by the expression of His will. He is clearly omnipotent, and everything that He brings into being is 'very good'.[1] Most important
of all, He is well disposed towards Man, for whose sake He appears
to have made the world and everything in it. Nor is Man himself
presented any less idealistically. God makes him in His own image,
appointing him as master of all the other creatures and binding him
only by the command to propagate his kind. In all this, it will soon
become evident, P differs from J as decisively as in matters of style
and standpoint.

There is still a considerable measure of disagreement among Old
Testament specialists as regards the source or sources of the Priestly
document, and unless fresh evidence is unearthed it seems unlikely
that the question will ever be conclusively settled. Nevertheless, it is
worth drawing attention to one especially popular theory for the sake
of the interesting parallel it affords to the idea of the Satanic Fall
which was first elaborated in Jewish Apocrypha and then adopted
by the Church Fathers. Its basis is the association of the Hebrew
word *tehom* (chaos) with Tiamat, the primeval monster of Babylonian mythology, who, after a prolonged conflict with Marduk, was
finally subdued and used to provide the material for the creation
of the cosmos.[2] References in the Old Testament to a combat with
Leviathan or Rahab have been taken to allude to a similar legend
in Jewish tradition,[3] thus leading some scholars to the view 'that a
fight with a dragon-like creature lay in the background of the
Hebrew story of the creation, though it was eliminated from the
Priestly version in the book of Genesis'.[4] More recently A. Heidel
has protested against the presuppositions on which this theory rests
and advanced several convincing arguments for abandoning the
whole hypothesis.[5] While I am not competent to take sides in the
controversy it does seem to me remarkable that both Judaism and

version of the Creation. It seems more likely, however, that this is an instance of what
S. R. Driver has called 'the plural of majesty', used to convey ideas of dignity in much
the same way as the English 'royal plural'. It would surely be strange to find such
obvious traces of polytheism in an account which is otherwise so remarkable for its strict
monotheism.

[1] Gen. i. 31.

[2] See *Enuma Elish*, tablet IV, 135–8. The whole work is translated, together with the
Gilgamesh Epic and other relevant material, in J. B. Pritchard's *Ancient Near Eastern
Texts* (2nd edn.), Princeton, 1955.

[3] Cf. Job vii. 12; Isa. xxvii. 1, li. 9; Ezek. xxix. 3, xxxii. 2.

[4] E. O. James, *Myth and Ritual in the Ancient Near East*, 1958, p. 168. For other
discussions of possible Babylonian analogues see Bibliography, p. 294.

[5] *The Babylonian Genesis* (2nd edn.), Chicago, 1950, ch. iii.

Christianity eventually found it necessary to postulate just such a combat prior to the making of the world, thereby either restoring the original outlines of the Hebrew story or bringing it into line with parallel versions in related mythologies.

The Jahwist document, which extends from the fourth verse of the second chapter to the end of the third, is considerably older than P. In its written form it dates from the ninth or tenth century B.C., but behind it there probably lies an oral tradition still more ancient. Indeed the suggestion has often been made that J itself represents an amalgamation of at least two separate stories, one involving the tree of knowledge and the other the tree of life.[1] This would certainly account for the many inconsistencies and repetitions in the narrative, but although several attempts have been made to disentangle them the two strands remain inextricably knotted. On the other hand, it is almost certain that the portion of J concerning the Fall was set down in its present form by one man, for it is characterized by an individual and very effective style, which has drawn universal praise from commentators. The crucial opening verses of the third chapter offer a good example:

Now the serpent was more subtil than any beast of the field which the Lord God had made. And he said unto the woman, Yea, hath God said, Ye shall not eat of every tree of the garden?

And the woman said unto the serpent, We may eat of the fruit of the trees of the garden:

But of the fruit of the tree which is in the midst of the garden, God hath said, Ye shall not eat of it, neither shall ye touch it, lest ye die.

And the serpent said unto the woman, Ye shall not surely die:

For God doth know that in the day ye eat thereof, then your eyes shall be opened, and ye shall be as gods, knowing good and evil.

And when the woman saw that the tree was good for food, and that it was pleasant to the eyes, and a tree to be desired to make one wise, she took of the fruit thereof, and did eat, and gave also unto her husband with her; and he did eat.[2]

The passage is a model of economy, bringing the characters vividly to life in their brief conversation and carrying the action forward with every phrase. Only the essentials of the story are emphasized, yet we carry away from it a profound sense of underlying complexity.

---

[1] The various theories are well summarized in J. Coppens, *La Connaissance du bien et du mal et le péché du paradis*, Gembloux, 1948, Appendix i.

[2] Gen. iii. 1–6.

By these qualities alone the Jahwist is clearly to be distinguished from the pedantic author of the Priestly document, with its stereotyped formulae and monotonous redundancies of expression. But the differences between them are more than stylistic. A great deal of the Jahwist's narrative energy derives from the material he is dealing with. If P is a crude form of chronicle, J is a full-blooded myth, and legendary elements such as the speaking serpent and the magical trees play a prominent part at every stage of the plot. Its deity, as I noted earlier, is not a concept (*Elohim*) but a person (*Jahweh*), who forms Man from the earth with his own hands, breathes life into his nostrils, plants the garden of Eden, walks in it to converse with its inhabitants, and manufactures clothes for them when they become aware of their nakedness.

The distinction between this concrete figure and the lofty abstraction who dictates events in P is further evident when we come to examine their respective characters. For Jahweh is not merely described anthropomorphically; his very nature is revealed by his shortcomings to be more human than divine. He makes mistakes, as in the episode of Adam's mate; he appears to be jealous in denying his creatures knowledge; he is not omniscient, and has to be told where Adam and Eve are hiding and why; he is envious and fearful in his desire to prevent them from eating of the tree of life and so becoming like him. He is, in fact, the complete antithesis of the benevolent and omnipotent Elohim of the Priestly document. And just as P's perfect man reflected the perfection of his Creator, so J's is made in the image of the primitive Jahweh. In striking contrast to P's idealistic view of Adam's original status and destiny J pictures him as a childlike innocent being, not far above the animals either mentally or physically. Like the beasts of the field he is formed from the dust of the ground, and it is among them that Jahweh first thinks of finding a suitable companion for him.[1]

As in the case of P, the question of sources has never been satisfactorily settled. Ever since the publication of S. Langdon's *The Sumerian Epic of Paradise* in 1915 Babylonian mythology has been ransacked for possible analogues to the Genesis account. While no narrative has yet been discovered which bears any detailed resemblance to the Hebrew version of the Fall, enough isolated parallels

---

[1] Cassuto has objected to this interpretation, but his general description of the Jahwist's view of Man's first condition is in accordance with the one presented here. See op. cit., pp. 113–14, 127–8.

have been found to establish the probability that at least some of its elements are of Babylonian origin. The creation of Enkidu in the *Gilgamesh Epic*, for instance, recalls that of Adam:

> When Aruru heard this,
> A double of Anu she conceived within her.
> Aruru washed her hands,
> Pinched off clay and cast it on the steppe.
> On the steppe she created valiant Enkidu . . .
> With the gazelles he feeds on grass,
> With the wild beasts he jostles at the watering place.[1]

He is made in order to rival Gilgamesh, but the hero forestalls Aruru's plan by sending a harlot to seduce him. When she has succeeded in doing so, she persuades Enkidu to abandon his primitive life among the animals for the more refined society of the city of Uruk:

> [The harlot] says to him, to Enkidu:
> 'Thou art wise, Enkidu, art become like a god!'[2]

Later in the poem her lover curses her, blaming her above all for his liability to death. Clearly the general outlines of this episode are somewhat similar to those of the Biblical story, and S. G. F. Brandon has recently revived the theory, widely canvassed by earlier scholars, that the Jahwist adapted the Babylonian myth in his presentation of Adam and Eve's experiences in Eden.[3] Studied more closely, however, the parallel is doubtful at best: there is no mention of a forbidden tree, Enkidu is not the first man, and even the notion that his 'Fall' consisted in his acquisition of civilization depends on the dubious symbolic value of Uruk. Consequently it still seems fair to describe it in W. L. Wardle's words as a 'somewhat remote correspondence to the idea that sexual knowledge deprives man of innocence and felicity.[4]

In another part of the same poem the hero, Gilgamesh, sets off in search of a tree which will renew his youth:

> Gilgamesh says to him, to Urshanabi, the boatman:
> 'Urshanabi, this plant is a plant apart,
> Whereby a man may regain his life's breath.
>
> .   .   .
>
> Its name shall be "Man Becomes Young in Old Age".'[5]

---

[1] Tablet I, i. 33–40.   [2] Tablet I, iv. 33–34.
[3] *Creation Legends of the Ancient Near East*, 1963, p. 132.
[4] *Israel and Babylon* (3rd edn.), 1925, p. 191.   [5] Tablet XI, 277–81.

Eventually he finds it, only to have it stolen by a serpent when he is on his way back:

> A serpent snuffed the fragrance of the plant;
> It came up [from the water] and carried off the plant.
> Going back it shed [its] slough.[1]

There is certainly no denying that this magical plant bears a distinct likeness to the tree of life, but the inference drawn by W. O. E. Oesterley and J. G. Frazer that the original version of J must have concerned the serpent's theft of the fruit of immortality goes far beyond the immediate evidence.[2]

Finally, it is worth drawing attention to an interesting analogue which has been found for the names given to Eve. The Sumerian words for 'rib' (*ti*) and 'life' (*til*) were depicted by the same ideogram, so the goddess Nin-ti could have been either 'the lady of the rib' or 'the lady who gives life'. This ancient pun, some scholars have suggested, was carried over into the Hebrew story, thus giving rise to Eve's alternative titles in Genesis.[3] Like all the others, however, this is only an isolated parallel, and the fact remains that over half a century of research has failed to produce any large-scale source for the Jahwist narrative. Indeed, the possibility that such a source ever will be found seems minimal, for, as Heidel has pointed out, Babylonian mythology did not need a Fall to account for the ills of human life. Man was created from the blood of the wicked Kingu, and his mortality was ensured from the very beginning:

> When the gods created mankind,
> Death for mankind they set aside,
> Life in their own hands retaining.[4]

The absence of any consistently analogous story in related mythologies makes it difficult to interpret the second and third chapters of Genesis with any degree of certainty. The profusion of subsequent theological and poetical elaborations which surround it obscures the issue still further. On the one hand, a would-be interpreter must

---

[1] Tablet XI, 287–9.

[2] *Immortality and the Unseen World*, 1921, ch. xii; *Folk-Lore in the Old Testament*, 1918, vol. i, ch. ii.

[3] Cf. S. N. Kramer, *Enki and Ninhursag*, New Haven, 1945, p. 9; Brandon, op. cit., p. 127.

[4] *Gilgamesh Epic*, tablet X, iii. 3–5.

beware of twisting the meaning in order to make it correspond with such vaguely similar ideas as do exist; on the other, he must be careful to avoid reading into the text notions that have developed since. The only external evidence available to him is the occurrence of various key phrases and concepts elsewhere in the Old Testament, and even this has to be used with some caution. What follows, therefore, is nothing but a most tentative exegesis of the Jahwist document.

As I mentioned earlier, the Fall story was originally designed to explain such phenomena as the need to labour. What still remains a matter for dispute is whether or not it was ever intended to explain human mortality. F. R. Tennant insists that it was not. According to J, he argues, Adam was created mortal in the first instance, and Jahweh's threat when he forbade the tree of knowledge referred only to premature death. The presence of the tree of life, too, further confirms that Man had not yet acquired immortality.[1] In opposition to this view Oesterley and Frazer have urged that the central theme of the narrative is nothing less than the origin of death. Although their over-reliance on Babylonian analogues makes their position suspect from the start, they do at least account for the awkward fact, ignored by Tennant, that Jahweh found it necessary to condemn Adam and Eve to die. The Jahwist's real meaning perhaps lay somewhere between these two extremes. I am not sure that he would have regarded the first pair as either mortal or immortal. They seem to have been potentially capable of being either; the tree of life offered them immortality, the tree of knowledge death. Consequently, when they had chosen the latter, Jahweh both sentenced them to return to the dust *and* deprived them of the tree of life. Until they decided to eat the fruit of one of the two trees they would have gone on living, but they were never immortal in the sense that they could not die.[2]

Be that as it may, it does seem certain that the story was not written to account for the existence of sin, for although Adam and Eve's disobedience was the first sin, there is no suggestion in the Biblical narrative that it in any way vitiated the moral nature of their descendants. In the very next chapter, for instance, the

---

[1] *The Sources of the Doctrines of the Fall and Original Sin*, 1903, p. 119. Cf. N. P. Williams, *The Ideas of the Fall and of Original Sin*, 1927, pp. 53–54.

[2] This is, in fact, the view taken by the Rabbis, the Greek Apologists, and Augustine. See below, pp. 41–42, 78, 93–94.

responsibility for Cain's wickedness is placed firmly on his own shoulders: 'If thou doest well, shalt thou not be accepted? and if thou doest not well, sin lieth at the door. And unto thee shall be his desire, and thou shalt rule over him.'[1] The development of the Christian belief that Adam's Fall produced an inherited bias or compulsion towards evil in his posterity is perhaps the classic example of *post hoc ergo propter hoc* reasoning.

Bearing these points in mind it should now be possible to make a more detailed approach to the primary significance of the Jahwist document. Before the Fall Adam and Eve lived in the garden of Eden in a state of innocence. Their mental and physical condition was not far above that of the animals, from whom they were distinguished only by their consciousness of the moral obligation to preserve the pristine beauty of their paradise and to abstain from the tree of the knowledge of good and evil. That they were already aware of these two duties would seem to preclude any possibility that the forbidden fruit conferred the power to discriminate between right and wrong, and the use of the phrase 'to know good and evil' elsewhere in the Old Testament[2] suggests that the kind of knowledge prohibited to them was scientific rather than ethical in character. As N. P. Williams has pointed out, the original Hebrew words for 'good' and 'evil' might better be translated 'weal' and 'woe', and taken to connote the physical well-being or hardship associated with the acquisition of the arts of civilization. Jahweh, according to this interpretation, desired 'to keep them in happy, childlike ignorance, infinitely inferior to himself, but safeguarded from the sorrows which the increase of knowledge brings in its train'.[3] The following chapters of Genesis confirm this impression, for it is with the development of civilized society that the first two acts of cruelty are connected. And when the story of the Watcher angels, recorded in Genesis vi, was amplified in Jewish Apocrypha and Pseudepigrapha it was made to yield the same grim warning that (in the words of Ecclesiastes) 'in much wisdom is much grief: and he that increaseth knowledge increaseth sorrow'.[4]

So long as Adam and Eve observed Jahweh's commandment they would go on living; if they broke it they would die. Yet in spite of this threat the woman was lured by the serpent's promises of divinity into eating the fruit of the tree of knowledge, and persuaded her

[1] Gen. iv. 7. [2] 2 Sam. xiv. 17, xix. 35; Deut. i. 39; Isa. vii. 15–16.
[3] Op. cit., p. 43. [4] Eccles. i. 18. See below, Ch. II, pp. 29, 33.

husband to do the same. The identity of her tempter is still a matter for dispute—he has been associated with the snake who stole the magical plant from Gilgamesh, with the cult figures of various fertility goddesses, and, most convincingly, with the malevolent reptiles of Semitic demonology—but all scholars are agreed that the Jahwist did not have in mind the later association of the serpent with Satan. In the story as we have it there is nothing to suggest that it was anything but a particularly clever animal.[1]

The immediate consequence of their disobedience was that Adam and Eve's eyes were opened, as the tempter had promised they would be, and that they saw that they were naked. S. R. Driver has shown that the opening of the eyes is used in other Old Testament contexts to express any sudden or miraculous enlightenment.[2] The Jahwist has supplemented the metaphor by making the fallen pair's realization of their nudity the first result of their new vision. This vivid illustration of the loss of innocence again suggests that change from childish ignorance to adult sophistication which was already inherent in the concept of the knowledge of good and evil. Thus, according to J, the Fall does not seem to have been a *fall* at all. On the contrary, it was an over-abrupt *rise*, a momentary transition from a state of naïve innocence to one of precocious maturity; it was a cautionary tale of a child who grew up too quickly, not a demi-god who fell.

Although this reading of the story is by no means unanimously accepted by students of the Old Testament,[3] it has to commend it the advantage of being the only interpretation to make any sense at all of Jahweh's conduct after the Fall. Fearing that, since Man had now 'become as one of us, to know good and evil',[4] he might also eat of the tree of life and so become immortal, he expelled Adam and Eve from the garden and set an angelic guard to ensure that they did not steal back in. If the phrase 'to know good and evil' refers to

[1] Cassuto has suggested that the conversation is an internal dialogue taking place within Eve herself, but it seems very unlikely that the Jahwist would have resorted to the sophistications of allegory in this period. Cf. op. cit., p. 142.

[2] *The Book of Genesis* (14th edn.), 1943, p. 46. See Gen. xxi. 19; Num. xxii. 31; 2 Kings vi. 17.

[3] The most recent dissentient is Brandon, who argues most ingeniously that the whole burden of the story consists in Jahweh's desire to prevent Adam and Eve from acquiring sexual knowledge and thus becoming like gods in their ability to reproduce life. They are punished with death because once Man has learned to propagate himself human mortality is necessary to prevent the earth from becoming overcrowded. But if this is the case it is difficult to see why Jahweh gave Adam a partner of a different sex in the first place. Cf. op. cit., pp. 135-7.

[4] Gen. iii. 22.

anything other than scientific knowledge it is not easy to understand the motives which prompted this action.[1] The serpent, it appears, was telling at least half the truth; the eyes of Adam and Eve were opened, and we have it on the authority of Jahweh himself that they became as gods. The only point on which the tempter misled Eve concerned Man's subsequent immortality; in spite of his assurances to the contrary, she and her husband did in fact die. In the serpent's defence, however, it should be added that Adam and Eve did not die immediately, as the terms of the threat had implied they would, nor was their mortality the direct result of eating the fruit. They died simply because their jealous creator ordained that they should. Thus in the light of the final verses of the third chapter of Genesis we are forced to admit that the subtle serpent's analysis of the fruit and the motives underlying its prohibition was perfectly accurate. His one mistake was to underestimate Jahweh's temper. This may be an unpalatable conclusion, but the reasons given for Adam and Eve's expulsion make it hard to escape the inference that partaking of the tree of knowledge had improved their intellectual stature.

Such, then, is the nature of the two documents which compose the Biblical account of the Creation and Fall. It now remains to study the various questions which they pose. The foregoing examination of J has revealed the source of at least some. They stem from the legendary elements contained in the narrative, and in particular from doubts concerning the precise significance of the serpent and the two trees. These symbols were probably old even at the time the Jahwist was writing. As J. Skinner has said, they are 'all emblems derived from a more ancient religious tradition', and it is their incomplete assimilation into the structure of a monotheistic and ethical theology which makes some of J's features so puzzling.[2] In a recent study of this conflict between the story and the mythical relics it preserves B. S. Childs has remarked that 'behind the figure of the serpent shimmers another form still reflecting its former life. A tension exists because this independent life of the original figure still struggles against the framework of a simple snake into which it has been recast.' In this case, he argues, the tension is a calculated one, used by the Jahwist to 'define the limits without giving the answer

---

[1] Coppens's contention that the phrase simply means 'to sin' (op. cit., pp. 1–18) can hardly be reconciled with this later occurrence of the expression.

[2] *A Critical and Exegetical Commentary on Genesis* (2nd edn.), 1930, p. 52.

to the problem of the origin of sin'. Rejecting, on the one hand, the possibility that God created evil and, on the other, the concept of cosmic dualism, the author was content merely to give expression to the complexity of the problem by means of the myth.[1] While it is debatable whether the Jahwist would have been satisfied with such an ambiguous solution or have been likely to present it in so subtle a manner, it is certainly true that whatever the reason for their presence the serpent and two trees constitute a grave difficulty for any commentator.

In ages less concerned than ours with the original meaning of the text the problem presented itself rather differently. At first the Fathers and the Rabbis seem to be asking the same questions as contemporary readers: who or what is the serpent, and how do the trees of knowledge and life relate to the rest of the story? They did not, however, want the same kind of answers, for their primary concern was not with the discovery of the Jahwist's intention, but with the reinterpretation of his symbols for cultures which had forgotten the ancient Hebrew background. We want to find out the old meaning; they were looking for a new one through which to articulate a new doctrine. Indeed, the ambiguity of these legendary elements was, if anything, an advantage, from their point of view, allowing them as it did to read into them whatever doctrinal significance they wished to find there. It was this kind of question that the bulk of Christian exegesis set itself to answer, and in this kind of way.

The main function of this first group of questions is interpretative. They take the story as a story for granted and explore only the meaning of the persons and objects involved in it, directing our attention into and beyond the actual events rather than at and around them. The latter function was performed by a second type of question which I shall call 'narrative'. In a most stimulating essay E. Auerbach has compared the styles of Homer and the Old Testament author known as the Elohist, whose writing, he states, is characterized by:

the externalization of only so much of the phenomena as is necessary for the purpose of the narrative, all else [is] left in obscurity; the decisive points of the narrative alone are emphasized, what lies between is non-existent; time and place are undefined and call for interpretation; thoughts

[1] 'Myth and Reality in the Old Testament', *S.B.T.* xxvii (1960), 45–48.

and feelings remain unexpressed, are only suggested by the silence and
the fragmentary speeches; the whole . . . remains mysterious and 'fraught
with background'.[1]

These remarks could equally well be applied to the Jahwist's style.
He too tells us simply what happens, and his account of the Fall is
full of lacunae of motive and of circumstance. The third chapter of
Genesis positively bristles with questions that have been unasked
and unanswered. How did Eve know that the tree of knowledge was
forbidden when she was created after the prohibition? How did she
come to be alone when the serpent tempted her? How could the
serpent speak? Why did he want her to break Jahweh's commandment and why did he approach her rather than Adam? How did
Eve manage to persuade Adam to eat the fruit with her? Why did
Jahweh not interrogate the serpent? These difficulties are bound to
emerge as soon as the myth is taken seriously as a narrative. They
have to do not so much with its meaning as with its integrity,
probing the purely narrative coherence of the account, the motives
of the characters and the circumstances in which they acted, as
opposed to any doctrinal significance to be derived from them.
Consequently, as the following chapters will reveal, while the
Christian Fathers were generally more interested in interpretative
questions, the Rabbis, whose theology did not place so much emphasis on the Fall, tended to concentrate more on these narrative
problems.[2]

The two kinds of questions I have so far been discussing have
related to the J document alone. The third, and most perplexing,
was created by the combination of J with P. This redaction, which
probably took place during the fifth century B.C., was an event of the
greatest importance in the history of the Fall story. As I have shown,
the two documents offered profoundly contradictory views of the
natures of both God and Man, the first idealistic, the second
primitive. While each view was perfectly consistent within the
framework of its own suppositions, once the two collided they struck
off problems like sparks. P's position at the beginning of the story as
well as developments in the concept of the Deity made it virtually
inevitable that the idealistic view would predominate. But although

---

[1] *Mimesis* (trans. W. R. Trask), Princeton, 1953, pp. 11–12.
[2] In practice interpretative and narrative questions often overlap. Any discussion of
the serpent's motive, for instance, is bound to depend on the identity assigned to him.

there were two alternative accounts of the Creation there was only one of the Fall, and that was J's. Thus there arose the difficulty of reconciling the characters of God and Man as they were portrayed in P with their behaviour as it was related in J. This is the root of what I shall call the 'metaphysical' sort of question.

First, if Adam was created perfect in the image and likeness of a perfect God, as in P, how could he possibly have behaved so foolishly and sinfully as he did according to J? The defection of an innocent childlike creature poses no great problem; the disobedience of a demigod does. The introduction of the concept of free will into the argument is of very little help in this case, for, granted that he enjoyed the freedom to choose, one would still expect a perfect being freely to choose the good. In practice any thoroughgoing attempt to deal with the problem ultimately involves a reduction of Adam and Eve's intellectual or moral stature before the Fall. If Man was morally perfect he must have fallen because he was deceived, not tempted, by a superior intelligence which directed his good impulses to an evil end. If, on the other hand, he was intellectually invulnerable he could have fallen only because his reason was overcome by his sinful nature. If he had been perfect in both respects he would not have fallen at all.

The difficulties with regard to God are no less serious. Over the greater part of the period which this study covers the character attributed to the Deity remained fairly constant; He was regarded as being benevolent, just, omnipotent, and omniscient, as He was in the Priestly document. But, as my earlier discussion of J has shown, these qualities did not receive the same emphasis at the time the Fall story was composed, and as a result it has always been notoriously difficult to reconcile the behaviour of Jahweh in this episode with the more idealized notions of the Deity which have developed since. For instance, if God was omniscient, how could He have so misunderstood Adam's nature and needs as to consider the animals as potential companions for him? Why did He have to be told where Adam was hiding? Above all, if He was benevolent, why did He forbid the first pair to eat of the tree of knowledge, and why did He display such envy in expelling them from the garden? Indeed, if Adam was either morally or intellectually imperfect, to punish him was not only envious but flagrantly unjust. This type of question had to be faced by Christian Father and Jewish Rabbi alike in succeeding centuries; the ways of Jahweh to Adam needed justification in any comparatively sophisticated interpretation of the Fall.[1]

All three kinds of question are bound to arise in any literary elaboration of the myth as well as in any theological exegesis of it, though they take a somewhat different form. Interpretative questions, to begin with, become for the poet or dramatist problems of background. Once the corpus of Hebrew or Near Eastern legend has been forgotten, new terms of reference have to be found to make the ancient story meaningful to a contemporary audience. The mysterious figure of the serpent needs a fresh identity if he is to make any imaginative impact on readers who know nothing of Semitic demonology, and the garden of Eden has to be transplanted to a recognizable landscape, whether mythical or actual. The writers of each successive literary milieu encountered these problems anew, and one of the most interesting aspects of the history of the story is the way in which their various solutions qualified the Jahwist's original meaning.

Narrative questions likewise have a literary aspect. In a dramatic treatment, for example, an episode has to be invented to get Adam off the stage while Eve is being tempted, and a motive has to be supplied for the serpent's hostility to Man and God. Neither can Eve's corruption of Adam be left in its original obscurity; any treatment of the story with pretensions to credibility must explain both why and how she persuaded him to eat the fruit with her. Thus out of the silences and discontinuities of the Scriptural account there grew a varied pattern of speech and incident invented to answer the literary demands of different ages. These additions could, and often did, transform the whole significance of the Biblical account.

Finally, the metaphysical questions resolve themselves into problems involving the consistency of characterization. A realist-narrative author, in whatever genre he may be writing, has always been required to establish an observable connexion between a character's nature and actions; where this connexion or, to give it its more technical name, motivation is absent the actions are said to be 'out of character'. Clearly the incompatibility of the natures of God and Man as recorded in P with their actions as portrayed in J raises just such a problem for a narrative author. There would

---

[1] The Gnostics, who equated Jahweh with the Devil, would form the one exception, although this equation itself was the result of such difficulties as those discussed here. See below, Ch. III, pp. 62–68.

appear to be two possible solutions; he must either modify the characters to conform with their deeds or find some explanation not given in the text, some concealed motive, which will account for their unexpected behaviour. The third theoretical possibility of altering the plot to suit the characters is ruled out by the nature of his material; Scriptural texts can be reinterpreted but not drastically emended. In practice, however, he does not have even this limited choice. In the case of God the first alternative is out of the question, for the nature of the Deity is no less sacrosanct than His actions. Somehow the apparently malicious behaviour of Jahweh must be made to seem benevolent.[1] In the case of Adam, on the contrary, the second alternative is excluded. No possible motive could make the transition from perfection to sinfulness entirely credible, no conceivable explanation could ever account for the downfall of the perfect image of God. Consequently any author who faces this problem squarely is forced back upon the first solution; he has to account for the Fall by showing Adam and Eve to be in some way imperfect from the outset. What is more, he must do this without drawing attention to the dangerous corollary that God and not Adam would then be ultimately responsible for their sin.

All three kinds of questions, then, interpretative, narrative, and metaphysical demand an answer from the poet as well as from the commentator. The difference between the purely theological and the purely literary issues is largely one of form, and, as the history of Milton criticism has amply illustrated, it is not always easy to make any clear-cut distinction between the two. All the diverse answers which were evolved in rabbinic and patristic writings could, therefore, be applied to the solution of the corresponding literary problems. Poets and dramatists who subsequently treated the story of the Fall of Man had at their disposal a vast body of exegesis in which many of their most acute difficulties had been faced, and to varying degrees overcome. In the following two chapters I shall explore the two main branches of this exegetical tradition, the Jewish and the Christian.

[1] The problem, it seems, is perennial. Only recently *The Times* reported that during a performance in Tel Aviv of a contemporary play based on the story of Adam and Eve the Minister for Religious Affairs took violent exception to the description of God as 'a cunning old man', and left the theatre when the Creator was asked if He was jealous.

II

THE JEWISH INTERPRETATIONS

THE theological significance of 'Man's first disobedience' was never very precisely determined in Jewish writings on the subject. For the early Christian Church the actual incarnation of Christ served to establish Adam's sin as the fundamental cause of His mission, but Judaism had no comparable historical event to define the Fall's doctrinal position, and as a result the Old Testament, its Apocrypha and Pseudepigrapha, and the rabbinic tractates exhibit a wide variety of attitudes towards the story's form and meaning. As Williams has shown,[1] up to the time of the composition of the Syriac Apocalypse of Baruch (*post* A.D. 70) and the Fourth Book of Ezra (*c.* A.D. 50–120) the defection of the lustful Watcher angels related in the sixth chapter of Genesis was commonly regarded as the explanation of the existence of evil. Then, just as the Adam story was beginning to emerge in these later works as the official account of the origin of human wickedness, the destruction of Jerusalem by Titus and the overthrow of Bar Kokhba by Hadrian destroyed the millennial hopes embodied in apocalyptic Jewish literature and brought about the virtual disappearance of that genre. With it disappeared the doctrine of the Adamic Fall which it had gradually evolved. Thereafter orthodox Jewish thought fixed upon the rabbinic theory of the *yezer-ha-ra* (evil imagination), a primitive and potentially destructive impulse implanted in every man at his birth,[2] as the answer to the problem of sin, while the notion of the Adamic Fall passed into Christianity via the Epistles of St. Paul.

1. *The Old Testament and its Apocrypha and Pseudepigrapha*

One of the most remarkable features in the history of the Fall story is the complete absence of any explicit reference to it in the rest of the Old Testament. By this I mean reference to the *events*

---

[1] *Ideas of the Fall*, chs. i–ii.

[2] For a full account of this theory, which somewhat resembles the Jungian view of the libido, see N. P. Williams, op. cit., pp. 51–91; F. R. Tennant, *Doctrines of the Fall*, ch. vii; W. D. Davies, *Paul and Rabbinic Judaism*, 1948, ch. ii.

recounted there. For since the Jahwist, as we have seen, incorporated into his narrative several *emblems* derived from an older and wider Semitic tradition, their appearance in isolation cannot be taken as proof that a writer is necessarily alluding to the story as a whole.[1] The tree of life, for instance, is mentioned in a variety of contexts which have not the remotest connexion with the third chapter of Genesis; wisdom, the fruit of the righteous, hope, and a wholesome tongue are all described as a tree of life in Proverbs,[2] without any attempt being made to link them, however tenuously, with Adam's experience in Eden. And the image of the garden itself is no less common; Isaiah and Joel both contrast it with the desolation of the wilderness,[3] while Ezekiel's vision of the promised land strongly suggests the scenery of paradise:

And by the river upon the bank thereof, on this side and on that side, shall grow all trees for meat, whose leaf shall not fade, neither shall the fruit thereof be consumed: it shall bring forth new fruit according to his months . . . and the fruit thereof shall be for meat, and the leaf thereof for medicine.[4]

In another passage the same prophet depicts the Prince of Tyre in terms which have seemed to some scholars to contain a reference to the Fall:

Thou sealest up the sum, full of wisdom, and perfect in beauty. Thou hast been in Eden the garden of God; every precious stone was thy covering, the sardius, topaz, and the diamond, the beryl, the onyx, and the jasper, the sapphire, the emerald, and the carbuncle, and gold: the workmanship of thy tabrets and of thy pipes was prepared in thee in the day that thou wast created.

Thou art the anointed cherub that covereth; and I have set thee so; thou wast upon the holy mountain of God; thou hast walked up and down in the midst of the stones of fire.

Thou wast perfect in thy ways from the day that thou wast created, till iniquity was found in thee . . .

[1] The generality of some of the terms of reference—Adam means simply 'Man' and Eden 'delight'—complicates the matter still further, for it is often difficult to determine when a Hebrew author is using them in their specialized and when in their wider senses.

[2] Cf. iii. 13–18, xi. 30, xiii. 12, xv. 4.

[3] Isa. li. 3; Joel ii 3.

[4] Ezek. xlvii. 12. Rev. xxii. 2, which appears to derive from this passage, makes the reference still more explicit: 'In the midst of the street of it, and on either side of the river, was there the tree of life, which bare twelve manner of fruits, and yielded her fruit every month: and the leaves of the tree were for the healing of the nations.'

Thine heart was lifted up because of thy beauty, thou hast corrupted thy wisdom by reason of thy brightness: I will cast thee to the ground, I will lay thee before kings, that they may behold thee.[1]

If Ezekiel did have the Genesis account in mind then it is clear that he must have known it in a very different form from the extant version. The Jahwist's Adam was a man, not a cherub, he was hardly distinguished for his wisdom, and he did not fall because he was dazzled by his own beauty. It seems fair, therefore, to conclude with U. Cassuto that although Ezekiel's description offers a few points of similarity to the Fall story its divergences are far more striking.[2] Significantly enough, later patristic commentators applied the passage to Satan rather than Adam, using it to provide what became the standard motive for the rebellion of the beautiful Lucifer.[3]

On the other hand, there does seem to be a certain amount of implicit reference to the Fall in the Old Testament by way of quasi-typological parallels between the Messianic Age and the garden of Eden, and between the Messiah and Adam. The first-quoted passage from Ezekiel is one obvious example, and if J. Daniélou's reading of them is correct the prophetic books contain several other instances.[4] The existence of such parallels may well suggest that the idea of a Fall was associated with Man's original estate in Eden, but this is merely an inference, and the fact remains that nowhere in the Old Testament is there any specific allusion to the events related in the Genesis narrative.

It is not until the composition of the Ethiopic Book of Enoch (c. 200–170 B.C.) that the Fall story reappears in Jewish religious literature:

And I came to the Garden of Righteousness, and saw beyond those trees many large trees growing there and of goodly fragrance, large, very beautiful and glorious, and the tree of wisdom whereof they eat and know great wisdom.

That tree is in height like the fir, and its leaves are like [those of] the Carob tree: and its fruit is like clusters of the vine, very beautiful: and the fragrance of the tree penetrates afar.

Then I said: 'How beautiful is the tree, and how attractive is its look.'

Then Raphael the holy angel, who was with me, answered me and said: 'This is the tree of wisdom, of which thy father old [in years] and

---

[1] Ezek. xxviii. 12–17. [2] *Commentary*, pp. 75–81.
[3] See below, Ch. III, p. 87.
[4] *Sacramentum Futuri*, Paris, 1950, pp. 4 et seq.

thy aged mother, who were before thee, have eaten, and they learnt wisdom and their eyes were opened, and they knew that they were naked and they were driven out of the garden.'[1]

This short passage is of crucial importance in the history of the interpretation of the Jahwist document, for it reveals that as late as the second century B.C. the moral and physical ills of life were still not associated with the story of Adam's disobedience. The fall of the Watcher angels, which is elaborated earlier in the same work, is regarded as the cause of evil; the Adam story is mentioned here only in passing, and without any doctrinal comment. Further, this Apocryphon confirms that the tree of knowledge was taken to confer wisdom rather than moral consciousness, and that the tree of life existed as an independent feature of Hebrew mythology: it is described as growing on a mountain whose summit is the throne of God and whose location is quite different from that of the garden of Eden.[2]

Dating from roughly the same period, the Book of Sirach (c. 180–175 B.C.) gives a complementary account of Man's original condition which is again based on Genesis:

> God created man out of dust,
> And turned him back thereunto.
> He granted them a [fixed] number of days,
> And gave them authority over all things on the earth.
> He clothed them with strength like unto Himself,
> And made them according to His own image.
> He put the fear of them upon all flesh,
> And caused them to have power over beasts and birds.
> With insight and understanding He filled their heart,
> And taught them good and evil.
> He created for them tongue, and eyes, and ears,
> And He gave them a heart to understand,
> To show them the majesty of His works,
> And that they might glory in His wondrous acts;
> That they might evermore declare His glorious works,
> And praise His holy name.[3]

Here the chief point of interest is the obviously perfectionist view that is taken of Adam's nature. Already, it appears, the Priestly

---

[1] xxxii. 3–6. The work contains sections dating from different periods. The passage I quote here is from one of the oldest parts of the book.

[2] xxiv–xxv.   [3] xvii. 1–10.

document has imposed its exalted conception of Man upon the entire story, with the result that the Jahwist's insistence on Adam's original ignorance of good and evil has to be denied. Far from prohibiting men to eat of the tree of the knowledge of good and evil God gives them this knowledge in the first place.

By far the fullest account of the Fall story in the centuries preceding the birth of Christ, however, is to be found in the Book of Jubilees (*c.* 153–105 B.C.), a Pharisaic work described by its most recent translator as an enlarged Targum of Genesis and Exodus 'in which difficulties in the Biblical narrative are solved, gaps supplied, dogmatically offensive elements removed, and the genuine spirit of later Judaism infused into the primitive history of the world'.[1] As such it offers a most interesting indication of the kind of problem that the Genesis narrative posed for orthodox Judaism in the second century B.C. The most serious appears to have been the Jahwist's anthropomorphic conception of God, for this is modified in at least two important ways. First, certain trivial tasks such as the parading of the animals and the instruction of Adam are delegated to the angels,[2] who were created on the first day.[3] Second, those parts of the narrative which reveal Jahweh's ignorance, jealousy, or envy are expunged: the prohibition of the tree of knowledge, the questioning of Adam and Eve after their Fall, the fears expressed lest Adam should eat of the tree of life, all these episodes are omitted by the Pharisaic redactor. The general intention behind, and the partial effect of, these alterations is to reconcile the Jahwist's account of God's actions with the Priestly writer's description of His nature, to solve, that is, one of the two major metaphysical difficulties inhering in the combination of the two documents. Similarly, the Jahwist's primitive Adam is elevated to accord with the Priestly estimate of his original dignity. This is done by reorganizing the episode of the naming of the animals in such a way that it is no longer implied that a mate for Adam was first sought among the beasts of the field:

And Adam named them all by their respective names, and as he called them, so was their name. And on these five days Adam saw all these, male and female, according to every kind that was on the earth, but he was alone and found no helpmeet for him. And the Lord said unto us: 'It is not good that the man should be alone: let us make a helpmeet for him.'[4]

---

[1] R. H. Charles, *Apocrypha and Pseudepigrapha of the Old Testament*, 1913, ii. 1.
[2] iii. 1; iii. 15.   [3] ii. 2.   [4] iii. 2–4.

By placing God's words after instead of before the naming of the other creatures the author of Jubilees avoids the suggestion that Eve was created as an alternative to them.

One or two minor narrative difficulties also receive attention in this treatment. According to Genesis, one of Adam's tasks was to guard the garden, but it was not made clear what he had to guard it against. Jubilees explains that he was commanded to protect it from the birds, beasts, and cattle.[1] Again, Genesis did not tell us how it was that the serpent could talk, so Jubilees suggests that before the Fall all the animals enjoyed the gift of speech; it was only after the condemnation that

was closed the mouth of all beasts, and of cattle, and of birds, and of whatever walks, and of whatever moves, so that they could no longer speak: for they had all spoken one with another with one lip and with one tongue.[2]

Finally, in Genesis the realization of nakedness was postponed until Adam had eaten the forbidden fruit with Eve. Jubilees does away with this unaccountable delay by making Eve clothe herself with fig-leaves before she approaches her husband.[3]

There remain a number of modifications which were produced not by any problem, but by the desire to furnish authority for some aspect of Hebrew law, or simply to follow up the implications of a particular phrase in the Biblical story. Of the former kind are the notions that Adam spent forty days alone in Eden before Eve joined him,[4] and that he was tempted only after a further seven years;[5] of the latter, the belief that the serpent originally had feet, which he lost as a result of God's condemnation to crawl on his belly,[6] and that after the expulsion 'Adam and his wife went forth from the Garden of Eden, and they dwelt in the land of Elda in the land of their creation'.[7]

The next treatment of the subject, the Book of the Secrets of Enoch (c. 30 B.C.–A.D. 70), is the product of a totally different intellectual environment, of Hellenistic rather than Pharisaic Judaism. Nevertheless, its presentation of the Fall is not so much the

---

[1] iii. 16. [2] iii. 28. [3] iii. 21. [4] iii. 9–14.
[5] iii. 17.

[6] In a note to iii. 23 Charles says that the lacuna in the extant text is to be filled with some such statement as that in Syncellus that the serpent's feet were cut off. The condemnation of the serpent to crawl on its belly was evidently taken to mean that formerly he walked on his feet like other animals.

[7] iii. 32. Presumably this depends on Gen. iii. 23: 'Therefore the Lord God sent him forth from the garden of Eden, to till the ground from whence he was taken.'

beginning of a new line of development as a continuation of those
trends I have already noted in more purely Hebrew works. God
explains to Enoch what happened after He had commanded His
wisdom to create Adam out of seven substances:

> I gave him seven natures: to the flesh hearing, the eyes for sight, to the
> soul smell, the veins for touch, the blood for taste, the bones for endurance,
> to the intelligence sweetness.
>
> I conceived a cunning saying to say, I created man from invisible and
> from visible nature, of both are his death and life and image, he knows
> speech like some created thing, small in greatness and again great in
> smallness, and I placed him on earth, a second angel, honourable, great
> and glorious, and I appointed him as ruler to rule on earth and to have
> my wisdom,
>
> and there was none like him of earth of all my existing creatures. And
> I appointed him a name, from the four component parts, from east, from
> west, from south, from north, and I appointed for him four special stars,
>
> and I called his name Adam, and showed him the two ways, the light
> and the darkness, and I told him: 'This is good, and that bad,' that I
> should learn whether he has love towards me, or hatred, that it be clear
> which in his race love me.
>
> For I have seen his nature, but he has not seen his own nature, there-
> fore through not seeing he will sin worse, and I said: 'After sin what is
> there but death?'
>
> And I put sleep into him and he fell asleep. And I took from him a
> rib, and created him a wife, that death should come to him by his wife,
>
> and I took his last word and called her name mother, that is to say, Eva.[1]

Although this passage is somewhat obscure in places, the conception of Adam's original nature it outlines is clearly in the tradition of
Sirach and Jubilees, that is to say in the perfectionist tradition.
Here he is a second angel, a notion which may have developed from
the use of plural verbs in the description of Adam's creation in the
first chapter of Genesis; given the belief in the prior existence of the
angels which had already been developed in Jubilees, 'in our image'
could be taken to mean 'in the image of the angels'. This insistence
on Man's first perfection did not merely contradict the Jahwist's
view of his nature; it made it quite impossible to accept the implications of the story as a whole, for the over-sudden growth of a childlike creature from ignorance to maturity could hardly be reconciled
with an angelic protoplast. Further, the growing emphasis on God's
benevolence, together with the glorification of wisdom evident in

[1] xxx. 9–18.

both Hebrew wisdom literature and Hellenistic philosophy, militated against the idea that the Deity would have wished to deny His creatures knowledge. Hence here, as in Sirach, the prohibition and violation of the tree of knowledge have completely disappeared. In their place the Hellenistic author introduces a literal seduction of Eve by a fallen angel:

Adam has life on earth, and I created a garden in Eden in the east, that he should observe the testament and keep the command.

I made the heavens open to him, that he should see the angels singing the song of victory, and the gloomless light.

And he was continuously in paradise, and the devil understood that I want [*sic*] to create another world, because Adam was lord on earth, to rule and control it.

The devil is the evil spirit of the lower places, as a fugitive he made, he made Sotona from the heavens as his name was Satomail, thus he became different from the angels, but his nature did not change his intelligence as far as his understanding of righteous and sinful things.

And he understood his condemnation and the sin which he had sinned before, therefore he conceived thought against Adam, in such form he entered and seduced Eva, but did not touch Adam.[1]

This extraordinary innovation may perhaps represent the final fusion of the Watcher story with that of Adam and Eve. In one of the later portions (94–64 B.C.) of the Ethiopic Book of Enoch one of the Watcher angels is described thus: 'And the third [of the fallen angels] was named Gadreel: he it is who showed the children of men all the blows of death, and he led astray Eve.'[2] As the Watchers fell through lusting after the daughters of men, it is possible that this passage refers to a sexual encounter between the angel and Eve. Once the tree of knowledge and the episode involving it became unacceptable for the reasons I have given, it was only natural that a substitute should be sought in the rival Fall story, the Watcher legend, which revolved around the lust of the angels. Earlier in the Secrets of Enoch, Satomail, or Sotona, is described as the leader of the Watchers.[3] His seduction of Eve, therefore, is quite in character with his legendary function.

He is also described as the leader of one of the ten troops of angels who were created on the second day:

And one from out the order of angels, having turned away with the order that was under him, conceived an impossible thought, to place his throne higher than the clouds above the earth, that he might become equal in rank to my power.

And I threw him out from the height with his angels, and he was flying in the air continuously above the bottomless.[1]

Behind this account of the Devil's rebellion and fall there lies the famous passage in Isaiah in which the King of Babylon is compared to the morning star:

How art thou fallen from heaven, O Lucifer, son of the morning! how art thou cut down to the ground, which didst weaken the nations!

For thou hast said in thine heart, I will ascend into heaven, I will exalt my throne above the stars of God: I will sit also upon the mount of the congregation, in the sides of the north:

I will ascend above the heights of the clouds; I will be like the Most High.

Yet thou shalt be brought down to hell, to the sides of the pit.[2]

Prompted by the Vulgate translation of 'morning-star' as 'Lucifer', which the Authorized Version follows, and further encouraged by centuries of patristic commentary, the modern reader naturally assumes that these verses concern Satan's primordial conflict with his Creator, but in this he is almost certainly mistaken. As L. Jung has demonstrated, the Old Testament Satan was no more than a kind of celestial prosecutor, whose function it was to test Man's virtue and accuse him when it was found wanting; nowhere is he portrayed as acting independently of, or contrary to, the wishes of God.[3] The Isaiah story is simply an ancient astral myth, based on the disappearance of Venus at the break of day, which has been used by the prophet to illustrate the inevitability of Babylon's downfall.[4] By misinterpreting this myth, and by associating the rebellious angel thus produced with Satan, the serpent, and the Watcher angels, the author of the Secrets of Enoch initiated the spectacular developments in the history of the Devil which took place in both Judaism and Christianity, and finally culminated in the celestial warfare of *Paradise Lost*.

The character of the Deity, too, is of interest in this work. Adam and Eve could hardly be blamed for their Fall as it is presented in

---

[1] xxix. 4–5. [2] Isa. xiv. 12–15.

[3] 'Fallen Angels in Jewish, Christian and Mohammedan Literature', *J.Q.R.*, N.S. xv (1924), 489–94.

[4] See G. W. Wade, *The Book of the Prophet Isaiah*, 1911, p. 100; G. B. Gray, *A Critical and Exegetical Commentary on the Book of Isaiah*, 1912, p. 255.

the Secrets of Enoch, so their subsequent condemnation posed a distinct problem if the Divine justice was to be preserved. It is solved by interpreting the episode semi-allegorically, thereby minimizing the terms of the sentence and maximizing God's mercy:

> But I cursed ignorance, but what I had blessed previously, those I did not curse, I cursed not man,
>> nor the earth, nor other creatures, but man's evil fruit, and his works.
>> I said to him: 'Earth thou art, and into the earth whence I took thee thou shalt go, and I will not ruin thee, but send thee whence I took thee. Then I can again take thee at My second coming.'
> And I blessed all my creatures visible and invisible. And Adam was five and half hours in paradise. And I blessed the seventh day, which is the Sabbath, on which he rested from all his works.[1]

Benediction rather than condemnation is the dominant theme in this version of the episode. The curse on ignorance, indeed, is scarcely a curse at all so far as Adam is concerned, and it reveals by implication an attitude very similar to that expressed in the Wisdom of Solomon (*post* 50 B.C.):

> She [Wisdom] guarded to the end the first formed father of the world, that was created alone,
> And delivered him out of his transgression,
> And gave him strength to get dominion over all things.[2]

Out of these two trends in Jewish thought, the insistence on God's benevolence and the ever-growing emphasis on the desirability of wisdom, there grew the Gnostic inversion of the Fall story which I shall be discussing at the beginning of the following chapter.

The Wisdom of Solomon also contains the oft-quoted verse:

> But by the envy of the devil death entered into the world,
> And they that belong to his realm experience it.[3]

Neither here nor in the Book of Sirach, where death is stated to be the consequence of a woman's sin,[4] is there any certainty that the reference is to the disobedience of Adam and Eve; both passages could equally well apply to the Watcher story. In the sister works, the Syriac Apocalypse of Baruch and the Fourth Book of Ezra, however, there is abundant evidence that by the end of the first century of our era the Fall of Adam and Eve had come to be

---

[1] xxxi. 7–xxxii. 2. Presumably the curse on Adam's evil fruit is an allegorical interpretation of the curse on the earth.

[2] x. 1–2.   [3] ii. 24.   [4] xxv. 24.

regarded by orthodox Jewish thinkers as the cause not only of Man's mortality but also of his hereditary sinfulness:

This is my first and last word; better had it been that the earth had not produced Adam, or else, having once produced him, (for thee) to have restrained him from sinning.

For how does it profit us all that in the present we must live in grief and after death look for punishment?

O thou Adam, what hast thou done! For though it was thou that sinned, the fall was not thine alone, but ours also who art thy descendants!

For how does it profit us that the eternal age is promised to us, whereas we have done the works that bring death?

And that there is foretold to us an imperishable hope, whereas we so miserably are brought to futility?[1]

Whereas all the earlier Apocrypha, even those which, like Jubilees, treated the Fall narrative at length, traced the origin of human misery back to the sexual corruption of mankind by the Watcher angels, these two, influenced perhaps by the fusion of the Watcher with the Adam story accomplished in the Secrets of Enoch, pointed for the first time to the violation of the tree of knowledge as the source of 'all our woe'.[2] In the process they also invoked the theory of the *yezer-ha-ra* to explain how Adam's sin was passed on to his descendants, so reconciling the rabbinic diagnosis of evil with the apocryphal account of the cause of the malady. But, as I have said, the disasters of A.D. 70 and 135 brought about the disappearance of the genre to which all these works belong. It was left to St. Paul to refine and develop the doctrinal synthesis which apocalyptic Judaism had achieved just before its final destruction.[3]

2. *The Rabbinic Literature*

Unlike the various Apocrypha and Pseudepigrapha the majority of the rabbinic tractates do not represent the writings or the ideas of any one man. Even works attributed to a single author, the *Pirkê de Rabbi Eliezer* (ninth century), Rashi's *Commentary on the Pentateuch* (eleventh century), Maimonides's *Guide for the Perplexed* (twelfth century), and *The Chronicles of Jerahmeel* (fourteenth century), are in

---

[1] 4 *Ezra* vii. 116–20. See also Syriac Baruch xvii. 3, xix. 8, xxiii. 4.

[2] Syriac Baruch, it should be added in qualification, is careful to stress Man's free will, viz. liv. 19: 'Adam is therefore not the cause, save only of his own soul, But each of us has been the Adam of his own soul.'

[3] See below, Ch. III, pp. 60–61.

fact little more than collections of Biblical interpretations culled from earlier periods. Their Christian equivalents would be the medieval *compendia* and *florilegia* rather than the commentaries of great original thinkers like Origen. The dates given for their composition, therefore, indicate only the time at which the material they contain was assembled and written down; the material itself often ante-dates the compilation by several centuries.[1]

As a result, it would serve no useful purpose to treat these works one by one in chronological order. They can be more profitably discussed as a whole, representing as they do an organically related body of oral and literary tradition, but even this method has its dangers. The portions of rabbinic lore relating to the Fall story belong to what is known as the *haggadah*, which is primarily explanatory and imaginative in nature, as opposed to the *halakhah*, which is legalistic and logical. Haggadic amplifications of the Scriptural text are scattered here and there throughout the *Talmud* (sixth century) and the *Midrash Rabbah* (sixth to twelfth century), the two most comprehensive compilations of rabbinic beliefs, wherever the *Mishna* or the Bible itself suggested a particular illustration or allusion. To try to reduce them to a dogmatic system, as some scholars have done, can be extremely misleading, for, as Jung has emphasized, the Rabbis themselves made no attempt to weave their stories into a consistent doctrinal or narrative pattern; contradictory versions of the same episode and incompatible theories derived from the same passage often exist side by side in this literature, and in reading it we have constantly to remind ourselves that 'there is no such thing as a systematic Jewish theology'.[2] This is at once the strength and the weakness of rabbinic speculation. It presents a complex picture, but the picture is whole.

Rabbinic statements regarding the consequences of the Fall illustrate the point very clearly. On the one hand, it was categorically asserted that Adam 'received the penalty of death and caused the pangs of death to be brought upon the world';[3] on the other, that the righteous 'are punished with death for slight transgressions' so that 'Adam might not be called to account by them'.[4] For every

---

[1] The date of a Rabbi to whom a saying is ascribed offers a rough guide. See the index of Rabbis in I. Epstein, *The Babylonian Talmud*, vol. xxxv.

[2] L. Lung, op. cit., pp. 469–72.

[3] *Num. Rab.* x. 2. See also *Ex. Rab.* xxxviii. 2; *Deut. Rab.* ix. 8; *Ecc. Rab.* vii. 13; *Shabb.* 55b.

[4] *Num. Rab.* xix. 18. See also ibid. xvi. 24; *Lev. Rab.* xxvii. 4.

passage which claims that the Fall caused human mortality another can be found which denies that it did anything of the kind.

Rabbinic methods of exegesis, however, were by no means as arbitrary as these contradictions might suggest. From the effort to prove the oral law by reference to the *Torah* and the Pentateuch there arose certain *middoth* or exegetical rules, which, although they were originally intended for halachic application, were also employed in haggadic discussions.[1] In general, these rules made for the most minute quasi-logical exposition of the Biblical text, and their application to the first three chapters of Genesis created a whole host of new developments in the elaboration of the story of the Fall of Man.

As we have already seen, the plural verbs in the Priestly account of Man's creation had been taken by both Jubilees and the Secrets of Enoch to imply the prior existence of the angels. According to the former they were created on the first day, according to the latter on second. *The Targum of Jonathan* (pre-seventh century) and *Genesis Rabba* (one of the older books in the *Midrash Rabbah*) were inclined to agree with the latter on the grounds that God's sole authorship of the Creation might otherwise be called into question:

> When were the angels created? R. Johanan said: They were created on the second day, . . . R. Hanina said: They were created on the fifth day, . . . R. Luliana b. Tabri said in R. Isaac's name: Whether we accept the view of R. Hanina or that of R. Johanan, all agree that none were created on the first day, lest you should say, Michael stretched [the world] in the south and Gabriel in the north.[2]

From this basic situation, possibly from the hortative verb in 'Let us make',[3] there developed the idea that the angels were not altogether convinced of the wisdom of making Man:

> [R. Hanina said that] when He [God] came to create Adam, He took counsel with the ministering angels, saying to them, 'Let us make man.' 'What shall his character be?' asked they. 'Righteous men shall spring from him' He answered. . . . He revealed to them that the righteous would arise from him, but He did not reveal to them that the wicked would spring from him, for had He revealed to them that the wicked would spring from him the quality of Justice would not have permitted him to be created.[4]

---

[1] For a detailed account of these rules see H. L. Strack, *Introduction to the Talmud and Midrash*, Philadelphia, 1945, ch. xi.

[2] *Gen. Rab.* i. 3. See also *Targ. Jon.* i.

[3] *Gen.* i. 26.

[4] *Gen. Rab.* viii. 4.

The difficulty at the root of this *haggadah* is precisely that which was to trouble generations of Christian theologians: if God could foresee the Fall and the ensuing wickedness of Man, why did He create him at all? The answer here and elsewhere in Jewish writings on the subject is that His love of righteousness was greater than His hatred of sin. Occasionally the conflict was put in dramatic form, consisting of a debate between either the angels or the four daughters of God:

R. Simon said: When the Holy One, blessed be He, came to create Adam, the ministering angels formed themselves into groups and parties, some of them saying, 'Let him be created,' whilst others urged, 'Let him not be created.' Thus it is written, *Love and Truth fought together, Righteousness and Peace combatted each other* [Ps. lxxxv. 11]: Love said, 'Let him be created, because he will dispense acts of love'; Truth said, 'Let him not be created, because he is compounded of falsehood'; Righteousness said, 'Let him be created, because he will perform righteous deeds'; Peace said, 'Let him not be created, because he is full of strife.' What did the Lord do? He took Truth and cast it to the ground.[1]

In some sources the debate was simplified by putting the objections of Truth and Peace in the mouth of the *Torah* and the answers of Love and Righteousness in the mouth of God,[2] while in several others the basis of the conflict was omitted, leaving only the unmotivated opposition of the angels.[3] In none of them, however, is there to be found any trace of the Satanic rebellion as related in the Secrets of Enoch.

The angelic counsel preceding the creation of Man was one of those seminal episodes out of which grew a wide variety of subsidiary legends. The popular medieval theme of the debate of the four daughters of God is dependent on it, and the motive for Satan's rebellion in the Vita Adae et Evae is only another variation.[4] In strictly rabbinic works, on the other hand, it came to be associated with Adam's ability to name the animals:

'And he was wiser than all' [1 Kings iv. 31]—this means than the first man: and what was his wisdom? You find that when the Holy One, Blessed be He, sought to create man, He took counsel with the ministering angels. He said to them, 'Let us make man in our own image' [Gen. i. 26]. They said before Him, 'What is man that Thou art mindful of him?' He

---

[1] Ibid. viii. 5.   [2] *Jer.* vi. 8; *P.R.E.* xi.   [3] *Sanh.* 38b; *Jer.* vi. 3.
[4] See below, Ch. II, p. 56; Ch. IX, pp. 232–41.

said to them, 'The wisdom of man whom I desire to create in my world will be greater than yours.' What did He do? He gathered all the living beasts and birds and caused them to pass before them. He said to them, 'What are the names of these?' and they did not know.[1]

Only Adam succeeded in giving the creatures their names, thereby winning the contest and justifying his creation. Thus the episode which in Genesis had illustrated Adam's primitive nature came to be read in exactly the opposite way as an example of his original perfection.

Once the plurals which God had applied to Himself in Genesis had been taken to refer to the angels, the phrase 'in our image' naturally invited the interpretation 'in the image of the angels'. This development, which had taken place by the time of the composition of the Secrets of Enoch, played a great part in shaping rabbinic ideas on the subject of Man's unfallen condition, as the following comment reveals: 'I made him equal to the ministering angels—for it says, *Behold, the man was as one of us* [Gen. iii. 22].'[2] Like the angels he was created fully formed and mature in every respect:

R. Judah b. R. Simon said: . . . he was created as a young man in his fulness. R. Eleazer b. R. Simeon said: Eve too was created fully developed. R. Johanan said: Adam and Eve were created as at the age of twenty.[3]

His beauty was such that his heel out-dazzled the light of the sun itself:

Rabbi Levi said in the name of Rabbi Simeon B. Menasya, 'The heel of the first man made the sun look dark, and do not be surprised at this, for it is usual among men that one makes for oneself two vessels, one for one's own use and one for that of some member of the household. For whom would he make a more beautiful one? Surely for himself. Even so, the Holy One, Blessed be He, created the first man for His own purposes, and the circle of the sun for the use of the creatures: by analogy He would make the sun darker; and seeing that the heel is such, how much brighter will be the face of the first man?'[4]

---

[1] *Pesikta*, 34a, quoted in W. D. Davies, op. cit., Appendix C. See also *Gen. Rab.* xvii. 4; *Num. Rab.* xix. 3; *Ecc. Rab.* vii. 23; *Jer.* xxii. 1; *P.R.E.* xiii.

[2] *Ex. Rab.* xxxii. 1.

[3] *Gen. Rab.* xiv. 7. See also *S.S.Rab.* iii. 11. *Hull.* 60a extends the idea to cover the animal creation as well: 'All the animals of the creation were created in their full-grown stature.'

[4] *Pesikta*, 36b, quoted in W. D. Davies, loc. cit. See also *Lev. Rab.* xx. 2; *Ecc. Rab.* viii. 1; *B.B.* 58a; Sirach xlix. 16.

So great was Adam's beauty, indeed, that although some men inherited particular characteristics of his, none possessed them all:

Six people were similar to the first man, and they were all slain. They were: Samson with his might . . . Saul with his stature . . . Asahel with his swiftness . . . Josiah with his nostrils . . . Zedekiah with his eyes . . . Absolom with his hair.[1]

But if the Priestly document, with its pregnant phrases concerning the divine or angelic image, gave rise to the concept of Man's original perfection, the Jahwist document, with its assertion that Adam was formed out of earth, made it necessary to modify that concept in certain respects; although Adam was created in the image of the angels, there was no escaping the fact that he was also a quintessence of dust. Consequently his status was most frequently defined as being somewhere between that of the angels, on the one hand, and the animals, on the other. The Secrets of Enoch had already dwelt on this fusion of earthly and angelic, and the Rabbis pursued the idea in some detail:

R. Joshua b. R. Nehemiah said in the name of R. Hanina b. R. Isaac, and the Rabbis in the name of R. Leazer said: He [God] created him with four attributes of the higher beings [i.e. angels] and four attributes of the lower beings [i.e. beasts]. [The four attributes of] the higher beings are: he stands upright, like the ministering angels; he speaks, like the ministering angels; he understands, like the ministering angels; and he sees, like the ministering angels. . . . He has four attributes of the lower beings: he eats and drinks, like an animal; procreates, like an animal; excretes, like an animal; and dies, like an animal.[2]

This analysis, of course, was to be strictly distinguished from any form of dualism, a point made forcibly by R. Amemar:

A *magi* once said to Amemar: From the middle of thy [body] upwards thou belongest to *Ormuzd*; from the middle downwards, to *Ahriman*. The latter asked: Why then does *Ahriman* permit *Ormuzd* to send water through his territory?[3]

[1] *P.R.E.* liii, See also *Sot.* 10a. Philo puts the matter succinctly in *De Op. Mun.* xlix: 'Such was the first man created, as I think, in body and soul, surpassing all the men that now are, and all that have been before us.'

[2] *Gen. Rab.* viii. 11. In *Hag.* 16a these four *differentia* become three; sight is omitted from the angelic and death from the bestial attributes. The reason may be that before the Fall Adam did not possess the angelic power of sight, for his eyes had not been opened and he was not yet 'as one of us'. And he did not become mortal until he ate the forbidden fruit.

[3] *Sanh.* 39a. A *magi* is a Zoroastrian, according to whose beliefs there were two co-eternal and mutually antagonistic deities, the good Ormuzd and the evil Ahriman.

Applied to the question of Adam's mortality, the combination of angelic and animal attributes produced a theory very similar to the one which may have been in the Jahwist's mind:

R. Tifdai said in R. Aha's name: The Holy One, blessed be He, said: 'If I create him of the celestial elements he will live [for ever] and not die, and if I create him of the terrestrial elements, he will die and not live [in a future life]. Therefore I will create him of the upper and of the lower elements: if he sins he will die; while if he does not sin, he will live.'[1]

Before the Fall Adam was poised between heaven and earth, between mortality and immortality. In spite of his many perfections his destiny was in the balance.

Adam's origin in the dust of the earth was also the occasion of several haggadic amplifications concerning his microcosmic nature. This had already been explored in the Secrets of Enoch, according to which his name was derived from the initials of the four compass points,[2] and his constituent parts from the earth, dew, sun, cloud, stones, grass, wind, and God's breath.[3] The Rabbis went even further, claiming that the dust of which Adam was made was collected from the four corners of the world:

R. Meir used to say: The dust of the first man was gathered from all parts of the earth. . . . R. Oshaiah said in Rab's name: Adam's trunk came from Babylon, his head from *Erez Yisrael*, his limbs from other lands, and his private parts, according to R. Aha, from Akra di Agma.[4]

In an attempt to provide an explanation for this complicated procedure later sources suggested that God collected earth from all

[1] *Gen. Rab.* viii. 11. Philo had expressed the same idea in *De Op. Mun.* xlvi: 'man is the borderland between mortal and immortal nature, partaking of each so far as is needful.' However, he related this relative condition to Man's constitution of spirit and flesh: 'he was created at once mortal and immortal, mortal in respect of the body, but in respect of the mind immortal.' In his *Leg. All.* i. xxix–xxx he went on to apply this idea to Man's moral nature, claiming that he is 'neither good nor bad but midway between these.' See also Rashi, *On Genesis*, ii. 7.

[2] xxx. 13–14. *Sot.* 5a, on the other hand, derived Adam's name from the Hebrew words for 'dust, blood, and gall', while in *Antiquities*, I. i. 2 Josephus connected it with red earth (*adamah*), from which, he claimed, Adam was created.

[3] xxx. 8. See my note on 'Microcosmic Adam' in *Medium Ævum*, xxxv (1966), 38–42, for the subsequent history of this idea. *A.R.N.* xxxi elaborated the same basic notion in terms of correspondences rather than ingredients:
R. Eliezer the son of R. Jose the Galilean said: . . . He [God] created the heavens and the earth in the upper and lower regions, and created in man all that he created in his world; the world contains forests, so also does man, viz., his hair; the world contains evil beasts, so also does man, viz., lice.

[4] *Sanh.* 38a–b. A note explains that Akra di Agma was a town notorious for its loose morals. See also *P.R.E.* xi; *Jer*, vi. 6; *Targ. Jon.* ii; Rashi, *On Genesis*, ii. 7.

over the world, in order that 'wherever he [Adam] should die there he should be received for burial'.[1] At its most extreme Adam's microcosmic nature was taken to imply that he literally filled the entire world: 'Rab Judah said in Rab's name: The first man reached from the one end of the world to the other. . . . R. Eleazer said: The first man reached from earth to heaven.'[2]

The creation of Eve was no less fruitful in the production of extra-Biblical legends. The abrupt change from singular to plural in Genesis i. 27 led several Rabbis to the conclusion that Adam and Eve were originally created as a unity: 'R. Jeremiah b. Leazer said: When the Holy One, blessed be He, created Adam, He created him an hermaphrodite . . . for it is said, *Male and female created He them and called their name Adam*'.[3] But it was the account of Eve's birth from Adam's rib in the second chapter of Genesis which proved to be most amenable to creative interpretation. *Jerahmeel*, for instance, recorded the story that Adam's original majesty was so great that:

All the creatures saw him and were afraid of him; they thought he was their creator, and prostrated themselves before him. Adam then said to the animals: 'Why do you come and prostrate yourselves before me? Come, let us all go and invest Him who created us with majesty and strength, and crown Him King over us.'[4]

Eve was created in order to avoid any possible recurrence of the creatures' mistake:

Now Adam walked about the Garden of Eden like one of the ministering angels. God said: 'Just as I am alone in My world, so is Adam; just as I have no companion, neither has Adam. Tomorrow the creatures will say, 'He does not propagate, he is surely our creator.' It is not good for man to be alone, I will make a helpmeet for him.'[5]

---

[1] Rashi, *On Genesis*, ii. 7. See also *P.R.E.* xi; *Jer.* vi. 9.

[2] *Sanh.* 38b. See also *Gen. Rab.* viii. 1; *Lev. Rab.* xiv. 1; *Hag.* 12a; *A.R.N.* vii.

[3] *Gen. Rab.* viii. 1. See also Rashi, *On Genesis*, i. 27; *Guide*, ii. 30. *Lev. Rab.* xiv. 1 suggests that Adam and Eve were created like Siamese twins in the first instance and separated later.

[4] *Jer.* vi. 12. See also *P.R.E.* xi.

[5] *Jer.* vi. 13. See also Rashi, *On Genesis*, ii. 18. The reason offered in *Gen. Rab.* viii. 10 and *Ecc. Rab.* vi. 10 for Adam's sleep during Eve's creation was based upon the same circumstance:

When the Holy One, blessed be He, created Adam, the ministering angels mistook him for a divine being and wished to exclaim 'Holy' before him. . . . What did the Holy One, blessed be He, do? He caused sleep to fall upon him, and so all knew that he was [but mortal] man.

More commonly the Rabbis emphasized God's benevolence rather than His jealousy at this point of the story. Rabban Gamaliel explained that if Adam had witnessed the making of Eve he would have found her loathsome,[1] and R. Jose went so far as to posit that this had actually happened on a previous occasion: 'At first He created her for him and he saw her full of discharge and blood; thereupon He removed her from him and created her a second time.'[2] Adam was put to sleep, therefore, so that Eve would attract him. The Creator's choice of a rib was dictated by equally benevolent motives:

R. Joshuah of Siknin commenced in R. Levi's name: . . . Said He: 'I will not create her from [Adam's] head, lest she be lightheaded [frivolous]; nor from the eye, lest she be a coquette; nor from the ear, lest she be an eavesdropper; nor from the mouth, lest she be a gossip; nor from the heart, lest she be prone to jealousy; nor from the hand, lest she be light-fingered; nor from the foot, lest she be a gadabout. But [I will create her] from the modest part of man, for even when he stands naked, that part is covered.[3]

Unhappily, another sage went on to observe, the plan misfired, and all these undesirable qualities are to be found even in the best of women.[4] In similar vein the differences between the male and female temperaments were traced to the respective origins of Adam and Eve in earth and bone:

And why is a man easily pacified and a woman is not easily pacified? He (derives his nature) from the place from which he was created and she (derives hers) from the place from which she was created.[5]

When Adam first saw his newly created wife two kinds of reaction were ascribed to him. Rashi claimed that 'his heart's longings were not satisfied . . . until he met Eve',[6] but *Genesis Rabba*, referring to the story of Eve's previous creation, interpreted Adam's waking words as meaning: 'This is she of the previous occasion; this is she who is destined to strike the bell and to speak [in strife] against me

[1] *Sanh.* 39a. See also Rashi, *On Genesis*, ii. 21.

[2] *Gen. Rab.* xvii. 7. The Roman lady to whom this story is told remarks: 'I can corroborate your words . . . It had been arranged that I should be married to my mother's brother, but because I was brought up with him in the same home I became plain in his eyes and he went and married another woman, who is not as beautiful as I.'

[3] *Gen. Rab.* lxxx. 5. See also ibid. xviii. 2.

[4] *Deut. Rab.* vi. 11.

[5] *Nid.* 31b. See also *Gen. Rab.* xvii. 8.   [6] Rashi, *On Genesis*, ii. 22.

... it is she who troubled me ... all night.'[1] By far the most popular *haggadah* to grow out of this episode, however, concerned the subsequent union of the first pair. God Himself, it was taught, adorned Eve as a bride and brought her to her future husband:

> For R. Simeon b. Menasia expounded: What is meant by the words, '*And the Lord God built the rib*'? It teaches that the Holy One, blessed be He, plaited Eve's hair and brought her to Adam; for in the seacoast towns 'plaiting' is called 'building' ... *And he brought her to the man.* R. Jeremiah B. Eleazer said: This teaches that [God] acted as best man to Adam.[2]

The whole incident was embroidered with all the trappings of a formal Jewish wedding, with the result that the first meeting of Adam and Eve became an actual marriage:

> The Holy One, blessed be He, made ten wedding canopies for Adam in the garden of Eden.... The ministering angels were going to and fro and walking before him like friends who guard the wedding canopies.[3]

These comments on Man's unfallen experiences are notable for their continual emphasis on the physical aspect of things, and the same is true of the rabbinic interpretations of the two trees, the tree of knowledge and the tree of life. Nowhere is it asked or explained what kind of knowledge or immortality they conferred. The Rabbis were interested only in determining their physical nature and appearance. The most frequent remark to be made on the tree of life, for example, was that it was of immense size, so huge, in fact, that it would have taken a journey of five hundred years' duration to encompass it.[4] As regards the tree of knowledge, it was its species which was the chief point of interest. One school of thought inferred from the fact that Adam and Eve clothed themselves with the leaves of a fig-tree when they had fallen that the forbidden fruit too must have been a fig:

> R. Jose said: They were figs. He learns the obscure from the explicit, and [the meaning of] a statement from its context, thus: This may be compared to a royal prince who sinned with a slave girl, and the king on

---

[1] *Gen. Rab.* xviii. 4.

[2] *Ber.* 61a. See also *Gen. Rab.* xviii. 1; *Er.* 18a–b; *Jer.* vii. 2; *P.R.E.* xii; passages cited in C. G. Montefiore and H. Loewe, *A Rabbinic Anthology*, 1938, p. 281.

[3] *P.R.E.* xii.

[4] *Gen. Rab.* xv. 6; *S.S.Rab.* vi. 9; *Targ. Jon.* ii. This rather strange idea may be connected with the fact that the olive-tree, with which the tree of life was often associated, is reputed to live for 500 years.

learning of it expelled him from court. He went from door to door of the
slaves, but they would not receive him; but she who had sinned with him
opened her door and received him. So when Adam ate of that tree, He
expelled him and cast him out of the garden of Eden; and he appealed to
all the trees, but they would not receive him. . . . But because he had
eaten of its fruit, the fig-tree opened its doors and received him.[1]

The Ethiopic Enoch, on the other hand, had likened the tree of knowledge to a vine, and several Rabbis accepted this association, taking
the opportunity to draw the inevitable moral that wine is the ultimate
cause of human misery: 'R. Meir holds that the tree of which Adam
ate was the vine, since the thing that most causes wailing to a man
is wine.'[2]

Of more immediate interest is the rabbinic solution to the problem
of the serpent's identity. As we have seen, the Secrets of Enoch had
effected a fusion of the Watcher with the Adam story by portraying
the Fall as a sexual assault on Eve by the fallen Sotona. While
insisting that the serpent was only a serpent the Rabbis incorporated
the sexual motif into their version of the temptation by attributing
to the snake the lustful intentions of the leader of the Watcher
angels:

Said R. Joshuah b. Karhah: It teaches you through what sin that wicked
creature inveigled them, viz. because he saw them engaged in their natural
functions, he [the serpent] conceived a passion for her [Eve].[3]

This account of the tempter's reason for corrupting Eve clearly
implied that she and Adam had sexual relations before the Fall, and
the point was reinforced by Rashi, who noted that the pluperfect
form of the verb 'knew' at the beginning of the fourth chapter of
Genesis proved that Cain's conception must have taken place before
the expulsion.[4]

---

[1] *Gen. Rab.* xv. 7. See also *Ber.* 40a; *Sanh.* 70a–b; Rashi, *On Genesis*, iii. 7.

[2] *Ber.* 40a. See also Ethiopic Enoch xxxii. 3–6; *Num. Rab.* x. 2; ibid. x. 4; *Es. Rab.* v.
1; *Sanh.* 70a–b. This idea produced an interesting subsidiary *haggadah* connecting
Adam's vine with Noah's in Gen. ix. 20. *Targ. Jon.* ix and *P.R.E.* xxiii state that Noah's
vine was carried to him from Eden by a river, and according to *Sanh.* 70a–b God
reproved Noah for his drunkenness by reminding him of Adam's lapse. Christian treatments of the subject, on the other hand, saw in Noah's drunkenness not a second Fall
but a figure of the Redemption (see H. Gardner, *The Limits of Literary Criticism*, 1956,
ch. i).

[3] *Gen. Rab.* xviii. 6. See also Rashi, *On Genesis*, iii. 1. In *Sot.* 9a–b the serpent is said
to have even contemplated marriage with Eve.

[4] Rashi, *On Genesis*, iv. 1.

To return to the serpent, however, he resembled Sotona not only in the nature of his designs but also in his success in carrying them out: 'R. Johanan stated: When the serpent copulated with Eve, he infused her with lust.'[1] Popular though this legend was, one or two Rabbis were not content with concupiscence as a motive for the reptile's hostility to Adam. They suggested instead that all Man's material benefits in Eden were the object of his envy:

R. Judah b. Tema said: Adam reclined in the Garden of Eden, whilst the ministering angels roasted flesh and strained wine for him. Thereupon the serpent looked in, saw his glory, and became envious of him.[2]

The existence of such characteristically human feelings in a mere beast of the field was rendered less fantastic by the semi-human form with which he was invested in these sources. Taking up the hints dropped in Jubilees, the Rabbis asserted that before the Fall the serpent walked and talked like a man. Rabbi Joshua of Siknin, for example, commented on God's curse: 'And what did God do unto him? He severed his feet and cut off his tongue, so that he should no [longer] be able to speak.'[3] The conversation with Eve thus presented no problems, for the 'first serpent possessed the power of speech like human beings'.[4]

This general conception of the tempter's appearance and nature may, perhaps, represent a compromise between the Secrets of Enoch and Genesis, between that is to say, the angelic and the serpentine assaults on Man's innocence. Later treatments, on the contrary, broke the equation back down into its constituent elements and maintained a very clear distinction between the angel and the animal:

Sammael had twelve wings. What did Sammael do? He took his band and descended and saw all the creatures . . . and he found among them none so skilled to do evil as the serpent. . . . Its appearance was something like that of the camel, and he mounted and rode upon it.[5]

But once the angel was introduced into the story as an independent figure a motive had to be provided for him too. It was found in the naming contest between Adam and the angels. According to

[1] *Yeb.* 103a–b. See also *Shab.* 145b–146a; *Ab. Z.* 22b.
[2] *Sanh.* 59b. See also Josephus's *Antiquities*, I. i. 4; *A.R.N.* i.
[3] *Deut. Rab.* v. 10. See also *Gen. Rab.* xix. 1, xx. 5; *Ecc. Rab.* x. 11; *Targ. Jon.* iii; Rashi *On Genesis*, ii. 14; *P.R.E.* xiv.
[4] *Deut. Rab.* v. 10.
[5] *P.R.E.* xiii. See also *Guide*, ii. 30; *Jer.* xxii. 2.

Jerahmeel, when Adam had won the competition, 'The angels then began to envy him, saying, "Indeed, God will now love him more than He does us: if we can entice him to sin he will be destroyed from the earth."'[1] Again there is no trace of any premundane rebellion as such; Sammael, the leader of these envious but still unfallen angels,[2] was condemned *because* he tempted Adam and Eve.

From the examples of rabbinic exegesis already quoted it is obvious that the literal meaning of the Biblical text took pride of place, and that as a result the story's narrative problems received more attention than its interpretative or metaphysical difficulties. Nowhere is this clearer than in the rabbinic interpretation of the temptation itself. The first problem here was Adam's absence at the crucial moment:

Now where was Adam during this conversation? Abba Halfon b. Koriah said: He had engaged in his natural functions and then fallen asleep. The Rabbis said: He [God] took him and led him all round the world.[3]

The second was the serpent's decision to approach Eve rather than Adam. Those Rabbis who accepted the sexual version of the episode could, of course, assume that he chose her because it was she that he desired, but when the sexual interpretation was abandoned the choice of Eve demanded some other explanation: 'At that time the wicked serpent said to himself: "As it is impossible for me to make Adam stumble, [for he himself received the words from the Lord], I will make Eve stumble."'[4] His reasoning was based on the fact that, according to the sequence of events in Genesis, Eve had not yet been created when God forbade the tree of knowledge.[5] The commentator therefore assumed that Adam must have informed Eve of the command on some later occasion, so that she received it at second hand. When she repeated it to the serpent, however, she inserted the additional phrase 'neither shall ye touch it'.[6] From these two incidental details the Rabbis deduced that Adam must have deliberately exaggerated the terms of the prohibition when he passed them on to Eve:

[1] *Jer.* xxii. 1. See also *P.R.E.* xiii.

[2] The divine suffix '-*el*' indicates that he is still an inhabitant of heaven.

[3] *Gen. Rab.* xix. 3. This passage confirms my statement that the Rabbis assumed that Adam and Eve enjoyed sexual relations before the Fall.

[4] *A.R.N.* i. See also *P.R.E.* xiii.

[5] See Gen. ii. 16–17.

[6] Gen. iii. 3.

We see, then, that Adam did not want to give Eve the exact words he received, but he added: 'Ye shall not eat of it, neither shall ye touch it, lest ye die', in order that they should take care even not to touch the tree.[1]

This minor *haggadah* became in turn the basis of the entire temptation in those sources which retained the verbal encounter:

when he [the serpent] saw her thus lying, he took and thrust her against it [the tree]. 'Have you then died?' he said to her; 'just as you were not stricken through touching it, so you will not die when you eat of it.'[2]

In a more complex account of the incident the serpent himself touched the tree:

He said to her: 'As thou sayest that the Holy One, blessed be He, has forbidden thee to touch it, see that I am touching it and will not die, and the same will be with thee.' And so he did; he arose and shook the tree with his hands and feet till the fruit fell down. . . . The serpent said again to her: 'If thou sayest that the Holy One, blessed be He, forbade to eat it, see I eat of it, and do not die, and thou mayest do the same and thou wilt not die.' So Eve said to herself, the injunctions of my master are unfounded.[3]

Eve's transgression, then, was the result of a trick whereby the serpent, by proving to her that a part of the command as transmitted by Adam was unfounded, led her to believe that the prohibition as a whole was groundless. In this form the Fall became perfectly credible and the transition from perfection to sinfulness quite natural. What is more, the real responsibility for it was transferred from Eve to Adam: 'And who caused all this? The words that Adam added: " 'Ye shall not touch it.' "[4] There was an obvious moral here, and the Rabbis were not slow to draw it:

But a man should not make a fence higher than the object which it is to guard, lest the fence fall and crush the plants. This is what Adam did, who added the prohibition against touching the tree; he made a fence higher than the object, and the fence fell and crushed the plants.[5]

[1] *A.R.N.* i. See also Rashi, *On Genesis*, iii. 3.
[2] *Gen. Rab.* xix. 3. See also Rashi, *On Genesis*, iii. 4. The translator, J. H. Lowe, was apparently unaware of this tradition and mistakenly added 'by persuasive words' after 'pushed her'.
[3] *A.R.N.* i. See also *P.R.E.* xiii; *Jer.* xxii. 2–3.   [4] *A.R.N.* i.
[5] Quoted in Montefiore and Loewe, op. cit., pp. 156–7. These editors add a note to the effect that it was really Eve who made this mistake, but their correction is surely misconceived. The whole point of the story is that Adam brought about the Fall by exaggerating the command, not that Eve did so when she spoke to the serpent.

If Adam was typical of his sex in his over-solicitous warning to his wife, she was no less typical of hers in her motives for persuading her husband to fall with her:

As soon as she had eaten thereof her teeth were set on edge, and she saw the angel of death with drawn sword standing before her. She then said in her heart, 'Woe unto me that I have eaten of this death, for now I will die; and Adam, my husband, who has not eaten of it will live for ever, and God will couple him with another woman. It is better that we die together, for God has created us together even unto death.' So when her husband came she gave him some of the fruit to taste.[1]

The similarity between this Eve and Milton's needs no stressing. Equally feminine was the manner of her persuasion:

R. Simlai said: She came upon him with her answers all ready, saying to him: 'What think you: that I will die and another Eve will be created for you?' . . . The Rabbis said: She began weeping and crying over him.[2]

The two major narrative difficulties of the Biblical story, Eve's submission to the serpent and Adam's to Eve, were thus solved by a combination of exegetical ingenuity and shrewd insight into the respective natures of the masculine and feminine temperaments.

The immediate consequences of the Fall were threefold: Adam and Eve's eyes were opened, they perceived that they were naked, and they concealed themselves among the trees. Each of these incidents raised a possible difficulty for the literal-minded reader. First, if their eyes were opened, in what sense had the first pair been blind? The standard reply to this question was that they became aware of the repercussions of their disobedience on future generations,[3] but Maimonides and Rashi took advantage of the opportunity to expatiate on the nature of the knowledge contained in the forbidden fruit. The former cited an objector who anticipated much recent criticism of *Paradise Lost* by arguing that:

It would at first sight . . . appear from Scripture that man was originally intended to be perfectly equal with the rest of the animal creation, which is not endowed with intellect, reason, or the power of distinguishing between good and evil: but that Adam's disobedience to the command of

---

[1] *Jer.* xxii. 4. See also *P.R.E.* xiii; Rashi, *On Genesis*, iii. 6.

[2] *Gen. Rab.* xix. 5. See also *Deut. Rab.* iv. 5.

[3] *Gen. Rab.* xix. 6. In *Q.A.* i. 39 Philo explains: 'That they were not created blind is evident from the fact that even all the other beings were created perfect. . . . Or it may be that by eyes Scripture symbolically indicates the vision of the soul, through which alone are perceived all good and bad.'

God procured him that great perfection which is the peculiarity of man, viz., the power of distinguishing between good and evil. . . . It thus appears strange that the punishment for rebelliousness should be the means of elevating man to a pinnacle of perfection to which he had not attained previously.[1]

In reply Maimonides employed Rashi's argument that before the Fall Adam's purely intellectual knowledge was complete. His gain in moral knowledge was made only at the expense of a large part of his other philosophical powers: 'Then he fully understood the magnitude of the loss he had sustained, what he had forfeited, in what situation he was thereby placed.'[2] It may be doubted whether this explanation satisfied the anonymous inquirer any more than it has contemporary students of Milton's epic.

The second question was created by the answer to the first. If, as the commentators insisted, Adam and Eve had not been blind before the Fall, how could they have remained oblivious to their nakedness? One possible solution to this problem was that they had previously been clothed: 'And the eyes of both were enlightened, and they knew that they were naked, divested of the purple [or onyx-coloured] robe in which they were created.'[3] A more convincing one was that their nakedness was merely the symptom of their moral poverty: 'Even of the one precept which they had possessed they had stripped themselves.'[4] The third question was of much the same kind. If Adam's stature had been such that he filled the whole world, how could he possibly have concealed himself under a tree? Obviously, the answer came, he must have shrunk in a literal as well as a metaphorical way:

Before Adam sinned he could listen to the divine utterance standing upright and without being afraid, but after he had sinned, when he heard the divine voice he was frightened and hid himself. . . . R. Aibu said: On that occasion Adam's stature was lessened and reduced to a hundred cubits.[5]

The problems involved in the subsequent interrogation and condemnation of Adam and Eve were of a far more serious order, for it was in this section of the story that God's behaviour was most open to criticism. To begin with, His questions to the fallen pair seemed to imply that He was not omniscient, that He had to extract a

[1] *Guide*, i. 2.   [2] Ibid.   [3] *Targ. Jon.* iii. See also *P.R.E.* xiv.
[4] *Gen. Rab.* xix. 6. See also Rashi, *On Genesis*, iii. 7.
[5] *S.S. Rab.* iii. 7. See also *Gen. Rab.* xix. 8; *Hag.* 12a; *Sanh.* 38b; *P.R.E.* xiv.

confession before He knew what crime had been committed. The
Rabbis consequently took some pains to point out that the Deity's
ignorance was only apparent; He was really offering the sinners an
opportunity to repent:

> R. Tanhuma b. Abba expounded: . . . When Adam transgressed the
> Commandment of the Holy One, blessed be He, and ate of the tree, the
> Holy One, blessed be He, desired that he should repent, and He gave him
> an opening, but Adam did not do so.[1]

Indeed, in the biblical text there was more than a hint of petulance
in Adam's replies, and at least one source took it up and made it
explicit: 'Adam said before the Holy One, blessed be He: Sovereign
of all worlds! When I was alone, I did not sin against Thee. But the
woman whom Thou hast brought to me enticed me away from Thy
ways.'[2] On the other hand, it was noticed that God failed to question
the serpent, who had been the prime mover in the tragedy. This the
Rabbis accounted for by the reptile's readiness to defend itself:

> With Adam He [first] discussed the matter, with Eve He [first] dis-
> cussed the matter, but with the serpent He entered into no discussion.
> The reason is that the Holy One, blessed be He, said: 'This serpent is
> ready with his answers.' . . . Therefore He pronounced his sentence
> summarily.[3]

So far as the curses themselves were concerned, the problem was
to demonstrate their justice. The terms of the serpent's condemnation
seemed to imply that all the animals had shared to some extent in
his punishment, so it became necessary to suppose that they too had
sinned: '[Eve] gave the cattle, beasts, and birds to eat of it [the
forbidden fruit]. All obeyed her and ate thereof, except a certain
bird named *hol* [phoenix].'[4] Nevertheless, the serpent's sentence
was the most severe:

> Because the wisdom of the serpent was so great, therefore was the
> penalty inflicted upon it proportionate to its wisdom. . . . Consequently
> he was cursed above all cattle and all beasts of the field.[5]

---

[1] *Num. Rab.* xiii. 3. See also Rashi, *On Genesis*, iii. 9. In *Q.A.* i. 45 Philo had offered a
similar explanation: 'The things said appear to be not a question but a kind of threat
and reproach: where art thou now, from what good hast thou removed thyself, O man!'

[2] *P.R.E.* xiv.

[3] *Gen. Rab.* xx. 2. See also *Sanh.* 29a–b; *Leg. All.* III. xxi; Rashi, *On Genesis*, iii. 14.

[4] *Gen. Rab.* xix. 5. The exception made of the phoenix suggests that this *haggadah*
was invented to account for the mortality of the animals. See also *Jer.* xxii. 5; Rashi,
On Genesis, iii. 6.   [5] *Ecc. Rab.* i. 18. See also *Gen. Rab.* xix. 1.

The curse on the ground also demanded some explanation, and it was soon forthcoming: 'accursed is the ground, in that it did not show thee thy guilt.'[1] Adam's punishment, conversely, appeared to be too lenient rather than too harsh: God had threatened that he would die on the day he ate the forbidden fruit,[2] yet Genesis made it quite clear that in fact he continued to live for some considerable time after he had fallen. Two explanations were offered: first, that God took pity on Adam,[3] and second, that one day of God's was equivalent to a thousand years:

Said the Holy One, blessed be He, to them: '. . . Now ye do not know whether that means one day of Mine or one day of yours. But behold! I will grant him one day of Mine, which is a thousand years, and he will live nine hundred and thirty years and leave seventy for his children.'[4]

The subsequent expulsion received comparatively little attention, in spite of the unfavourable light it cast on the Divine mercy. In general the Rabbis were content to examine only the question of the coats of skins with which the fallen pair were clothed. Since the animals had only just been condemned, it was inferred, they could not have provided the necessary materials; the only possible source was the serpent's slough:

And the Lord God made unto Adam and to his wife vestures of honour from the skin of the serpent which he had cast from him, upon the skin of their flesh, instead of that adornment which had been cast away.[5]

And the same work also perpetuated the idea first developed in Jubilees that Adam and Eve were expelled into the land in which the former had originally been made: 'and he went and dwelt on Mount Moriah, to cultivate the ground from which he had been created.'[6]

The Scriptural account had had relatively little to say about Adam and Eve's experiences once they had been cast out of the garden of Eden, but the rabbinic tractates dwelt on this period of their lives at some length. The starting-point of these elaborations was the commonly held assumption that the Fall took place on the sixth day: 'You have followed the course of Adam who did not withstand his

---

[1] *Targ. Jon.* iii. See also *P.R.E.* xiv; Rashi, *On Genesis*, i. 12. Thus the earth's forebodings as expressed in *Gen. Rab.* ii. 2 are justified: 'Because she [the earth] knew that she was fated to receive punishment at his hand. Thus the earth foresaw that she was destined to meet her doom at the hand of man.'

[2] Gen. ii. 17. [3] *Num. Rab.* xxiii. 13.

[4] *Gen. Rab.* xix. 8. See also *Num. Rab.* v. 4. This depends on Ps. xc. 4: 'For a thousand years in thy sight are but as yesterday when it is past.'

[5] *Targ. Jon.* iii. See also *P.R.E.* xx. [6] *Targ. Jon.* iii.

trials for more than three hours, and at nine hours death was decreed upon him.'[1] According to this time-table Adam and Eve's first experience of night must have followed almost directly on their condemnation. Out of this rapid sequence of events the Rabbis constructed an imaginative and beautiful legend to illustrate the fear and loneliness of fallen Man:

Our Rabbis taught: When Adam, on the day of his creation, saw the setting of the sun he said: 'Alas, it is because I have sinned that the world around me is becoming dark; the universe will now become again void and without form—this then is the death to which I have been sentenced from Heaven!' So he sat up all night fasting and weeping and Eve was weeping opposite him. When however dawn broke, he said: 'This is the usual course of the world!'[2]

Other versions of the story pictured Adam reciting the words of Psalm cxxxix as he saw the sun disappearing,[3] or joining the angels in singing Psalm xcii to welcome the new dawn:

It is a good thing to give thanks unto the Lord, and to sing praises unto thy name, O Most High:
To show forth thy loving-kindness in the morning, and thy faithfulness every night.[4]

A second school of thought claimed that immediately after the Fall God comforted Adam with 'knowledge of a kind similar to Divine [knowledge]'.[5] This Divine revelation is a constant feature of rabbinic speculations on the Fall, although it was located at different points of the story by different commentators. Some believed that 'While Adam was still a lifeless mass, God showed him all the righteous people that would descend from him',[6] some construed the opening of his eyes as marking the moment at which he saw into the future,[7] while others linked the idea with the mention of a book at the beginning of the fifth chapter of Genesis:

But did not Resh Lakish [himself] say, What is the meaning of the verse *This is the book of the generations of Adam*? Did Adam have a book? What it implies is that the Holy One, blessed be He, showed to Adam every [coming] generation with its expositors, every generation with its sages, every generation with its leaders.[8]

[1] *Ex. Rab.* xxxii. 1. Compare Secrets of Enoch, xxxii. 2; Rashi, *On Genesis*, iii. 8.
[2] *Ab. Z.* 8a. See also *A.R.N.* i; *Gen. Rab.* xi. 2; ibid. lxxxii. 14.
[3] *Gen. Rab.* xi. 2; ibid. lxxxii. 14. [4] See *A.R.N.* i; *P.R.E.* xviii.
[5] *Pes.* 54a. [6] *Ex. Rab.* xl. 3. [7] *Gen. Rab.* xix. 6.
[8] *Ab. Z.* 5a. See also *Sanh.* 38b.

Finally something should be said of the rabbinic view concerning the parentage of Cain and Abel. The sexual interpretation of the Fall adapted from the Secrets of Enoch became the basis of a theory that the Tempter not only seduced Eve but actually begot a child by her:

And Adam knew Hava his wife, who had desired the angel; and she conceived and bare Kain; and she said, I have acquired a man, the Angel of the Lord. And she added to bear from her husband Adam his twin, even Habel.[1]

This passage admittedly is somewhat ambiguous, but a later source makes it quite clear that Cain was thought to be the Devil's son: '(Sammael) riding on the serpent came to her, and she conceived [first editions add 'Cain'].'[2] Thus it was that: 'From Seth arose and were descended all the generations of the righteous. From Cain arose and were descended all the generations of the wicked, who rebel and sin.'[3] These two tribes were related in turn to the 'sons of God' and the 'daughters of men' mentioned in the sixth chapter of Genesis, so producing a version of the Watcher story according to which the lustful offspring of the diabolic Cain ravished the virtuous offspring of Seth and thereby introduced the poison of evil into the human stock for ever.[4]

3. *The Vita Adae et Eve and Apocalypsis Mosis*

The post-lapsarian experiences of Adam and Eve also provided the subject-matter for the sister works generally known as the Vita Adae et Evae and the Apocalypsis Mosis. In essence they are two redactions of a common Hebrew original written during the early centuries of our era, but the variations between them are many and both show signs of considerable revision and contamination. Their subsequent popularity, particularly the Vita's, was immense,[5] and for that reason I have reserved them for independent study.

After their expulsion from the garden of Eden, the Vita narrates, the fallen pair looked in vain for food, until Eve was driven to ask in despair:

'Wilt thou slay me? that I may die, and perchance God the Lord will bring thee into paradise, for on my account hast thou been driven

---

[1] *Targ. Jon.* iv.   [2] *P.R.E.* xxi.   [3] Ibid. xxii.   [4] Loc. cit.
[5] See E. C. Quinn, *The Quest of Seth*, Chicago, 1963, and my review in *Medium Ævum*, xxxiv (1965), 85–88.

thence.' Adam answered: '. . . How is it possible that I should stretch forth my hand against my own flesh? Nay, let us arise and look for something for us to live on, that we fail not.'[1]

In order to placate their Creator they decided to do penance, but the Devil, disguised as an angel, persuaded Eve to abandon hers and led her back to her husband, who reproached her bitterly for being deceived a second time. In her distress she asked the Tempter why he persecuted them thus. He replied that it was on their account that he was cast out of heaven, for when Man was created in the image of God the angels were assembled to worship him:

And Michael went out and called all the angels saying: 'Worship the image of God as the Lord God hath commanded.'

And Michael himself worshipped first; then he called me and said: 'Worship the image of God the Lord.'

And I answered, 'I have no (need) to worship Adam.' And since Michael kept urging me to worship, I said to him, 'Why dost thou urge me? I will not worship an inferior and younger being (than I). I am his senior in the Creation, before he was made was I already made. It is his duty to worship me.'

When the angels, who were under me, heard this, they refused to worship him.

And Michael saith, 'Worship the image of God, but if thou wilt not worship him, the Lord God will be wrath with thee.'

And I said, 'If He be wrath with me, I will set my seat above the stars of heaven and will be like the Highest.'

And God the Lord was wrath with me and banished me and my angels from our glory; and on thy account were we expelled from our abodes into this world and hurled on the earth.

And straightway we were overcome with grief, since we had been spoiled of so great glory.

And we were grieved when we saw thee in such joy and luxury.

And with guile I cheated thy wife and caused thee to be expelled through her (doing) from thy joy and luxury, as I have been driven out of my glory.[2]

Basically this looks very much like an adaptation of the rabbinic theory that the angels opposed the creation of Man, but it has been combined most ingeniously with the story of Lucifer's pre-mundane rebellion, which the Secrets of Enoch had extrapolated from Isaiah's prophecy of the downfall of the King of Babylon.

[1] Vita, iii. 2–3.　　　　　　　　　　　　　[2] Ibid. xiv–xvi.

Filled with repentance, Eve banished herself from Adam's company. In self-imposed exile she bore Cain and, after Adam had been reunited with her, Abel. There followed the murder of Abel by Cain, anticipated by Eve in a dream, and the begetting of Seth, to whom Adam related a vision (based on the rabbinic legends) concerning his foreknowledge of the future wickedness of the world, the coming of the Messiah, and the Last Judgement, which he was given after the condemnation.[1] He then went on to tell his son of the Fall itself:

But God gave a part of paradise to me and (a part) to your mother: the trees of the eastern part and the north, which is over against Aquilo he gave to me, and to your mother he gave the part of the south and the western part.

(Moreover) God the Lord gave us two angels to guard us.

The hour came when the angels had ascended to worship in the sight of God; forthwith the adversary [the devil] found an opportunity while the angels were absent and the devil led your mother astray to eat of the unlawful and forbidden tree.

And she did eat and gave to me.[2]

In the fuller account in the Apocalypsis it was Eve who described her own deception. She too explained that Adam and she were given charge of two separate parts of the garden, but she offered a rather different version of the incident of the angels' worship:

And instantly he [the serpent] hung himself from the wall of paradise, and when the angels ascended to worship God, then Satan appeared in the form of an angel and sang hymns like the angels. And I bent over the wall and saw him, like an angel. But he saith to me: 'Art thou Eve?' And I said to him 'I am.' 'What art thou doing in paradise?' And I said to him, 'God set us to guard and to eat of it.' The devil answered through the mouth of the serpent: 'Ye do well, but ye do not eat of every plant.'[3]

After a further conversation, modelled closely on the Biblical account, the Tempter made Eve promise to persuade Adam to eat the fruit with her:

And when he had received the oath from me, he went and poured upon the fruit the poison of his wickedness, which is lust, the root and beginning

---

[1] Ibid. xxv–xxix.   [2] Ibid. xxxii–xxxiii.

[3] Apoc. Mos. xvii. 1–3. The abrupt transition from angel to serpent suggests that a certain amount of textual contamination has taken place at this juncture of the narrative, and indeed the Armenian recension of this work omits the phrase 'through the mouth of the serpent' altogether.

of every sin, and he bent the branch on the earth and I took of the fruit
and I ate.[1]

Here again rabbinic ideas have been adapted and synthesized. The
notion that the serpent actually touched the forbidden tree has been
combined with the belief that he infused Eve with his lust, though
the sexual element has been abandoned in its cruder form and
expressed only through the infection of the fruit.

When Eve had finally eaten of the tree she immediately realized
that she was naked, and began to search for leaves with which to
clothe herself. However, all the trees except the fig had shed their
foliage when she ate the fruit, so she was forced to use fig-leaves.[2]
This too appears to be a refinement of a rabbinic story, while the
belief that Eve covered her nakedness before approaching Adam
derives from Jubilees. The subsequent condemnation is also described along rabbinic lines in this account. The serpent was
punished by being deprived of its hands and feet,[3] and Adam was
told that he would henceforth have to suffer the enmity of the wild
beasts.[4]

Both the Vita and the Apocalypsis, then, are very closely related
to orthodox rabbinic speculations on the Fall. It was through them
that many of these ideas reached the Middle Ages.

---

[1] Apoc. Mos. xix. 3.   [2] Ibid. xx. 4–5.   [3] Ibid. xxvi. 2.
[4] Ibid. xxiv. 4.

III

THE CHRISTIAN INTERPRETATIONS

THE amount of sheer ingenuity expended by the Rabbis on the exposition of the Fall story might at first suggest that they accorded it an importance which a closer study of their comments reveals it did not really have for them. For the interpretations they drew out of it were generally of such a kind as to justify Williams's conclusion 'that this narrative was never taken in earnest by the Rabbis as the explanation of the ultimate origin of sin'.[1] Imaginative and humane as it was, their treatment of Eve's encounter with the serpent and Adam's with Eve, to take two outstanding examples of what their exegetical methods could produce, contributed little or nothing to the doctrinal meaning which had been read into those events by the authors of the Syriac Apocalypse of Baruch and the Fourth Book of Ezra. This comparative indifference to the story's doctrinal implications is probably to be accounted for by the close relationship that has always existed between the supposition of a Fall and the expectation of a Messiah. When the Jewish millennial vision was shattered by the persecutions of Titus and Hadrian, the corresponding belief in original sin perished with it, and the Rabbis turned instead to the concept of the *yezer-ha-ra* for their explanation of Man's enduring wickedness.

Christianity, on the other hand, was founded on the claim that with the incarnation of Christ the Messianic prophecies had come true, that His life, death, and resurrection constituted the historical fulfilment of the promises made in the Old Testament and its Apocrypha. Given the evident interdependence of Adamic and Messianic speculations, it was only to be expected that a religion which taught that the Redemption had actually taken place should very soon come to emphasize the significance of the Fall which had made that Redemption necessary.

[1] *Ideas of the Fall*, p. 72.

1. *The New Testament*

Surprisingly enough the Gospels themselves do not record any direct reference by Christ to the disobedience of Adam and Eve. He was more concerned, perhaps, with the practical remedies for sin than with any theoretical arguments about its origin. Or, as certain of His sayings indicate, He may simply have accepted the Watcher story or the rabbinic notion of the *yezer-ha-ra*.[1] It was St. Paul who first set the Fall opposite the Redemption, and thereby established once and for all its unique position in the structure of Christian theology. Following in the tradition of Jewish Messianic typology, he created an unequivocal connexion between Adam's sin and Christ's sacrifice: 'For since by man came death, by man came also the resurrection of the dead. For as in Adam all die, even so in Christ shall all be made alive.'[2] Nor was death the only consequence of the Fall, as this passage taken by itself might seem to imply; in the fuller discussion of the question in the Epistle to the Romans hereditary sinfulness was declared to be the primary result of Adam's transgression and death the consequent punishment. The Fall implanted in Man an inclination to evil (possibly the *yezer-ha-ra*) which the Law (probably the *Torah*) could reveal but not cure. Only the Grace of God operating through the Atonement could perform the latter function.[3] St. Paul thus took over the synthesis of apo-

---

[1] The former possibility is suggested by Matt. xii. 40–45, xiii. 38–39; John xii. 31, xiv. 30, xvi. 11; the latter by Mark vii. 21–22. One or two other sayings could be taken to allude to the story, if not the doctrine, of the Fall. The best case can be made for John viii. 44: 'Ye are of your father the devil, and the lusts of your father ye will do. He was a murderer from the beginning, and abode not in the truth, because there is no truth in him. When he speaketh a lie, he speaketh of his own: for he is a liar, and the father of it.' Yet even here, the terms are so general that no specific allusion can safely be read into them. The verse was taken by some later commentators as authority for the idea that the Devil had a son. See my article on '*Genesis B* and its Background', *R.E.S.* N.S. xiv (1963), 6.

[2] 1 Cor. xv. 21–22.

[3] For a full analysis of these chapters see N. P. Williams, op. cit., pp. 112 et seq.; F. R. Tennant, *Doctrines of the Fall*, ch. xi; W. Sanday and A. C. Headlam, *A Critical and Exegetical Commentary on the Epistle to the Romans*, 1895. St. Paul's synthesis of apocryphal and rabbinic views on the origin of evil has an interesting corollary. The doctrine of the *yezer-ha-ra* applied to each individual man, whereas the doctrine of the Adamic Fall applied to Man in general. Their combination, therefore, could produce not only a psychological account of Adam's disobedience but also an Adamic account of the individual's. Hence in the seventh chapter of Romans St. Paul seems to have used the historical Fall story as a means of analysing his own personal experience, thus exemplifying the implications of the pregnant phrase in the Syriac Apocalypse of Baruch, liv. 19: each of us 'has been the Adam of his own soul'.

cryphal and rabbinic views on the origin of evil which had evolved by the first century A.D., and adapted it to fit the Christian context.

Non-canonical Jewish works may also have provided the Apostle with one especially vivid detail in his treatment of the Genesis narrative. Addressing the Church at Corinth he wrote:

> For I am jealous over you with godly jealousy: for I have espoused you to one husband, that I may present you as a chaste virgin to Christ.
> But I fear, lest by any means, as the serpent beguiled Eve through his subtilty, so your minds should be corrupted from the simplicity that is in Christ.[1]

In both the Secrets of Enoch and a number of the rabbinic tractates Eve's corruption by the tempter had been expressed in sexual terms, and it seems very likely that this legend lay behind St. Paul's analogy.[2] But he did not adopt the Jewish tradition in its entirety. The idea of Man's original perfection, for instance, is conspicuous by its absence in his writings, and the trees of life and knowledge are nowhere mentioned. However, these are minor considerations compared with his major contribution to the history of the story, his incorporation of the apocryphal doctrine of the Fall into the body of Christian dogma.

This crucial development served only to intensify many of the problems inhering in the first three chapters of Genesis. As Williams again has observed, the transplantation of Christianity from Israel to the world of Graeco-Roman culture 'inevitably involved the subjection of its main constitutive ideas to a process of intellectual scrutiny, analysis, and discussion' that went far beyond anything it had previously experienced.[3] In such an environment the contradictions and discontinuities in the Fall story, with which Judaism had been wrestling for at least three centuries, were magnified still further. For the adoption of the Jahwist's unsophisticated myth as the official Christian explanation of the existence of evil exposed it to all the philosophical difficulties entailed in the reconciliation of a perfect Creator with an imperfect Creation. That this issue

---

[1] 2 Cor. xi. 2–3.

[2] See H. St. John Thackeray, *The Relation of St. Paul to Contemporary Jewish Thought*, 1900, pp. 52–55. A. Plummer's *A Critical and Exegetical Commentary on the Second Epistle of St. Paul to the Corinthians*, 1915, p. 295, on the other hand, expresses some doubts about this hypothesis. Other Pauline passages cited by Thackeray to illustrate his theory are: 2 Cor. xi. 13–14; 1 Tim. ii. 13–14. See above, Ch. II, pp. 33, 46–47.

[3] Op. cit., p. 167.

was being hotly debated we have the evidence of Tertullian (d. *post* A.D. 220), who caught the prevalent mood of the time in his exasperated comment: 'The same subject-matter is discussed over and over again by the heretics and the philosophers; the same arguments are involved. Whence comes evil? Why is it permitted? What is the origin of man?'[1] In the new role which St. Paul had assigned to it the Scriptural account of the Creation and Fall purported to answer all these questions, and as a result it was bound to attract a great deal of close and often hostile criticism. In particular, the opponents of the new religion inquired, how could the acquisition of moral consciousness or, indeed, of any other kind of knowledge have been the cause of human misery? Why should a benevolent God have wished to deny Man the one gift that distinguishes him from the animals? And even if a satisfactory answer could be found to these questions, what possible motive could have induced a perfect creature to sin?[2]

2. *The Gnostic and Manichean Reading*

The one great stumbling-block to the solution of these problems was monotheistic Christianity's insistence on God's omnipotence and benevolence. Remove that and the problems evaporated. This is precisely what the two dualistic sects, the Gnostics and the Manichees, set themselves to do. Jahweh, they contended, was clearly neither omnipotent nor benevolent; rather, he was a subordinate and malicious deity who created Man for his own selfish ends and attempted to keep him in ignorance of the supreme Deity by forbidding him to eat of the fruit of the tree of knowledge. Once this step was taken the rest of the story presented no great difficulty. The tree of knowledge was good and Jahweh was both envious in prohibiting it and jealous in punishing Adam for disobeying him. The serpent, on the contrary, was the first pair's best friend; by persuading them to transgress the commandment he made them aware that there was a better and more kindly God set above Jahweh, and that it was to union with Him that they should aspire.

Several interrelated trends in the thought of the period combined to produce this reading of the Fall story. The three most potent

---

[1] *De Praescr.* vii.

[2] I have drawn these questions not only from my earlier analysis of the Jahwist and Priestly documents but also from contemporary criticisms recorded by the Fathers. See below, pp. 71, 79–80, 87.

were: first, the Ptolemaic theory that the cosmos was made up of a series of concentric spheres with the earth at their centre; second, the Platonic view that between the perfect Creator and his imperfect Creation there existed a gap inhabited by some intermediary power (Demiurge) or powers; and third, the Stoic corollary that the human soul, whose true home lay above the material world, consisted of a spark of pure spirit imprisoned in a corporeal and therefore evil body. Superimposed on each other these three widely held beliefs amounted to a fairly comprehensive interpretation of Man's predicament. Having fallen from its divine birthplace into the centre of the physical universe, his soul was now obliged to free itself from its mortal coil and reascend to its original state of beatitude in Heaven.[1]

This world-view found perhaps its most systematic expression in the *Hermetica*, a collection of Greek and Latin writings dating from the second or third century of our era.[2] The most influential of them, the *Poimandres*, described in terms often reminiscent of Genesis the fall of a Primal Man who, having been created in the image of God and endowed with the various natures of the seven planetary administrators, was captivated by the beauty of Nature and so became confined in the terrestrial sphere:

And that is why man, unlike all other living creatures upon earth, is twofold. He is mortal by reason of his body; he is immortal by reason of the Man of eternal substance. He is immortal, and has all things in his power; yet he suffers the lot of a mortal, being subject to Destiny. He is exalted above the structure of the heavens; yet he is born a slave of Destiny. He is bisexual, as his Father is bisexual, and sleepless, as his Father is sleepless; yet he is mastered by carnal desire, and by oblivion.[3]

Man's one hope of salvation was to abjure the pleasures of the flesh, which only bound him more firmly to his earthly habitation, and to seek instead that redemptive knowledge (*gnosis*) which could lead him back to the realm of spirit:

And the vice of the soul is lack of knowledge. A soul that has gained no knowledge of the things that are, and has not come to know their nature, nor to know the Good, but is blind . . . carries the body as a

---

[1] This brief summary is based largely on F. C. Burkitt, *Church and Gnosis*, 1932, ch. ii; R. McL. Wilson, *The Gnostic Problem*, 1958, chs. ii–iii.

[2] See art. on 'Hermetic Books' in *O.D.C.C.*

[3] *Poimandres*, 15. For the parallels between this and the Biblical account of Adam's Fall see C. H. Dodd, *The Bible and the Greeks*, 1935, ch.ᵛⁱⁱ

burden and is ruled by it, instead of ruling it. . . . On the other hand, the virtue of the soul is knowledge. He who has got knowledge is good and pious; he is already divine.[1]

That, as C. H. Dodd has pointed out, was the whole burden of the serpent's words to Eve.[2]

It was in an intellectual atmosphere permeated with this kind of thinking that the Gnostic reading of the Fall story was conceived— hence the marked similarities that exist between the system of the Ophites, one of the earliest Gnostic sects, and that of the *Poimandres*. According to the two most detailed extant accounts of Ophite beliefs, the *Apocryphon of John* (pre-180) and the summary given by Irenaeus (*c*. 130–*c*. 202) in his *Against the Heresies*,[3] a certain sub- ordinate deity called Ialdabaoth came to imagine that he was the master of the universe. When his mother, Sophia, informed him that in fact there existed a superior Being, he decided to create the world in order to draw attention to himself. With the help of the seven planetary administrators, each of whom contributed something of his own nature, he also formed Adam in the image of God.[4] But although the figure he fashioned was of great size and beauty it was unable to move. To remedy this defect Ialdabaoth imparted to it all of his divine energy, with the result that Adam came to possess life and intelligence. Having thus emptied himself of his former power, Ialdabaoth wished to ensure that it remained ensnared in the material world, so he placed Adam amid the physical delights of Eden and kept him in ignorance both of the spiritual element within him and of the existence of the supreme God. He then created Eve in the hope that by propagating the human race she and her husband would prevent the celestial spark from ever returning to its heavenly home.[5] However, Christ[6] persuaded the first pair to eat of the tree of knowledge, a source of spiritual illumination which God had placed in the garden to liberate men from the domination of their

---

[1] *Libellus*, x. 8b–9. See also *Libellus*, i. 27, vii. 1a, iv. 4-5.

[2] Op. cit., p. 169.

[3] Irenaeus's account appears to be based on a recension of the *Apocryphon of John*. The latter work was immensely popular in Gnostic circles. Three versions of it were recently discovered in the Nag Hammadi library, for instance. See H. C. Puech, G. Quispel, W. C. Van Unnik (trans. F. L. Cross), *The Jung Codex*, 1955, ch. i; A. D. Nock, 'A Coptic Library of Gnostic Writings', *J.T.S.* N.S. ix (1958), 314–24.

[4] Both versions quote Gen. i. 26–27.

[5] According to Irenaeus's account the planetary powers seduced Eve and begot sons by her in much the same way as the Watcher angels corrupted the daughters of men.

[6] Irenaeus's account has Sophia (Wisdom), the *Apocryphon*, Christ.

creator, and as a result they became aware of their true nature. In his jealous rage Ialdabaoth cast them out of their paradise, seduced Eve,[1] who subsequently bore Cain and Abel by him, and kindled sexual passion in Adam.[2] All their descendants, therefore, are corrupted by carnal desire. Not until men abandon the desires of the flesh for the knowledge of God will Ialdabaoth's evil plans finally be frustrated.

Here the tendencies we have already noted in the Jewish Apocrypha and the Hermetic writings have been carried to their logical conclusion. The problem of accounting for Jahweh's apparent ignorance and malice, for instance, has been solved by equating him with the wicked son of Sophia,[3] the Ophite counterpart of the Platonic Demiurge, while the serpent has been cast as hero in the consequent reversal of roles. The forbidden tree, which had been forced out of the story during the second century B.C. by the difficulty of believing that the acquisition of knowledge could be harmful,[4] has reappeared as a purely beneficial agent. And the sexual corruption of Eve which had been invented to take its place[5] has been postponed until after the expulsion. Several rabbinic notions, too, have been incorporated into the narrative: such ideas as the enormous size of the first man, the use of subordinates during his creation, and the diabolic parentage of Cain and Abel, all have parallels in the rabbinic tractates.[6] Indeed, if Hellenistic modes of thought shaped the general outlines of the Ophite version of the Fall story, Jewish sources seem to have furnished many of its most striking details.

Of course the Ophite was only one of many Gnostic schools, but to judge by the number of refutations it provoked it was certainly the most vigorous. For Irenaeus was not alone in taking issue with it; both pseudo-Tertullian and Origen (d. 253–4) found it necessary to discredit it. Listing the various heresies of his day, the former wrote: 'To these are added those heretics likewise who are called Ophites: for the serpent they magnify to such a degree, that they prefer him

---

[1] Irenaeus's account claims that although Ialdabaoth lusted after Eve his desires were never fulfilled. She had previously been seduced by the planetary powers.

[2] This view is peculiar to the *Apocryphon*.

[3] Marcion's distinction between the wicked God of the Old Testament and the good God of the New may have contributed to this development, but as R. M. Grant has shown in his *Gnosticism and Early Christianity*, 1959, pp. 57–59, Judaism had attributed some of the Deity's less acceptable deeds to the Devil as early as the second century B.C.

[4] See above, Ch. II, pp. 29–33.   [5] See above, Ch. II, pp. 33, 46–47.

[6] See above, Ch. II, pp. 38–39, 43, 55.

even to Christ Himself; for it was he, they say, who gave us the origin of the knowledge of good and evil.'[1] And in his *Contra Celsum* Origen complained that his opponent 'ought to have known that those who espoused the cause of the serpent, because he gave good advice to the first human beings, and who go far beyond the Titans and Giants of fable, and are on this account called Ophites, are so far from being Christians that they bring accusations against Jesus to as great a degree as Celsus himself.'[2] The most significant evidence of its popularity, however, was provided by the Manichees, who adopted the Ophite reading of the Fall story as the basis of their entire philosophical system.

During the third and fourth centuries this sect emerged as an even more powerful dualistic rival to the orthodox Church than its predecessor. Like Gnosticism its theory was based on the twin concepts of the inherent evil of matter and the consequent duty of Man to free himself from his bondage by means of spiritual knowledge.[3] By applying these principles to the first three chapters of Genesis it evolved an interpretation of Adam's transgression which amounted to a complete inversion of the traditional meaning assigned to that event. According to the *Acta Archelai* and Theodore bar Khoni's *Book of Scholia* (late sixth or early seventh century),[4] Adam and Eve were formed by the Prince of Darkness and his companions, who had previously brought about, by their rebellion against the god of light, the existence of the physical universe:

Furthermore, as regards the manner of the creation of Adam, he tells us that he who said, 'Come and let us make man in our image, after our likeness,' or 'after the form which we have seen,' is the prince who addressed the other princes in terms which may be thus interpreted: 'Come, give me of the light which we have received, and let us make man after the form of us princes, even after that form which we have seen, that is to say, the first man.' And in that manner he (or they) created the man. They created Eve also after the like fashion, imparting to her of their

---

[1] *Adv. Omn. Haer.* ii.

[2] *Con. Cels*, vi. 28. See also Epiphanius, *Panarion*, xxxvii. 3. Origen's statement that the Ophites 'bring accusations against Jesus' suggests that he knew the version of the story in the *Apocryphon* according to which it was Christ who persuaded Adam and Eve to eat the forbidden fruit.

[3] See H. C. Puech, *Le Manichéisme*, Paris, 1949, p. 70.

[4] F. Cumont has suggested that, like Irenaeus's account of Ophite beliefs and the *Apocryphon*, these two works are two versions of a common original, which may have been the *Epistula Fundamenti* of Mani himself. See *Recherches sur le Manichéisme*, Brussels, 1908, i. 3.

own lust, with a view to the deceiving of Adam. And by these means the construction of the world proceeded from the operations of the prince.[1]

The resemblances between this and the Ophite version of the same episode are clear. In both Man is made by some subordinate power in the image of a deity who himself belongs to the purely spiritual sphere; in both they impart to their creation, though only to Eve in this account, something of their own nature; and in both they infect the woman with lust. The result, as in the *Apocryphon of John*, is a reading of the Fall story which focuses on the struggle by the two opposing supernatural powers for possession of the divine essence in Man. The Prince of Darkness, hoping to keep it permanently trapped in matter, denied Adam the knowledge which might have led him back to the Prince of Light and gave Eve the desire which would bring about the multiplication of mankind. But Christ intervened:

And he (Mani) says: Jesus the Luminous approached Adam the Innocent and woke him from the sleep of death in order that he might be delivered from the [two?] great (?) spirit(s). . . . Then Adam examined himself and recognized what he was. And He (i.e. Jesus) showed him the Fathers in the Height, and His own self thrown in all unto the teeth of leopards . . . and mixed and imprisoned in all that exists and bound in the pollution of Darkness. And (Mani) says, that He (Jesus) raised him (Adam) up and made him taste of the Tree of Life. And then Adam looked and wept; and he raised his voice mightily, like a lion that roars and ravens; he loosened (his bosom) and smote (his breast) and said, 'Woe, woe! to the fashioner of my body and to the binder of my soul, and to the rebels who enslaved me!'[2]

The one major difference between this and the Ophite account of the incident is that now it is the tree of life which is forbidden. The reason for this change is given in the *Acta Archelai*:

Now, with respect to paradise, it is not called a cosmos. The trees that are in it are lust and other seductions, which corrupt the rational powers of those men. And that tree in paradise, by which men know the good, is Jesus Himself, (or) the knowledge of Him in the world. He who partakes thereof discerns the good and the evil.[3]

---

[1] *Acta Archelai*, x.

[2] *Book of Scholia*, trans. in A. V. W. Jackson, *Researches in Manichaeism*, New York, 1932, pp. 249–54.

[3] *Acta Archelai*, x. The one feature of the Ophite account to be omitted is the episode in which Adam lies inert and has to be filled with divine power before he is able to move.

The Ophite view that the tree of knowledge was a divine source of wisdom evidently led the Manichees to equate it with Christ Himself. Thus the original Biblical narrative was made to yield the moral that, in F. Cumont's words, by making him taste of the fruit of knowledge 'Jesus and not the Tempter revealed to Adam the depth of his misery. But man will also know henceforth the means of freeing himself from it.'[1]

I have dwelt on these heretical interpretations of the story at such length because they played a large part in determining the course which orthodox Christian speculations were to take. The overwhelming advantage of the doctrine of the Fall so far as the Church was concerned was that it explained the existence of evil within the framework of a strictly monotheistic universe. It was the one firm bulwark against dualistic arguments which inferred from the coexistence of evil with good in the world the coexistence of an evil with a good deity. The first three chapters of Genesis, therefore, had to be defended at all costs, and in the first five centuries a good deal of the Fathers' energies were devoted to demonstrating the essential integrity of the Priestly and the Jahwist documents.

They attempted to do so in three distinct ways, or to use the terminology of Scriptural exegesis, at three different 'levels': the literal, the allegorical, and the typological.[2] The first was designed to engage rationalistic criticism on its own ground, the literal meaning of the text; the second, to harmonize the story's morality with Hellenistic beliefs by transferring its meaning to the realm of abstract ethical concepts; and the third, to reveal the historical signi-

It is missing, I believe, because it has been combined most ingeniously with a similar incident in the *Apocryphon* where Ialdabaoth puts Adam to sleep in order to prevent him from becoming aware of his true nature. These two episodes are amalgamated in turn with the account of Adam's slumber in Genesis, thus producing a version of the story according to which it is Christ who awakens Adam from his initial oblivion and thereby brings him truly to life.

[1] Op. cit. i. 49.

[2] These three levels are variously designated. Philo referred to them as the literal, the moral, and the anagogical, and Origen elaborated on this distinction by relating the three levels to the three elements in Man: the literal sense, he claimed, speaks to Man's flesh, the moral to his soul, and the anagogical to his spirit. Later a fourth level was added by splitting Philo's anagogical level into two. Thus Cassian distinguished between the historical sense (literal), the tropological (Philo's 'moral' and my 'allegorical'), the allegorical (one aspect of Philo's 'anagogical' and my 'typological'), and the anagogical (the other aspect of Philo's 'anagogical' and my 'typological'). Jewish exegetes found these four levels in the Hebrew word for paradise, *pardes*, and termed them *peshat* (Cassian's 'historical'), *remez* (Cassian's 'allegorical'), *derush* (Cassian's 'tropological'), and *sod* (Cassian's 'anagogical').

ficance of Adam's sin by relating it to the over-all sequence of the Christian scheme of salvation. In the following sections of this chapter I shall study patristic interpretations of the Fall at these three levels from the second to the fifth century.[1] During this period the Church's ideas on the subject were relatively fluid, consisting of a continual process of action, reaction, and synthesis. After Augustine, and chiefly on his account, they became hardened and tended to degenerate into mere permutations of older theories, with scarcely any new additions or amplifications. It was left to the poets rather than the theologians of succeeding ages to enrich the original design yet further.

3. *The Allegorical Reading*

The allegorical reading[2] deserves to be given chronological precedence over the other two for several reasons—its roots were more ancient and its influence more pervasive—but the most important is its intimate connexion with the heretical versions of the Fall story we have just been examining. For both the problems it dealt with and the presuppositions it brought to their solution were in all essentials the same as those which had led to the Gnostic and Manichaean distortions of the Genesis narrative. Philo (*c.* 20 B.C.– *c.* A.D. 45), from whose works almost all the later allegorists quarried

[1] I pursue the allegorical tradition beyond this point because it was still in the process of development right up to the time of Erigena. I have chosen to categorize this material according to exegetical technique rather than doctrinal school because the various readings of the Genesis narrative constantly overlapped the generally accepted divisions between one group of Fathers and another. Admittedly, few if any of them confined their attention to any one level of the story, and in that sense the three 'levels' cannot be regarded as mutually exclusive either. But whereas the commentators were always aware of, and distinguished carefully between, the methods they employed to explicate the Biblical text, it is less certain whether they thought of themselves as being bound by the divisions that separate, say, the Alexandrian from the Cappadocian school of thought, even if they recognized them.

[2] I include Philo in this category because his exegesis has far more in common with patristic than with rabbinic interpretations of Genesis. By grouping him together with Origen, Ambrose, Augustine, Isidore, and the pseudo-Bede I do not mean to suggest that they formed an exclusive and clearly defined school of thought of the kind discussed in the foregoing section. I mean simply that there is to be observed running through their works a distinctive interpretation of the Fall story which differs both in content and in exegetical technique from the Gnostic, the literal, and the typological interpretations. In the commentaries of several of these Fathers this particular interpretation constitutes only one level of the total meaning they give to the story, and is to be found side by side with literal and typological explanations. At this one level, however, the interpretations of all the writers listed above are similar enough to be described as an exegetical tradition.

their material, and Origen, his first Christian disciple, accepted not only the dichotomy between matter and spirit upon which the dualistic theories rested but also the consequent importance attaching to *nous*, the source of *gnosis*. In their view the existence of evil was to be explained by some premundane descent of celestial energy from the supersensible world into the physical universe. According to Philo, for instance, the subordinate beings who inhabited the gap between God and the Creation, and had assisted in the making of Adam, were solely responsible for Man's wickedness: 'It is to the end that, when man orders his course aright, when his thoughts and deeds are blameless, God the universal Ruler may be owned as their Source; while others from the number of His subordinates are held responsible for thoughts and deeds of a contrary sort: for it could not be that the Father should be the cause of an evil thing to His offspring.'[1] But whereas the Gnostics, having disposed of the question of human sinfulness by means of a similar hypothesis, went on to read the Biblical account of Adam's disobedience as the beginning of our Salvation, Philo and Origen saw in this event a further example of the decline from the spiritual to the corporeal, asserting that the coats of skin with which the fallen pair were clothed were in fact their physical bodies: 'But according to the deeper meaning, the tunic of skin is symbolically the natural skin of the body. For when God formed the first mind, He called it Adam; then He formed the sense, which He called Life; in the third place, of necessity He made his body also, calling it symbolically a tunic of skin.'[2] In its earliest form, at least, the allegorical reading of the Fall could equally well be called the 'semi-Gnostic' interpretation.

The adoption of the allegorical method itself by Philo and his patristic successors was also, in a sense, an outcome of the philosophical milieu in which the dualistic sects had evolved. In the comparatively sophisticated world of the Graeco-Roman empire at the beginning of our era the Jahwist's crude anthropomorphisms were unlikely to be taken very seriously by any but the most naïve reader. The reaction of Celsus to the description of Eve's creation was probably typical; he ridiculed it, Origen protested, 'without

---

[1] *De Op. Mun.* xxiv.

[2] *Q.A.* i. 53. Compare Origen's *Con. Cels.* iv. 40: 'And the expulsion of the man and woman from paradise, and their being clothed with tunics of skins (which God, because of the transgression of men, made for those who had sinned), contain a certain secret and mystical doctrine (far transcending that of Plato) of the soul's losing its wings, and being borne downwards to earth, until it can lay hold of some stable resting-place.'

quoting the words, which would give the hearer the impression that they are spoken with a figurative meaning. He would not even have it appear that the words were used allegorically, although he says afterwards, that "the more modest among Jews and Christians are ashamed of these things, and endeavour to give them somehow an allegorical signification".[1] And he heaped still greater scorn on the episode of the temptation:

> But as Celsus makes a jest also of the serpent, as counteracting the injunctions given by God to the man, taking the narrative to be an old wife's fable, and has purposely neither mentioned the paradise of God, nor stated that God is said to have planted it in Eden towards the east ... and the other statements which follow, which might of themselves lead a candid reader to see that all these things had not inappropriately an allegorical meaning.[2]

The best defence against this kind of criticism, as Origen indicated in these passages, was allegory. From the fifth century B.C. onwards Greek philosophers had been reinterpreting the myths of Homer and Hesiod to their own taste by means of this device; confronted with an offensive or absurd story concerning the gods and heroes of antiquity, they simply injected into it whatever wholesome moral truths they wished to find there, and then pretended to discover them beneath the literal meaning of the text. By the first century A.D. the technique was fully developed and widely practised, and, as the heirs of Hellenistic Alexandrian culture, first Philo and then Origen inherited it as part of their intellectual patrimony. It was only natural, therefore, that for their defence of the Old Testament they resorted to a method of interpretation so well equipped to deal with rationalistic attacks on myth.

The foundation of Philo's interpretation of the Fall story was his equation of Eden with the rational soul, with what a present-day psychologist might call the psyche. In this region lived the passions, represented by the animals, and the virtues and opinions, represented by the plants:

> Moses evidently signifies by the plesaunce the ruling power of the soul which is full of countless opinions, as it might be of plants; and by the tree of life he signifies reverence toward God, the greatest of the virtues, by means of which the soul attains to immortality; while by the tree that is cognisant of good and evil things he signifies moral prudence,

---

[1] *Con. Cels.* iv. 38.   [2] Ibid. iv. 39. See also *De Princ.* IV. i. 16.

the virtue that occupies the middle position, and enables us to distinguish things by nature contrary the one to the other.[1]

As in the Book of Sirach and the Secrets of Enoch, Man was thus endowed with the knowledge of good and evil *before* the Fall, for the virtue attaching to moral prudence made it impossible to believe that God would have forbidden him to partake of it. The Fall, it followed, must have consisted in something other than the violation of the tree of knowledge, and this consideration was the determining factor in Philo's exegesis of the rest of the story.

The master of the rational soul, he stated, was the mind, represented by Adam, whose task it was to take care of the plants, that is, to guard his virtues.[2] Eve stood for the soul's sense or sense-perception of the physical world: 'In the allegorical sense, however, woman is a symbol of sense, and man, of mind.'[3] Sense-perception was born when the mind relaxed its attention, when, as Genesis had it, Adam fell asleep,[4] and his waking words meant that: 'For the sake of sense-perception the Mind, when it has become her slave, abandons both God the Father of the universe, and God's excellence and wisdom, the Mother of all things, and cleaves to and becomes one with sense-perception.'[5] Adam's recognition of Eve, then, constituted the beginning of the Fall, revealing that the mind was ready to abandon its natural authority for the sake of physical sensation. And the Fall itself took just this form. The serpent, which symbolized pleasure,[6] attacked the mind via the senses: 'Pleasure does not venture to bring her wiles and deceptions to bear on the man, but on the woman, and by her means on him. This is a telling and well-made point: for in us mind corresponds to man, the senses to woman.'[7] Here lay the key to the serpent's prior approach to Eve: 'Now of necessity sense comes into contact with the sense-perceptible; and by the participation of sense, things pass into the mind; for sense is moved by objects, while the mind is moved by sense.'[8] As we have seen, Philo followed the later Jewish Apocrypha in making the knowledge of good and evil a part of the mind's original condition, and as a result was forced to find a substitute for

---

[1] *De Op. Mun.* liv. See also *Leg. All.* ii. iv; *Q.A.* i. 6–10.
[2] *Leg. All.* i. xvi–xvii.   [3] *Q.A.* i. 37.
[4] *Leg. All.* ii. vii.   [5] Ibid. ii. xiv. See also *De Op. Mun.* liii.
[6] *De Op. Mun.* lvi. The serpent is said to be an apt symbol of pleasure because it crawls on its belly, eats earth, and has venomous teeth. See also *Leg. All.* ii. xviii.
[7] *De Op. Mun.* lix.   [8] *Q.A.* i. 37.

the eating of the forbidden fruit as the occasion of the Fall. Faced
by the same problem, the author of the Secrets of Enoch had made
use of the idea that Eve was literally seduced by an angel. Philo's
theory of the sense's corruption by pleasure may well have been an
allegorization of this legend, for after reviewing the various senses
which are susceptible to pleasure he concluded: 'those connected
with sexual intercourse prove themselves the most violent of all in
their intensity.'[1] Be that as it may, his account of the temptation had
nothing at all to do with the violation of the tree of knowledge.
Rather, he located the origin of sin in the mind's relationship with
sense-perception, in Adam's submission to his wife. It was left to
the Christian allegorists to solve the difficult problem of reintegrat-
ing the forbidden tree into the allegorical design handed down to
them by their Jewish predecessor.

The first of them, Origen, attempted to do nothing of the kind.
On the contrary, he pushed the sexual implications of Philo's reading
even further:

Our interior man consists of spirit and heart. The spirit can be taken
as the male and the heart as the female. If these two elements agree and
accord with each other, they will grow and multiply as a result of their
union; they will beget good children: . . . If it happens that the heart,
which is united to the spirit and, so to speak, married to it, inclines towards
corporeal pleasures and is carried away by the delights of the flesh . . . this
heart, soiled by the adultery of the body, cannot beget and multiply
legitimately.[2]

In this version the tree of knowledge still had no part to play in the
main action of the story; indeed, so long as it retained the allegorical
identity assigned to it by Philo it was bound to remain outside the
basic allegorical pattern. Origen merely extrapolated from the
original equation the corollary of the bastard offspring of pleasure's
union with the heart.[3]

The later Christian allegorists, however, did not pursue this
refinement. Ambrose (339–97), for example, by-passed the Greek

---

[1] *Leg. All.* II. xviii. See also *De Op. Mun.* lvii.   [2] *Homil. in Gen.* i. 15.
[3] This extrapolation may have been, like the seduction motif itself, an allegorization
of a literal Jewish *haggadah*. Those Rabbis who had followed the Secrets of Enoch in
picturing the Fall as a sexual corruption inferred that Cain and Abel must have been the
serpent's children. Once the seduction was allegorized it would have been only natural
to treat this subsidiary legend in the same way, thus producing the concept of the illegi-
timate offspring of pleasure's union with the heart. Compare Justin Martyr, *Dial.* c, and
Tertullian's *De Carne Christi*, xvii, quoted below, pp. 100–101.

Father completely and went back directly to Philo: 'For there was one before us who has claimed that the sin had been committed by the man as a result of the pleasure of the senses, seeing in the serpent the symbol of pleasure, in the woman the feeling that the Greeks call *aisthesis* (perception or sensation), and in the man who was deceived the spirit which the Greeks call *nous* (mind).'[1] In a letter to Sabinus, who, after reading his *Hexaemeron*, had requested further elucidation on the topic of paradise, Ambrose developed an interpretation of Eden which was little more than a concise summary of Philo's views. The real paradise, he wrote, 'is no earthly one which can be seen; . . . Hence also Paradise is in our highest part, thick set with the growth of many opinions, and wherein chiefly God hath placed the Tree of life, that is, the root of piety. . . . He has likewise planted within us a seedplot of the knowledge of good and evil; . . . Divers other plants are also there, whose fruits are virtues.'[2] The serpent was associated more directly with lust, but otherwise his role, too, was much the same: 'well therefore has holy Moses represented lust under the similitude of a serpent; for it creeps upon its belly like a serpent, not walking on foot, nor raised upon legs, gliding along by the sinuous contortions, as it were, of its whole body.'[3] The one original feature of Ambrose's treatment of the story was his interpretation of the Fall itself:

Now since God knew that man's affections, once endued with knowledge, would more readily incline towards craft than towards perfect prudence. . . . He desired to cast out craft from Paradise, and as the provident Author of our salvation, to place therein the desire of life and the discipline of piety. Wherefore He commanded man to eat of every tree which is in Paradise but that of the tree of knowledge of good and evil he should not eat.[4]

Here for the first time there appears a hint of the difficulty of relating the tree of knowledge and its violation to the allegorical meanings of the garden and its inhabitants. Although Ambrose by no means solved the problem, his vague association of the forbidden tree with craft represented at least an attempt to restore it to its position at the centre of the narrative.

The next step in this direction was taken by Ambrose's most famous pupil, Augustine: 'No one then denies that Paradise may

[1] *De Par.* ii.
[2] *Ep.* xlv. 3–8.
[3] Ibid. xlv. 10. Compare *De Op. Mun.* lvi.
[4] Ibid. xlv. 9.

signify the life of the blessed; its four rivers the four virtues . . . its trees all useful knowledge; its fruits the customs of the godly; the tree of life, wisdom herself, the mother of all good; and the tree of the knowledge of good and evil, the experience of a broken commandment.'[1] While the details of this passage clearly derive from Philo, the scene in which they are set has been shifted from the psyche to a wider area of reference, 'the life of the blessed'. In his *De Genesim contra Manichaeos* Augustine worked out this new scheme more elaborately. Interpreting the physical delights of the garden as Adam's spiritual blessings, he claimed that the position of Eden in the East signified its proximity to the source of the light of wisdom, that the trees represented spiritual joys, the four rivers the four virtues, and the tree of life wisdom itself. Adam's duty was to cultivate these spiritual benefits with the help of Eve.[2] In this modified version of the allegorical reading the actual *personae* thus retained their literal identities; only the scenery among which they moved was figurative.

This drastic reorganization created in turn two fresh problems: a literal identity had to be found for the serpent, and the psychological meaning of the story had to be either abandoned or modified. The first was easily solved by the association of the serpent with the Devil,[3] but the second involved more far-reaching changes, as the following passage reveals:

for if a heart which ought to be looking forward to what is ahead—that is, to God—and forgetting what is behind—that is, the delights of the body—leaves God and turns in upon itself in the desire to bear fruit of its own power . . . pride then swells up within, and pride is the beginning of every sin. And with this, the sin of the heart will bring on its own punishment, for by experience it will learn what is the difference between the good it has forsaken and the evil into which it has fallen. And this will be to that soul the tasting of the fruit of the tree of the discernment of good and evil.[4]

What Augustine has done here is to synthesize the allegorical patterns worked out by his predecessors and bring them to bear on the literal episode at the centre of the story. The rejection of the spiritual for the carnal, which Philo had read into Adam's attitude to Eve, is now implicit in the violation of the tree of knowledge, and the

[1] *De Civ. Dei*, xiii. 21.   [2] *De Gen. con Man.* II. ix–xi.
[3] Ibid. II. xiv. See below, pp. 87–88.   [4] Ibid. II. ix.

generation of evil or self-begotten deeds, which Origen had taken to be the result of the Fall, is now one of the motives which caused that violation. The doctrinal focus has thus been shifted back to the forbidden tree, the symbol of Man's relationship with God.

By the time Isidore of Seville (560–636) came to write his *Mysticorum Expositiones Sacramentorum* this new interpretation was fully developed. Paradise again is 'the blessed life', the fruit of the trees 'the customs of the pious', the tree of life 'wisdom, the mother of all good',[1] and the serpent the Devil.[2] But the tree of knowledge no longer represents 'the experience of a broken commandment'; it is now more specifically 'free will':[3] 'And we must not touch the tree of the knowledge of good and evil which is planted in the middle of Paradise, that is, we must not take pride in the nature of our will which is in the middle of us lest, deceived by knowledge, we should experience evil.'[4] This is a great improvement on Augustine's designation, for by defining the tree of knowledge more precisely Isidore is able to reassign their allegorical identities to Adam and Eve without detracting from the importance of the tree itself. According to this version of the story, then, the Devil deceives the carnal sense into persuading reason to abandon the will of God for its own desires, to eat, that is to say, of the forbidden fruit.[5] Pseudo-Bede's *In Pentateuchum Commentarii* contains much the same interpretation.[6] Adam's task is to guard himself in his paradise of spiritual delights,[7] and to abstain from the tree of knowledge, 'that is, not to take pride in the nature of our will, which is in the middle of us, lest deceived by the present good we experience evil also'.[8] The Devil attacks reason through carnal pleasure and persuades it to exult in its own authority.[9]

In the exegesis of these two commentators the wheel has come full circle. The Augustinian synthesis, which in its attempt to plant the tree of knowledge back in the middle of the story had sacrificed the Philonic allegory of Adam and Eve, has been revised in such a way that the reason–sense–pleasure equation is preserved and related directly to the eating of the fruit. The only important feature

---

[1] *Myst. Ex. Sac.* In Gen. i. 17.   [2] Ibid. iv. 2.   [3] Ibid. iii. 4.
[4] Ibid. iv. 2.   [5] Ibid. iv. 3–4.
[6] At one point Origen's version of the story is quoted in Rufinus's translation: 'The spirit is called the masculine, the heart can be called the feminine. Those, if they accord with each other, can beget as children good and useful senses, with which they fill the earth, that is, the flesh' (*In Pent. Comm.*, In Gen. i).
[7] *In Pent. Comm.*, In Gen. ii.   [8] Ibid. iii.   [9] Loc. cit.

of Philo's interpretation to be omitted is his explanation of Adam's initial reaction to Eve as the mind's surrender to the charms of the senses. This surrender now takes place at the Devil's instigation, when the tree of knowledge, the free will of the individual, is abused.

John Scotus Erigena (b. *c.* 800–15), on the other hand, developed the Philonic tradition in exactly the opposite direction, placing all the emphasis on Eve's creation and largely ignoring the forbidden tree. Paradise, he stated,[1] was human nature in its original state, Adam the mind, Eve the sense, the serpent pleasure, and the four rivers the four cardinal virtues. Up to this point his exegesis was more or less in accordance with that of his predecessors, but instead of adopting their interpretation of the tree of knowledge he located the Fall in Adam's sleep, the soul's descent to carnal pleasures. The division of Man into two sexes was the first result of the Fall, not one of the preliminaries to it. Gregory of Nyssa (d. 394), one of Erigena's chief sources, had suggested that God created Eve because, foreseeing the Fall, He wished to make provision for the subsequent procreation of mankind. Before the Fall, 'if there had not come upon us as the result of sin a change for the worse, and removal from equality with the angels, neither should we have needed marriage that we might multiply; but whatever the mode of increase in the angelic nature is . . . it would have operated also in the case of men'.[2] Erigena took over this idea, but omitted the qualifying element of God's foreknowledge. Hence the change from angelic to human modes of reproduction was not something which God anticipated by creating Eve; it was an actual consequence of Adam's sin. The creation of Eve, therefore, must have taken place after the Fall, after, that is to say, Adam's sleep.

This apparently eccentric exposition of the Genesis narrative was quite as dependent on the Philonic interpretation as the more orthodox ones had been. The only difference between Erigena and the earlier commentators is that whereas they grouped the Philonic allegories around the tree of knowledge, he brought out the implications of the Philonic treatment of Adam's sleep, and chose that as the focal point of his exegesis. Both versions of the story stemmed ultimately from those two seminal works, the *Legum Allegoria* and *De Opificio Mundi.*

---

[1] For this summary I have relied chiefly on the synthesis of *De Divisione Naturae* given in H. Bett, *Johannes Scotus Erigena*, 1925, pp. 56–67. For a rabbinic equivalent of Erigena's interpretation see *Gen. Rab.* xxi. 5.   [2] *De Hom. Op.* xvii. 2.

4. *The Literal Reading*

Like the allegorical, the literal reading originated in the need to explain away the difficulties of the Fall story without relapsing into metaphysical dualism. But it set itself the infinitely harder task of resolving them at the literal level. The criticisms attributed to thinkers like Simon Magus and Celsus were aimed primarily at the surface meaning of the narrative, and it was this meaning which the Greek Apologists of the second century, Tatian, Justin Martyr, Theophilus of Antioch, and their successors made it their business to defend. In the process of doing so they did not hesitate to borrow liberally from the other great tradition of literal commentary, the rabbinic.

However, in one vital respect the interpretation evolved by the first Christian school of literal exegesis differed wholly from the Jewish. Whereas the Apocrypha and the rabbinic tractates laid a great deal of emphasis on the perfections bestowed on Adam by his Creator, the earliest patristic writings on the subject portrayed him as an imperfect childlike creature serving a spiritual apprenticeship before his destined elevation to angelic status. Since only God was perfect from the very beginning, the creatures, as Tatian said, could have been created with no more than the possibility of becoming so: 'And each of these two orders of creatures [the angels and man] was made free to act as it pleased, not having the nature of good, which again is with God alone, but is brought to perfection in men through their freedom of choice.'[1] Theophilus applied this principle to the question of Adam's mortality, arguing that he was given: 'means of advancement, in order that, maturing and becoming perfect, and being even declared a god, he might thus ascend into heaven in possession of immortality. For man had been made a middle nature, neither wholly mortal, nor altogether immortal, but capable of either.'[2] And Irenaeus in turn derived from it the following estimate of Man's original nature: 'So, having made the man lord of the earth and everything in it, He made him in secret lord also of the servants in it. They, however, were in their full development, while the lord, that is the man, was a little one; for he was a child and had need to grow so as to come to his full perfection.'[3]

---

[1] *Orat. con Graec.* vii.

[2] *Ad Autol.* ii. 24. See also ibid. ii. 27; Justin Martyr's *Frag.* xi. In this alone did the early patristic idea of Adam resemble the Jewish. Compare above, Ch. II, p. 42.

[3] *Dem.* xii.

Consequently in their unfallen state the first pair, 'having been created a short time previously, had no understanding of the pro-creation of children: for it was necessary that they should first come to adult age'.[1] Their very lack of shame at their nakedness showed that their physical development was not yet complete: 'For this reason they *were not ashamed*, as they kissed each other and embraced with the innocence of children.'[2] All this was a far cry from the Jewish conception of Adam's initial maturity and his pre-lapsarian sexual relations with Eve. In fact these early Fathers reverted, per-haps unconsciously, to the Jahwist's picture of Man's primitive condition in Eden, thus solving the most difficult single problem of the story: how could Adam fall? 'But man was a little one, and his discretion still undeveloped, wherefore also he was easily misled by the deceiver.'[3] Clement of Alexandria (d. pre-215) brought this point out clearly in his attacks on the 'heretics': 'By which consideration is solved the question propounded to us by the heretics, Whether Adam was created perfect or imperfect? Well if imperfect, how could the work of a perfect God—above all, that work being man—be imperfect? And if perfect, how did he transgress the command-ments? For they shall hear from us that he was not perfect in his creation, but adapted to the reception of virtue.'[4]

What is more, the related problem of the prohibition of the tree of knowledge could be solved along the same lines. In its running battle with the dualistic sects the Church found itself committed to two seemingly contradictory tenets: that the fruit of the tree was not in itself evil or deadly, and that God was not envious in forbidding Adam and Eve to eat of it. The Gnostic and Manichaean way out of the dilemma, to accept the first proposition and deny the second, was clearly out of the question, for it involved the association of Jahweh with the wicked Ialdabaoth. But so was the converse, to deny the first and accept the second, for that implied that God had deliberately introduced an evil element into the world. If Adam was childlike and imperfect, however, the goodness of the fruit could be reconciled with the benevolence of the prohibition without resorting to either of these unpalatable alternatives:

The tree of knowledge itself was good, and its fruit was good. For it was not the tree, as some think, but the disobedience, which had death in it.

---

[1] *Adv. Haer.* III. xxii. 4. See also Justin Martyr's *Dial.* c.
[2] *Dem.* xiv.   [3] Ibid. xii.   [4] *Strom.* vi. 12.

For there was nothing else in the fruit than only knowledge; but knowledge is good when one uses it discreetly. But Adam, being yet an infant in
age, was on this account as yet unable to receive knowledge worthily. For
now, also, when a child is born it is not at once able to eat bread, but is
nourished first with milk, and then, with the increment of years, it ad-
vances to solid food. Thus, too, would it have been with Adam; for not
as one who grudged him, as some suppose, did God command him not to
eat of knowledge. But He wished also to make proof of him, whether he
was submissive to His commandment.[1]

Only if Adam was in some way immature could his Maker have
commanded him to abstain from something which was in essence
good. As in the Jahwist document, therefore, the Fall consisted in
eating the fruit too soon and so growing up too quickly.

In many ways this was the most satisfactory exegesis of the story
ever offered by patristic commentators, and it was certainly one of
the most influential. The dietetic image which Theophilus had used
to illustrate his thesis was repeated by Irenaeus, Gregory of Nazianzus (c. 329–c. 390), and John of Damascus (c. 680–c. 760),[2] while the
notion that the Fall consisted in some kind of anticipation provided
at least two later Fathers with a means of integrating the allegorical
interpretation with the literal. Philo, as we have seen, had elaborated
two incompatible allegorical patterns, the first concerning the
relationships between Adam, Eve, and the serpent, and the second
concerning the significance of the tree of knowledge. Clement of
Alexandria superimposed the first of these on the literal events of the
narrative by suggesting that the first act of disobedience was the
premature sexual union of Adam and Eve. Having dismissed as
blasphemous the Gnostic and Manichaean doctrine that intercourse
is inherently sinful, he pointed out that, 'if nature led them [Adam
and Eve], like the irrational animals, to procreation, yet they were
impelled to do it more quickly than was proper because they were
still young and had been led away by deceit. Thus God's judgement
against them was just, because they did not wait for his will. But
birth is holy.'[3] Gregory of Nazianzus, on the other hand, attempted
to harmonize Philo's view, that the tree of knowledge represented
'the science of knowing', with Adam's violation of it thus:

This Law was a commandment as to what plants he might partake of,
and which one he might not touch. This latter was the Tree of Know-

[1] *Ad Autol.* ii. 25.
[2] *Adv. Haer.* IV. xxxviii. 1; *Orat.* xlv. 8; *Orth. Fid.* ii. 11.   [3] *Strom.* iii. 17.

ledge; not, however, because it was evil from the beginning when planted; nor was it forbidden because God grudged it to men—let not the enemies of God wag their tongues in that direction, or imitate the serpent. But it would have been good if partaken of at the proper time; for the Tree was, according to my theory, Contemplation, which it is only safe for those who have reached maturity of habit to enter upon; but which is not good for those who are still somewhat simple and greedy.[1]

In both cases the bridge between the allegorical and the literal level was the 'anticipation theory' first put forward by Theophilus.

The third major criticism advanced by the 'heretics' was directed at the absurdity of the temptation itself; a story in which a mere serpent defied the will of God, Celsus had asserted, was more like an old wives' tale than divinely inspired history.[2] For this reason alone the identity of the tempter required some clarification—a beast endowed with the power of speech did smack of fable rather than fact—so the early Fathers, taking the New Testament's loose association of the serpent with Satan as their point of departure,[3] invented a version of the episode according to which Eve's assailant was an angel who was expelled from Heaven after he had persuaded her to eat the forbidden fruit. The first step was again taken by Tatian:

And, when men attached themselves to one who was more subtle than the rest, having regard to his being the first-born, and declared him to be God, though he was resisting the law of God, then the power of the Logos excluded the beginner of the folly and his adherents from all fellowship with Himself. And so he who was made in the likeness of God . . . becomes mortal; but that first-begotten one through his transgression and ignorance becomes a demon.[4]

On the basis of this admittedly vague description of the tempter's activities Irenaeus then constructed the following account of the Fall:

This commandment the man did not keep, but disobeyed God, being misled by the angel, who, becoming jealous of the man and looking on him with envy because of God's many favours which He had bestowed on the man, both ruined himself and made the man a sinner, persuading him to disobey God's command. So the angel, having become by falsehood the head and fount of sin, both was himself stricken, having offended against God, and caused the man to be cast forth out of Paradise.[5]

---

[1] *Orat.* xlv. 8.   [2] *Con. Cels.* iv. 39. See above, p. 71.
[3] Rev. xii. 9, xx. 2.
[4] *Orat. con. Graec.* vii. See also Justin Martyr's *Dial.* cxxiv.   [5] *Dem.* xvi.

The motive of envy, which had originally been attributed to the
Devil in the Wisdom of Solomon and to the serpent in the rabbinic
tractates,[1] was thus introduced into the earliest patristic interpretation of the third chapter of Genesis in order to provide an explanation for the unfallen angel's hostility to Man.

Although the precise nature of the 'favours' which provoked this
feeling was never very clearly defined by Irenaeus, it is probably safe
to assume that he shared the opinion of the Rabbis that the material
delights of Eden were the primary object of the tempter's envy, for,
like them, he portrayed Adam's benefits in largely physical terms:

> And so that he might have nourishment and grow up in luxury, a place
> was prepared for him better than this world, well-favoured in climate,
> beauty, light, things good to eat, plants, fruit, water, and all other things
> useful to life; and its name is the Garden. And so fair and goodly was the
> Garden, the Word of God was constantly walking in it; He would walk
> round and talk with the man, prefiguring what was to come to pass in the
> future.[2]

Several later commentators, however, explored this question in
more detail. Tertullian, for example, taught that the Devil took
offence at Man's lordship over the earth: 'Therefore I detect the
nativity of impatience in the devil himself, at that very time when he
impatiently bore that the Lord God subjected the universal works
which He had made to His own image, that is, to man.'[3] Cyprian
(d. 258), on the other hand, adopted the view expressed in the Vita
Adae et Evae that the angel 'suffered with impatience that man was
made in the image of God'.[4] And Methodius of Olympus (d. c. 311)
and Gregory of Nyssa, influenced perhaps by the Johannine description of Satan as 'the prince of this world',[5] suggested that he saw in
Adam a potential rival to his own majesty: 'He to whom the adminis-
tration of the earth has been consigned takes it ill and thinks it not
to be borne, if, of that nature which has been subjected to him, any
being shall be exhibited bearing likeness to his transcendent dignity.'[6]
Diverse as they were, all these analyses of the tempter's reasons for
bringing about the Fall rested on the assumption that he was not
cast down into Hell until he had succeeded in leading Adam and
Eve astray. In spite of the subsequent emergence of the legend of
Lucifer's premundane rebellion, this theory persisted for a long

---

[1] See above, Ch. II, pp. 35, 47–48.   [2] *Dem.* xii.   [3] *De Pat.* v.
[4] *De Bon. Pat.* 19. Compare above, Ch. II, p. 56.   [5] John xvi. 11.
[6] *Orat. Cat.* vi. See also Methodius's *De Resurr.* vii.

time in the Western Church. Even as late as the fifth century Cassian (*c.* 360–435) found it necessary to refute it:

Germanus: Up till now we used to believe that the reason and commencement of the ruin and fall of the devil, in which he was cast out from his heavenly estate, was more particularly envy, when in his spiteful subtelty he deceived Adam and Eve . . . Serenus: . . . the occasion of the envy and seduction, which led him to deceive man, arose from the ground of his previous fall, in that he saw that man, who had but recently been formed out of the dust of the ground, was to be called to that glory, from which he remembered that he himself, while still one of the princes, had fallen. And so that first fall of his, which was due to pride, and which obtained for him the name of the serpent, was followed by a second owing to envy.[1]

Up to this point the Fathers were concerned with altogether a different kind of question from that which the Rabbis had undertaken to answer; whereas the latter had interested themselves chiefly in narrative problems, the former paid more attention to interpretative and metaphysical difficulties. But as regards the events which took place after the temptation the interests of the two schools more or less coincided. It was during the interrogation and condemnation, they both realized, that God's conduct was most vulnerable to the kind of criticism that had led the Gnostics to equate Him with the ignorant and malicious Ialdabaoth. The mere fact that He found it necessary to ask Adam and Eve where they were hiding, for example, suggested that He was not after all omniscient. Like the Rabbis, therefore, Theophilus insisted that He called out to them not because He did not know where they were but because He wished to offer them an opportunity to repent: 'And as to God's calling, and saying, Where art thou, Adam? God did this, not as if ignorant of this; but, being long-suffering, He gave them an opportunity of repentance and confession.'[2] Mercy, too, was the theme of Irenaeus's interpretation of the questions God put to the fallen pair when they eventually stood before Him: 'For this purpose, too, He interrogates them, that the blame might light upon the woman; and again, He interrogates her, that she might convey the blame to the serpent.'[3] And mercy was mingled with justice in the same

---

[1] *Coll.* viii. 9–10.
[2] *Ad Autol.* ii. 26. See also Hilary of Poitiers, *Hom. in Ps.* i. 24. Compare above, Ch. II, p. 52.
[3] *Adv. Haer.* III. xxiii. 5.

commentator's explanation of the omission of any question to the serpent: 'But He put no question to the serpent; for He knew that he had been the prime mover in the guilty deed; but He pronounced the curse upon him in the first instance, that it might fall upon man with a mitigated rebuke.'[1] As the Rabbis had noticed, the terms of this curse seemed to imply that the other animals were included in it. Their consequent assumption that Eve must have distributed the forbidden fruit to all the beasts of the field was perhaps in Theophilus's mind when he wrote: 'The animals are named wild beasts, from their being hunted, not as if they had been made evil or venomous from the first . . . but the sin in which man was concerned brought evil upon them. For when man transgressed, they also transgressed with him.'[2]

The similarities between the two schools are even more marked when we come to the expulsion, the episode to which Simon Magus had taken such strong exception: 'in his saying respecting Adam, "Let us drive him out, lest he put forth his hand and touch the tree of life, and eat, and live for ever"; in saying *lest* he is ignorant; and in driving him out . . . he is also envious.'[3] In one of his rare excursions into literal exegesis Philo had provided a characteristically ingenious answer to the second and more serious of these charges: 'The Deity, however, is without any part in evil and is not envious of immortality or anything else whatever in the case of the good man . . . he (Adam) failed to obtain immortality for it is unseemly to immortalize evil, and it is unprofitable for him to whom it happens.'[4] If Adam had been allowed to stay in the garden of Eden and eat of the tree of life he would have found himself condemned to an eternity of sinfulness. To expel him, if followed, was yet another demonstration of the divine wisdom and mercy, and Theophilus was careful to emphasize this point in his adaptation of Philo's argument: 'And God showed great kindness to man in this, that He did not suffer him to remain in sin for ever; but, as it were, by a kind of banishment, cast him out of Paradise, in order that, having by punishment expiated, within an appointed time, the sin, and having been disciplined, he should afterwards be restored.'[5] The Jewish commentator's allegorical exposition of the coats of skins as Man's

---

[1] Loc. cit.   [2] *Ad Autol.* ii. 17. See above, Ch. II, p. 52.

[3] *Clem. Hom.* iii. 39.   [4] *Q.A.* i. 55.

[5] *Ad Autol.* ii. 26. See also Gregory of Nazianzus's *Orat.* xlv. 8; Methodius's *De Resurr.* iv.

body was less acceptable, implying as it did that matter was inherently evil, so Methodius modified it to accord with earlier patristic statements concerning the benevolent motives lying behind the expulsion: 'God for this cause pronounced him [Adam] mortal and clothed him with mortality. For this is what was meant by the coats of skins.'[1] Yet despite these proofs of God's good will towards men, the fact remained that He had threatened them with death on the day they ate the forbidden fruit. To explain Adam and Eve's survival Irenaeus again had recourse to Jewish ideas: 'And there are some, again, who relegate the death of Adam to the thousandth year; for since "a day of the Lord is as a thousand years" [2 Peter iii. 8], he did not overstep the thousand years.'[2] Apart from the substitution of a New for an Old Testament reference—2 Peter iii. 8 has replaced Psalm xc. 4—this view was substantially the same as that expounded by the Rabbis. The one distinctively Christian comment on this part of the story related to God's instigation of the future enmity between Adam's offspring and the serpent: 'For from that time, He who should be born of a woman, [namely] from the Virgin, after the likeness of Adam, was preached as keeping watch for the head of the serpent.'[3] Beneath the curse lay the promise of Man's ultimate salvation.

Thus the problems which had produced the dualistic and allegorical readings of the scriptural text were also instrumental in shaping the literal reading as it appeared in the works of this first group of Fathers. In order to justify God's ways to Adam they were driven back to an interpretation of the Fall which in many ways resembled that of the Jahwist himself. Like him they saw Adam's disobedience as a *péché d'enfant*, a premature acquisition of knowledge by an immature and childlike creature, who consequently grew up too soon. The chief virtue of their version of the story, which may most conveniently be designated by Williams's term 'minimal', was that it reconciled the Priestly document's account of God's omniscience and benevolence with the Jahwist document's concept of Adam's nature and sin. But although it was both literally consistent and morally acceptable this minimal estimate of the first transgression had a corresponding disadvantage: it reduced it to such small proportions that it hardly seemed important enough to warrant the

---

[1] *De Resurr.* iv.   [2] *Adv. Haer.* v. xxiii. 2.
[3] Ibid. v. xxi. 1. He may have been anticipated by St. Paul in Rom. xvi. 20: 'And the God of peace shall bruise Satan under your feet shortly.'

sacrificial agony of the Redemption. The two events did not form a
real balance, and the typological parallels between them worked out
by the same Fathers, perhaps to remedy this disparity,[1] were not
sufficient to offset the apparent triviality of the first when compared
with the gravity of the second. It was not long, however, before this
difficulty was resolved by an interpretation which gave full weight
to the seriousness of Adam's sin, the 'maximal' interpretation.

The basic difference between the two schools is clearly reflected
in their respective views of Man's original condition. The minimal
commentators had emphasized Adam's ignorance and innocence;
their maximal successors laid all the stress on his perfections. For
just as the inference that the plurals in the first chapter of Genesis
referred to the angels had led the Rabbis to portray Adam's nature
as angelic, so the assumption that these same plurals referred to the
Trinity[2] ultimately led the Fathers to dwell on his likenesses to God:
'for he [Adam] was appointed king over the earth and all things on
it; he was beautiful in his form, being created an image of the
archetypal beauty; he was without passion in his nature, for he was
an imitation of the unimpassioned.'[3] Adam was not merely destined
to achieve angelic status, as Theophilus had believed; he was the
equal of the angels already: 'His eyes were fixed steadfastly on
heaven, he was full of joy in the things he beheld, since he loved to
the full the giver of these things, who graced him with eternal life,
and placed him amid the delights of paradise, giving him moreover
higher authority than the angels, so that he was able to feed with
archangels.'[4] In the Christian tradition, as in the Jewish, the Priestly
writer's exalted description of Man soon came to impose itself on
the Jahwist's more primitive account.

This fundamental change in perspective naturally affected the
way in which the rest of the story was interpreted. For instance,
whereas the Greek Apologists had seen Adam's sexual innocence as
no more than a symptom of his physical immaturity, these later
commentators singled it out as a vital aspect of his original per-

---

[1] See below, pp. 99–104. It is perhaps no coincidence that those Fathers with the
greatest penchant for typological interpretation were also those who took a minimal view
of the Fall.

[2] See Basil's *Hex.* ix. 6; Gregory of Nyssa's *De Hom. Op.* vi. 3.

[3] *Orat. Cat.* vi. Gregory of Nyssa insisted in *De Hom. Op.* xvi. 1 that Man's glory lay
in his likeness to God rather than his likeness to the world. Compare Gregory of Nazianzus, *Orat.* xlv. 7.

[4] Basil's *Quod Deus*, vii. See also Chrysostom's *Hom. in Gen.* xvi. 1.

fection: 'For it was after the transgression that these things (sexual acts) took place. But until this time they were living in Paradise like angels, not moved by lusts, nor plagued by other emotions, not under the pressure of their nature's demands, but uncorrupt in every respect, as they were created, and immortal.'[1] Gregory of Nyssa, indeed, went so far as to suggest that had it not been for the Fall the human race would have been propagated in some non-carnal way.[2]

The same Father also raised the crucial question that was bound to be revived as soon as the minimal conception of pre-lapsarian Man had been abandoned: 'Whence, then, comes it, you will ask, that he who had been distinguished throughout with excellent endowments exchanged these good things for worse?'[3] Irenaeus and Clement of Alexandria had been able to answer quite simply that Adam was led astray because he was still in his infancy, but Gregory of Nyssa and those of his persuasion had to account for the corruption of a demi-god. In order to do so they first blackened the character of his antagonist by picturing him not as an unfallen angel but as the rebellious Lucifer invented by the author of the Secrets of Enoch. Origen had prepared the ground for this development by relating both the fourteenth chapter of Isaiah, from which the apocryphal legend had been derived, and the twenty-eighth of Ezekiel to the Satan of the New Testament, thus passing on to Christianity the idea of the Devil's premundane conflict with his Creator. Of the first passage he wrote: 'In this manner, then, did that being once exist as light before he went astray, and fell to this place, and had his glory turned into dust . . . whence, too, he was called the prince of this world.'[4] Of the second: 'We have shown, then, that what we have quoted regarding the prince of Tyre from the prophet Ezekiel refers to an adverse power, and by it it is most clearly proved that that power was formerly holy and happy; from which state of happiness it fell from the time that iniquity was found in it, and was hurled to the earth, and was not such by nature and creation.'[5] Origen's primary purpose, no doubt, was to refute the dualistic theogonies of Gnosticism, and he did not go on to equate this rebellious angel with the tempter in Eden—his allegorical interpretation of the Fall in any case precluded such an

---

[1] Chrysostom's *Hom. in Gen.* xv. 4.
[2] *De Hom. Op.* xvii. 2. See above, p. 77.
[3] *Orat. Cat.* v.
[4] *De Princ.* I. v. 5. See above, Ch. II, pp. 33–34.
[5] Ibid. I. v. 4.

equation. But for the maximal Fathers of the third and fourth centuries who interpreted the story literally the legend offered a welcome opportunity of making the Fall more credible by transforming Adam's adversary into a sufficiently powerful and evil character to have been able to overcome his unfallen perfection. Moreover, it provided a rather less recondite motive for the temptation itself than any of those previously put forward: Lucifer envied Adam because he saw him enjoying the advantages that he himself had just lost: 'Thus he was not instituted as our enemy from the outset; he is driven to become our enemy through envy. For, having been made aware that he is an outcast from the angelic ranks himself, he finds it insupportable to him to see man, who is of the earth, exalted to angelic status.'[1] No sooner, then, did Adam's disobedience come to be regarded as something more than a childish lapse than the tempter's downfall was considerably magnified, and transferred from after to before the temptation.

Most Fathers who accepted this view of Man's seducer simply read 'Satan' or 'Lucifer' for 'serpent' in the Genesis narrative, but John Chrysostom (c. 344–407) insisted on defining the relationship between the two more precisely. He concluded that Satan had insinuated himself into a real serpent in order to gain access to Eve: 'But it may be that someone reading this account may wonder whether the serpent was a partaker in rational nature. But it was not like this at all; far from it. The scriptures should always be understood in this way—that the words are the Devil's own. . . . He was using the beast as a convenient organ for his purpose, by means of which he might dangle the bait.'[2] Influenced perhaps by the explanation of the serpent's appropriateness as a symbol of lust given by the allegorists, Gregory of Nyssa refined this idea still further: 'And he, that evil charmer, framing his new device of sin against our race, drew along his serpent train, a disguise worthy of his own intent, entering in his impurity into what was like himself— dwelling, earthly and mundane as he was in will, in that creeping thing.'[3] The serpentine disguise, as in *Paradise Lost*, indicated the depth to which the former archangel had sunk.

Finally, the idealistic conception of Adam's nature made it necessary to re-examine the meaning of the tree of knowledge. No

[1] Basil's *Quod Deus*, viii. See also Cyril of Jerusalem's *Cat.* ii. 4, xii. 5; Chrysostom's *Hom. in Gen.* xvi, xxii; *Hom. in Joh.* liv.
[2] *Hom. in Gen.* xvi. 2.   [3] *De Bapt. Chr.*, p. 519. Compare above, p. 74.

longer could the goodness of the tree be reconciled with the benevolence of God by assuming that Adam was forbidden to eat its
fruit only because he was too young to put the knowledge it conferred to its proper use. An angelic man would have known the
difference between right and wrong from the outset, so he could
hardly have acquired this or indeed any other intellectual ability
prematurely. Consequently the maximalists were forced to deny
that the tree contained the knowledge of good and evil at all: 'Why
is it called the tree of knowledge of good and evil? There are many
contentious people who dare to say that after the eating of the fruit
of the tree, Adam had the power to discern good and evil. That
would be the very height of madness. . . . For how could He have
given a commandment to one who was in ignorance that transgression was a bad thing?'[1] In fact Adam and Eve's moral awareness
was complete before the Fall, and the reason they were prohibited
from partaking of this one tree was 'so that they might know that
they enjoyed the fruition only by God's grace and charity, and that
He is the Lord and Creator of all things'.[2] Thus the tree of knowledge
retained its significance as the token of Man's obedience, while losing
the supernatural properties which had formerly been ascribed to it.
Gregory of Nyssa, however, was not content to let the matter rest
there. He argued that, 'since the majority of men judge the good to
lie in that which gratifies the senses . . . for this reason that desire
which arises towards what is evil, as though towards good, is called
by Scripture "the knowledge of good and evil"'.[3] The forbidden
tree, he maintained, was essentially evil; its apparent goodness was
merely an illusion created by the Devil, who 'obtained credence for
his counsel, covering over the fruit with a fair appearance and the
show of pleasure, that it might be pleasant to the eyes and stimulate
the desire to taste'.[4] Although this interpretation answered his own
earlier question concerning the possibility of a perfect creature's
choosing to sin, it posed in turn a still more difficult one, which he
resolutely ignored: why should God have planted such a tree in the
garden of Eden in the first place?[5]

What Gregory seems to have been attempting here was to relate
the Philonic allegory of reason's deception by the senses to the

[1] *Hom. in Gen.* xvi. 5.   [2] Ibid. xiii. 4.   [3] *De Hom. Op.* xx. 3.
[4] Ibid. xix. 5. See also xx. 4. Compare *Apoc. Mos.* xix. 3.
[5] In fact Gregory has opted for the second of the two alternatives I mentioned
above, p. 79, that is, he has denied that God was envious in prohibiting the fruit, but
asserted that the fruit was evil.

literal violation of the tree of knowledge. In this he was typical of the
maximal school of commentators, for when the minimal estimate of
Adam's original condition, and thus of his subsequent lapse, came
to be rejected, it was essential that some more serious interpretation
should be found to take its place. Stripped of its allegorical complications, Philo's theory that the Fall consisted in the abandonment
of spiritual virtue for fleshly pleasure offered a convenient and
thoroughly acceptable alternative, and it was enthusiastically adopted
by at least two of Gregory's contemporaries, Basil the Great (c.
330–79) and Athanasius (295–373). The former gave the following
account of the first transgression: 'He [Adam] soon reached the
point of satiety with these things [spiritual pleasures], and becoming
insolent in his sufficiency, he preferred what seemed good to his
carnal eyesight to what was of spiritual worth, and he placed the
satisfaction of his gluttonous appetite before the fruits of the
spirit.'[1] And the latter this very similar one: 'For he [Adam] also,
as long as he kept his mind to God, and the contemplation of God,
turned away from the contemplation of the body. But when, by
counsel of the serpent, he departed from the consideration of God,
and began to regard himself, then they not only fell to bodily lust,
but knew that they were naked, and knowing, were ashamed.'[2] In
both these passages the allegorical meaning elaborated by Philo has
been transferred to the literal level of the story, so paving the way
for Augustine's final synthesis.

But these later Fathers did not reject the minimal reading in its
entirety. Cyril of Jerusalem (d. 386), for example, reproduced
Gregory of Nazianzus's explanation of the tempter's reasons for
approaching Eve rather than Adam: 'Not daring to accost the man
because of his strength, he accosted as being weaker the woman, still
a virgin.'[3] And Gregory of Nyssa followed Methodius in interpreting
the skins with which Adam and Eve were clothed as the tokens of
their mortality: 'But since all skin, after it is separated from the
animal, is dead, I am certainly of opinion that He who is the healer
of our sinfulness, of His foresight invested man subsequently with

---

[1] *Quod Deus*, vii.
[2] *Con. Gent.* iii. 3. Committed as they were to the maximal reading, these Fathers
could not make use of Gregory of Nazianzus's earlier synthesis of the allegorical and
literal interpretations. In order to avoid Gregory of Nyssa's extremely unsatisfactory
conclusion that the fruit of the tree was evil, therefore, they expressed the Philonic idea
of a descent from the spiritual to the material in the vaguest possible terms.
[3] *Cat.* xii. 5. Compare Gregory of Nazianzus's *Orat.* xlv. 8.

that capacity for dying which had been the special attribute of the brute creation.'[1] Nor were they afraid to make use of rabbinic material when it suited their purposes. Chrysostom, in particular, seems to have been thoroughly familiar with the *haggadah*, for at least three of his most distinctive comments on the story were derived from it. First, he assumed like the Rabbis that Eve did not try to deceive Adam as the serpent had deceived her—rather, she employed her feminine wiles to persuade him to fall with her:

The woman said, *The serpent beguiled me.* But the man did not say, The woman deceived me, but, *she gave me of the tree* . . . Now it is not the same thing to be deceived by a fellow creature, one of the same kind, as by an inferior and subordinate animal. This is truly to be deceived. Compared therefore with the woman, he is spoken of as *not deceived.* For she was beguiled by an inferior and subject, he by an equal. Again, it is not said of the man, that he *saw the tree was good for food,* but of the woman, and that she *did eat, and gave it to her husband*: so that he transgressed, not captivated by appetite, but merely from the persuasion of his wife.[2]

Second, he concurred with the Jewish commentators that Adam and Eve's new vision after the Fall was not to be taken to imply that they had been blind before it: 'For it is not in fact the eating of the tree's fruit which opened their eyes, for indeed they saw perfectly well before they had eaten of it.'[3] And third, he adopted the rabbinic belief that the fallen pair's nakedness was a metaphor for their moral depravity: '[They were] naked, because of the transgression of the commandment, of the glory from above, receiving the realization of their sense of nudity so that they might understand through the growing sense of their nakedness to what ruin their transgression of the Lord's command had brought them.'[4]

The maximal version of the story, then, was distinguished from the minimal primarily by its more exalted conception of Adam's original condition. The other features that set it apart from the earlier reading, its association of the serpent with Lucifer and its attempt to draw from the Philonic allegories a more serious account of the Fall, followed naturally from the initial modification. For its exegesis of the post-lapsarian section of the narrative, on the other hand, it relied largely on the minimal and rabbinic analyses of God's justice

---

[1] *Orat. Cat.* viii. See also Cyril of Jerusalem's *Cat.* ii. 7. [2] *Hom. in Tim.* ix.
[3] *Hom. in Gen.* xvi. 5. Compare above, Ch. II, p. 50.
[4] Loc. cit. Several other commentators made the idea still more explicit. See Athanasius's *Con. Gent.* iii. 3; Gregory of Nyssa's *Orat. Cat.* viii.

and mercy. But in heightening the sinfulness of the Fall, while at the same time minimizing its results, it created a fresh problem: if Adam's disobedience was so grave, why, even making due allowance for God's mercy, were its effects so comparatively trivial? The third and last school of interpretation, the Augustinian, soon set the balance right once and for all.

Like the earlier readings, Augustine's was worked out in an atmosphere permeated with the ever-present threat of dualism. By the fourth century, as I remarked earlier, Manichaeism had replaced Gnosticism as the chief exponent of this philosophy, which, for a short period in his youth, even numbered the future Bishop of Hippo among its adherents. But the situation was now complicated by the appearance of a Pelagian Scylla opposite the Manichaean Charybdis. This new ultra-optimistic heresy was based on the belief in the complete freedom of Man's will and in the consequent possibility of human perfection.[1] Adam's failure to observe the prohibition of the tree of knowledge injured no one but himself, and he could not be blamed either for human mortality or for human sinfulness.[2] The Fall was merely the first historical example of sin, not its cause.[3] Hence each child, according to Pelagius and his disciples, is born in a state of original innocence such as Adam once possessed. The only difference is that it has to grow up in a world where the habit of sin prevails; we sin, therefore, by imitation rather than necessity: 'Nothing good, and nothing evil . . . is born with us, but is done by us: for we are born not fully developed, but with a capacity for either conduct; we are formed naturally without either virtue or vice.'[4]

Against the background of this and the Manichaean heresy

---

[1] For this summary I have relied chiefly on G. de Plinval, *Pélage*, Lausanne, 1943; J. Ferguson, *Pelagius*, 1956; R. W. Battenhouse, *A Companion to the Study of St. Augustine*, 1955, ch. viii.

[2] See Pelagius, *On Romans*, v. 12.   [3] Ibid. v. 12, 16, 19.

[4] Augustine's *De Grat*. ii. 14. In essence this view of the human condition was no more than an extension of the minimal interpretation of the Fall. Substitute 'Man' for 'Adam'—which is only to translate the Hebrew word literally—and the comments of the Greek Apologists become Pelagian. As Williams has pointed out (op. cit., pp. 349 et seq.) the Pelagian view of the Fall as the first example of sin implies a view of the Redemption as the first example of goodness. The successful resistance of the temptations in the wilderness would thus be more important than the sacramental remedy on the Cross. Irenaeus's doctrine of the Atonement is sometimes perilously close to this examplarist view, and may well be accounted for by his interpretation of the actual Fall. It is also worth remarking that the subject of *Paradise Regained* is not, as one might expect, the Crucifixion, but the temptation in the wilderness.

Augustine worked out a reading of the Fall story which incorporated many of the ideas originally propounded by the maximal and minimal schools of thought. Indeed, taken point by point his comments are not particularly remarkable for their novelty; one finds a notion drawn from Theophilus here, a distinction first made by Tertullian there, and one is always very much aware of the four centuries of Christian speculation lying behind his writings. What is new is the synthesis of these earlier elements in a whole which is considerably more than the sum of its parts. In Augustine's version of the Genesis narrative the diverse and often contradictory interpretations of his predecessors were welded together in a firm and systematic pattern which was to dominate the Church's thinking on the subject for the next thirteen centuries and longer.

Nowhere is the essentially synthetic nature of his exegesis clearer than in his discussion of Man's unfallen condition. For Williams's contention that his opinions 'represent the culminating point of that tendency to exalt it to the highest pitch of original righteousness and perfection'[1] does less than justice to their subtlety. To be sure, Augustine dwelt at length on the material benefits bestowed on the first man: 'He feared no inward disease, no outward accident. Soundest health blessed his body, absolute tranquillity his soul. As in Paradise there was no excessive heat or cold, so its inhabitants were exempt from the vicissitudes of fear and desire. No sadness of any kind was there, nor any foolish joy; true gladness ceaselessly flowed from the presence of God.'[2] And there is no denying that he laid a great deal of stress on Adam's bodily perfections, 'since he was not made an infant, but in the perfection of a full-grown man'.[3] But in several more important respects his views were closer to those of the minimal than to those of the maximal Fathers. He rejected out of hand, for instance, the maximal belief that Adam was already angelic, asserting with Theophilus that he was destined to achieve this dignity only if he preserved his innocence: 'He [God] gave him free will, so as still to guide him by His command and to deter him by the menace of death; and He placed him in the happiness of Paradise, in a life of security, as it were, whence, provided he preserved his innocence, he was to rise to better things.'[4] His conception

---

[1] *Ideas of the Fall*, p. 360. See also J. N. D. Kelly's echo in *Early Christian Doctrines*, 1958, p. 362.　　　　[2] *De Civ. Dei*, xiv. 26. See also ibid. xiv. 10.

[3] *De Pecc. Mer.* i. 68. See also *De Gen. ad Litt.* VI. xiii.

[4] *Ench.* viii. See also ibid. xxviii.

of Adam's immortality, too, was virtually identical with that of the Greek Apologists. Distinguishing between the states of 'posse non mori' and 'non posse mori' he wrote: 'So, too, it was an inferior form of immortality—but immortality it was—by which man was also able to avoid death; though the immortality of the life to come is of a higher order, one in which it is impossible for man to die.'[1] It was this conditional status which distinguished Adam so clearly from the celestial orders: 'For God had not made man like the angels, in such a condition that, even though they had sinned, they could none the more die. He had so made them, that if they discharged the obligations of obedience, an angelic immortality and a blessed eternity might ensue, without the intervention of death; but if they disobeyed, death should be visited on them with just sentence.'[2] In the light of these passages and others like them the statement that Augustine adopted the idealistic estimate of prelapsarian Man needs considerable modification. His teaching was in fact a blend of minimal and maximal ideas.

So far as the sexual innocence of the first pair was concerned, Augustine followed Chrysostom in regarding it as a vital aspect of their unfallen happiness, but he vigorously repudiated Gregory of Nyssa's corollary that had it not been for the Fall men would have propagated in some non-sexual way. The command to be fruitful and multiply proved that procreation was a part of God's original plan and so could not have been sinful in itself. Adam and Eve's lack of shame at their nakedness indicated simply that they were unsullied by lust or concupiscence: 'And certainly, had not culpable disobedience been visited with penal disobedience, the marriage of Paradise should have been ignorant of this struggle and rebellion, this quarrel between will and lust, . . . but those members, like all the rest, should have obeyed the will.'[3] Augustine also agreed with Chrysostom in his interpretation of the naming of the animals, an episode calculated to embarrass any but the most minimal com-

---

[1] Ibid. xxviii. See also *De Civ. Dei*. xiii. 1, xiii. 19; *De Pecc. Mer.* i. 2–5; *De Gen. ad Litt.* VI. xxv.

[2] *De Civ. Dei*, xiii. 1. See also Gregory the Great's *Mor.* iv. 54, ix. 5. The presence of the tree of life complicated this view somewhat. Why, the question arose, did God not forbid Adam to eat of it, and why did not Adam do so and so obtain true immortality? Augustine solved this problem by taking over Ambrosiaster's rather unusual interpretation of the tree, according to which it offered not immortality but merely the postponement of death (*Quaest. in Vet. Test.* xix). See *De Pecc. Mer.* i. 3, ii. 35; *De Civ. Dei*, xiii. 20; *De Gen. ad Litt.* VIII. iv–v.

[3] *De Civ. Dei*, xiv. 23. See also *De Gen. ad Litt.* IX. iii; *De Grat.* ii. 40; *De Nupt.* ii. 37.

mentator, implying as it did that Adam's nature was not far removed from that of the other creatures. Like the Rabbis, Chrysostom had seen in Adam's ability to provide names for the various creatures a convincing demonstration of his superior wisdom, and in the same vein Augustine wrote: 'First then, God showed man how superior he was to the beasts and to all irrational forms of life, and this is implied when it is said that all living things were brought to him that He might see what he should call them.'[1] The incident further revealed that Adam had not been created blind as the *Clementine Homilies* had suggested.[2]

On the question of the tempter's motives and identity Augustine had rather less room in which to manœuvre, for the legend of Lucifer's premundane rebellion and downfall was by now firmly established in the body of Christian doctrine. The only point on which there was some doubt was the precise time at which the Devil's attempted usurpation had taken place. Under the influence, perhaps, of his earlier involvement with the Manichees, Augustine interpreted the division of light from darkness on the second day of the Creation as the division of the good from the bad angels.[3] In every other regard he was content to recapitulate the maximalist version of the story: 'But after that proud and therefore envious angel . . . preferring to rule with a kind of pomp of empire rather than to be another's subject, fell from the spiritual Paradise, and essaying to insinuate his persuasive guile into the mind of man, whose unfallen condition provoked him to envy now that himself was fallen, he chose the serpent as his mouthpiece in that bodily Paradise.'[4] Satan chose the serpent 'because, being slippery, and moving in tortuous windings, it was suitable for his purpose. And this animal being subdued to his wicked ends by the presence and superior force of his angelic nature, he abused as his instrument.'[5] The serpent was called the subtlest of all the beasts of the field because the Devil was concealed inside him, forcing him, like a man possessed, to speak things which he did not himself understand.[6]

---

[1] *De Gen. con. Man.* II. xi. See also *De Pecc. Mer.* i. 67. Compare Chrysostom's *Hom. in Gen.* xvi.

[2] *Clem. Hom.* iii. 42.

[3] *De Civ. Dei*, xi. 33. See also ibid. 9; *De Gen. ad Litt.* XI. xvi, xxvi.

[4] Ibid. xiv. 11. See also *De Nat.* xxxiii.

[5] *De Civ. Dei*, xiv. 11. Elsewhere (*De Gen. ad Litt.* XI. xxvii–xxix) he suggested that the serpent was the only beast Satan was allowed to use.

[6] *De Gen. ad Litt.* XI. xxvii–xxix.

Augustine's analysis of the reasons why the tempter chose to approach Eve rather than Adam was equally conventional: '[Satan] first tried his deceit upon the woman, making his assault upon the weaker part of that human alliance, that he might gradually gain the whole, and not supposing that the man would readily give ear to him, or be deceived, but that he might yield to the error of the woman.'[1] But in his exposition of the actual temptation he went into far greater detail than any of his predecessors. His point of departure was Chrysostom's assertion that the tree of knowledge was no more than a token of Man's obedience. Adam and Eve were

prohibited from a tree which had no inherent evil. For God forbid that the Creator of all good, who made all things . . . should plant anything evil amidst the fertility of even that material Paradise. Still, however, it was well to show man, whose submission to such a Master was so very useful to him, how much good belonged simply to the obedience. . . . They were in fact forbidden the use of a tree, which, if it had not been for the prohibition, they might have used without suffering any evil result whatever; . . . the tree did not produce it to their detriment from any noxious or pernicious quality in its fruit, but entirely from the fact of their violated obedience.[2]

Yet if this were so why should the tree of the knowledge of good and evil have been so called? Augustine explained that its name was derived from the effect it produced: 'He called [it] the tree of knowledge of good and evil, to signify by this name the consequence of their discovering both what good they would experience if they kept the prohibition, and what evil if they transgressed it.'[3] The Fall, therefore, consisted primarily in disobedience, but Augustine did not let the matter rest there. Tertullian had claimed that the law prohibiting the tree contained in embryo the precepts of the entire Decalogue, and Augustine's interpretation of its violation was no less comprehensive. Among the sins subsumed in Adam's disobedience he listed pride, blasphemy, murder, spiritual fornication, theft, and avarice.[4] Indeed, he seems to have regarded the physical trespass as the symptom of sin rather than the sin itself: 'The wicked deed, then—that is to say, the transgression of eating the forbidden fruit —was committed by persons who were already wicked. . . . The

---

[1] *De Civ. Dei*, xiv. 11. See also Gregory the Great's *Mor.* iii. 12.
[2] *De Pecc. Mer.* ii. 35. See also *De Civ. Dei*, xiii. 20; *De Gen. ad Litt.* VIII. xiii; Gregory, *Mor.* XXXV. 29.
[3] Ibid. ii. 35. See also *De Civ. Dei*, xiii. 21, xiv. 17; *De Gen. ad Litt.* VIII. xiv–xv.
[4] *Ench.* xiii. Compare Tertullian's *Resp.* ii.

devil, then, would not have ensnared man in the open and manifest sin of doing what God had forbidden, had man not already begun to live for himself.'[1] This nascent 'evil will'[2] he defined elsewhere as pride: 'Under what circumstances would the woman believe these words, namely that they had been prohibited from a good and useful thing by Divine influence, unless there were already in her mind a certain love of her own power and a certain proud self-presumption which should have been defeated and humiliated through the temptation?'[3] The passage is a crucial one, for it indicates that Eve was at least potentially sinful before she ever touched the forbidden fruit. Although it solves the problem of accounting for her defection, it does so by casting the gravest doubts on her original integrity, and, by implication, on the benevolence and justice of her Creator. As I remarked in the first chapter, any thoroughgoing attempt to make the Fall seem plausible ultimately involves a reduction of Adam and Eve's intellectual or moral stature prior to it. Augustine was no exception to this rule.

The idea of the 'evil will' may well have been an adaptation of the rabbinic concept of the *yezer-ha-ra*, and Augustine's treatment of Eve's subsequent corruption of her husband also had affinities with rabbinic comments on the episode. Like Chrysostom, he adduced a passage from St. Paul's second Epistle to Timothy to show that Adam ate the forbidden fruit not because he believed the serpent's promises but because his wife urged him to do so:

so we cannot believe that Adam was deceived, and supposed the devil's word to be truth, and therefore transgressed God's law, but that he by the drawings of kindred yielded to the woman, the husband to the wife, the one human being to the only other human being. For not without significance did the apostle say, 'And Adam was not deceived, but the woman being deceived was in the transgression'; but he speaks thus, because the woman accepted as true what the serpent told her, but the man could not bear to be severed from his only companion, even though this involved a partnership in sin. He was not on this account less culpable, but sinned with his eyes open.[4]

And he made Adam's acquiescence still more credible by adding that Eve gave him the fruit, 'possibly with some persuasive words which the Scripture has left out though it is to be understood. But surely there was no need for the man to be persuaded when he saw

---

[1] *De Civ. Dei*, xiv. 13. [2] Loc. cit. [3] *De Gen. ad Litt.* XI. xxx.
[4] *De Civ. Dei*, xiv. 11. See also *De Gen. ad Litt.* XI. xlii.

that she was not dead from eating the fruit.'[1] Out of this synthesis of Jewish, Pauline, and patristic ideas developed the brilliant scene in Book IX of *Paradise Lost*.

Augustine's most significant and lasting contribution to the history of the Fall story, however, was his exegesis of the events which followed upon Adam's disobedience. There already existed, as we have seen, a strong tradition of sexual interpretation, both allegorical and literal, attaching to Eve's submission to the tempter. Its most recent exponent was Methodius of Olympus, who attempted to combine the two branches of the tradition by presenting the episode as a psychological seduction: 'For thus a commotion was stirred up, and we were filled with agitations and foreign imaginations, being emptied of the divine inspiration and filled with carnal desire, which the cunning serpent infused into us.'[2] In support of his interpretation he invoked the seventh chapter of St. Paul's Epistle to the Romans: 'For this saying of his (Paul's), "I was alive without the law once", refers to the life which was lived in Paradise before the law ... by our first parents ... for we lived without concupiscence, being altogether ignorant of its assaults.'[3] Here, I believe, is the key to Augustine's doctrine of concupiscence, for it is in the Apostle's description of his own fall that the results of sin are defined as the rebellion of the flesh and the impotence of the will. Around this Pauline framework Augustine built his analysis of Adam's postlapsarian condition. The eyes of the fallen pair were opened, he noted, in the sense that they became aware that their sexual organs were no longer under the control of their higher faculties; the war between the flesh and the spirit had begun: 'and then the man and the woman grew ashamed of their nakedness, when they perceived the rebellious motion of the flesh, which they had not perceived before. This discovery is called "the opening of their eyes".'[4] Augustine's insistence on the possibility of pure conjugal relations between Adam and Eve before the Fall can now be seen to form an essential part of his total exegesis. Indeed, without it his attitude towards carnal intercourse would have come dangerously close to the Manichaean view that the generative act is inherently sinful.

---

[1] *De Gen. ad Litt.* XI. xxx.

[2] *De Resurr.*, Synopsis, ii. The reference to the 'foreign imagination' may be an adaptation of the rabbinic notion of the *yezer-ha-ra*.

[3] Ibid. i.

[4] *De Pecc. Mer.* ii. 36. See also ibid. i. 21; *De Nupt.* i. 7; *De Civ. Dei*, xiii. 13, xiv. 17; Gregory, *Mor.* xxxvi. 28.

In this way he solved the problem of relating the sexual motif to the story as a whole by using it as a particularly vivid image of Adam's state of mind. The split between his reason or will and his sexual appetite was both the first consequence of the Fall and an illustration of the general inability of his rational faculties to retain their authority over his bodily ones. As a result of this split 'the good that I would I do not: but the evil which I would not, that I do'.[1] The Fall consisted not in a descent from spirit to matter, not in reason's submission to the pleasures of the senses, not in the premature acquisition of knowledge, not even in the rejection of the heavenly for the earthly; it consisted in one act of disobedience that involved all those things, an act which created at the macrocosmic level a gulf between Man and his Maker, and at the microcosmic a gulf between his own will and appetite. All the various and conflicting elements of four centuries of patristic thought were thus fused in a reading of the story which was to be the basis of Fall speculations for the next thirteen centuries and more.

5. *The Typological Reading*

Typology has been variously defined. R. P. C. Hanson states that it is the interpretation of an event belonging to the present or the recent past as the 'fulfilment of a similar situation recorded or prophesied in Scripture'.[2] Approaching the question from the opposite end, Auerbach sees it as a connexion between two historical persons or events 'the first of which signifies not only itself but also the second, while the second encompasses and fulfills the first'.[3] And J. N. D. Kelly relates it to the difficulty of reconciling the Old with the New Testament, finding in it a technique 'for bringing out the correspondence'[4] between them. As all these definitions imply, typology is based upon the belief in the symmetry of sacred history. It is, quite simply, an aspect of prophecy. A type or figure,[5] like a prophecy, looks forward to a future fulfilment, the only difference being that, whereas prophecy is explicit and verbal, typology is implicit and historical. Both can exist only in a universe in which the progress of events follows a discernible and meaningful pattern, in which prophecies come true and types are fulfilled.

---

[1] Rom. vii. 19. [2] *Allegory and Event*, 1959, p. 7.
[3] *Scenes from the Drama of European Literature*, New York, 1959, p. 53.
[4] *Early Christian Doctrines*, p. 71.
[5] I make no distinction between the terms 'type' and 'figure'.

The connexion between the type and its fulfilment is, it should be stressed, purely analogical. The relationship of the one to the other is that of likeness or parallel, not of cause and effect. Noah's drunkenness, for example, may have been a figure of Christ's Passion,[1] but it was certainly not its cause. The one exception to this rule is the typology of the Fall. In this case the relationship between the type and its fulfilment is both analogical and causal, for the persons and events involved in the Fall story both foreshadowed and made necessary the persons and events involved in the Redemption. Fall typology, therefore, is of a very special kind, and the complex and unique relationships which it explores are altogether different from those normally denoted by the term.

To trace its source we have to go back, significantly enough, to the prophetic books of the Old Testament, in which the Messiah and the Messianic Age were pictured as a return to the perfections attendant upon Adam in the garden of Eden.[2] This basic theme was adopted and Christianized by St. Paul, who, as we saw earlier in this chapter, linked the sin of Adam with the sacrifice of Christ:

For as by one man's disobedience many were made sinners; so by the obedience of one shall many be made righteous.[3]

To this he added, inspired possibly by Canticles, the interpretation of Adam's union with Eve as a figure of Christ's union with the Church:

For this cause shall a man leave his father and mother, and shall be joined unto his wife, and they two shall be one flesh.
This is a great mystery; but I speak concerning Christ and the Church.[4]

Around these two isolated passages was woven the intricate design of Christian Fall typology.

The first elaboration appeared in the works of Justin Martyr and Tertullian, who worked out a parallel between Eve and the Virgin Mary on the pattern of the Pauline parallel between Adam and Christ:

He [Christ] became man by the Virgin, in order that the disobedience which proceeded from the serpent might receive its destruction in the same manner in which it derived its origin. For Eve, who was a virgin and

---

[1] See H. Gardner, *The Limits of Literary Criticism*, 1956, pp. 11–16.
[2] J. Daniélou lists all the relevant examples in *Sacramentum Futuri*, ch. i.
[3] Rom. v. 19. See also 1 Cor. xv. 21–22.   [4] Eph. v. 31–32.

undefiled, having conceived the word of the serpent, brought forth disobedience and death. But the Virgin Mary received faith and joy, when the angel Gabriel announced the good tidings to her.[1]

Tertullian was also responsible for the development of the second Pauline parallel, that between Adam and Eve, on the one hand, and Christ and the Church, on the other. Adam's sleep, he pointed out, foreshadowed the death of Christ, while the birth of Eve from Adam's rib prefigured the birth of the Church from the wound in Christ's side: 'From this, then, we are led to trace even the image of death in sleep. If Adam is a type of Christ, then Adam's sleep is a symbol of the death of Christ, and by the wound in the side of Christ was typified the Church, the true mother of all living.'[2]

In the works of Irenaeus several other new strands were woven into the design. The concept of Christ as the second Adam, for example, was embroidered with a secondary theme: 'For as by the disobedience of the one man who was originally moulded from virgin soil, the many were made sinners, and forfeited life; so was it necessary that, by the obedience of one man, who was originally born from a virgin, many should be justified and receive salvation.'[3] The tree of knowledge was also worked into the pattern: 'And the sin that was wrought through the tree was undone by the obedience of the tree, obedience to God whereby the Son of man was nailed to the tree, destroying the knowledge of evil, and bringing in and conferring the knowledge of good.'[4] And a further likeness was established between the days on which these events took place: 'the Lord suffered death, in obedience to his Father, upon the day on which Adam died while he disobeyed God.'[5] Indeed, of all the early Fathers Irenaeus seems to have been most deeply imbued with the typological view of sacred history. It shaped not only his interpretation of individual incidents in the Fall story but also his entire doctrine of the Redemption, according to which Christ's life was a

[1] *Dial.* c. See also Tertullian's *De Carne Christi*, xvii: 'As Eve had believed the serpent, so Mary believed the angel . . . But [it will be said] Eve did not at the devil's word conceive in her womb. Well, she at all events conceived; for the devil's word afterwards became as seed to her that she should conceive as an outcast, and bring forth in sorrow. Indeed, she gave birth to a fratricidal devil.' The image implicit both in this passage and in the one from Justin Martyr may well be an allegorical adaptation of the Jewish *haggadah* according to which Cain and Abel were the product of a sexual union between Eve and the serpent. See above, p. 55.

[2] *De An.* xliii. [3] *Adv. Haer.* III. xviii. 7. [4] *Dem.* xxxiv.

[5] *Adv. Haer.* v. xxiii. 2. This parallel depends on the rabbinic belief that Adam fell on the day on which he was created. Compare *Stanzaic Life of Christ*, 65–68, 6141–4.

'recapitulation' or summing-up of Adam's.[1] In order to achieve the salvation of mankind Christ had to neutralize the Fall by living out a perfected version of Adam's life. This theory combined the causal and analogical connexions between the Fall and the Redemption, and as a result the unique *rationale* underlying Fall typology was very clearly defined in Irenaeus's writings. The similarities between the events in Eden and on Calvary were there because they were absolutely necessary to the whole scheme of the Atonement: 'for Adam had necessarily to be restored in Christ, that mortality be absorbed in immortality, and Eve in Mary, that a virgin, become the advocate of a virgin, should undo and destroy virginal disobedience by virginal obedience.'[2] In the typological parallels between the two sequences lay the key to Man's salvation.

The last great typological innovator was Cyril of Jerusalem. To the existing design he added analogies between the thorns promised in God's sentence on the earth and the thorns in Christ's crown, the garden of Eden and the garden of Gethsemane,[3] and the fig-tree which clothed Adam and Eve and the fig-tree cursed by Christ: 'At the time of the sin, they clothed themselves with fig-leaves; for this cause Jesus also made the fig-tree the last of His signs. For when about to go to His passion, He curses the fig-tree, not every fig-tree, but that one alone, for the sake of the figure.'[4] These new symmetries he set against the background of the earlier patterns, and his writings thus contain perhaps the fullest typological account of the Genesis narrative to be found among the early Fathers. At this point, however, the figural interpretation of the Fall appears to have been exhausted, for during the following twelve centuries little or nothing was added to the scheme of types which had been evolved during the first four. Different writers highlighted different parts of the total design, but the design itself remained substantially the same. A survey of Fall typology in the Dark and Middle Ages would consist merely of endless repetitions of the same basic themes. I propose to turn, therefore, to a second and lesser known typological tradition associated with the Fall, the tradition which linked the temptation of Adam with the temptation of Christ in the wilderness.

Several scholars have suggested that the Marcan account of the latter event was written with the second and third chapters of Genesis

---

[1] For a detailed discussion of this theory see N. P. Williams, *Ideas of the Fall*, pp. 196–9.

[2] *Dem.* xxxiii.   [3] *Cat.* xiii. 18–19.   [4] Loc. cit.

in mind.[1] The presence of the wild beasts and the ministrations of the angels, they have observed, recall the Jewish elaborations of Adam's original condition, and to this might be added the parallel between the forty days which Adam spent alone in Eden, according to Jubilees, and the forty days which Christ spent in the wilderness. Whether or not this hypothesis is true, the similarities between the two temptations were sufficient to attract the attention of Irenaeus:

> For as at the beginning it was by means of food that (the enemy) persuaded man, although not suffering hunger, to transgress God's commandments, so in the end he did not succeed in persuading Him that was an hungered to take of that food which proceeded from God. . . . The corruption of man, therefore, which occurred in paradise by both (of our first parents') eating, was done away with by (the Lord's) want of food in this world.[2]

By the time of Gregory the Great (540–604) this initial parallel had been extended to cover all three aspects of the temptation:

> Our ancient enemy set himself against the First Man, our parent, with three temptations; for he tempted him by gluttony, by vainglory, and by avarice; and tempting him defeated him; for by consenting to the temptation he placed himself under the power of the devil. . . .
> But by the very means which he laid low the First Man, by these same did he himself succumb to the Second Man.[3]

The temptation of the stones, that is to say, corresponded to Adam's gluttonous desire to eat the fruit, the temptation of the temple to his vainglorious desire to be as God, and the temptation of the kingdoms to his avaricious desire for knowledge.

In this way the account of Christ's ordeal at the hands of the Devil came to furnish a psychological analysis of Adam's overthrow in Eden. The three stages of which the Fall was thus seen to consist were linked with the oft-quoted passage in the First Epistle of John: 'For all that is in the world, the lust of the flesh [gluttony], and the lust of the eyes [avarice], and the pride of life [vainglory], is not of the Father, but is of the world.'[4] But this triad recalled yet another, for the allegorists had equated the serpent with pleasure [the lust of the flesh], Eve with sense-perception [the lust of the eyes], and Adam with reason [the seat of pride]. Superimposed on each other these

---

[1] See W. D. Davies, *Paul and Rabbinic Judaism*, p. 42; J. Daniélou, op. cit., pp. 8–9.
[2] *Adv. Haer.* v. xxi. 2.
[3] *Sermon on the Gospel of the Sunday*, 2–3. [4] 1 John ii. 16.

three interpretations produced a version of the Fall which fused the allegorical with the literal and typological patterns:

Now sin is committed in the heart in four ways, and in four ways it is consummated in act. . . . The serpent tempted, in that the secret enemy silently suggests evil to man's heart. Eve was pleased, because the sense of the flesh, at the voice of the serpent, presently gives itself up to pleasure. And Adam, who was set above the woman, yielded consent, in that whilst the flesh is carried away in enjoyment, the spirit also being deprived of its strength gives in from its uprightness. And Adam when called in question would not confess his sin, in that, in proportion as the spirit is by committing sin severed from the Truth, it becomes worse hardened in shamelessness at its downfall.[1]

Suggestio comprehends the typological gluttony, the Johannine lust of the flesh, and the allegorical pleasure. Similarly, *delectatio* involves the typological avarice, the Johannine lust of the eyes, and the allegorical sense-perception, while *consentio* sums up the typological vainglory, the Johannine pride of life, and the allegorical surrender of reason. Here, then, the typological parallels between the temptations of Christ and Adam provided the fundamental framework around and within which the moral and psychological account of the Fall came to be constructed.

It was also the basis for an influential though eccentric doctrine of the Redemption.[2] Just as Irenaeus, by integrating the causal and analogical connexions between Adam's life and Christ's, had evolved a theory of the Redemption which depended on them, so some later Fathers, by linking the two temptations together in the same way, produced a theory of the Atonement which centred on the events which took place in the wilderness. The Devil, they taught, had acquired certain clearly defined legal rights over Man as a result of the Fall, so in order to free Adam's offspring it was necessary to persuade him to abuse these rights and so forfeit them. This God achieved by disguising Himself as a man and enticing Satan to tempt him; by so doing the Devil exceeded his proper powers, and, by failing to corrupt Christ, lost them. The Fall was thus neutralized not on the Cross but in the desert. It is in this typological tradition that *Paradise Regained* had its origins, but that is another story.[3]

---

[1] *Mor.* iv. 49. Compare *Stanzaic Life of Christ*, 5253 et seq.

[2] For a detailed account of this doctrine see H. Rashdall, *The Idea of the Atonement*, 1919.

[3] See B. Lewalski, *Milton's Brief Epic*, 1966, part ii.

PART TWO

The Literary Tradition

IV

THE NEO-CLASSICAL TREATMENTS

'WHAT has Ingeld to do with Christ?' demanded Alcuin (735–804) in his famous letter to those monks of Lindisfarne with a taste for secular poetry. The question was by no means a new one. 'What indeed has Athens to do with Jerusalem?' asked Tertullian some six centuries earlier.[1] 'What has Horace to do with the Psalter, or Virgil with the Gospels, or Cicero with the Apostle?' echoed Jerome.[2] In one form or another this problem was to occupy the Church throughout its entire history. Wherever and whenever Christianity collided with a vigorous pagan culture, Greek, Roman, Germanic, or Celtic, it had somehow to come to terms with the literature in which that culture found expression. The idols could be smashed and the temples destroyed, but the old gods and heroes lived on in the poetry which enshrined them. As long as this poetry was read, paganism would remain a potent force. At the turn of the second century the Christian apologist, Minucius Felix, stated the issue with characteristic clarity. Seeking to explain the persistence of heathen myths, he remarked:

These fables and errors we both learn from ignorant parents, and, what is more serious still, we elaborate them in our very studies and instructions, especially in the verses of the poets, who as much as possible have prejudiced the truth by their authority. . . . By these fictions, and such as these, and by lies of a more attractive kind, the minds of boys are corrupted; and with the same fables clinging to them, they grow up even to the strength of mature age.[3]

In practice the question posed in varying ways by Tertullian, Jerome, and Alcuin turned out to be more than merely rhetorical; it had to be answered if the new religion was to make any lasting impression on the minds of its converts.

Christianity evolved two solutions. The first was to turn the Devil's own technique against him, that is, to quote pagan 'scripture' in support of Christian doctrine. Perhaps the earliest example

---

[1] *De Praescr.* vii.   [2] *Epist.* xxii. 29.   [3] *Octavius*, xxii.

of the application of this device, and one much quoted in the Middle Ages and the Renaissance, occurs in a sermon preached by St. Paul to the Athenians, in which he alluded to a third-century Greek poem on astronomy to reinforce his point.[1] In the centuries following it became one of the most widely used weapons in the formidable armoury of Christian apologetics. For instance, the same Minucius Felix who had pointed to the dangers of pagan poetry cited Virgil, Homer, and Ennius in support of his refutation of Epicurean philosophy.[2] By the fourth century this method of argument was almost standard practice, approved of by Augustine himself; in a simile that was to become one of the great commonplaces of the Middle Ages he claimed that Christianity should adopt all that was best in the pagan tradition, just as the Jews had carried off and used the gold and silver vessels of the enemy in their flight from Egypt.[3]

If this were merely a polemical technique it would be of little permanent interest or significance. But it was more. It went hand in hand with a way of reading and a way of thinking which had a profound effect on the development of Christian thought. If pagan philosophers and poets had expressed many ideas agreeing so closely with Christian doctrine that they could be quoted to support it, then, it was urged, perhaps the pagans had been striving towards the Christian truth; perhaps their legends and stories were vague fore-shadowings, albeit unenlightened by revelation, of the Christian fact. The classic example of this attitude is the Messianic inter-pretation of Virgil's fourth *Eclogue*, according to which the wonder-child who will usher in the Golden Age is the Christ-child of Isaiah's prophecy. Such, then, was the first answer to the problem of pagan culture. Virgil had a great deal to do with the Gospels; he anti-cipated them.

The second, and for the purposes of this study the more important, solution grew out of the first. Whereas the first was to read pagan poetry in Christian terms, the second was to write Christian poetry in pagan terms. In the late Roman Empire, as well as in the Re-naissance, Christian humanism had both a passive and an active aspect, the one a way of reading, the other a way of writing. In practice, however, the distinction between the two was not always so clear, for the latter could, and often did, imply the former. To

---

[1] Acts xvii. 28. See Ralegh's comment in his *History of the World*, I. i. 2, and Vincent of Beauvais's argument for the use of pagan literature in his *Speculum Historiale*, i. 8.

[2] *Octavius*, xix.   [3] *De Doct. Christ.* ii. 40.

describe the garden of Eden in terms usually associated with the Golden Age is already to suggest a certain identity between them. Although it was left to the humanist writers of the Renaissance to make this idea fully explicit, it was always present within the technique itself. Possibly in an age in which both the heathen and the Christian sides of the equation were equally viable there was no need to make the obvious deduction. It was enough for the poet to set them opposite each other; the cultivated reader, accustomed to syncretistic modes of thought, would do the rest for himself.

In many ways this second answer was more satisfactory than the first. Even the most tortured ingenuity could not impose a Christian interpretation on more than a fraction of pagan literature. Yet this was the only literature available, and the Church could not afford to divorce itself entirely from classical culture. The new Christian-Latin poetry that evolved provided at least some Christian alternative. Here was a literature which attempted to preserve the sophistication of classical letters while at the same time being morally and theologically acceptable. It revealed that the truths of the new religion offered sources of inspiration no less fertile than the fictions of the old. As Juvencus put it in the preface to his epic on the Gospel story early in the fourth century:

> Quod si tam longam meruerunt carmina famam,
> Quae ueterum gestis hominum mendacia nectunt,
> Nobis certa fides aeternae in saecula laudis
> Inmortale decus tribuet meritumque rependet.
> Nam mihi carmen erit Christi uitalia gesta,
> Diuinum populis falsi sine crimine donum.[1]

What is more, such poetry was a subtle and effective form of missionary technique; putting the new wine in old bottles might have altered the taste a little, but it made it far more likely that it would be drunk. Consequently, this second solution proved to be most popular, and it had a long-lasting influence on Christian thought, a great deal of whose richness derives from its ability to absorb and transform not only individual minds but whole mythologies and languages. From each different culture with which it has come in

---

[1] *Evangeliorum Libri Quatuor*, 15–20. 'For if poems that weave lying fictions with the deeds of the ancients have deserved such a long-lasting reputation, our unshakeable faith will earn for us the immortal glory of eternal praise for ever and ever and will repay our deserts. For the subject of my song will be the life-giving deeds of Christ, the Divine gift to the nations, without the stain of falsehood.'

contact Christianity has inherited a fresh body of legend, imagery, and diction in and through which to express itself.

One of the first and most remarkable products of this creative synthesis was the corpus of Christian-Latin poetry which appeared during the fourth, fifth, and sixth centuries. A comparatively large proportion of it was written on the theme of the Creation and Fall, and it is with these poems in particular that this chapter will be concerned. In probable order of composition they comprise the following: the *Cento* of Valeria Faltonia Proba (late fourth or early fifth century); the *Metrum in Genesim* of Hilarius Arelatensis (first half of the fifth century); Claudius Marius Victor's *Alethia* (first half of the fifth century); the *Carmen de Deo* of Blossius Aemilius Dracontius (end of the fifth century); the *Poematum de Mosaicae Historiae Gestis Libri Quinque* of Alcimus Ecdicius Avitus (first published at the beginning of the sixth century); and Cyprianus Gallus's *Heptateuchos* (middle of the sixth century).[1]

Four of these poets lived in Gaul—Hilary was Bishop of Arles, Victor Rhetor of Marseilles, Avitus Bishop of Vienne, while Cyprian's surname speaks for itself—and it is, perhaps, no mere coincidence that they chose the Fall as the subject of their poems, writing as they were at the very time and in the very area in which the Semi-Pelagian controversy was raging. This concerned Augustine's doctrines of Grace, Free Will, and Predestination. His dispute with Pelagius had emphasized the full rigour of his views on these questions, and his death in 430 did not see the end of the argument. The idea that fallen Man is incapable of any good on his own initiative militated against the very principles upon which the monastic life was founded. Not surprisingly, therefore, there was a vigorous reaction in the ascetic communities of Southern Gaul in the fifth century, a reaction generally known as the Semi-Pelagian movement, although, as several scholars have pointed out, it owed little or nothing to the ideas of Pelagius himself; the designation 'Anti-Augustinian' would better define its purpose and nature. The two most prominent exponents of this school, Cassian and Faustus of Riez, taught that although the Fall had weakened Man's will it had not made it completely ineffectual. As a result of Adam's sin Man inherited a bias towards evil, but he was still capable at times

---

[1] Scholars of this period are by no means unanimous in their dating of these works. I have followed the chronology given in W. Kirkconnell's *The Celestial Cycle*, Toronto, 1952.

of doing good without any exterior help. Thus there began a lively
controversy, which was never really satisfactorily settled in the
Western Church. At the Synod of Arles in 475 the '*error praedestina-
tionis*' was condemned, but at the Council of Orange in 529 a
modified form of Augustinianism was reasserted.[1]

The issues involved in this dispute are obviously related to the
interpretation of the Fall story itself, and the poems of Hilary,
Victor, Avitus, and Cyprian may quite possibly reflect the renewal
of interest in the subject. Before going on to examine them, however,
it would be as well to explore at least one example of the Semi-
Pelagian exegesis of the Fall, for their doctrinal implications have
often been seen as a reflection of Semi-Pelagian ideas. The fullest
account of the story is to be found in Cassian's *Conferences*. There
he stated that the angels were created before the work of the six
days, and that the Devil fell before the creation of Adam.[2] As I noted
in the last chapter, he found it necessary to refute the old idea of the
Greek Apologists that the Devil fell *because* he tempted Adam;
he may also have had in mind the older Greek notion of Adam's
original imperfection when he wrote: 'For we cannot think that
before [the Fall], he [Adam] was such as to be altogether ignorant of
good. Otherwise we should have to admit that he was formed like
some irrational and insensate beast: which is sufficiently absurd
and altogether alien from the Catholic faith.'[3] On the contrary, he
maintained that Adam was perfect in wisdom before the Fall,
'inasmuch as he had seen the infancy of this world, while still as it
were tender and throbbing and unorganized; and as there was in
him not only such fullness of wisdom, but also the grace of prophecy
given by Divine inspiration, so that while he was still an untaught
inhabitant of this world he gave names to all living creatures.'[4]
Up to this point there is nothing in his interpretation to offend even
the most strict Augustinian. It is only after the Fall that the Semi-
Pelagian view affects the reading of the story: 'For Adam who was
deceived, or rather (to use the Apostle's words) "was not deceived",
but, acquiescing in the wishes of her who was deceived, seems to
have come to yield a consent that was deadly, is only condemned to
labour.'[5] There is nothing here of the Augustinian theory of Man's

[1] For this summary I have relied largely on A. Harnack's *History of Dogma*
(trans. J. Millar), 1898, v. 245–529, and O. Chadwick's *John Cassian*, 1950, ch. iv. See
below, Ch. V, p. 166 for the later history of the argument in the Saxon Church.
[2] *Coll.* viii. 9–10.   [3] *Ibid.* xiii. 12.   [4] *Ibid.* viii. 21.
[5] *Ibid.* viii. 11.

loss of Free Will and his consequent inability to do good: 'for they came, as has been said, to know good and evil. Adam therefore after the fall conceived a knowledge of evil which he had not previously, but he did not lose the knowledge of good which he had before.'[1] The Semi-Pelagian version of the Fall, then, differs from the Augustinian only in its minimization of the effects of Adam's disobedience, and it is well to remember this when searching, as some scholars have done, for Semi-Pelagian elements in such poems as the *Alethia*.

A second and far more dangerous force which might have focused the attention of Christian poets on the Fall story was the renewed outbreak of dualism, Augustine's other major adversary. The sacking of Rome in 410, lamented so eloquently by Jerome in his letters, and the widespread havoc and destruction wrought by the barbarian invasions led many men to see the world in terms analogous to Yeats's vision in 'The Second Coming':

> Things fall apart; the centre cannot hold;
> Mere anarchy is loosed upon the world.
> The blood-dimmed tide is loosed, and everywhere
> The ceremony of innocence is drowned;
> The best lack all conviction, while the worst
> Are full of passionate intensity.

Rome, the centre, had fallen, and from every part of the Empire, and from Gaul in particular, came testimony to the anarchy loosed by Vandal, Hun, and Goth. Paulinus, Bishop of Beziers, and Orientus, Bishop of Auch, for example, gave moving poetic expression to the calamities of the times, while exhorting their readers to bear them with Christian fortitude.[2] But in the face of the invaders' passionate intensity many civilized men did seem to lack all conviction, and the author of the *Carmen de Providentia Divina*, written in about 415 and attributed to Prosper of Aquitaine, revealed at least one form this intellectual despair could take. Sceptics, he claimed, were using the disasters of that period as evidence that the world could not possibly be governed by the will of the Christian God. Pointing to the past as well as to the present, they demonstrated that throughout the whole course of human history the good have suffered while the wicked have triumphed. If there were a benevolent, just, and omnipotent Deity, they concluded, He would not permit sin to go unpunished and virtue unrewarded. In answer to

---

[1] *Coll.* xiii. 12. [2] *Epigramma*, passim; *Commonitorium*, passim.

this timeless argument the poet himself offered the classic Christian answer: God does in fact govern the universe, as the ordered existence of Nature proves, but He gave Man a free will, the abuse of which is the cause of his present misery.[1]

From the kind of scepticism expressed by the author's antagonists in this poem it was but a short step to dualism, to the belief that there are two coeternal and mutually antagonistic deities at work in the universe, one good and one evil, the latter being responsible for the sufferings Man undergoes. That this view was being canvassed we have the evidence of Prudentius's *Hamartigenia*, in which the poet expounded and refuted the dualistic heresy as preached by the famous Gnostic advocate Marcion. Having summarized the Marcionite belief that Man and his world were the creation of the evil god who coexisted with the good one, Prudentius countered it very neatly by asserting that the so-called malign deity was no other than the Devil of orthodox Christian theology. Indeed, Satan himself was the first dualist, for he imagined that he was self-begotten, and hence attempted to assume equality with his Maker:

> persuasit propriis genitum se viribus ex se
> materiam sumpsisse sibi, qua primitus esse
> inciperet, nascique suum sine principe coeptum.[2]

He it was who tempted Adam and Eve to eat the forbidden fruit and thus bring on themselves and their posterity the evils we now see around us. Thus the motive which Milton was eventually to attribute to the Devil in *Paradise Lost* was originally inspired by the need to find a convincing rebuttal of the dualistic theogonies of Gnosticism and Manichaeism.

In the light of these disputes it is not hard to see why a Christian poet of the fifth century might have chosen the Fall of Man as his subject. As I remarked in the previous chapter, the story and doctrine of the Fall were Christianity's chief bulwark against dualism in all its forms, for it was only by positing some primal catastrophe that theologians could reconcile the wickedness of the world with the goodness of its Creator. The arguments of Prudentius and the author of the *Carmen de Providentia Divina* both hinged on Adam's

---

[1] *Carmen de Providentia Divina*, 97–266.
[2] *Hamartigenia*, 171–3. 'He persuaded [himself] that he was created by his own strength and took on substance of himself, whereby he first began to be, and that his beginning derived from no creator.'

disobedience, which brought 'death into the world and all our woe'. In the turmoil of the decaying Empire, therefore, it was only to be expected that a substantial part of its religious poetry should be devoted to that ultimate source of all subsequent hardships.

The interest these poems have for us, however, is not primarily doctrinal. Their significance lies rather in their being the first large-scale attempts at a poetic re-creation of the myth of the Fall. They grew not only out of the need to reinforce the case against dualism but also, as I showed earlier, to meet the ever-present threat of pagan literature by providing a more edifying alternative, and in this regard there is one last factor to be taken into consideration. For the fusion of Christian content and classical colouring in which they consist had a literary as well as a didactic purpose. When the events of Genesis were first related by the Jahwist they were set against the then familiar background of ancient Near Eastern legend. By the fifth century A.D. that background had been almost completely forgotten, leaving the story in a mythological vacuum. This may have been a distinct advantage in the eyes of the commentators, for it left them free to interpret the narrative according to their own doctrinal convictions. For the poets, on the other hand, it created a serious problem. In order to bring the myth back to imaginative life a new frame of reference had to be found, a recognizable mythological backcloth provided. The actors could not perform effectively on a bare stage.

The pagan concept of the Golden Age, as it was pictured in Ovid's *Metamorphoses*, Virgil's fourth *Eclogue*, and Lucretius's *De Rerum Natura*, offered a solution to both the doctrinal and the poetic problem. It was this 'fable' that Minucius Felix had singled out as being especially insidious,[1] and the reason is readily apparent. The description of the Golden Age in the *Metamorphoses*, for instance, is remarkably similar to the Genesis account of the Creation. In this similarity lay the danger. By it an unwary reader might be deluded into accepting the Stoic philosophy lurking below the surface. Yet this pagan concept could provide the poet with a widely known and vivid poetic hinterland for the Fall narrative. If he placed Adam in the Golden Age he could 'convert' the heathen legend, and at the same time give the ancient Hebrew myth a local habitation and a name. Thus there evolved a body of poetry exemplifying both the active and the passive aspects of Christian humanism.

[1] *Octavius*, xxii.

The characteristic features of the Golden Age as described by Virgil, Ovid, and, with qualifications, Lucretius may be synthesized as follows. The earth brought forth its fruits spontaneously in a climate of eternal spring. The meadows were full of flowers which had not been planted, and the fields with corn which did not have to be cultivated. No hoe or mattock disturbed the soil, no pruning knife trimmed the vine, and no yoke weighed down the oxen. Men lived happily, content with the honey-dew exuding from the trunks of the oak trees, the arbute berries growing in profusion, the acorns clustered on the trees, and the grapes and blackberries hanging amid the thorns. The air was filled with perfumes which breathed from every hedge.[1] These are precisely the features attributed by Victor, Dracontius, and Avitus to the garden of Eden. Their accounts, indeed, are so similar to each other that one may stand for all:

> Non hic alterni succedit temporis unquam
> Bruma, nec aestivi redeunt post frigora soles,
> Excelsus calidum cum reddit circulus annum,
> Vel densante gelu canescunt arva pruinis.
> Hic ver assiduum coeli clementia servat:
> Turbidus Auster abest, semperque sub aere sudo
> Nubila diffugiunt jugi cessura sereno.
> Nec poscit natura loci quos non habet imbres,
> Sed contenta suo dotantur germina rore.
> Perpetuo viret omne solum, terraeque tepentis
> Blanda nitet facies; stant semper collibus herbae,
> Arboribusque comae; quae cum se flore frequenti
> Diffundunt, celeri confortant germina succo.
> Nam quidquid nobis toto nunc nascitur anno,
> Menstrua maturo dant illic tempora fructu.
> Lilia perlucent nullo flaccentia sole,
> Nec tactus violat violas, roseumque ruborem
> Servans perpetuo suffundit gratia vultu.
> Sic cum desit hiems, nec torrida ferveat aestas,
> Fructibus autumnus, ver floribus occupat annum.
> Hic quae donari mentitur fama Sabaeis
> Cinnama nascuntur . . .
> Illic desudans fragrantia balsama ramus
> Perpetuum promit pingui de stipite fluxum,
> Tum si forte levis movit spiramina ventus,
> Flatibus exiguis, lenique impulsa susurro,

---

[1] See *Metam.* i. 101 et seq.; *Ec.* iv. 26–41; *De Rer. Nat.* v. 933–42.

Dives silva tremit foliis, ac flore salubri,
Qui sparsus late suaves dispensat odores.
. . . varios dant arva colores,
Et naturali campos diademate pingunt.[1]

The Christian poet pays more attention, perhaps, to the horticultural than to the agricultural advantages of Eden, but with that reservation the passage could come straight out of a classical description of the Golden Age.

The use to which these Christian poets put their pagan antecedents, however, went far beyond the mere transplantation of scenery. The first of them, Proba, constructed a lengthy Biblical poem made up entirely of lines and phrases culled from the works of Virgil and arranged in the form of a continuous narrative. The general effect is that of a badly stitched patchwork quilt, but, while there is no denying Jerome's opinion that the author's ingenuity rather than the end to which it was put deserves our admiration,[2] it must be admitted that her account of the Creation and Fall is astonishingly lively, given the inherent limitations of the *cento* form. Her description of the work of the days, which lies behind many subsequent treatments of the subject, offers a good example of her quality:

fundit humus flores et frondes explicat omnes
sanguineisque inculta rubent auiaria bacis,
non rastris, hominum non ulli obnoxia curae.

---

[1] *De Mos. Hist.* i. 218–57. 'Winter never comes here with change of season, nor do the summer suns return after the cold when the lofty circle [of the sun] brings back the warm year, nor do the meadows grow white with frosts and thickening ice. Here the mildness of the sky maintains a perpetual spring. The blustering south wind is absent, and yielding clouds drift ever away under the pure sky in perennial calm. Nor does the nature of the place need showers, which it does not have, but the contented plants are dowered with their own dew. All the ground is perpetually green, and the gentle face of the warm earth shines. Grasses always stand on the hills and leaves on the trees, which when they spread themselves with abundant blossom renew their shoots with quickening sap. For whatever is produced during the whole year with us a month's time there brings to full fruition. The lilies shine forth undrooping in the sun, whose touch does not harm the violet, while the perpetual grace of its face spreads out, preserving the roses' blush. Thus when there is no winter, and the torrid summer does not burn, autumn fills the year with its fruits and spring with its flowers. Here grow cinnamons which tradition falsely assigns to the Sabaeans. . . . There a tree exuding fragrant balms pours forth an endless flow from its fruitful stem. If a light breeze happens to stir its pores then the luxurious forest with gentle breaths, stirred with a low murmur, trembles throughout its leaves and healthful blossom, which dispenses sweet odours far and wide. . . . The fields display various colours and paint the meadows with a natural diadem.' Compare *Alethia*, i. 233–47.

[2] *De Vir. Illust.* xviii.

tertia lux gelidam caelo dimouerat umbram.
auia tum resonant auibus uirgulta canoris
et liquidas corui presso dant gutture uoces
nec gemere aëria cessauit turtur ab ulmo.
quarto terra die uariarum monstra ferarum
omnigenumque pecus nullo custode per herbam
educit siluis subito mirabile uisu.
tum demum mouet arma leo, tum pessima tigris
squamosusque draco et fulua ceruice leaena
saeuire ac formae magnorum ululare luporum.
cetera pascuntur uirides armenta per herbas,
nec gregibus liquidi fontes nec gramina desunt.[1]

For anyone at all familiar with the *Georgics* and *Eclogues* reading such a passage is rather like looking into a literary kaleidoscope.

The events of the second and third chapters of Genesis are dealt with no less ingeniously. Adam is created 'os umerosque deo similis',[2] and the beauty and maturity of Eve are depicted in lines which had originally done service for such diverse characters as Aeneas, Scylla, and Lavinia:

> claraque in luce refulsit
> insignis facie et pulchro pectore uirgo,
> iam matura uiro, iam plenis nubilis annis.[3]

After God has forbidden the pair to eat the fruit of the tree of knowledge Proba proceeds to paint the garden of Eden in colours that again call up memories of the Golden Age:

> hic uer purpureum atque alienis mensibus aestas,
> hic liquidi fontes, hic caeli tempore certo

---

[1] *Cento*, 92–106. 'The earth pours forth flowers and unfolds all her leaves, and the wild haunts of birds grow red with blood-coloured berries without the aid of rakes or any human care. The third day had taken away the chill shadow from the sky. Then the pathless thickets resound with tuneful birds, and crows pour out their clear voices from their contracted throats and the turtle-dove has cooed unceasingly from the lofty elm. On the fourth day the earth brings forth monstrous wild beasts of all kinds and every species of cattle, without any keeper, in the fields, suddenly from the woods, a wondrous sight. Then the lion begins to fight, then the most deadly tigress, the scaly serpent, and the tawny-necked lioness begin to rage and huge wolves to howl. All the other cattle graze among the green grass, and there is no lack of fodder or of clear fountains for the flocks.'

[2] Ibid. 120. 'Like a god in countenance and stature.' Virgil had originally used the phrase to describe Aeneas. Cf. *Aeneid*, i. 589.

[3] Ibid. 130–2. 'And the maiden, wondrous in countenance and lovely breast, shone forth in the clear light, already ripe for a husband and clearly of marriageable age.' Cf. *Aeneid*, i. 588, iii. 426, vii. 53.

dulcia mella premunt, hic candida populus antro
inminet et lentae texunt umbracula uites.
inuitant croceis halantes floribus horti
inter odoratum lauri nemus ipsaque tellus
omnia liberius nullo poscente ferebat.[1]

Then comes the temptation itself. The serpent begins by praising the delights of the garden, but this proves to be only the prelude to his real purpose. The prohibition and the threat attendant on it, he claims, vitiate the gifts Man has received. What is the use of immortality if it is compromised by even the possibility of death? If Eve eats the fruit Adam surely will do the same, for, as Venus had said to Juno, 'tu coniunx, tibi fas animum temptare precando'.[2] When Eve has yielded to these persuasions the serpent's prophecy comes true; as she offers the fruit to Adam 'animum subita dulcedine mouit'.[3] Despite the crudity of its form, Proba's *Cento* is by no means lacking in interest for students of *Paradise Lost*.

The next poem, Hilary's *Metrum in Genesim*, represents a far more sophisticated attempt to incorporate elements derived from the literature of paganism. Based largely on Virgil's fourth *Eclogue* and the first book of Ovid's *Metamorphoses*, it brings to bear on the Genesis narrative not the actual words but the broader intellectual concepts of these two famous accounts of perfected Nature. The creation of the world, for instance, is described thus:

pecudumque larem requiemque uolucrum
planescunt campi, colles tumor arduus effert.
subsidunt ualles, florentia prata uirescunt
saxaque durantur, pinguis se gleba resoluit,
rumpuntur fontes, fluuiis genus arduum unde est.[4]

This looks very much like a combination of two ideas found in Ovid's portrayal of the same events:

---

[1] *Cento*, 163–9. 'Here is purple spring, and summer in months not her own; here are clear fountains; here at the prescribed time of the year they press out sweet honey, here the white poplar towers over the cave and supple vines weave patches of shade. Gardens fragrant with yellow flowers beckon them amid the perfumed grove of laurel, and the earth bore everything of itself more freely and quite spontaneously.'

[2] Ibid. 194. 'You are his wife and it is your prerogative to tempt his heart with your pleas.' Cf. *Aeneid*, iv. 113.

[3] Ibid. 205. 'She moved his heart with sudden sweetness.'

[4] *Met. in Gen.* 96–100. 'The plains level out as a home for the herds and a perch for the birds, and high swellings produce hills. Valleys sink down, the flowering meadows bloom, rocks harden, the fertile clods crumble, and springs burst forth, the lofty source of rivers.'

iussit et extendi campos, subsidere valles,
fronde tegi silvas, lapidosos surgere montes.

> . . .

cesserunt nitidis habitandae piscibus undae
terra feras cepit, uolucres agitabilis aer.[1]

Hilary's picture of the world's original fecundity, on the other hand, vividly recalls that of Virgil's fourth *Eclogue*, emphasizing as it does the earth's innocence of cultivation:

herbarum uaria consurgunt gramina campis.
Iamque seges tenera fructum fundebat arista,
cum iuga nulla forent nec uomis nullus aratro,
mugiret nullus proscissis taurus in aruis.
ecce etiam uitis madido iam plena racemo,
expers falcis adhuc et duri nescia ferri,
pampineas celsis texebat collibus umbras.[2]

Purely verbal parallels are few, but the identity of general concept with the following passage from the *Eclogue* is clear enough:

molli paulatim flavescunt campus arista,
incultisque rubens pendebit sentibus uva.

> . . .

non rastros patietur humus, non vinea falcem;
robustus quoque iam tauris iuga solvet arator.[3]

When he comes to the creation of Man, Hilary reverts to Ovid. Adam, he states, was made in order that he should govern the world and give praise to his Creator:

His ubi perfectis genitor iam diuite mundo
cuncta uidet curam magni deposcere regis,

---

[1] *Metam.* i. 43–75. 'Then the god further ordered plains to unroll, valleys to sink down, woods to be clothed with leaves, and rocky mountains to rise up. . . . The waters afforded a home to gleaming fishes, earth received wild beasts, and the yielding air welcomed the birds.'

[2] *Met. in Gen.* 101–7. 'Grassy meadows of all kinds spring up in the plains. And the cornfield was already bringing forth fruit from tender ears of grain, while no yokes existed nor any ploughshare for the plough, and no bull lowed in the furrowed fields. Lo, even the vine already laden with juicy clusters of grapes, not having felt the pruning fork and still without knowledge of the hard iron, was weaving shades of vine-leaves on the high hills.'

[3] *Ec.* iv. 28–41. 'and the fields become golden with soft corn and the ripening grape will hang from the unpruned thorn . . . the soil will not suffer the ploughshare or the vine the pruning-knife; and then too the sturdy ploughman will untie the yoke from his oxen.'

> qui mare, qui terras atque omnia nata gubernet,
> quique altum spectet caelum laudetque potenter
> munera magna dei, ne sint haec condita frustra.[1]

He was distinguished by his Divine likeness, his hands, his reason, his voice, his conscience, and his upright gait:

> aetheriam primum faciem uultumque paternum
> incessumque pedum rectum, sublimia colla,
> ne qua mora in caelum oculis spectantibus esset.[2]

The treatment of Man's creation in the *Metamorphoses* stresses exactly the same points:

> sanctius his animal mentisque capacius altae
> derat adhuc et quod dominari in cetera posset.
> natus homost . . .
> pronaque cum spectent animalia cetera terram,
> os homini sublime dedit caelumque videre
> iussit et erectos ad sidera tollere vultus.[3]

In more specifically Christian vein Hilary interprets the verbs in the first chapter of Genesis as referring to the Father and Son. Eve was made 'cupito . . . vultu'[4] from Adam's rib so that she would be the more dear to her husband, and the poet concludes his account of the unfallen world by drawing attention to the spiritual benefits which stem from Man's possession of a soul.

At this point of the story one would expect to find a description of the Fall, but Hilary completely omits this crucial episode. Instead he presents a contrasting picture of Adam's post-lapsarian condition, which is characterized by weakness, cold, and hunger, the very three features marking the transition from the Golden to the Silver Age in

---

[1] *Met. in Gen.* 111–15. 'Now that this has been completed, the Father perceives that in so rich a world all these things need the care of a great king, who would rule the sea, the land, and all things that had been born, and would behold the lofty sky and offer worthy praise to the great gifts of God, so that these things should not have been made in vain'

[2] Ibid. 132–4. 'First a heavenly countenance and a face like the Father, an upright gait on thy feet, a neck uplifted on high, lest there should be any delay in thine eyes beholding heaven.'

[3] *Metam.* i. 76–86. 'There was as yet no living thing which was more akin to the gods than these, none more capable of intelligence, none that could be master over the rest. Man was born. . . . Whereas all other living creatures hang their heads and look at the ground, he gave to man an uplifted countenance, bidding him look up to heaven, and lift his face up to the stars.'

[4] *Met. in Gen.* 122–3. 'With the desired . . . face.'

the *Metamorphoses*.[1] He continues with a survey of the increasingly wicked races which descended from Adam. As a punishment for their sins God inflicted on them the hostile elements of Nature— frost, rain, and thunder—but the only result was that men grew still more depraved, rejoicing in war and slaughter, perjury and theft. This vision of human degeneration corresponds in turn with Ovid's conception of the Bronze and Iron Ages, which brought with them violence, war, and deceit.[2] Finally, Hilary relates how the Flood washed away the wickedness of the earth, thus prefiguring the sacrament of baptism and initiating a new and better phase of human history. Only a drop of the ancient poison now remained, to be cleansed eventually by the yet purer flood of Christian baptism.

In the light of these parallels it seems very likely that Hilary had Ovid's poem in mind when, at Pope Leo's request, he composed the *Metrum in Genesim*, and this, I think, explains why he omitted the episode of the Fall. There is no equivalent event in the *Metamorphoses*, and Hilary's chief concern appears to have been to translate that work's account of the four Ages into Christian terms. The real meaning of the *Metrum in Genesim* lies in the contrast between the pre- and post-lapsarian worlds, between, that is to say, the Golden Age, on the one hand, and the Silver, Bronze, and Iron, on the other. The Fall itself is important only in so far as it is the hinge upon which the contrast turns. It can, therefore, be assumed rather than portrayed. One of the most interesting features of the later poems by Dracontius, Avitus, and Cyprian is the way in which the treatment of the Fall grows more elaborate as the direct influence of Ovid, Lucretius, and Virgil diminishes. In general it appears to be true that the more freely these classical sources are adapted the more fully the Fall is described.

The minimal view he took of the evil remaining after the Flood is enough in itself to suggest that Hilary may have had Semi-Pelagian leanings, and N. K. Chadwick has shown that he did in fact belong to that party.[3] The author of the third of these Christian Latin poems on the Fall, Claudius Marius Victor, has often been suspected of harbouring like sympathies. More recently, however, P. F. Hovingh, while admitting its emphasis on the freedom of the will, has convincingly demonstrated the *Alethia*'s essential orthodoxy.[4]

---

[1] *Metam.* i. 113 et seq.   [2] Ibid. i. 137–74.
[3] *Poetry and Letters in Early Christian Gaul*, 1955, pp. 181–3.
[4] *Claudius Marius Victorius Alethia*, Groningen, 1955, Introduction.

That this poem more than the others should have been submitted
to doctrinal scrutiny is scarcely surprising, for it is by far the most
obviously didactic in intention. Indeed, Victor expressly states in
his Preface that it was composed for the edification of the young,[1]
who, it may be recalled, were the particular concern of Minucius
Felix. It is didactic in a very special way, however. Rather than
adapting the terms and concepts of Ovid and Virgil to his Biblical
theme Victor has undertaken a detailed refutation of Lucretius's
ideas concerning the origin of the world as they appeared in the
De Rerum Natura. Although this poem was principally directed
against the Stoics, many of its arguments could well have been
written with Genesis in mind. For example, Lucretius heaped scorn
on the idea that the world could have been created by any god or
gods for the sake of Man, or that Man himself could have been
formed by the gods—they had no pattern on which to model him.[2]
Neither could any one man have given things their names, for he
would have had no one to instruct him:

> proinde putare aliquem tum nomina distribuisse
> rebus et inde homines didicisse vocabula prima,
> desiperest.[3]

Victor, on the contrary, insists on Man's dignity in the Creation. He
was modelled according to a pre-existent image in the mind of
God, who made him as a witness to the glory of the Divine works:

> ni spectator adest, quem tantae gloria molis
> impleat atque oculis auidum per singula ducat,
> quid possint conferre deo?[4]

And it was God, too, who gave Adam the wisdom to name the
animals.[5] In addition to these fundamental points the Christian
poet takes issue with his pagan predecessor on the question of the
discovery of the various metals. Lucretius's theory was that they
came to light as a result of a forest fire, started by lightning or some
other accidental means, which burned down the vast forests covering

---

[1] Alethia, precatio, 103–6.   [2] De Rer. Nat. v. 156–86.

[3] Ibid. v. 1041–3. 'Then it would be foolish to think that someone had at that time
given names to things and that from him men had learned the elements of language.'

[4] Alethia, i. 155–7. 'What use could these things be to God unless there is a spectator,
whom the glory of so great a fabric might fill and conduct the eager man's eyes over
every part?'

[5] Ibid. i. 339 et seq. Cf. Cyprian's Hept. i. 42–44. The Rabbis, as I mentioned in the
second chapter, held a similar opinion.

the mountains.[1] Victor asserts that the fire was in fact started by Adam, who, after his expulsion from the garden of Eden, threw a stone at the serpent, thereby striking the first spark and setting the trees alight.[2] Finally, as S. Gamber has remarked, the *Alethia* contains a vigorous attack on Atomism, a theory closely associated with Lucretius and his *De Rerum Natura*.[3] Victor's poem, then, exemplifies a second possible kind of pagan influence: a Christian poet could be provoked to refute as well as to imitate.

The *Alethia* opens with a formal prayer, in the course of which the fall of Satan is mentioned for the first and only time. Man, it is explained, was created to overcome him, but was defeated by the serpent and condemned to death, a punishment which turned out to be a 'felix poena':

> iamiam nemo patrem temerarius arguat Adam,
> quod leue praescriptum uiolata lege resoluens
> ad letum patefecit iter. poena illa parentis
> prima fuit tanti, quia plus est uincere mortem
> quam nescisse mori.[4]

This passage, which has often been taken as an example of Victor's alleged Semi-Pelagian tendencies, is in fact little more than a variation of Augustine's distinction between the states of 'posse non mori', in which Adam was created, and 'non posse mori', which the elect will enjoy in heaven.

The first book begins with an account of the work of the first five days, which is brief in proportion to the poem as a whole, and it is not until the formation of Man on the sixth day that there appears any development of real interest:

> facilem nam cedere limum
> et flexum formamque sequi qua ducitur arte
> arripit ac sacra qualem iam mente gerebat
> explicat in speciem, flatuque immissa uaporo
> uita rigauit humum. tellus mollita liquore
> partim facta caro est, sanguis, qui lubricus umor,

---

[1] *De Rer. Nat.* v. 1241 et seq.
[2] *Alethia*, ii. 90 et seq.
[3] *Le Livre de la 'Genèse' dans la poésie latine au cinquième siècle*, Paris, 1899, pp. 62–63.
[4] *Alethia, precatio*, 92–96. 'Let no imprudent person now blame Adam, the father of men, because by breaking the law, transgressing an easy precept, he opened the way to death. The first punishment of the father of men proved to be so valuable for the reason that it is a greater thing to conquer death than not to have known it.'

> distendit mollis per nota foramina uenas,
> et mentis iam plenus homo est terraque repulsus
> exilit ac dominum prudens rationis adorat.[1]

This vivid, almost visceral, picture of the gradual transformation of earth into living flesh was bettered only by Dracontius, whose description of the same event could well have been inspired by Victor's.[2] After a long typological digression connecting Adam's creation from the earth with the final bodily resurrection, the poet goes on to portray the garden of Eden in terms very similar to those used by Avitus in the lines quoted earlier in this chapter. In the mild sunlight of an eternal spring the trees and flowers blossom all the year round, and the scents of the various herbs are mingled in one perfect fragrance. Stirred by gentle breezes, the woods sing in praise of their Creator:

> sonat arbore cuncta
> hymnum silua deo modulataque sibilat aura
> carmina.[3]

Here Victor digresses once more, this time to suggest that the various trees may be taken to represent different virtues, an idea deriving from Philo and popular among the allegorical school of commentators.[4] There follow the prohibition of the tree of knowledge, the naming of the animals, and the creation of Eve. She is made from Adam's rib for two reasons: first, lest Nature should presume that man is born from man alone; second, in order that Adam should recognize her as part of himself and so love her, as he does:

> tetigit noua gratia mentem
> affectusque oculis in uiscera nota receptus
> irruit et tanto penetrauit in ossa calore.[5]

---

[1] *Alethia, precatio*, i. 204–12. 'He snatches up the clay, which yields easily and readily follows the shape and form in which it is moulded, and kneads it into whatever shape He was already pondering in His sacred mind, and life, injected with a vaporous breath, moistened the clay. Softened by the moisture, the earth is partly made flesh, and blood, the smooth liquid, swells the soft veins through the well-known apertures. And now the man is filled with a mind and springs forth, pushed out of the earth, and, intelligent by virtue of his reason, adores the Lord.'

[2] See below, p. 128.

[3] *Alethia*, i. 249–51. 'With every tree the forest sings a hymn to God, and the breeze whispers harmonious songs.'

[4] See above, pp. 71–72.

[5] *Alethia*, i. 382–4. 'A new pleasure touched his mind, and a feeling of love, conveyed by his eyes to his inmost parts, rushed in upon him and penetrated his bones with great warmth.'

Unlike Hilary, Victor does describe the actual temptation, and in some detail. The serpent in this version of the episode elaborates an argument that anticipates Milton's view of the dilemma of fallen Man as set out in *Areopagitica*. His chief point is that knowledge of good depends on knowledge of evil:

> o uitae melioris inops rerumque bonarum
> gens ignara homines! nam qui dinoscere nescit,
> quo distent diuersa bonis, hic nec bona nouit.[1]

God, he insinuates, forbade His creatures to acquire such knowledge because He was afraid that they might so become gods themselves. Convinced by this doubtful logic, Eve eats the fruit and hastens to persuade Adam to do the same:

> experti iam docta mali, solacia culpae
> quaerit et in crimen facilem tractura maritum,
> qua periit prior, arte petit.[2]

As soon as she has succeeded they are assailed by shame, the symptom of concupiscence, and cover themselves with fig-leaves. In vain they try to hide from their Maker. He seeks them out to condemn them to their respective punishments, and Victor takes great pains to demonstrate the justice of His sentence. The serpent, who brought about the beginning of sin by means of food, is condemned to eat earth; Eve, who multiplied sin by corrupting her husband, is condemned to the pain of natural multiplication; and Adam, who rebelled against God, is condemned to suffer the rebellion of the earth.[3] The fallen pair are then expelled from the garden by a whirlwind, lest by eating of the tree of life they should perpetuate their sin for ever, another idea taken over from the commentators.

At this juncture Victor pauses to examine the psychological condition of the exiles. They are tormented by all kinds of doubt, fearful of what lies in store for them and bitterly regretful for what they have lost. They wonder how much they themselves have been

---

[1] Ibid. i. 398–400. 'O race of men, you lack a better life, you are ignorant of good things! For he who cannot distinguish how evil differs from good does not really know what good is either.'

[2] Ibid. i. 413–15. 'Now well-versed in the evil which she has experienced she seeks consolation for her sin, and she attacks her pliable husband in order to draw him into sin by means of the same guile to which she first succumbed.'

[3] Ibid. i. 486–522.

changed by their disobedience and its consequences, and they
ponder:

> an hoc esse mori, uel, si grauiora supersunt,
> an detur reditus miseris, an fine perenni
> perdant quod superest, an cum uia mortis amarae
> per lignum ingruerit mundo populisque futuris,
> possit adhuc aliquod per lignum uita redire.[1]

Here for the first time the poem really comes to life. Just as Dracontius was to excel the other poets in his portrayal of Adam's state
of innocence, so Victor is distinguished by his presentation of Man's
state of guilt. Outside the garden they fall to the ground in silent
prayer until Adam rises to ask God for guidance in the fulfilment of
his sentence. Readily admitting the guilt which he has incurred 'per
affectum, quem sexus sentit uterque',[2] he asks for no more than the
opportunity to undergo his punishment to the full. Only when the
effects of the Fall on its perpetrators have thus been made clear does
Victor pass on to describe its consequences for mankind at large.

The background of violence and suffering against which all these
poems were written reaches to the very origins of the next of them,
Dracontius's *Carmen de Deo*, for it was composed, like Boethius's
Consolatio, while its author was languishing in the prison of a
barbarian emperor. Less didactic than the *Alethia* and more dis-
cursive than the *Metrum in Genesim*, it contains one of the most
memorable treatments ever produced of Man's unfallen condition.
That this particular aspect of the story should have stimulated
Dracontius's imagination more than any other is partly to be
explained by the circumstances in which he was writing—physical
captivity has often prompted the human mind to seek a compensating
freedom in the creation of some ideal world, as the works of Boethius,
Malory, and Bunyan attest—but it is also to be accounted for by the
nature of his poetic gifts themselves. Unlike those of his immediate
successor, Avitus, they were descriptive rather than dramatic, and
they flowered in a poem of wide-eyed wonder and breathless silences
which, in its ability to evoke the freshness of Nature while it was

---

[1] *Alethia*, i. 543–7. 'Whether this is what it means to die or, if a heavier punishment
awaits them, whether in their misery they will ever be allowed to return or whether they
have lost Heaven for ever, or whether, since the path to bitter death first came on the
world and future generations through a tree, so life could still return by means of some
tree.'

[2] Ibid. ii. 61. 'Through the yearning that each sex feels for the other.' This clearly is
Victor's equivalent of the Augustinian 'drawings of kindred'. See above, p. 97.

still, in Cassian's phrase, 'tender and throbbing and unorganized', has no rival in this or any other period.

The distinctive quality of Dracontius's descriptive powers emerges early in the first book with these lines on the first appearance of the vine:

> Torta per obliquos it vitis in orbe corymbos,
> Verberat et palmes ramos fluitante flagello;
> Vinea pampineos subarundinat ebria campos,
> Munera laetitiae spondens pendentibus uvis,
> Fructibus et variis redolent florentia rura.[1]

The gradual unfolding of the laden shoots is mirrored by the syntactical structure itself, with the powerful verbs straining against the heavily balanced nouns and adjectives surrounding them. In a later passage on the creation of the birds, on the other hand, the verbs are placed at the beginning of the phrases to create a sense of rapid movement and excitement:

> Exsilit inde volans gens plumea laeta per auras,
> Aera concutiens pennis crepitante volatu:
> Ac varias fundunt voces modulamine blando,
> Et, puto, collaudant Dominum meruisse creari.[2]

Whereas in the description of the vine the feeling was one of slow, ponderous growth, here everything is speed, noise, and delight. One can almost hear the rustle of innumerable wings in 'crepitante volatu'. In both accounts there is an underlying suggestion of parturition, inspired perhaps by Lucretius's claim that the animals were quite literally born from the earth, and this image becomes explicit when Dracontius comes to the same event:

> Sexta dies phoebi rutilo processerat ortu,
> Cum natura parens gignit animantia terris.
> Cornibus erumpunt armata fronte juvenci.
> Et per prata vagum sequitur sua bucula taurum.

---

[1] *Carmen*, i. 169–73. 'The twisted vine circles around the slanting clusters of fruit, and the vine-shoot lashes the branches with its waving tendril. The drunken vineyard spreads its shoots right through the fields, which are filled with vine-leaves, promising joyful gifts with the hanging grapes, and the luxuriant countryside is filled with the scent of various fruits.'

[2] Ibid. i. 240–3. 'Thence springs forth the plumed species, flying joyously through the breezes, shaking the air with their wings in rustling flight: and they pour out various notes in pleasant cadence, and, I think, praise the Lord together because they have deserved to be created.'

> Cervus in arva fugax palmatis cornibus errat,
> Et velox prorumpit equus, pecus utile bellis.
> Impia terribiles producit terra leones.[1]

Here and elsewhere in the poem Dracontius creates a temporal perspective, not by means of typological elaborations such as Avitus was to employ, but by constant reminders of the use to which these new-born plants and animals will be put: the horse will be useful in war, the laurel leaves will honour poets, the vine will produce wine. By thus keeping before the reader's eyes the destiny of these things in a fallen world the poet subtly captures something of their original freshness.

All this, however, is merely the prelude to the creation of Man, which Dracontius pictures with a vitality equalled only by Avitus— and that because the latter poet probably borrowed from him. The miraculous moments in which clay was transmuted into flesh have never been more perfectly realized:

> Conspicitur nova forma viri, sine mente parumper,
> Spiritus infusus subito per membra cucurrit,
> Et calefacta rubens tenuit praecordia sanguis.
> Mox rubuere genae, totos rubor inficit artus,
> Iam cutis est, qui pulvis erat, jam terra medullas
> Ossibus includit, surgunt in messe capilli,
> Orbe micant gemino gemmantia lumina visus,
> Et vocem compago dedit, nova machina surgens
> Auctorem laudare suum, gavisa quod esset.[2]

The slowly gathering momentum of the process is echoed by the enjambment, rare in this poet; beginning with short staccato bursts, the phrases gradually gain in complexity until they culminate in the first sound of the newly created man, a sound, characteristically

---

[1] *Carmen*, i. 271–7. 'The sixth day had appeared with the red dawn of Phoebus when mother Nature brings forth the living creatures on the earth. The young bulls break forth with forehead armed with horns, and the heifer follows her wandering mate through the meadows. The swift stag roams through the fields with spreading antlers, and the speedy horse breaks forth, the breed useful in war. The cruel earth bears the terrible lions.'

[2] Ibid. i. 339–47. 'The new form of a man appears, without a soul for the moment; a spirit, which has been infused, has suddenly run through his limbs, and red blood has occupied his warm breast. Soon his cheeks have grown red, a redness colours all his limbs; now what used to be dust is skin, now earth confines the marrows in bones, hair rises up in a crop, the jewelled lights of sight shine with twin orbs, and the whole frame has given voice, a new device rising to praise its Author, rejoicing in its creation.' Compare *De Mos. Hist.* i. 116–20.

enough, of praise. (Indeed, one of the most notable features of these poems is the recurrence of this theme. Hilary's Adam was formed in order to give praise to his Maker, and Victor's adored his Lord as soon as he had received the gift of reason; even the trees in the *Alethia* sang hymns to their Creator, while the birds in the *Carmen de Deo* gave thanks for their existence. Not only the heavens but all created beings declare the glory of God.)

So far, I have drawn attention chiefly to Dracontius's visual and auditory imagination. Still more striking is the psychological insight with which he portrays the unfallen innocence of the first pair. Of all the various parts of the Genesis narrative the pre-lapsarian life of Adam and Eve has always been the most difficult to re-create, for moral and intellectual perfection is hard to conceive, and impossible to describe, without resort to allegory. Dracontius, however, does not conceive the state of innocence in perfectionist terms. His Adam is more like a lost little boy than the governor of the world, an *'animal rationis amicum'*[1] rather than the Aristotelian *'animal rationale'*:

> Tunc oculos per cuncta jacit, miratur amoenum
> Sic florere locum . . . camposque virentes
> Miratur: sed quid sit homo, quos factus ad usus,
> Scire cupit simplex, et non habet unde requirat:
> Quo merito sibimet data sit possessio mundus,
> Et domus alma nemus per florea regna paratum;
> Ac procul exspectat virides jumenta per agros,
> Et de se tacitus, quae sint haec cuncta requirit,
> Et quare secum non sint haec ipsa, volutat.[2]

A fifth-century Christian ivory depicts an Apollonian Adam reclining in the top right-hand corner staring into space as the animals play around him,[3] and it is just such a moment of awed solitude that Dracontius has caught here. Set beside Victor's account of Adam's doubts after the Fall, the passage offers a good indication of where the relative strengths of the two poets lay.

---

[1] Ibid. i. 329. 'An animal friendly towards reason.' Compare *Metam.* i. 76.

[2] Ibid. i. 348–58. 'Then he casts his eyes over all, wonders that the pleasant place flowers thus . . . marvels at the green fields: but in his simplicity he desires to know what man is, for what purposes he was made, and has no one to ask: for what merit the world was given to him to possess, and the kind home, the grove prepared in the flowering kingdoms; and from afar he gazes at the animals in the green fields and silently asks himself what all these things are, and ponders why these very things are not with him.'

[3] Reproduced in K. Clark, *The Nude*, 1960, p. 47.

Eve is created from Adam's rib for the same reason as in several others of these poems, that Adam should recognize her as his own flesh and blood and so love her the more. She is created physically mature, and Dracontius reminds us that she will soon bear children. With Adam we see her for the first time as he awakens from his sleep:

> Constitit ante oculos nullo velamine tecta,
> Corpore nuda simul niveo, quasi nympha profundi.
> Caesaries intonsa comis, gena pulchra rubore,
> Omnia pulchra gerens, oculos, os, colla manusque,
> Vel qualem possent digiti formare Tonantis.[1]

There is nothing in the whole literature of the Fall to match this picture of Eve, unashamedly sensuous yet without the slightest hint of sensuality. As in the description of Adam, these lines convey something of the passionate purity of a classical Greek nude; if he is Apollonian there is more than a suggestion of the Nereid about his wife. The two are commanded to live in 'honesta voluptas',[2] a paradox which reflects the whole tone of the description.

At this point of the story Dracontius introduces a brilliantly conceived episode to illustrate the first pair's gradual awakening from ignorance to experience. Lucretius and Statius had recorded a legend according to which the first men were afraid of the night, and the Rabbis had related the idea to the fallen Adam's first experience of the dark.[3] Dracontius places this experience before the Fall, using it to express not the apprehensions of a sinful man but the innocence of a sinless one:

> Mirata diem, discedere solem,
> Nec lumen remeare putat terrena propago;
> Solanturque graves lunari luce tenebras,
> Sidera cuncta notant coelo radiare sereno.
> Ast ubi purpureum surgentem ex aequore cernunt
> Luciferum vibrare jubar, flammasque ciere,
> Et reducem super astra diem de sole rubentem
> Mox revocata fovent hesterna in gaudia mentes,

---

[1] *Carmen*, i. 393–7. 'She stood before him uncovered by any veil, with her snowy body naked like a nymph of the sea. The hair of her head was unshorn, her cheeks were made lovely with a blush, and everything about her was beautiful, eyes, mouth, neck and hands, even as the fingers of the Thunderer could make her.'

[2] Ibid. i. 414. 'Honest pleasure.'

[3] *De Rer. Nat.* v. 973–6; *Thebaid*, iv. 282–4. See above, Ch. II, p. 54.

Temporis esse vices noscentes, luce diurna
Coeperunt sperare dies, ridere tenebras.[1]

On the following day Adam and Eve wander through their new-found realm, marvelling at the wonders around them:

Ibant per flores, et tota rosaria bini
Inter odoratas messes lucosque virentes
Simpliciter pecudum ritu, vel more ferarum,
Corporibus nudis, sed nescia corda ruboris.

.   .   .

Publica jungebant affectibus oscula passim,
Nec rubor ullus erat.[2]

This clearly has much more in common with the Lucretian than with the Ovidian conception of Man's original state, and the numerous parallels I have already noted between the *Carmen de Deo* and the *De Rerum Natura* raise the possibility that, whereas Victor set himself to refute, Dracontius chose to adapt, the pagan poem. For the Golden Age as pictured by Lucretius was essentially a primitive period, when men and women wandered at large like wild beasts, taking their pleasures wherever and whenever nature inclined them.[3] It is in this light that Dracontius seems to have seen Adam and Eve, although he has omitted the grosser and more savage aspects of the Epicurean account.

Poetically the description of the temptation itself is far less satisfying; not until Avitus did the episode receive any really articulate treatment. Nevertheless, it is worth remarking that, as might be expected from his previous portrayal of Adam's condition, Dracontius presents the first act of disobedience in its minimal form:

Quaerit opem sceleri, per quam fallatur honestas,
Simplicitasque cadat, vel credula corda reatum

---

[1] *Carmen*, i. 417–26. 'Having marvelled at the day, the earthly creation thinks that the sun has disappeared and that the light will not return; they find consolation for the heavy shades in the light of the moon, and observe all the stars shining in the clear sky. But when they see glowing Lucifer rising from the sea kindling his light and rousing his flames, and the daylight, reddened by the sun, returning brighter than the stars, at once they cherish their minds with the joys of yesterday which have come back, knowing that there are alternations in time, and they begin to look forward to the days with their daily light and to laugh at the darkness.'

[2] Ibid. i. 437–45. 'The two of them would walk through the flowers and the rose-gardens everywhere, through the scented crops and the green groves, innocently, like the tame herds or the wild animals, with naked bodies, but their hearts were unaware of shame. . . . Here and there they would kiss each other affectionately in public, nor was there any shame.'   [3] *De Rer. Nat.* v. 925–73.

Incurrant non fraude sua, sed clade perenni.
Fortia corda viri non expugnanda per anguem
Praesensit pietatis inops, et conjugis aures
Aggreditur sub voce pia, sermone maligno
Insidiosus adit heu! mollia corda puellae,
Ingerit ore cibos crudeli funere plenos.[1]

'Simplicitas' and 'honestas' are the key words here; the soft heart of
Eve is deceived, not tempted, by the pious voice which conceals its
malevolent intention, and there is a note of real pity in the poet's
voice as the serpent approaches her. The effect of the fruit leads her
to tempt Adam, as in the *Alethia*, but the incident is not elaborated.
And again as in the *Alethia* the immediate result of the Fall is the
birth of concupiscence. The real tragedy of the story, however, is
summed up in one line which might stand as the motto of the whole
poem: 'Cognita simplicitas, sed mox est corde fugata.'[2] 'Simplicitas',
not 'perfectio', lies at the heart of Dracontius's vision.

The next poem, the *De Mosaicae Historiae Gestis*, complements
the *Carmen de Deo* in almost every respect, for if Avitus did not
possess Dracontius's descriptive powers he was gifted with those
dramatic abilities which the latter so obviously lacked. Although
his account of the unfallen world cannot compare with his predecessor's, his treatment of the temptation far surpasses any we have
so far examined. He is further distinguished from the other poets by
his self-conscious attempt to achieve epic dignity and complexity.
Taking Virgil's *Aeneid* as his model rather than Ovid's *Metamorphoses* or Lucretius's *De Rerum Natura*, he wrote in deliberate
imitation of the Roman poet's 'high style' and incorporated into his
narrative all those literary devices which we think of as being
characteristically Virgilian. The elaborate Virgilian simile, for
instance, has many counterparts in Avitus's poem: God is compared
to a sculptor as he creates Adam, and the Devil's serpentine disguise
is made the occasion of a detailed description of a viper that has
just sloughed its skin.[3] The other outstanding feature of the epic,

---

[1] *Carmen*, i. 465–72. 'He seeks a chance of doing evil, by which honesty should be
deceived and innocence should fall, or by which credulous hearts might incur guilt, not
through their own treachery, but by an eternal disaster. The pitiless devil foresees that
the man's brave heart may not be overcome by a serpent, so, under cover of pious voice,
he approaches the ears of his wife; with his wicked speech the deceiver comes to the soft
heart of the girl, alas, bringing food full of cruel death in his mouth.'

[2] Ibid. i. 484. 'As soon as simplicity was recognized it fled from the heart.'

[3] *De Mos. Hist.* i. 73 et seq.; ii. 126 et seq.

those extensive digressions on the history of some important object or character, was clearly out of the question in a work which dealt with the beginning of things, but Avitus found an equivalent in the typological system of correspondences developed by the Fathers. Instead of invoking the sense of the past by tracing something or someone's history he created a forward-looking perspective by revealing their fulfilment: Adam's sleep during the creation of Eve anticipated the death of Christ and the birth of the Church, the forbidden tree foreshadowed the tree of Calvary.[1] The temporal relationship is still insisted on, but it is a relationship with the future, not the past. The exegetical technique worked out by the Church in its attempt to reconcile the two Testaments has become in a literary context a quasi-epic device for heightening the significance of the Jahwist's simple story.

Nor is this epic quality limited to the surface of the poem. It goes deeper, affecting the presentation of the actual characters. Thus Avitus's Adam and Eve are far removed from the innocent children who roamed the fields like animals in the *Carmen de Deo*. On the contrary, they are dignified adults, the formality of whose union contrasts vividly with the ignorant sensuality of Dracontius's pair:

> Taliter aeterno conjungens foedere vota,
> Festivum dicebat hymen, castoque pudori
> Concinit angelicum juncto modulamine carmen.
> Pro thalamo paradisus erat, mundusque dabatur
> In dotem, et laetis gaudebant sidera flammis.[2]

Here Avitus might have had in mind the 'marriage' of Dido and Aeneas, in which Nature provided all the usual concomitants of a Roman wedding:

> prima et Tellus et pronuba Iuno
> dant signum: fulsere ignes et conscius aether
> conubiis, summoque ulularunt vertice Nymphae.
> ille dies primus leti primusque malorum
> causa fuit.[3]

---

[1] Ibid. i. 160–9, iii. 17–23. See also ii. 24–26, 32–65, iv. 352–87.

[2] Ibid. i. 188–92. 'Uniting their desires thus in an eternal covenant Hymen proclaimed festivity, and with chaste modesty sang an angelic song with blended harmony. Paradise was their marriage chamber, and the world was given as dowry, and the stars rejoiced with glad flames.'

[3] *Aeneid*, iv. 166–70. 'First Earth and Juno, presiding over the marriage, give the sign: fires flash and the air is aware of their wedlock, and the nymphs wail from the topmost peak. That day first was the cause of death and of evils.'

Juno gives way to Hymen, the nymphs to the angels, and the lightning to the twinkling of the stars, while the final lines take on an added resonance if they are recalled in the new context. Less probably, Avitus may have been influenced by the rabbinic elaborations of the marriage of Adam and Eve, in which the distinctive features of a Jewish wedding, the canopy, the precentor, the ritual adornment of the bride, all found a place in the union of the first pair.[1] In any case, the effect in the Christian version is remarkable: by finding natural counterparts to the traditional accessories the poet has given the scene an unaffected dignity and formality equalled only by Milton.

The Adversary, too, has undergone several significant modifications. For the first time in a literary treatment the patristic association of Satan with the serpent has been used. In the other poems the serpent was merely a mysterious creature such as we might expect to find in a mythological landscape, but here the tempter is a figure of epic proportions, a ruined archangel who fell because, like the Devil in Prudentius's *Hamartigenia*, he deluded himself that he was self-created and therefore aspired to be the equal of God:

> Se semet fecisse putans, suus ipse Creator
> Quod fuerit, rabido concepit corde furorem,
> Auctoremque negans, Divinum consequar, inquit,
> Nomen, et aeternam ponam super aethera sedem,
> Excelso similis, summis nec viribus impar.[2]

Though he has fallen, we are reminded, he still retains many of his angelic qualities, and he makes the same point himself in the course of a fine soliloquy in which he explains his reasons for corrupting Man:

> Proh dolor, hoc nobis subitum consurgere plasma,
> Invisumque genus nostra crevisse ruina!
> Me celsum virtus habuit, nunc ecce rejectus
> Pellor, et angelico limus succedit honori.
> Coelum terra tenet, vili compage levata
> Regnat humus, nobisque perit translata potestas.

---

[1] See above, Ch. II, p. 45.

[2] *De Mos. Hist.* ii. 40–44. 'Thinking that he had made himself, that he was his own creator, he conceived a frenzy in his rabid heart, denying his Maker. I will achieve the title of a god, he cried, and place my eternal throne above the heavens, like unto the Most High and equal to His omnipotence.'

Non tamen in totum periit; pars magna retentat
Vim propriam summaque cluit virtute nocendi.

. . .

Haec mihi dejecto tandem solatia restant.
Si nequeo clausos iterum conscendere coelos,
His quoque claudentur: levius cecidisse putandum est,
Si nova perdatur simili substantia casu,
Si comes excidii subeat consortia poenae
Et quos praevideo nobiscum dividat ignes.[1]

In his motives both for this rebellion and for his temptation of Man this Devil is clearly an ancestor, albeit a distant one, of Milton's Satan in *Paradise Lost*.

The temptation itself is conceived in far greater detail and with far more subtlety than in any other of these poems. Here it is an epic event, and as such it cannot be merely assumed, as in the *Metrum in Genesim*, or glossed over, as in the *Alethia* and the *Carmen de Deo*. Having first taken on the form of a serpent, the Devil climbs a tree so that he can reach the ear of Eve—he fears that Adam would not succumb to his poison—and proceeds to flatter her in terms again reminiscent of *Paradise Lost*:

O felix, mundique decus pulcherrima virgo,
Ornat quam roseo praefulgens forma pudore.
Tu generi ventura parens, te maximus orbis
Expectat matrem: tu prima et certa voluptas
Solamenque viri, sine qua non viveret ipse,
Ut major, sic jure tuo subjectus amori
Praedulcis conjux, reddes cui foedere prolem.[2]

---

[1] Ibid. ii. 89–112. 'Woe is me that this sudden creature of clay should rise in our place, and a hated race benefit from our fall. Courage once held me exalted, but lo, now I am banished as an exile and clay succeeds to my angelic honour. Earth grasps heaven, and dust, raised by the base creature, rules, and the power which has been transferred from us [to Man] is lost to us. Not all is lost, however; a great part still retains its own strength, renowned for its supreme power to harm. . . . At least these consolations are left to me as an outcast. If I cannot mount again to the heavens that are now closed to me, they shall be closed to men as well: it will seem a lighter loss to have fallen if the new creation should be lost in a like disaster, if, as a comrade in my destruction, it should suffer a partnership of punishment and share with us the flames which I foresee.'

[2] Ibid. ii. 145–51. 'O happy one, ornament of the world, most beautiful maiden, whom refulgent beauty adorns with blushing modesty; you are the future parent of the race, the mighty world awaits you as its mother: you are the first and certain joy and comfort of man, without whom he could not live; though he to whom you will bear children by your union is greater than you, most gentle wife, he is subjected to your law by love.'

If all the world is theirs, he inquires, why has God forbidden one tree? Although the poet himself breaks in to reprove Eve for conversing with so unnatural a thing as a speaking serpent, she accepts its praise and goes on to ask him the meaning of the threat of death:

> Quid vocitet mortem tu nunc, doctissime serpens,
> Pande libens, quoniam rudibus non cognita res est.[1]

The question allows the serpent to bring the conversation round to his real purpose: God, he claims, is jealous and forbade the fruit of the tree of knowledge only to prevent men from becoming as gods. Hereafter, no more words are spoken, but Avitus conveys Eve's gradual submission by means of an eloquent series of visual images:

> Talia fallaci spondentem dona susurro
> Credula submisso miratur femina vultu.
> Et jam jamque magis cunctari ac flectere sensum
> Incipit, et dubiam letho plus addere mentem.
> Ille ut vicino victam discrimine sensit,
>
> .   .   .
>
> Unum de cunctis lethali ex arbore malum
> Detrahit, et suavi pulchrum perfundit odore,
> Conciliat speciem, nutantique insuper offert.
>
> .   .   .
>
> Naribus interdum labiisque patentibus ultro
> Jungit, et ignorans ludit de morte futura.
> O quoties ori admotum compuncta retraxit,
> Audacisque mali titubans sub pondere dextra
> Cessit, et effectum sceleris tremefacta refugit.[2]

Eventually, however, she finds the courage to eat the fruit, and Avitus crowns his picture of this stage of the temptation with a lovely moment as Adam returns:

---

[1] *De Mos. Hist.* ii. 181–2. 'Most erudite serpent, be so kind as to explain what He means by death, for the uninstructed do not know what it is.'

[2] Ibid. ii. 204–19. 'As he promises such gifts with a fallacious whisper the credulous woman marvels at him with a yielding look, and now she begins to hesitate more and more and relax her feelings, and she inclines her wavering mind towards death. When he perceived that she was overcome by the crisis at hand he pulled down one apple out of all from the fatal tree . . . and poured a sweet odour over the beautiful fruit, making it look attractive, and offered it to her while she was wavering over it. . . . Meanwhile with nostrils open and lips parted she takes it willingly and ignorantly plays with impending death. O how often, overcome by remorse, has she withdrawn the apple as it approached her mouth, and, her, hand hesitating under the weight of reckless evil, retires and shaking shirks the outcome of the crime in terror.'

Ignarus facti diversa parte revertens
Adam diffusi laetus per gramina campi
Conjugis amplexus atque oscula casta petebat.[1]

Immediately Eve assails him, reproaching him for his cowardice in abstaining from the forbidden tree for so long:

Sume cibum, dulcis, vitali ex germine, conjunx.

.   .   .

Crede libens, mentem scelus est dubitasse virilem
Quod mulier potui; praecedere forte timebas;
Saltem consequere, atque animos attolle jacentes.[2]

Overcome by this imputation on his valour, Adam, like a true epic hero, reacts without hesitation. As soon as he has done so the fallen pair perceive that they are naked, not, Avitus emphasizes, because they had been blind before, but because they now feel for the first time the pangs of concupiscence. After a short speech of triumph the Devil vanishes, and there follows a description of Adam and Eve's misery and desire for death very much like that in the *Alethia*. When they are questioned by God Adam blames Him for giving him Eve in the first place:

Atque utinam felix, quae quondam sola vigebat,
Caelebs vita foret, talis nec conjugis unquam
Foedera sensisset, comiti non subdita pravae.[3]

The patristic exegesis of Adam's unrepentant reply to God's questions has become a natural human sentiment; as it has throughout the whole poem, doctrine has been turned into poetry.

The last of these poems, Cyprian's *Heptateuchos*, has received rather less than its due in critical studies of the poetry of this period. It is generally regarded as a dull and unimaginative paraphrase of negligible literary merit.[4] On the contrary, unless my reading of the

---

[1] Ibid. ii. 235–7. 'Ignorant of what had been done elsewhere, Adam joyfully returned through the grass of the spacious field, seeking the embraces and chaste kisses of his wife.'

[2] Ibid. ii. 242–9. 'Sweet husband, take food from the seed of life. . . . Believe me willingly, it is wrong for a masculine spirit to hesitate to do what I, a woman, could; you were, perhaps, afraid to be the first; at least follow my example and rouse your downcast courage.'

[3] Ibid. iii. 105–7. 'Would that my happy life, which flourished previously in solitude, had continued single, and had never been united to such a wife nor subjected to so depraved a companion.'

[4] See, for instance, Gamber, op. cit., p. 55; F. J. E. Raby, *A History of Christian-Latin Poetry*, 2nd edn., 1953, p. 76; E. S. Duckett, *Latin Writers of the Fifth Century*, New York, 1930, p. 65.

poem is wholly misconceived, Cyprian has introduced several profoundly important and aesthetically satisfying modifications into the Genesis narrative. He begins, it is true, somewhat cautiously with a brief and very largely Scriptural account of the work of the first five days, though even this is occasionally illuminated by a particularly striking line or two. The creation of the trees and flowers, for instance, comes vividly to life in these lines:

> florea uentosis consurgunt germina campis
> pomiferique simul procuruant brachia rami.[1]

And the appearance of the reptiles and the animals is described with equal economy and skill:

> sexta pater gelidos in spiras lubricat angues
> quadrupedumque greges totos diffundit in agros.[2]

As in Dracontius's *Carmen de Deo* the carefully chosen verbs suggest the creative energy itself. Cyprian's poem may be the shortest of the six, but he is by no means the smallest poet.

With the creation of Adam the poetic narrative begins to break still further out of the framework of the Biblical text. Adam is made in the image of God, conventionally enough, in order to govern the rest of the creatures. But Cyprian has noticed the shift from the abstracted Elohim of the first chapter of Genesis, who created merely by the expression of His will, to the anthropomorphic Jahweh of the second, who fashioned Adam with his own hands, and he takes advantage of the contrast to comment on the special care lavished on Man by his Creator.[3] To judge from the evidence of the poem as a whole, Cyprian seems to have been a man especially sensitive to the benevolence of God, for this is but the first of many occasions on which he intervenes to draw the reader's attention to the Divine goodwill towards men. Indeed, the very next episode, the formation of Eve, is described in such a way as to make just this point:

> metitur solum mordaces uoluere curas.
> ilicet inriguo perfundit lumina somno,
> mollius ut uulsa formetur femina costa.[4]

---

[1] *Hept.* i. 13–14. 'Flowery plants spring up on the wind-swept plain, and at the same time fruit-bearing trees curve out their arms.'

[2] Ibid. i. 21–22. 'On the sixth day the Father slips icy snakes into coils, and pours forth flocks of animals on to all the fields.'   [3] Ibid. i. 29–31.

[4] Ibid. i. 33–35. 'God foresees that, alone, Adam would suffer gnawing cares. Therefore he pours trickling sleep over his eyes in order that the woman might the more gently be made from the rib He had reft.'

When Adam has named his wife and the animals, inspired by the wisdom his Maker has given him, he receives the command to increase and multiply. By postponing the injunction to fertility and the prohibition of the tree of knowledge, which follows shortly, until after the creation of Eve, the poet not only gives them added point; he establishes a nice balance between the positive and negative aspects of the pair's duty, between life and death. He then goes on to describe the forbidden tree in terms of the same balance:

> gignitur haec inter pomis letalibus arbos
> coniunctum generans uitae mortisque saporem.[1]

Like Prudentius and Dracontius, Cyprian appears to have held the 'cumulative' theory of the tree of knowledge expounded by Gregory of Nyssa, according to which the forbidden fruit contained a mixture of good and evil, life and death. The tree of life, which is nowhere mentioned in this version of the story, has in fact been combined with the tree of knowledge to form one tree, the double nature of whose fruit is further elaborated in the prohibition:

> solliciti, ne forte malum noxale legatis,
> quod uiret ex gemino discreta ad munia suco.[2]

During the course of the narrative up to this point Cyprian's departures from the Scriptural account have been growing increasingly adventurous, beginning with delicate but small-scale descriptive details, expanding to pious observations on God's conduct, and eventually developing into a reorganization of the story's chronology and a major reinterpretation of the forbidden tree. His treatment of the Fall itself marks the culmination of this process, for his presentation of the circumstances under which Adam and Eve sinned is by far the most original of those we have so far examined. The key to his version of the episode is to be found in the fact that the serpent approaches Eve during the night, 'nec minus interea caecos nox alta tenebat',[3] promising her not equality with the gods but simply the return of daylight:

---

[1] Ibid. i. 52–53. 'Among these there is created a tree with deadly apples, generating a sap conjoined of life and death.'

[2] Ibid. i. 68–69. 'Beware lest by chance you should pick the harmful evil which flourishes from a double sap for two different purposes.'

[3] Ibid. i. 70. 'While deep night held them blind.'

> atqui si studeas mellitos carpere uictus,
> aureus astrigero ridebit cardine mundus.[1]

At first Eve refuses, but when she has finally consented the light does return just as the serpent had promised: 'adfulsit nulla maculatum nube serenum.'[2] Convinced by this demonstration and corrupted by the effect of the fruit, she persuades Adam to eat with her, and again:

> quod simul ac sumpsit, detersa nocte nitentes
> emicuere oculi mundo splendente sereni.[3]

Later, when he is interrogated, Adam himself explains in more detail how Eve prevailed on him to transgress the prohibition:

> Tradidit haec mulier, dum dicit lumina promptim
> candenti perfusa die liquidumque serenum
> adfulsisse sibi solemque et sidera caeli.[4]

What Cyprian seems to have done here is to adapt the legend of primitive Man's fear of the night, which had appeared already in the *Carmen de Deo*, and apply it to the actual temptation. The serpent overcomes Eve by using her ignorance of the cycle of day and night to convince her that the forbidden fruit would bring back the light.[5] When, in the natural course of things, she does see a new day dawn, Adam is also assured of the tempter's good faith and eats the fruit with her. They are not tempted, merely deceived.

It is not, therefore, surprising that Cyprian emphasizes the mercy rather than the anger of God during the subsequent condemnation and expulsion. This he does by omitting any reference to God's fear that by eating of the tree of life the fallen pair would live for ever— an omission necessitated also by his previous amalgamation of the tree of life with the tree of knowledge—and by concentrating all his

---

[1] *Hept.* i. 79–80. 'But if you care to pluck the honeyed fruit the golden world will smile again with its star-bearing pole.'

[2] Ibid. i. 84. 'The clear sky shone out, unspotted by any cloud.'

[3] Ibid. i. 87–88. 'As soon as he took it their eyes shone out gleaming and clear over the resplendent world now that night had been effaced.'

[4] Ibid. i. 98–100. 'This woman gave them to me, saying that her eyes were immediately suffused with gleaming day, and that the clear sky and also the sun and stars of heaven had shone on her.'

[5] Possibly the literal meaning of 'lucifer' ('the bringer of light') contributed to this version of the temptation, but Cyprian's omission of any connexion between the serpent and the fallen angel makes this unlikely. Also the opening of Adam and Eve's eyes after the Fall may have suggested that if they were not previously blind—and the commentators insisted that they were not—the onset of night had prevented them from seeing.

attention on the clothing of Adam and Eve with coats of skins, which he uses as an illustration of the Creator's continued benevolence:

> quis dominus, pigro ne frigore membra rigerent,
> consuit euulsas pecudum de uiscere pelles,
> operiens nudos calidis de uestibus artus.[1]

The sum total of these far-reaching modifications of the Biblical story is a thoroughly minimal treatment of the Fall, dominated by an acute sense not of Man's sinfulness but of God's mercy.

These poems, then, all contain significant and often beautiful elaborations of the Genesis narrative. Sometimes these consist in the poetical presentation of a patristic interpretation, as in the case of Avitus's description of the Devil and his motives or Dracontius's emphasis on Adam and Eve's ignorance of lust. Sometimes they may have been inspired by rabbinic speculations, as in Avitus's account of the wedding of Adam and Eve or Dracontius's picture of the first night in Paradise. More often, however, they were simply the result of the endeavour to turn the Bible's terse phrases into poetry which would be both edifying and enjoyable. In this respect the Christian-Latin poets were trying to do what the author of *Genesis B* and Milton were to set themselves to achieve centuries later, and with no little success. Dracontius's portrayal of Man's original innocence and Victor's of his fallen misery can match anything outside *Paradise Lost*, while Avitus and Cyprian's versions of the temptation offered later poets two equally original ways of handling that episode. In conclusion, therefore, it is worth noting that these works were available to both Milton and the author of *Genesis B*. Of the six Dracontius's seems to have been the most immediately popular, for it was revised by Eugenius of Toledo between 642 and 672 at the express command of Chindasuindus, King of the Spanish Goths, and is mentioned in a catalogue of the monastic library of Reichenau dated 822. Avitus is included in Alcuin's list of the authors represented in the York library, and several Continental monastic catalogues of the ninth and tenth centuries refer to him. Later his poem was published in Paris, in 1508, and again in 1545. Cyprian's *Heptateuchos* was known to Bede, Alcuin, and Aldhelm, and is included in a tenth-century catalogue

---

[1] *Hept.* i. 131–3. 'And lest their limbs should be benumbed with sluggish cold, the Lord sewed together for them skins flayed from the bodies of animals, covering their naked limbs with warm clothes.'

of Lorsch. Victor may have been known to Bede, is mentioned in two Continental monastic catalogues of the tenth century, and was published in Paris in 1536. Hilary's poem was published in 1516, while Proba was one of the set authors listed in the syllabus of St. Paul's School at the time Milton was a student there. Finally, Morelle, the publisher of Du Bartas's *Sepmaine*, issued the works of Hilary, Victor, Dracontius, Avitus, and Cyprian in a combined edition in Paris in 1560.[1] It is more than possible, then, that these first poetic treatments of the Genesis narrative could have influenced Christian poets writing on the same subject in both the Carolingian and Elizabethan Renaissances.

[1] The facts assembled here are drawn from a number of different sources. For information on the availability of these works on the Continent and in England during the Dark Ages I have relied on G. Becker's *Catalogi Bibliothecarum Antiqui*, Bonn, 1885, and J. D. A. Ogilvy's *Books Known to Anglo-Latin writers from Aldhelm to Alcuin*, Cambridge, Massachusetts, 1936. For details concerning their publication in the Renaissance, on the other hand, I have consulted T. de Maisières's *Les Poèmes inspirés du début de la Genèse à l'époque de la Renaissance*, Louvain, 1931. The syllabus of St. Paul's School is reprinted in K. E. Hartwell's *Lactantius and Milton*, Cambridge, Massachusetts, 1929.

V

THE HEROIC TREATMENTS

IT was no coincidence that, as I remarked at the beginning of the last chapter, Alcuin's question concerning the relationship of secular to sacred literature echoed those of Tertullian and Jerome. For in the newly converted nations of the West the Church was again confronted with the problem of coming to terms with a long-established and widely read body of native poetry which celebrated the deeds of the gods and heroes of a pagan mythology. The fact that the poetry and the mythology were in this case Germanic rather than Greek or Roman did not make them any the less dangerous in the eyes of devout Christians. Ingeld and all he stood for could undo the work of the missionaries quite as effectively as Odysseus or Aeneas. Only the incidental factors had altered; the fundamental problem still remained.

But by the same token so did the solution. The aberrant monks of Lindisfarne might be persuaded to abandon heathen fiction for Scriptural truth by the well-tried technique of presenting the stories and doctrines of the new religion in the forms and diction of the old. If God could be described as '*summus tonans*' in fifth- and sixth-century Gaul, there was no reason why He should not be clothed in the garb of a '*wigfruma*' in seventh- and eighth-century England, and on the basis of this assumption a vigorous school of Anglo-Saxon religious poetry developed during the Dark Ages, dedicated to the same ends and produced by the same means as its Latin forerunner in the late Roman Empire. Its founder, according to the venerable Bede (673–735), was the cowherd Caedmon,[1] but while it is certainly possible that his brief hymn on the Creation became sufficiently popular to initiate the literary movement represented by

---

[1] *Hist. Ecc.* iv. 24. Both F. Palgrave in his Appendix to S. H. Gurteen's *The Epic of the Fall of Man*, 1896, and J. K. Bostock in *A Handbook on Old High German Literature*, 1955, pp. 145–6, have noted a similar legend on the Continent, according to which the religious literature of Saxony had its origin in the works of a divinely inspired peasant. Palgrave also remarks that Caedmon's name might be derived from the Chaldaic word 'Cadmon' (beginning) which was used as the title of Genesis.

poems like *Genesis A* and *Christ and Satan* in England, and *Genesis B* and the *Heliand* on the Continent, there is a great deal of concrete evidence to suggest that it was inspired by the example of the Christian-Latin poets, the popularity of whose works is in no doubt.[1] The 'Caedmonian Revolution', as it has been called, merely gave another turn to the wheel which had originally been set in motion some two or three hundred years earlier.

On the other hand, there is no denying the very distinctive character of the Anglo-Saxon treatments of the Biblical narrative. The differences between, say, *Genesis A* and the *Metrum in Genesim* are far more obvious than the underlying similarities of aim and method to which I have so far drawn attention. They derive, of course, from the use of the style, language, and concepts peculiar to Germanic Saga rather than those associated with Classical Epic.[2] The substitution of Ingeld for Aeneas and Odysseus may have been a peripheral consideration for the theologian, but for the practising poet it was absolutely central, involving as it did the application of a whole new terminology to the stories of the Old and New Testaments. This terminology was essentially heroic in nature. It reflected, that is to say, the values and conventions of a primitive society whose moral code was that of the *comitatus* and whose feudal structure revolved around the '*winsele*'.[3] The local warlord demanded unconditional loyalty from his retainers, in return for which he offered them a share in his booty and the protection of his court. Ties of kinship or nationality were, in the last resort, subordinate to those which bound a warrior to his chief,[4] and the worst crime the former could commit was to betray that allegiance. Conversely, the worst punishment was to be excluded from the *comitatus*, to be, like the speaker in the Old English poem *The Wanderer*, lordless and therefore friendless.[5]

When the vocabulary of such a society was superimposed on the Christian world-picture two things happened: first, the vocabulary

[1] See above, Ch. IV, pp. 141–2.

[2] I use the word 'Saga' in its most general sense, as a convenient means of distinguishing Germanic from Classical Epic.

[3] For a detailed account see D. Whitelock, *The Beginnings of English Society*, 1952, ch. ii.

[4] *The Parker Chronicle*, for instance, records under the year 755 that the followers of Cynewulf rejected Cyneheard's offers of conciliation, even though to do so involved fighting against their own kin, and *The Battle of Maldon* relates that the hostage Æscferð fought for his captors against the Danes.

[5] See especially ll. 19–48.

itself was modified and words like 'dom', 'lof', and 'wyrd' came to acquire a new resonance;[1] second, the more subtle and spiritual aspects of the Church's teaching were coarsened by the heroic emphasis on physical valour and material reward and punishment.[2] Heaven was transformed into an idealized wine-hall, presided over by a warrior God and inhabited by angelic thanes:

> þegnas þrymfæste þeoden heredon,
> sægdon lustum lof, heora liffrean
> demdon, drihtenes dugeþum wæron
> swiðe gesælige.[3]

To be a member of this celestial *comitatus* constituted the proper aspiration of the faithful, who earned their place in it by their military prowess in the terrestrial battle against Satan and his allies. Even a relatively passive saint like Guthlac was conscripted by the poets as 'godes oretta', 'meotudes cempa'.[4] Armed with 'gæstlicum wæpnum' against the 'færscytum' of the Devil's 'mægen'[5] he defended, like the heroes of *The Battle of Maldon* and *Waldere*, a difficult position against overwhelming odds, rejecting the offer of a safe-conduct no less steadfastly than the companions of Cynewulf and Cyneheard:

> We þe beoð holde gif ðu us hyran wilt,
> . . . We þas wic magun
> fotum afyllan; folc in ðriceð
> meara þreatum ond monfarum.[6]

In spite of all the adversary's threats:

> Dryhtnes cempa,
> from folctoga, feonda þreatum
> wiðstod stronglice.[7]

---

[1] See B. J. Timmer, 'Heathen and Christian Elements in Old English Poetry', *Neophil.* xxix (1944), 180–5.

[2] See A. R. Skemp, 'The Transformation of Scriptural Story, Motive, and Conception in Anglo-Saxon Poetry', *M.P.* iv (1907), 423–70.

[3] *Genesis A*, 15–18. 'Stout-hearted thanes worshipped their Prince, uttered praise gladly, glorified their Lord of Life, were very happy in their Lord's excellence.'

[4] *Guthlac*, 569, 576. 'God's warrior', 'the Lord's soldier'. See also 401–2, 580, 901.

[5] Ibid. 177, 186, 282. 'spiritual weapons', 'sudden shots', 'war-band'. In *Crist*, 779, it is said that the Christian need not fear the 'deofla strælas', 'devils' arrows'.

[6] Ibid. 280–6. 'We will be loyal to you if you will obey us. . . . We can tread this place down with our feet; the people will press in with troops of horses and with armies.'

[7] Ibid. 901–3. 'The Lord's warrior, the bold commander, firmly withstood the hosts of enemies.'

For his bravery he expected a warrior's reward, the heavenly 'sigorlean', which he eventually received after his death from his 'sigedryhten' among the angelic 'sibgedryht'.[1]

But if the saint's vocation lost much of its spirituality by being defined in these worldly terms, the Devil's activities gained fresh force and significance, for, as R. E. Woolf has noted,[2] the heroic formulae were far more appropriate to Satan and his followers than to Christ and His disciples. Set against the background of the code of allegiance which united a *comitatus*, the disloyalty of the rebel angel stood out very clearly; by revolting against his Lord and Creator he had disobeyed the most respected law of feudal society:

> Noldan dreogan leng
> heora selfra ræd, ac hie of siblufan
> godes ahwurfon. Hæfdon gielp micel
> þæt hie wið drihtne dælan meahton
> wuldorfæstan wic werodes þrymme,
> sid and swegltorht.[3]

In *Christ and Satan* the perversity of this initial act of rebellion was compounded by Lucifer's claim that he was the father of Christ, whose place he attempted to usurp in the celestial hierarchy:

> þa ic in mode minum hogade
> þæt ic wolde towerpan wuldres leoman,
> bearn helendes.[4]

His quarrel with his Maker thus assumed the proportions of the kind of feud over the succession that had disrupted so many dynasties in the Dark Ages; to a contemporary reader who knew anything at all of recent history his motives in this poem would have seemed only too familiar.

---

[1] *Guthlac*, 1366–75. 'triumphant reward', 'victorious Lord', 'peaceful band'.

[2] 'The Devil in Old English Poetry', *R.E.S.* N.S. iv (1953), 12.

[3] *Genesis A*, 23–28. 'They would no longer follow their own course, but turned away from the love of God. They made a great boast that they could share with their Lord the wondrous dwelling of the glorious host, spacious and radiant.'

[4] *Christ and Satan*, 84–86. 'Then I thought in my heart that I would overthrow the light of glory, the Son of God.' From the immediate context it is not clear whether 'bearn' is accusative singular or plural, but in another passage where there is no doubt about the reference Christ is called 'bearn waldendes' (l. 194), and when Satan recalls the incident for a second time he states: 'Ðæs ic wolde of selde sunu meotodes, / drihten adrifan', 'Whence I wished to drive the Son of God, the Lord, from His throne'. The author of the poem may have been led to this interpretation of the rebellion either by the account in the Vita Adae et Evae, according to which Satan was cast out of Heaven

So too would his behaviour after his expulsion from Heaven. Like the speaker in *The Wanderer*, he vividly recalled the joys he had lost:

> Byrhtword aras
> engla ordfruma, and to þæm æþelan
> hnigan him sanctas; sigetorht aras
> ece drihten, ofer us gestod
> and gebletsode bilewitne heap
> dogra gehwilcne.[1]

Now that he had forfeited his position 'in heofnum heahgetimbrad' and been cast out from the 'wloncra winsele', he was compelled to 'wadan wræclastas' as an exile,[2] lamenting his downfall in phrases which echoed those traditionally used by his human counterpart:

> Hwær com engla ðrym,
> þe we on heofnum habban sceoldan?
> Eala drihtenes þrym! Eala duguða helm!
> Eala meotodes miht! Eala middaneard!
> Eala dæg leohta! Eala dream godes!
> Eala engla þreat! Eala upheofon![3]

This tendency to reduce supernatural phenomena to the level of mundane experience is still more evident in the Anglo-Saxon poets' treatment of Adam and Eve. For example, the Church's doctrine that Man was created to replace the fallen angels was taken by the author of *Genesis A* to mean that the defection of Satan and his companions had literally left unsightly gaps in the heavenly ranks:

> Him on laste setl,
> wuldorspedum welig, wide stodan
> gifum growende on godes rice,
> beorht and geblædfæst, buendra leas,
> siððan wræcstowe werige gastas
> under hearmlocan heane geforan.

because he refused to worship Adam (see above, Ch. II, p. 56.), or more probably by Lactantius's theory that the Devil envied Christ (see below, Ch. IX, p. 226).

[1] Ibid. 236–41. 'The clear-voiced Leader of the Angels arose and the saints bowed down before the Noble One. The eternal glorious Lord arose, stood over us, and blessed the innocent host each day.' Compare *The Wanderer*, ll. 34–36, 41–44.

[2] Ibid. 29, 93, 120. 'high-timbered Heaven', 'wine-hall of the proud', 'travel the paths of exile'. Compare *The Wanderer*, l. 5; *The Seafarer*, l. 57.

[3] Ibid. 36–166. 'Where has the glory of the angels gone, which we used to have in Heaven? . . . Alas the protector of the hosts! Alas the might of the Lord! Alas the world! Alas the bright day! Alas the bliss of God! Alas the host of angels! Alas the high Heaven!' Compare *The Wanderer*, ll. 92–95.

þa þeahtode þeoden ure
modgeþonce, hu he þa mæran gesceaft,
eðelstaðolas eft gesette,
swegltorhtan seld, selran werode.[1]

And he found it necessary to supplement the orthodox view that
God had put Adam to sleep to prevent him from feeling any pain
while Eve was being created from his rib with the statement: 'ne þær
ænig com / blod of benne.'[2]

The same preoccupation with physical reality informs his account
of Adam and Eve's original happiness:

> Heo wæron englum gelice,
> þa wæs Eve, Adames bryd,
> gaste gegearwod. Hie on geogoðe bu
> wlitebeorht wæron on woruld cenned
> meotodes mihtum.[3]

Their outward beauty is what chiefly interests him, and when he
comes to describe the garden of Eden he again lays all the stress on
its natural advantages:

> Fægere leohte
> þæt liðe land lago yrnende,
> wylleburne. Nalles wolcnu ða giet
> ofer rumne grund regnas bæron,
> wann mid winde, hwæðre wæstmum stod
> folde gefrætwod.[4]

Clearly this is a far less sophisticated picture of the world's pristine
innocence than that in the *Metrum in Genesim* or the *Alethia*. Living
as he did in an environment more akin to the savage landscape of the
De Rerum Natura, the eighth-century poet had little time for the
refined delights of sight, smell, and sound elaborated in the Christian-

---

[1] *Genesis A*, 86–95. 'Behind them their dwellings, glorious in splendour, stood far and wide burgeoning with gifts in the kingdom of God, bright and glorious, lacking inhabitants, after the weary spirits had gone downcast to their place of exile under terrible confinement. Then our Lord planned in His mind how he would again establish the glorious creation, the homelands, the bright hall, with a better company.' See above, Ch. III, pp. 83, 88. Compare Ælfric, *Exameron*, 324–8; *De Init. Creat.*, p. 12.

[2] Ibid. 180–1. 'Nor did any blood issue from the wound.' See above, Ch. IV, p. 138.

[3] Ibid. 185–9. 'They were like angels when Eve, Adam's bride, was equipped with a soul. They were both born into the world young and glorious by God's might.' Compare *Phoenix*, 397 et seq.; *Crist*, 1379 et seq.

[4] Ibid. 210–15. 'The running water, the well-spring, flowed beautifully over that gentle land. The clouds did not yet bear rain over the spacious land, dark with the wind, but the earth stood decorated with blossoms.'

Latin poems. His idea of perfection extended little further than climatic stability and the absence of the bodily discomforts inflicted by Nature. Hilary's perfect farm and Victor's perfect garden consequently gave way to the more primitive ideal of an amenable countryside.[1]

The temptation itself was largely taken for granted in those poems which touched on the subject. The brief description of it in *Guthlac* is typical:

> Hy to ær aþreat
> þæt hy waldendes willan læsten,
> ac his wif genom wyrmes larum
> blede forbodene, ond of beame ahneop
> wæstm biweredne ofer word godes,
> wuldorcyninges, ond hyre were sealde
> þurh deofles searo deaðberende gyfl
> þæt ða sinhiwan to swylte geteah.[2]

The only embellishment of any real interest is to be found in a later passage from the same poem in which death is figured as an ale-cup:

> Bryþen wæs ongunnen
> þætte Adame Eue gebyrmde
> æt fruman worulde. Feond byrlade
> ærest þære idese, ond heo Adame,
> hyre swæsum were, siþþan scencte
> bittor bædeweg.[3]

Since Adam first tasted of it no man has been able to avoid

> þone bitran drync
> þone Eue fyrn Adame geaf,
> byrelade bryd geong.[4]

[1] If the description of Eden in the Old English *Phoenix* is compared with that in the Latin original this point emerges very clearly. The Anglo-Saxon poet amplifies the Latin account by emphasizing the climatic benefits of Paradise. See especially ll. 28-84.

[2] *Guthlac*, 844-51. 'All too soon they tired of performing God's will, and his [Adam's] wife took the forbidden fruit on the advice of the serpent, and plucked the forbidden fruit from the branch against the word of God, the King of glory, and as a result of the Devil's treachery gave the deadly food, which brought the married pair to death, to her husband.' Compare *Christ and Satan*, 408-16; *Juliana*, 499-505; *Crist*, 1392-1413; *Phoenix*, 400-8. The similarities between these accounts have led C. Abbetmeyer to the conclusion that they have a common source in some popular homily. See his *Old English Poetical Motives derived from the Doctrine of Sin*, Minneapolis, 1903, p. 28.

[3] *Guthlac*, 980-5. 'The brew was begun which Eve prepared for Adam at the beginning of the world. The Devil first gave it to the woman to drink, and she later poured the bitter drink for Adam, her dear husband.' Compare the *Eclogue* of Theodolus, 41-43.

[4] *Guthlac*, 868-70. 'the bitter drink that Eve gave to Adam long ago, the young wife served [him].'

The point of this metaphor is that in the Germanic wine-hall it was the wife's duty to pass the 'medoful' to her lord and his retainers;[1] by offering her husband and his descendants a poisoned drink Eve betrayed that elementary trust.

Not surprisingly, the moral and spiritual effects of Adam's disobedience were largely ignored in the literature of this period—the Augustinian doctrines of concupiscence and the depravity of the will, for example, are notable by their absence. During the Dark Ages it was the natural hazards of life rather than the metaphysical problems of conduct that needed explanation. A Christian reader wanted to know why he had to endure the miseries of rain, frost, wind, and snow, and the ultimate degradation of death; the theological complexities of sexual relationships and ethical responsibilities, even if he had been able to understand them, would have seemed far removed from the problems of the world in which he lived. As a result, the Anglo-Saxon poets confined their attention to the material consequences of the Fall, describing Adam and Eve in terms normally associated with the familiar figure of the exile. After their expulsion from the garden of Eden the first pair were 'dugeðum bedæled'[2] and forced to undertake a 'longne sið in hearmra hond'.[3] In their new habitation 'feond rixade'[4] and death came to saint and sinner alike.

Only *Genesis A* offered any consolation:

> ac he him to frofre let hwæðere forð wesan
> hyrstedne hrof halgum tunglum
> and him grundwelan ginne sealde;
> het þam sinhiwum sæs and eorðan
> tuddorteondra teohha gehwilcre
> to woruldnytte wæstmas fedan.[5]

Boniface had been advised by Bishop Daniel of Winchester to deal with the pagans 'not in an offensive and irritating way but calmly and with great moderation'. In particular, he was informed, 'their

---

[1] See *Beowulf*, 612–31.

[2] *Genesis A*, 930. 'deprived of blessings.' Compare *Crist*, 1407–8.

[3] *Phoenix*, 440–1. 'a long journey into the power of the hostile ones.' Compare *Crist*, 1414–18.

[4] *Guthlac*, 864. 'the Devil reigned.'

[5] *Genesis A*, 955–60. 'But He, however, let the roof [of Heaven] ornamented with holy stars remain as a consolation for them, and gave them the ample riches of the earth; He ordered each of the sea's and land's productive tribes to bring forth fruits for the married couple.' Compare Ælfric, *Exameron*, 490–3.

superstitions should be compared with our Christian dogmas and
touched upon indirectly'.[1] This, perhaps, is what the anonymous
poet was attempting to do here. The gods of Germanic mythology
were not especially distinguished for their goodwill towards men,
and by emphasizing the contrasting benevolence of the Christian
Deity he may have hoped to convince his audience of the superiority
of the new religion. Nevertheless, as Eve herself remarked earlier in
the poem, the tempter's successful assault on the garden of Eden
had brought about a long-lasting 'fæhðe'[2] that could only be settled
by the military conquest of Hell:

> Hwearf þa to helle hæleða bearnum,
> meotod þurh mihte; wolde manna rim,
> fela þusenda, forð gelædan
> up to eðle.[3]

Man's salvation was not finally assured until the warrior Christ broke
down the doors of Satan's fortress to release the souls imprisoned
there.[4]

In order, then, to make the Biblical history of the Fall and the
Redemption both attractive and comprehensible to those of his
contemporaries with a taste for pagan poetry, the Christian *scop*
adopted not only the literary conventions but also the moral values
of Germanic Saga. Certain episodes clearly lent themselves more
readily than others to heroic treatment, and on these he tended to
concentrate, often to the detriment of the story as a whole. But
although he thereby modified its doctrinal content he very rarely
tampered with the narrative structure of the sacred text; indeed,
so far as the Fall itself is concerned he was generally content to
paraphrase the account in Genesis.

The author of the ninth-century Saxon poem, *Genesis B*,[5] on the
other hand, described the first transgression in great detail, exploring
the motives and reactions of the tempter and the tempted with a
breadth of imagination unequalled in this or any earlier period.

---

[1] See C. H. Talbot, *The Anglo-Saxon Missionaries in Germany*, 1954, p. 77.

[2] *Genesis A*, 900. 'feud.' Compare *Crist*, 617.

[3] *Christ and Satan*, 398–401. 'Then the Lord by His might turned to Hell for the
sons of men; He wished to lead forth a multitude of men, many thousands, up to His
kingdom.'

[4] Ibid. 378–90, 463–7.

[5] On the basis of present critical opinion I assume that the Old English translation is
a more or less accurate version of the original Old Saxon poem, and that this original was
composed in Saxony in the mid ninth century.

J. K. Bostock has pointed out that the other religious poems written on the Continent in the ninth century are wholly dependent upon the standard theological works of the time. The *Heliand*, for instance, draws much of its material from the commentaries of Raban Maur (776–856), Bede, and Alcuin on the Gospels of Matthew, Luke, and John respectively, while Otfrid of Weissenburg's *Evangelienbuch* uses in addition to these some commentaries of Augustine, Jerome, and Gregory the Great.[1] In this respect, Bostock observes, these two poems are typical of their age, for independent speculation is hardly to be expected in a period 'when compilation from the accepted authorities was preferred to original thought'.[2] *Genesis B* is the one glowing exception. It owes little or nothing to the writings of the 'accepted authorities', and it makes substantial and far-reaching changes in the story's plot and characterization.

Its originality is all the more striking when the poem is set in the context of the orthodox interpretation of Genesis which would have been available to its author. For during the course of its transmission to northern Europe the Church's teaching on the subject had altered scarcely at all. Thanks first to the rapid expansion of the monastic libraries in this area[3] and second to the general reluctance of successive generations of commentators to venture beyond the limits set by Augustine, an English or Saxon poet wishing to treat the Fall of Man would have found substantially the same interpretation of the story whether he consulted Gregory the Great, Isidore of Seville, Bede, Alcuin, or Raban Maur. From the fifth to the ninth century there stretched an unbroken exegetical tradition, which consisted of little more than various permutations of Augustinian ideas. Nowhere is this clearer than in Alcuin's *Interrogationes et Responsiones in Genesin* which, together with his pupil Raban Maur's *Commentariorum in Genesim Libri Quatuor*, offers a convenient picture of those elements in patristic thought that were most potent on the Continent in the years immediately preceding the composition of *Genesis B*.

One of the first questions posed by Alcuin's interrogator, Sigewulf, concerned the omission in the Genesis narrative of any reference to the Devil's rebellion against his Maker. In reply Alcuin suggested

---

[1] J. K. Bostock, op. cit., pp. 155–6.   [2] Ibid., pp. 176–7.
[3] For detailed accounts see M. R. James, 'Learning and Literature till the death of Bede', *C.M.H.*, vol. iii, ch. xix; R. Irwin, 'In Saxon England, Studies in the History of Libraries—vii', *L.A.R.* lvii (1955), 290 et seq.; M. L. W. Laistner, *Thought and Letters in Western Europe*, 2nd edn., 1957, ch. v.

that the explanation was to be found in the difference between Adam's sin, which was redeemable, and Satan's, which was not: 'The angel was the author of his own crime, but the man was deceived by a trick. Also, the greater was the angel's glory, so much the greater was his downfall: but the frailer was the man's nature, so much the easier was his pardon.'[1] Adam was created with a free will, Alcuin went on to remark, in order that he should be morally responsible for his actions, and to this end the tree of life and the tree of knowledge were planted in the garden of Eden. The one offered him life, the other death: 'He had access to the tree of life as it were to a medicine, by means of which he might become incorruptible; he had access to the tree of knowledge as it were to a poison, by means of which he would die.'[2] In this the English commentator was something less than orthodox, for generations of Fathers, including Augustine, had insisted that the forbidden tree was not in itself harmful. Alcuin's most famous pupil, Raban Maur, may well have intended to refute his master's interpretation when he repeated the familiar argument that 'the fruit of the tree was not in itself poisonous. For clearly He who made everything in paradise good can hardly be thought of as having made something noxious there. But the evil came to man through his transgression of the commandment.'[3] And when Ælfric translated the *Interrogationes* into the vernacular some two centuries later he carefully expunged the offending passage. In a later section of the same work, however, Alcuin reverted to the generally accepted view that the tree of knowledge was so called merely because it enabled the first pair to realize when they had eaten of it the difference between the good of obedience and the evil of disobedience.[4] The prohibition was designed to teach them that they were subject to a higher authority, and so long as they observed it their bodies and their minds were in perfect harmony.

The serpent, according to Alcuin, was said to be more subtle than the other beasts of the field because it was filled with the spirit of the Devil, who spoke through his mouth just as a demon speaks through the mouth of a man possessed without his realizing it.[5] He tempted Adam and Eve 'on account of his hatred for the Creator, his envy of Man, and his despair of his own salvation',[6] and he was

[1] *Interr.* iv.   [2] Ibid. vi.   [3] *Comm. in Gen.* i. 12.
[4] *Interr.* lii. Compare Ælfric, *Exameron*, 438–43.
[5] *Interr.* lx, lxii; *Comm. in Gen.* i. 15, i. 18.
[6] *Interr.* xiii. Compare Ælfric, *Exameron*, 449–55; *De Init. Creat.*, p. 16.

permitted to do so in order to test their loyalty to God. Eve's ready acquiescence was to be accounted for by 'a certain love of her own power and a certain proud self-presumption' that already existed in her mind before the temptation ever took place.[1] When she saw nothing deadly about the fruit she ate of it quite confidently, as did Adam when he saw that Eve had not died as a result of her transgression.[2] Immediately they both became aware of their nakedness, for they were now subject to the pangs of carnal concupiscence. God called them out of the hiding-place in which they subsequently took refuge, not because He was ignorant of their whereabouts, but because He wished to show them how far they had removed themselves from Him by their act of disobedience. But neither of them took advantage of this opportunity for confession and repentance. Instead, Adam blamed God for giving him Eve as a companion, while she in turn attempted to exculpate herself by shifting the blame to the serpent, and so, by implication, to its Creator.[3]

Such, in brief, was the Church's teaching on the Fall story as it would have been available to a ninth-century Saxon. It was, as I have said, almost wholly Augustinian, and with the exception of Alcuin's somewhat unusual views on the tree of knowledge every single idea I have quoted can be found in the *De Civitate Dei* or the *De Genesi ad Litteram*. On the other hand, neither Alcuin nor Raban adopted Augustine's reading in its entirety; they borrowed only certain selected elements from his total interpretation, and as they both tended to choose the same elements their choice may reflect a significant change of emphasis in the explication of the Biblical text. For the questions posed by Sigewulf were primarily concerned with the integrity of the story as a story. Why did Genesis not mention the fall of the angels? Why were the trees of life and knowledge planted in the garden? Why was the Devil hostile towards Adam? Did the serpent understand what he was saying? What led Eve to believe him? Why did Adam eat the fruit with her? All these questions were directed not so much at the story's moral and theological meaning as at its shortcomings as a narrative. They had, in fact, more in common with rabbinic *haggadah*, which attempted to fill in the gaps in the Biblical account, than with patristic *exegesis*, which set out to examine the doctrinal implications of the story as it stood.

---

[1] *Interr.* lxvi; *Comm. in Gen.* i. 15.   [2] *Interr.* lxviii; *Comm. in Gen.* i. 15.
[3] *Interr.* lxix, lxxii, lxxiv; *Comm. in Gen.* i. 16, 17.

The reason for this new attitude towards sacred history lay in the nature of the heathen fiction which Alcuin himself had denounced so bitterly. To judge from the very few examples that have survived, Germanic Saga was distinguished from Classical Epic by its emphasis on situation as opposed to action; as W. P. Ker's criticism of *Beowulf* has demonstrated, the Aristotelian criterion of plot—men in action—cannot be fruitfully applied to it. It was concerned, on the contrary, with men in tension, and such action as it did contain was not so much an end in itself as the expression or resolution of that tension. The real centre of interest in the *Hildebrand*, for instance, was the predicament of the father and son who were forced to fight against each other, not the fight itself. In J. K. Bostock's words, the Germanic poets 'had a bent towards dialogue, for that form concentrates the interest most readily on situations and the psychological problems arising out of them'.[1] From what we know of the stories of Ingeld and Finn, their focal points, too, were the conflict of loyalties within a clearly illuminated situation rather than the actual events which those conflicts produced, and the chronicler who put together the story of Cynewulf and Cyneheard appears to have organized his material with a similar end in view.

This constant stress on situation gave Germanic Saga a very distinctive kind of plot structure. The story unfolds not in a continuous movement but in a series of vivid 'stills'. As each arrives it is given historical perspective and psychological depth by the author's comments or the speeches of the characters themselves. To take a particularly brilliant example from *Beowulf*, as Grendel approaches Heorot we see him first in 'longshot', a vague shadowy figure in the night: 'Com on wanre niht / scriðan sceadugenga.'[2] Then we are given a glimpse of the retainers sleeping in the hall, all except one, and the poet digresses to explain that they were able to sleep secure in the knowledge of God's power. Returning to the one, Beowulf, who was awake, the poet pictures him eagerly awaiting the coming ordeal. The next 'shot' of Grendel is in middle distance; now we can recognize him and make out the misty slopes of the moor: 'ða com of more under misthleoþum / Grendel gongan.'[3] The previous description of the mood of the retainers is then balanced by a statement of Grendel's relationship with God and of his intention to

---

[1] Op. cit. pp. 56–57.
[2] *Beowulf*, 702–3. 'The shadow-goer came gliding in the dark night.'
[3] Ibid. 710–11. 'Then Grendel came from the moor under the misty hill-sides.'

seize one of the hall's occupants. The 'sequence' concludes with a 'close-up' of Grendel as he gazes at Heorot, and the whole situation is put into temporal as well as psychological perspective by a reminder of his past attacks and a prophecy of his approaching doom:

> Wod under wolcnum to þæs þe he winreced
> goldsele gumena gearwost wisse
> fættum fahne. Ne wæs þæt forma sið,
> þæt he Hroþgares ham gesohte;
> næfre he on aldordagum ær ne siþðan
> heardran hæle, healðegnas fand![1]

Applied to the Fall story, in which the motives and interrelationships of the characters were so obscure, this kind of narrative technique could hardly fail to produce large-scale elaborations of the Biblical account. An audience familiar with works like *Beowulf* and *Waldere* would expect to be told not merely what happened but how, not merely who acted but why, yet these were precisely the questions left unasked in Genesis. They were also, as we have seen, the questions which most concerned Sigewulf in the *Interrogationes*, and it is not perhaps too fanciful to see in his inquiries the glimmerings of the typical Germanic reaction to the Jahwist's laconic myth.

The author of *Genesis B* attempted to provide typical Germanic answers. Unlike his English predecessors, who had been content simply to overlay the original text with a veneer of heroic diction and imagery, he imitated the more fundamental literary devices characteristic of the Saga, and wherever necessary invented the situations they were designed to explore. His use of 'flashback', for instance, recalls the same device in *Beowulf*, where, after tracing the genealogy of Hrothgar and describing the building of Heorot, the narrator interrupts the action to tell of the ancestry of Grendel, wherein lies the explanation of his hostility to the hall-dwellers. In much the same way the Saxon poet, having reached the focal point of the story with God's command to the first pair to abstain from the tree of knowledge, breaks off to relate in considerable detail the previous rebellion of Satan and his followers, wherein lies

---

[1] *Beowulf*, 714–19. 'He went under the clouds until he could see the gold-hall of the warriors very clearly, adorned with gold-plate. That was not the first time he sought Hrothgar's home; never in the days of his life, neither before nor since, did he find the hall-thanes with harder fortune.'

the explanation of their hostility to Man.[1] Indeed, the motives of the villains are very similar in the two poems; just as Grendel envies Hrothgar's thanes the delights of their 'winsele', so the banished Satan begrudges Adam and Eve the pleasures of Eden. The Devil's envy, of course, had long been a commonplace of Christian theology, but here it is set in the context of native Germanic notions of loyalty, exile, and revenge. His attempt to overthrow his Creator is pictured as a trusted retainer's attempt to supplant his lord and establish a rival hall with the help of his own *comitatus*:

> ahof hine wið his herran, sohte hetespræce,
> gylpword ongean, nolde gode þeowian.
> cwæð þæt his lic wære leoht 7 scene,
> hwit 7 hiowbeorht; ne meahte he æt his hige findan
> þæt he gode wolde geongerdome
> þeodne þeowian. þuhte him sylfum
> þæt he mægyn 7 cræft maran hæfde
> þonne se halga god habban mihte
> folcgestælna. feala worda gespæc
> se engel ofermodes, þohte þurh his anes cræft
> hu he him strenglicran stol geworhte,
> heahran on heofonum. cwæð þæt hine his hige speone
> þæt he west 7 norð wyrcean ongunne,
> trymede getimbro; cwæð him tweo þuhte
> þæt he gode wolde geongra weorðan.[2]

His plaints when he has been cast out of Heaven resemble in turn those traditionally expressed by the exile, while his hatred of God's new favourites injects into the poem the atmosphere of a dynastic feud such as that which eventually destroyed Heorot.

After his fall Satan is securely fettered in Hell, a prison with bonds of chain and locked doors. In order to compass his revenge, therefore, he has to rely on the assistance of one of his companions.

---

[1] The description of the creation of Eden and of Adam and Eve is not extant in the Old English translation, but it obviously prefaced the story of the fall of the angels, for our fragment begins with God's command to the newly created pair to abstain from the tree of knowledge.

[2] *Genesis B*, 263–77. 'He rose up against his Master and sought hostile speech, uttered a boast, would not serve God. He said that his body was bright and radiant, white and shining; he could not find it in his heart to serve his God with allegiance. It seemed to him that he had more strength and force than holy God could have war-companions. The angel spoke many words in his pride, he thought how through his own force he would build a stronger throne, higher in Heaven. He said that his heart prompted him to work west and north, to establish a building. He said it seemed doubtful to him whether he would be God's thane.'

Ironically, he appeals to the very concept of loyalty which he himself has just betrayed, offering the usual rewards for bravery to anyone who will undertake his mission for him:

> gif ic ænegum þegne þeodenmadmas
> geara forgeafe, þenden we on þan godan rice
> gesælige sæton 7 hæfdon ure setla geweald,
> þonne he me na on leofran tid leanum ne meahte
> mine gife gyldan, gif his gien wolde
> minra þegna hwilc geþafa wurðan
> þæt he up heonon ute mihte
> cuman þurh þas clustro . . .
> Se þe þæt gelæsteð, him bið lean gearo
> æfter to aldre, þæs we her inne magon
> on þyssum fyre forð fremena gewinnan.
> Sittan læte ic hine wið me sylfne, swa hwa swa þæt secgan cymeð
> on þas hatan helle, þæt hie heofoncyninges
> unwurðlice wordum 7 dædum
> lare [forlæten.]¹

At this point of the story there is a lacuna in the text, but it is probably safe to assume that one of his subordinates volunteered, for in the following lines we find another demon being armed with all the trappings of Teutonic mythology. This description suggests that his subsequent activities are to take the form of a military expedition; he is a warrior rather than a tempter. The scene concludes with his escape from Hell, as the fire magically parts for him just as the doors of Heorot had sprung open when Grendel touched them. Thus the stage is set for the central confrontation, which will be played out against this vividly painted backcloth of Germanic concepts.²

So far the poet's raw material had been readily amenable to such treatment. At this juncture, however, he was faced with the rather more difficult problem of presenting the disobedience of Adam and Eve in heroic terms. He solved it by abandoning the standard

¹ *Genesis B*, 409–41. 'If I formerly gave princely treasures to any thane, when we abode happy in the good kingdom and had power over our thrones, then he could not requite me with rewards for my gifts at a better time, if any of my thanes would yet consent that he might make his way up out of here through the barriers. . . . He that performs this, for him will reward be ready ever hereafter, whatever benefits we can gain henceforth in this fire. I will let him sit with myself, whosoever comes to say in this hot hell that they [Adam and Eve] have unworthily foresaken the law of the heavenly King in word and deed.'

² This is familiar critical ground, so I mention only the outstanding points. See C. C. Ferrell, *Teutonic Antiquities in the Anglo-Saxon Genesis*, Halle, 1893; B. J. Timmer, *The Later Genesis*, rev. edn., 1954, pp. 55–57.

patristic doctrine that the Fall consisted in pride and inventing a version of the episode based on the contrast between the angelic and human transgressions which Alcuin had elaborated in the *Interrogationes*: whereas the Devil was the author of his own destruction, Man was deceived by a trick. Although the particular kind of trick to which the first pair succumb in *Genesis B* is admittedly very different from anything Alcuin may have had in mind, it still depends on the crucial distinction between a moral *temptation* and an intellectual *deception*. For the Tempter's sartorial preparations in Hell, far from being a mere convention adopted from the sagas, prove to be the key to his eventual success; his assumption of a disguise. Masquerading as an angel, he tells Adam and Eve that God has sent him to instruct them to eat of the forbidden fruit after all; if they refuse to do so they will be punished. Consequently, the events leading up to the violation of the tree of knowledge can now be rendered consistent with the over-all military tone of the poem. The Fall is brought about not by a moral enticement but by a strategic manœuvre.

The ensuing encounter is broken down into three scenes, which, as in Germanic Saga, are treated dramatically, with the poet acting as a chorus to remind the audience of the motives, tensions, and implications lying beneath the surface of the action. The first of them portrays the Tempter's prior approach to Adam, an innovation necessitated by his pose as an angel: if he really were the emissary of God it would only be natural for him to deliver his message to the man in the first instance. Appealing to Adam's undoubted loyalty, he offers him the allurements of beauty, power, and wisdom as the fruits of virtue rather than of sin. God, he explains, has decided to let Man eat of the tree of knowledge:

> ic eom on his ærende hider
> feorran gefered. ne þæt nu fyrn ne wæs
> þæt ic wið hine sylfne sæt. þa het he me on þysne sið faran,
> het þæt þu þisses ofætes æte.[1]

He has sent a messenger because He did not want to trouble Himself with such a journey—a remark which is heavily ironical if we remember Satan's predicament in Hell. Adam's reply is measured and cautious. He cannot understand why God should have changed

---

[1] *Genesis B*, 496–9. 'I have journeyed far on his errand hither. It was not long ago that I sat with Him Himself. Then He ordered me to go on this journey, ordered that you should eat of this fruit.'

His mind, and he is by no means convinced by the self-styled angel's credentials. Until he has been offered some proof of his good faith he declines to obey.

This preliminary interview establishes two important points which determine the course of the following two scenes. First, Adam's refusal to believe him has given the Devil a weapon to use against Eve; he can appeal not only to her credulity but also to her desire to protect her husband from the consequences of his alleged disobedience. Second, Adam's request for a 'tacen' has taught the Devil how to accomplish his downfall; if Eve can be persuaded to eat the forbidden fruit by offering her some concrete assurance that she is fulfilling the will of God, it should not be difficult for her to convince Adam that the emissary is all he claims to be. The prior temptation of Adam, albeit unsuccessful, suggests the means by which he can finally be brought to destruction.

That the Devil has taken these lessons to heart is immediately evident when he comes to tempt Eve. Instead of repeating his earlier arguments he adopts a less direct approach, and appeals not to Eve's loyalty to God but to her love for Adam. If she will eat of the tree of knowledge and prevail on her husband to do likewise, he tells her, she will be able to avert God's wrath:

> þy ic wat þæt he inc abolgen wyrð
> mihtig on mode. gif þu þeah minum wilt,
> wif willende, wordum hyran,
> þu meaht his þonne rume ræd geþencan.
> gehyge on þinum breostum þæt þu inc bam twam meaht
> wite bewarigan, swa ic þe wisie.
> æt þisses ofetes![1]

She will, moreover, be given a vision of the heavens to confirm the virtue of her deed. At this critical moment the poet holds up the action to describe Eve's gradual submission to the Tempter's suggestions, pointing out that 'hæfde hire wacran hige / metod gemearcod'.[2] And as soon as she has actually partaken of the forbidden fruit he breaks in again to emphasize the irony of the situation, the contrast between the goodness of her motives and the wickedness of her action. Immediately afterwards, as the Devil had promised,

---

[1] *Genesis B*, 557–63. 'Whence I know that the Almighty will be angry with you both in His heart. If, however, you will obey my words willingly, woman, then you may fully consider His counsel. Ponder in your heart that you can ward off punishment from you both, as I shall show you. Eat of this fruit.'

[2] Ibid. 589–90. 'the Lord had endowed her with a weaker mind.'

she receives a vision whereby the heavens and the earth seem to her more spacious and beautiful than ever before. While she is still overwhelmed by this new insight he suggests that she should tell Adam of the power of the fruit. The first stage of the temptation has thus been successfully accomplished. It only remains to make a second assault on Adam, an assault which the Devil has every reason to believe will be more successful than the first, for Eve will be able to offer her husband the one thing which might sway him: the 'tacen' which he had demanded.

The third and final scene of the temptation reveals the importance of this point. After the poet has again intervened to underline the poignancy of the situation, drawing the audience's attention both to the dreadful consequences of what is about to happen and to the mitigating factor of the 'wifes wac geþoht',[1] Eve implores Adam to eat the forbidden fruit with her and describes her miraculous vision:

> Ic mæg heonon geseon
> hwær he sylf siteð, þæt is suð 7 east,
> welan bewunden, se ðas woruld gesceop.
> geseo ic him his englas ymbe hweorfan
> mid feðerhaman, ealra folca mæst,
> wereda wynsumast.[2]

Yet again the poet interrupts, this time to describe the Devil in the background, revelling in the disasters which will follow. When we return to Adam his resolution is weakening, but for the third time in this scene the poet intrudes:

> heo dyde hit þeah þurh holdne hyge, nyste þæt þær hearma swa fela,
> fyrenearfeða, fylgean sceolde
> monna cynne . . .
> Ac wende þæt heo hyldo heofoncyninges
> worhte mid þam wordum þe heo þam were swelce
> tacen oðiewde 7 treowe gehet.[3]

By now Adam has made up his mind, and falls with his wife. The entire episode is brilliantly conceived and executed. In a manner

---

[1] Ibid. 648. 'the woman's weak mind.'

[2] Ibid. 665-70. 'From here I can see where He Himself, who made this world, sits, that is south and east, surrounded with blessedness. I see his angels wheeling round him with their feather-coats, the greatest of hosts, most joyful of companies.'

[3] Ibid. 707-13. 'Yet she did it through loyal intent, she did not know that so many harms, grievous sufferings, would follow for mankind . . . But she thought that she was gaining the favour of the heavenly King with the words with which she showed such a token to the man and promised faith.'

M

very reminiscent of the account in *Beowulf* of Grendel's approach to Heorot, the 'camera' swings from Adam to the Devil, back to Adam, then off to Eve, and finally back to Adam again. The central dilemma of the hero is put into perspective by glances at the psychological forces surrounding him, and each 'shot' brings him closer to the deed itself.

The concluding sequence of the poem is taken up with the immediate reactions of the three protagonists. Whereas the previous scene had been shot in slow motion, with most of the movement coming from the camera, now the figures which had been frozen in a final 'still' suddenly come back to life and speech. The first to break the silence is the Devil. He gives a brief summary of the rebellion and fall of the angels, and offers Satan the consolation of Adam's disobedience to relieve his sufferings in Hell:

> nu hæbbe ic þine hyldo me
> witode geworhte 7 þinne willan gelæst
> to ful monegum dæge. men synt forlædde,
> adam 7 eue.[1]

Having delivered this triumphant 'gylpword', he returns to his master below. This speech, which recalls the similar one made by Satan in the *De Mosaicae Historiae Gestis*, both relieves the almost unbearable tension of the situation and prepares the way for the contrast, already sharpened by the juxtaposition of Satan's rebellion and Adam's disobedience, between the angelic and human falls upon which the structure of the poem rests. By reminding us of Satan's malevolence it sets Man's repentance directly opposite the Devil's envy.

When the Tempter has departed, the fallen pair, who have remained mute and motionless during his outburst, come slowly back to life. Eve realizes that her vision was no more than an illusion, and she and Adam fall to prayer. Adam, like his predecessor in Avitus's poem, reproaches her bitterly for the ills she has brought on them, but she replies with disarming humility and simplicity:

> þu meaht hit me witan, wine min adam,
> wordum þinum. hit þe þeah wyrs ne mæg
> on þinum hyge hreowan þonne hit me æt heortan deð.[2]

---

[1] *Genesis B*, 725–8. 'Now I have gained thy destined favour and performed thy will for full many a day. Men are led astray, Adam and Eve.'

[2] Ibid. 823–5. 'You may reproach me for it with your words, my beloved Adam, but it cannot grieve you in your heart more deeply than it does in mine.'

After another short speech of repentance they go off to clothe themselves and to pray that God should show them 'hu hie on þam
leohte forð libban sceolden'.[1] Here the Old English translation ends,
and if, as the Vatican fragment suggests, the Old Saxon poem
continued further, it must be admitted that the Anglo-Saxon editor
chose a good moment to conclude the translation. The description
of the interrogation and condemnation in *Genesis A* is necessarily
an anti-climax.

The differences between this version of the story and Alcuin's
exposition of the Biblical text in the *Interrogationes* are radical.
The seed of evil is in the tree of death, not in the heart of man, and
Eve partakes of it in the belief that she is saving her husband from
divine retribution, not because she aspires to equality with God.
Her motives are pure, with no suggestion of any 'love of her own
power' or any 'proud presumption'. Nor is Adam's decision to eat
the fruit any less praiseworthy; Eve's vision has assured him of the
messenger's authenticity, and his transgression is the natural consequence of his desire to obey his Maker's instructions. After the
Fall, far from being steadfastly impenitent, both he and Eve freely
acknowledge their guilt and seek for pardon without even the
provocation of God's questions. Nowhere is there even a hint that
they refused to take the responsibility for what they had done or
sought to transfer it to their Creator.

The general intention behind these changes is clear. At every
stage of the story the Saxon poet has gone out of his way to present
Adam and Eve in the most favourable possible light. It is, of course,
only too easy to over-read a work such as this, to educe from it
themes and ideas which would never have occurred to its author,
but the consistency with which the human pair are exonerated can
hardly be accidental. Throughout the poem there is a continual ironic
contrast between the catastrophic nature of the deeds themselves
and the goodness of the motives which inspired them. During Eve's
temptation, for instance, the narrator cannot forbear the comment:

> þæt is micel wundor
> þæt hit ece god æfre wolde
> þeoden þolian, þæt wurde þegn swa monig
> forlædd be þam lygenum þe for þam larum com.[2]

---

[1] Ibid. 850. 'how they were to live henceforth in the world.'
[2] Ibid. 594–7. 'That is a great wonder that eternal God, the Lord, should have
tolerated so many men to be betrayed with lies who came for instruction.'

Later, when she approaches Adam, he again reminds the reader

> þæt heo ongan his wordum truwian,
> læstan his lare, 7 geleafan nom
> þæt he þa bysene from gode brungen hæfde
> þe he hire swa wærlice wordum sægde.[1]

And just as Adam is about to eat the fruit we are told that Eve persuaded him to do so in good faith.

The theme of Eve's innocence in particular is further reinforced by three phrases which echo through the poem like a Wagnerian *leitmotif*. The first of them is introduced as she carries the apple to Adam:

> idesa scenost,
> wifa wlitegost þe on woruld come,
> forþon heo wæs handgeweorc heofoncyninges.[2]

It is repeated when she urges Adam to eat with her: 'idese sciene, wifa wlitegost . . . handweorc godes.'[3] And it appears yet again in the comment with which the poet offsets Adam's rebukes after the Fall:

> idesa scienost,
> wifa wlitegost. hie wæs geweorc godes,
> þeah heo þa on deofles cræft bedroren wurde.[4]

The second phrase is introduced by the Devil as he assures Eve that he serves God 'þurh holdne hyge'.[5] When she has heard him out she begins to trust him, because he has given her the vision as proof of 'his holdne hyge', and so she in turn tempts Adam 'þurh holdne hyge'.[6] The third, and in many ways the most crucial, phrase is stated four times. In answer to the Devil's arguments Adam objected that 'ne þu me oðiewdest ænig tacen / þe he me þurh treowe to onsende',[7] and the Devil puts this experience to good use when he comes to deal with Eve: 'iewde hire tacen 7 treowa gehet.'[8] Con-

---

[1] *Genesis B*, 648–51. 'that she began to trust in his words, to follow his advice, and believed that he had brought from God the command which he told her so truly.'

[2] Ibid. 625–7. 'the most radiant of ladies, most beautiful of women who had been born, because she was the handiwork of the heavenly King.'

[3] Ibid. 699–701. 'radiant lady, most beautiful of women . . . the handiwork of God'.

[4] Ibid. 820–2. 'most radiant of ladies, most beautiful of women. She was the handiwork of God, though she was seduced then into the Devil's power.'

[5] Ibid. 585. 'with loyal intent.'

[6] Ibid. 653, 707. 'his loyal intent'; 'through loyal intent'.

[7] Ibid. 539–40. 'you do not show me any token, that He has sent to me in good faith.'

[8] Ibid. 652. 'he showed her a token and promised good faith.'

vinced by the Tempter's proofs, 'heo þam were swelce / tacen oðiewde 7 treowe gehet.'[1] And when at last the whole deception is revealed the poet gives the phrase a final twist: 'hire þurh untreowa / tacen iewde se him þone teonan geræd.'[2]

But behind this sympathetic picture of the human pair and their motives we catch glimpses of the dark background of death and damnation. At every important crisis the narrator intervenes not only to relieve Adam and Eve of any moral blame but also to emphasize the terrible consequences of their actions. Just before commenting on Eve's innocence, for example, he pronounces that 'ne wearð wyrse dæd / monnun gemearcod'.[3] As she approaches Adam the action is again held up while the poet enlarges on the evils contained in the fruit,[4] and, when Adam is on the verge of eating, the description of Eve's good faith is balanced with the reminder that

> hit wæs þeah deaðes swefn 7 deofles gespon,
> hell 7 hinnsið 7 hæleða forlor,
> menniscra morð, þæt hie to mete dædon
> ofet unfæle.[5]

Thus although the Fall itself is softened its results are constantly highlighted. The figures in the foreground may be painted in gentle pastel colours, but they cast deep shadows on to the sombre landscape in which they move.

The literary effect of this is to create a profound sense of ambiguity. As in certain kinds of tragedy, the reader's response is divided between pity for the protagonists and fear at the outcome of their actions. We feel no more inclined to blame this Adam and this Eve than we do to blame Oedipus for his hideous mistakes; their errors are errors of judgement, not sins, and the nemesis which overtakes them is determined by a causal rather than a moral law. Good tragedy, however, is very rarely good theology, and the doctrinal implications of *Genesis B* are far more alarming than any that have been discovered by recent critics in *Paradise Lost*. The

---

[1] Ibid. 712–13. 'she showed the man such a token and promised good faith.'
[2] Ibid. 772–3. 'he showed her a token through bad faith, he who counselled the wrong to them.'
[3] Ibid. 593–4. 'A worse deed was not decreed for men.'
[4] Ibid. 633–45.
[5] Ibid. 719–22. 'But it was the sleep of death and the Devil's allurement, Hell and death and the perdition of Man, the destruction of humanity, which they took for food, the evil fruit.'

deed, it insists, was evil, and the deed is all that matters; the motives, the moral guilt or innocence of the agents, are totally irrelevant, for the law is implacable, and a certain action will be followed by certain inevitable consequences, regardless of the circumstances and characters of its perpetrators. The path to Hell is paved with good intentions.

To account for such a presentation of the story we have to turn to the poem's theological and literary context. I stated earlier that in the Dark Ages the Church's teaching on the Fall was almost purely Augustinian. So far as the exegesis of the narrative is concerned that is true. So far as the doctrine that was read into it is concerned, on the other hand, my original statement needs qualification. For Augustine's opinions on predestination and the depravity of the human will were never accepted in their full rigour by the Western Church. Cassian, Gregory the Great, Isidore of Seville, and Aldhelm all found it necessary to take a more optimistic view of Man's ability to contribute to his own salvation, and in ninth-century Saxony the same attitude is reflected in the dispute over the activities of the monk Gottschalk, who revived all the arguments which had been thrashed out in the Pelagian and Semi-Pelagian controversies by attempting to resurrect the Augustinian doctrine of predestination in its severest form. The reaction of the Saxon Church was swift: in 848 Gottschalk's ideas were condemned at the Synod of Mayence, while their propagator was committed to the care of Hincmar. At the Synod of Quierzy in 849 the condemnation was repeated, and Gottschalk himself was cast into prison, where he remained until his death in 869.[1] In the light of this affair *Genesis B* may be seen to be typical of its age in accepting the letter while excluding the spirit of Augustinianism. A minimizing account of the Fall would have been by no means out of place on the Continent in this period, particularly when it was interspersed with more strictly orthodox declarations concerning the disasters attendant on Adam's disobedience.

Still more potent, I believe, was the influence of the poem's literary environment. Its ambivalent attitude towards the Fall was the natural product of two conflicting strains in Germanic thought. On the one hand, there was the prevailing tendency, which we have already seen at work in Anglo-Saxon religious poetry, to define

---

[1] For a detailed account of this controversy see M. L. W. Laistner, op. cit., ch. xii; A. Harnack, op. cit. v. 292–302.

spiritual values in physical terms, to present the activities of God and His saints as heroic military exploits. To see Adam's transgression as an evil deed rather than a moral failure, therefore, would have been only natural; he was simply out-manœuvred and defeated by a more cunning enemy. On the other hand, there was the general predilection for studying motive, reflected in the structure of Germanic Saga and in Sigewulf's questions to Alcuin. This overriding concern with motive and circumstance was, of course, the exact converse of the purely pragmatic view of men's actions noted above. In moral and realistic terms what mattered was to do and die; in poetic and imaginative terms the real issue was the reason why. It is this strange paradox, perhaps, which is responsible for the ambiguities which lie at the heart of that complex and often beautiful poem, *Genesis B*.

VI

THE SCHOLASTIC TREATMENTS

THE nature and extent of the changes which took place in the interpretation of the Fall story during the transition from the Dark to the Middle Ages can readily be measured by setting beside Alcuin's *Interrogationes* the corresponding passages from the most influential and characteristic of the medieval Biblical commentaries, Peter Comestor's *Historia Scholastica*.[1] The popularity of this twelfth-century *compendium* exceeded even that of the *Glossa Ordinaria* itself, for whereas the latter consisted merely of a selection of patristic quotations appended to the text of the Vulgate, the *Historia*, like the Book of Jubilees, offered a connected and eminently readable paraphrase of the Scriptural narrative, filled out with legendary and theological amplifications, which could be enjoyed by the unlearned quite simply as a story.

According to Comestor, Adam was created in the image of God in so far as his soul and his reason were concerned. His possession of these faculties, together with the fact that the Trinity consulted over his creation and gave him mastery over the animals, was the chief indication of his original dignity.[2] Composed of red earth, as his name indicated,[3] he was first formed in the prime of life in a Damascene field, whence he was transferred to the garden of Eden.[4] There he was appointed to labour, not so much of necessity as for

---

[1] The Middle Ages produced, of course, several other detailed commentaries on Genesis, notably those of Bruno Astensis, Rupertus Tuitensis, Ernaldus of Bonneval, and Peter Abelard, but none of them was as influential as the *Historia*. Perhaps the most striking evidence of its popularity is furnished by Caxton. In the 1438 translation of the *Golden Legend* the life of Adam was a version of the Jewish Vita Adae et Evae almost exactly similar to that in the Wheatley Manuscript. This life Caxton replaced with a loose translation of the early chapters of the *Historia*, which, he evidently felt, was more in keeping with Christian ideas on the Fall. I say a 'loose translation' advisedly—in it the serpent is said to be 'hotter' than the other beasts of the field, the translator clearly having mistaken the Latin 'callidior' for 'calidior'.

[2] *Hist. Schol.*, Lib. Gen. ix.

[3] Ibid. xviii. Josephus had first connected the name Adam with the Hebrew *adamah* 'red earth' in his *Antiquities*. See above, Ch. II, p. 42.

[4] *Hist. Schol.*, Lib. Gen. xii–xiii. Compare *Genesis and Exodus*, 207; *Cursor Mundi*, 585–8; *Miroure*, p. 12; *Fall of Princes*, 505–8.

his own recreation and delight. God further hoped that 'he might subdue himself by discipline just as he subdued the land by tilling it, in order that he might submit himself to his Creator just as the earth submitted to him'.[1] The various fruits growing in the garden were planted there to provide him with food, even though he was in one sense already immortal: 'If you ask why man was given food before the Fall, though he was immortal, let us say that the immortality in which he was created had to be maintained by food, unlike the immortal life to come which will not require food. For the first is the possibility of not dying, the latter will be the impossibility of dying.'[2] Foreseeing the Fall, God also created the animals, who would eventually provide Adam with food, clothing, and help,[3] and paraded them before him so that he should realize that he was their master and that none of them was like him.[4]

Without Eve, however, Adam would have been incomplete. Her name 'virago' was derived from her origin 'a viro acta',[5] and she was made after her husband, not, as the Rabbis had suggested, together with him in the form of a hermaphrodite. Nor, as the Rabbis had also suggested, did God first make a woman out of the earth and form Eve from Adam's rib only when he had rejected his first companion.[6] The sleep which fell upon Adam during this operation was no ordinary slumber but 'an ecstasy, during which he is believed to have been in the heavenly meeting place. When he awoke from it he prophesied concerning the union of Christ and the Church and of the flood to come, and at the same time learned about the judgement through fire, and later he passed on this knowledge to his children.'[7] The subsequent command to be fruitful and multiply revealed that the heretics were mistaken in assuming that there could be no intercourse without sin.[8] On the contrary, Adam and Eve were naked and unashamed like children so long as their sexual impulses were under the control of their wills.[9]

The tree of life was so called 'from the effect which it had, furnishing the man who ate of it regularly with everlasting strength, so that no infirmity, neither old age nor worry, could cause him to deteriorate and die'.[10] But the tree of knowledge was named 'from

---

[1] *Hist. Schol.*, Lib. Gen. xv. [2] Ibid. x.
[3] Ibid. viii–ix. Compare *Genesis and Exodus*, 171–8.
[4] *Hist. Schol.*, Lib. Gen. xvi. [5] Ibid. xviii. [6] Ibid. ix, xvii.
[7] Ibid. xvi. This depends on the Septuagint's rendering of the Hebrew for 'sleep' as '*exstasis*'.
[8] Ibid. x. [9] Ibid. xx. [10] Ibid. xiii.

the events which followed the tasting of it. Before that man did not know what was evil, as he had not experienced it.' Alternatively, 'the evil may mean disobedience, the good, obedience, since after he had eaten of the fruit he came to know how much good there was in obedience and how much evil in disobedience'.[1] The command to abstain from this one tree was given before the creation of Eve; no doubt, therefore, 'it was given to the man that through him it might pass to the woman: or perhaps there is an anticipation, in that the command was given to both at the same time, after the creation of the woman'.[2] The threat of death which accompanied it meant only that if he disobeyed Adam would become mortal, not that he would die at once, and the command as a whole 'was given by some subject creature, just as divine commands have come to us through prophets and angels'.[3] The law governing Man's life in Eden thus consisted of two parts: the precept to be fruitful and multiply, and the prohibition of the tree of knowledge.[4]

Up to this point there has been little out of the ordinary about Comestor's interpretation of the story, but when he comes to discuss the temptation his comments become more original. For instance, though he maintains the traditional association of Satan with the serpent, he does so in a most unusual form: 'This Lucifer did through the serpent (the serpent then walked erect like a man; it was the curse that prostrated it). . . . Also he chose a kind of serpent, as Bede says, which had a face like a maiden's, since like approves of like, and he caused its tongue to speak although the creature was unaware of it (just as he speaks through fanatics and men possessed unbeknown to them).'[5] While the serpent's upright gait was a common rabbinic idea and the comparison with a man possessed of a demon was a standard patristic simile, the belief that the reptile had a woman's face has no known precedent. It appears in none of the extant works of Bede, whom Comestor cites as his authority, and it is not mentioned in any of the other major exegetical works on Genesis prior to the *Historia*. In more orthodox vein Comestor goes on to point out that the woman was chosen for the preliminary assault 'as she was less foreseeing and sure of herself'.[6] By posing the first

[1] Loc. cit. Comestor also distinguished between knowledge, '*scientia*', and experience, '*experientia*'. Adam knew the difference between good and evil but he had not yet experienced evil.

[2] *Hist. Schol.*, Lib. Gen. xv.   [3] Loc. cit.   [4] Ibid. xv.

[5] Ibid. xxi. In the *Glossa Ordinaria* there is a note of Nicholas of Lyra's that the serpent with the woman's face 'has no scriptural authority'.   [6] Loc. cit.

question, he adds, the Tempter hoped that 'the reply might give
him a chance to say what he had come to say. And so it happened.
For when the woman, as if in doubt, answered "Lest perchance we
die" the serpent said confidently of the command "By no means
will you die" because in her doubt she could easily be persuaded into
any opinion.'[1] The reason given here for the serpent's initial inquiry
concerning all the trees in the garden is almost certainly of Jewish
origin—in the previous century Rashi had observed that it began
the conversation with a deliberate mistake 'to compel her to reply
to him . . . and he would then go on to speak to her about that
particular tree'.[2] The attribution of doubt to Eve must, on the other
hand, be a Christian idea, for it depends on the Vulgate's rendering
of the Hebrew subjunctive by 'forte'. Thus Comestor's contemporary, Hildebert, explained in his *Tractatus Theologicus*: 'The temptation was carried out in this way: first he approached her with a
question in order to gather from her reply how he ought to converse
with her about the rest of the matter. . . . In these words, "Lest
perchance we die . . ." was given the ground for tempting her.'[3]
Both commentators, it may be remarked, are primarily interested in
the way in which Eve's decision was made rather than the sins it
involved, and the same is true of Comestor's treatment of Adam's
transgression: ' "and she ate, and gave of it to her husband", perhaps
beguiling him first with persuasive words, which the writer passes
over for the sake of brevity. He was easily persuaded by her because,
having previously believed that the woman would die forthwith,
following the edict of the Lord, and seeing that she had not died,
he considered that the Lord had uttered His threat only to frighten
them "and he ate of it".'[4] Although a very similar account of the
episode had been worked out by Augustine, Comestor gives it far
greater prominence than it had enjoyed in any earlier work.

Hereafter he is less imaginative. The fallen pair's awareness of
their nakedness, he asserts, was due to the onset of carnal concupiscence; God asked Adam where he was hiding in order to show
him his moral predicament; Adam and Eve did not take the opportunity to confess; and the serpent was not questioned because 'it
had done this not of itself, but the devil through it'.[5] More interesting

[1] Loc. cit.   [2] Rashi *On Genesis*, iii. 1.
[3] *Tract. Theol.* xxvi, translated in G. Boas and A. O. Lovejoy, *Essays on Primitivism*,
Baltimore, 1948, pp. 83–85.
[4] *Hist. Schol.*, Lib. Gen. xxii.   [5] Ibid. xxiii.

is his analysis of the appropriateness of the various curses: the serpent envied, lied, and deceived, so it was condemned to crawl, eat earth, and lose its voice; Adam who sinned only in eating the fruit, was sentenced only to a reduced diet; Eve, who sinned both in pride and in eating the fruit, was subjected to her husband and cursed in her fruit; and the earth was punished because the trespass arose from one of its trees.[1] Finally, Comestor interprets the coats of skins as the signs of Man's mortality, and emphasizes the mercy of the expulsion in the usual way.[2]

Both the differences and the similarities between this and Alcuin's exposition of the story are readily apparent. Like the *Interrogationes* the *Historia* is constructed on the Augustinian pattern: Comestor's views on Adam's original condition, the significance of the two trees, Eve's temptation of her husband, and the new sexual awareness that came with the Fall all derive ultimately from the works of the great Bishop of Hippo.[3] But into this orthodox design Comestor has woven many more exotic notions, the majority of them rabbinic. Sometimes ideas from the *Talmud* and the *Midrash Rabbah* are quoted only to be rejected, as in the case of Adam's androgynous nature and the prior creation of Lilith. More often, however, they are accepted, as in the case of the derivation of Adam's name, the belief that the serpent walked upright, the strategy of his opening question, and the reason for the curse on the earth.[4] Yet even when Comestor's use of Jewish material has been taken into account there still remains a world of difference between his exegesis and that of his predecessors; the distinctiveness of his commentary cannot be wholly explained away by his occasional excursions into the *haggadah*. The new element is the characteristically medieval concern for rationality. Comestor is constantly preoccupied with demonstrating the reason, or, as a Middle-English author would say, the 'skille', for every little detail of the story. The kind of reason he is interested in, moreover, has little or nothing in common with the kind Sigewulf had demanded from Alcuin. It is logical rather than psychological, it uncovers dialectical rather than human relationships, and it frequently has a forensic rather than a literary slant. The analysis of the commands given to Adam and of the justice of God's sentence, for instance, bespeaks not a poet's mind, nor even a moralist's, but a lawyer's.

---

[1] Loc. cit.   [2] *Hist. Schol.*, Lib. Gen. xxiv.   [3] See above, Ch. III, pp. 93–99.
[4] See above, Ch. II, pp. 47, 53.

This fundamental change of attitude on the part of the Biblical expositor reflects an equally fundamental change of attitude on the part of his audience. For by the Middle Ages, in Western Europe at least, paganism was no longer an active threat, and a medieval writer could safely assume that the overwhelming majority of his readers would be deeply imbued with Christian beliefs. As Boccaccio remarked in his *Genealogy of the Pagan Gods*:

Indeed, in the days when the Church was just taking root among the pagans, the Christians found it expedient to press hard against the pagan rites and observances, colored as men's notions of religion were by the origin and by the very perseverance of paganism. It was a precaution lest readers of pagan literature be caught by the claw of antiquity, and return as a dog to their vomit. But today, by the grace of Christ, our strength is very great; the universally hateful doctrine of paganism has been cast into utter and perpetual darkness, and the Church in triumph holds the fortress of the enemy.[1]

The great adversary now was not a rival religion but irreligion, not the myths of the heathen deities of Saga but the worldliness of the all too human heroes of Romance. Consequently it was more important to oust the values of secularism than the gods of paganism. The author of the fourteenth-century Biblical paraphrase, *Cursor Mundi*, for instance, noted regretfully that 'Man yhernes rimes for to here, / And romans red on maneres sere',[2] and went on to mention Alexander, Caesar, Brutus, Arthur, and Tristram as typical subjects. His poem on the contrary, he insisted, was dedicated to no worldly paramour but to the Virgin Mary:

> Off suilk an suld ȝe [mater] take,
> Crafty þat can rimes make;
> Of hir to mak bath rim and sang,
> And luue hire suette sun amang.[3]

It is not therefore surprising that just as the Germanic religious poets had expressed the Christian stories in terms associated with pagan Saga so their medieval successors superimposed the vocabulary of Romance on their Scriptural material. The Anglo-Saxon

[1] Charles Osgood, *Boccaccio on Poetry*, Princeton, 1930, pp. 123–4.
[2] *Cursor Mundi*, 1–2. I quote from the Cotton text.
[3] Ibid. 85–88. In similar fashion the author of a French versified Biblical paraphrase expresses his intention of treating the life of Christ rather than the adventure of Oliver and Roland. See J. Bonnard, *Les Traductions de la Bible en vers français au moyen âge*, Paris, 1884, ch. vi.

warrior-Christ living in the heavenly wine-hall thus gave way to the medieval conception of Christ as a knight and of Heaven as a 'hali ture' or 'hali palais',[1] in which God set Lucifer 'heist in his hall / Als prince and sire ouer oþer alle'.[2] When the rebel angel betrayed this trust he could no longer stay in 'þat curt, þat es sa clene'.[3] Again, a medieval sermon described the garden of Eden as 'a siker toure of Paradice',[4] and early in the fifteenth century Lydgate pictured it as the kind of idealized garden one might expect to find in a love-vision or a courtly Romance:

> The soil enbroudid ful off somer floures,
> Wher weedis wikke hadde noon interesse;
> For God and Kynde with fresshnesse off coloures
> And with ther tapitis & motles off gladnesse
> Had maad that place habounde in al suetnesse;
> And fresshe Flora, which is off floures queene,
> Hir lyuere made off a perpetuel greene.[5]

The Eden of Hilary's *Metrum in Genesim*, adapted from the classical concept of the Golden Age, was largely an agricultural paradise, while the Eden of *Genesis A* had been distinguished by the still more rudimentary advantages of clement weather and amenable country-side. Here the perfect farm and the perfect estate have been succeeded by the more sophisticated concept of the perfect garden.

Nor was this 'medievalization' merely a matter of such super-ficial features as descriptive vocabulary. It went considerably deeper, shaping the meaning that was given both to the Fall itself and to the nature of Man's subsequent predicament. The heroic values em-bodied in Germanic Saga had, as we have seen, put all the emphasis on military prowess, with the result that in *Genesis B* Adam's dis-obedience was presented as little more than a strategic blunder. For the medieval mind, however, pure violence had no such great appeal. In a universe governed by the laws of a rational Creator even the chaotic forces of lust and hate were expected to obey certain rules. The code of courtly love gave order and formality to con-cupiscence, while the elaborate etiquette of the chivalric joust imposed a measure of discipline on human irascibility. At a still more refined level, disputes were settled by verbal rather than

---

[1] *Cursor Mundi*, 418, 413.   [2] Ibid. 439–40.   [3] Ibid. 467.
[4] See W. O. Ross, *Middle English Sermons*, E.E.T.S. ccix, 1940, 313.
[5] *Fall of Princes*, 533–9.

physical encounters; indeed, if there is one thought-form characteristic of the Middle Ages that form is the debate, ranging from the
ribald invective of 'flyting' on the one hand to the chaste dialectic
of scholastic philosophy on the other. The natural outcome of these
tendencies was a widespread interest in judicial procedure, which
catered at one and the same time for the prevailing concern with law
and with argument, and the courtroom displaced the battlefield as
the setting for the Biblical drama.

The Anglo-Saxon concept of God as a war-lord consequently
gave way to the concept of God as a judge, the warrior-Christ
became Christ the advocate, and the rebel Satan reassumed his Old
Testament role of celestial prosecutor. Thus Hugh of St. Victor
worked out the problem of Man's salvation as a legal case:

> Were man, then, to have such an advocate that by his power the devil
> could be brought into court, man would justly speak against his dominion,
> since the devil had no just case for making a lawful claim on man. But
> no such advocate could be found save God alone. However, God was
> unwilling to take up man's case, because he was still angry at man for his
> sin. It was necessary, therefore, that man should first placate God, and
> thereafter, with God as his advocate, begin his suit against the devil.[1]

The problem was solved by Christ, who undertook to placate God
and defend Man. Peter Abelard, too, though writing from a different
theological standpoint, defined the situation in similar terms:

> And what right to possess mankind could the devil possibly have unless
> perhaps he had received man for the purposes of torture through the
> express permission, or even the assignment, of the Lord? . . . Where one
> slave was about to be set over the other and receive authority over him,
> it would never do for the more evil one who had absolutely no justification
> for preferment to be promoted; but it would be much more reasonable
> that the person who was seduced should possess a full claim for redress
> over the man who had caused the harm by his act of seduction.[2]

The ultimate value to which both these passages appeal is justice. In
the Middle Ages more than ever before theologians were concerned
with demonstrating not God's benevolence, nor even His omnipotence, but His justice. Believing as they did that justice had been
done, they set themselves the task of ensuring that it was seen to

---

[1] *On the Sacraments of the Christian Faith*, I. viii. 4, translated in L.C.C. x, 1956,
303–4.
[2] *Exposition of the Epistle to the Romans*, II. ii, translated in L.C.C. x, 1956, 281.

have been done, and this overriding purpose informs every major theological work produced from the twelfth to the fifteenth century. To justify the ways of God to Man became the aim of writers as disparate as Comestor, Abelard, and Aquinas, whose *Summa Theologica* is perhaps the greatest monument ever erected to the austere and implacable queen of the virtues.

The essentially forensic character of this way of thinking is evident at every stage of the medieval treatments of the Fall story. The rebellion of Lucifer, for instance, was frequently described as a trespass in the legal sense rather than as a military insurrection. In *Ðe Deuelis Perlament*, the *Canticum de Creatione*, and the *Towneley* and *Chester* plays on the subject the Devil does not attempt to overthrow God by force of arms; abusing his appointment as 'Govenour' and violating the ideal of 'lewtye',[1] he simply sits on His throne while He is engaged in creating the world.[2] His motive in the latter two works is the conventional one, pride, but in the *Canticum* he falls for the same reason as he had in the Vita Adae et Evae, because he refused to worship Adam:

> 'Ich was ar þe warld bigan,
> Er euer god maked man;
> þerfore', he seyd, 'so mot yt be:
> He schal first anoure me.'[3]

His refusal here to yield precedence to Man or do him homage accords perfectly with the *Cursor Mundi*'s picture of him as a proud knight, God's chief 'comandur'.[4]

Legalistic principles are still more prominent in the case of Adam's defection. Robert Grosseteste's *Chasteau d'Amour* portrays the first man as a serf who was given a beautiful estate to hold for his divine landlord:

> Now was þer a feyre franches,
> Was ordenyd to Adam & all hys,
> Sych an herytage euer-mo
> To haue wonyd in with-outen wo![5]

---

[1] *Chester*, i. 92, 153.

[2] *Ðe Deuelis Perlament*, 339–44; *Canticum de Creatione* (MS. Auch.), 27 et seq.; *Towneley*, i. 77–131; *Chester*, i. 69–192.

[3] *Canticum*, 3–6. See above, Ch. II, p. 56.

[4] *Cursor Mundi*, 453.

[5] *Chasteau d'Amour*, 115–18. I quote from one of the English versions of this work printed in C. Horstmann, *Altenglische Legenden*, Heilbronn, 1881.

He was bound to keep two laws, the 'naturall' and the 'posytyfe', that is, to obey God and to abstain from the forbidden tree. When he broke both commandments he lost his 'herytage':

> For defaute he lefte þe Joys suete,
> And þat was skyll: so do mene ȝete:
> For defaute euery wyght
> Hys herytage may lefe ryȝht;
> At kynges courte, in euery londe,
> ȝit men haue sych lawys fonde.[1]

Thanks to his disobedience,

> Now be we thrall þat are wer fre.
> Thrall he is þat to hym longys
> What seruys he vnderfongys.
>
> . . .
>
> When he seruys in seruage,
> He hade no franches of herytage:
> Than when he is all thrall become,
> Hys fre herytage is hym benome.[2]

The crux of the problem is that Man could not hope to win back his 'herytage' until he could find

> A man þat borne is of fre kynd,
> And þat he be of ryȝht lynage,
> Forto clame his herytage.[3]

Christ finally fulfilled these conditions and restored Man to his original inheritance. The over-all argument is much the same as Hugh of St. Victor's, but it is made still more pointed by being worked out in terms of feudal land-law.

Although this is perhaps the most elaborate example of the application of legal phraseology to the story, it is by no means the only one. The author of *The Stanzaic Life of Christ* claimed that by succumbing to the temptation Eve wrote the Devil a 'borogh' for her children, and that Christ

> for synne that ho borowet hade,
> sched his blode and whit hir dette
> and suche a manumissioun made.[4]

---

[1] *Chasteau d'Amour* 177–82. Compare *Cursor Mundi*, 9477–8.
[2] *Chasteau d'Amour* 186–94. Compare *Cursor Mundi*, 9482 et seq.
[3] *Chasteau d'Amour* 202–4. Compare *Cursor Mundi*, loc. cit.
[4] *Stanzaic Life of Christ*, 6406–8.

And a medieval preacher clarified the issues at stake in the Redemption by invoking the principles involved in the making and execution of wills. Birth, travail, and death, he stated, were the 'testament þat Adam, our formast fadyr, made to all his ospryng aftyr hym. . . . But Crist—blessyt most be he!—he come forto be executure of þys testament.'[1] Just as in the Anglo-Saxon treatments the etiquette of the wine-hall was used to illuminate the poignancy of the Fall, so here the medieval codes of serfdom and inheritance were adduced to demonstrate the impeccable justice of God's dealings with Man.

Of all the episodes in the story, however, the interrogation and condemnation were most obviously amenable to forensic treatment. As we have seen, Comestor went to some lengths to prove the appropriateness of the various curses, and several other medieval authors followed his example. The omission of any question to the serpent evidently seemed unjust to some of them, for in flat contradiction to the patristic view that God deliberately ignored him the authors of *Ludus Coventriae*, the *Norwich B* play on the Fall, the *Ordinale de Origine Mundi*, and *Ðe Lyff of Adam and Eve* in the Vernon MS. all claimed that God did in fact interrogate the reptile.[2] The latter two further refined the episode by making the curses follow the questions,[3] and the *Ludus Coventriae* and *Genesis and Exodus* (*c.* 1250) by reversing the order of the curses so that they corresponded to the order of the questions.[4]

More far-reaching in their implications were the various attempts to assess the relative guilt of the three protagonists. Comestor's analysis had hinted that Eve sinned more grievously than Adam, and Vincent of Beauvais took the same view. Eve, he showed, sinned in four ways: by desiring to be as God, by disobeying Him, by making her husband eat the fruit with her, and by refusing to acknowledge her guilt. Adam, on the other hand, did not aspire to divinity; he merely wished to avoid offending his wife. His sins, therefore, were only two: eating the apple and attempting to exculpate himself afterwards. For this reason the woman was punished more severely than the man. But in one important respect, Vincent noted, Adam's guilt did outweigh Eve's: whereas she was deceived,

---

[1] *Mirk's Festial*, p. 1.

[2] *Ludus Coventriae*, ii. 309–24; *Norwich B*, 79–82; *Ordinale*, 301–10; *Lyff of Adam and Eve*, in C. Horstmann, *Sammlung Altenglischer Legenden*, Heilbronn, 1878, p. 222.

[3] Horstmann, op. cit., p. 222; *Ordinale*, 261–316.

[4] *Ludus Coventriae*, ii. 325–48; *Genesis and Exodus*, 349 et seq.

he sinned in full knowledge of the facts.[1] Aquinas argued the case along very similar lines. So far as the actual circumstances were concerned Adam's sin was the greater, because 'it would seem that the woman sinned through ignorance, but the man through assured knowledge' and also because 'he was more perfect than the woman'.[2] Apart from that, however, Eve's sin was the more serious 'because she was more puffed up than the man. For the woman believed in the serpent's persuasive words. . . . On the other hand, the man did not believe this to be true.'[3] In the second place, not content with sinning herself, Eve made Adam sin with her. Finally, Adam's sin was ameliorated by the fact that he sinned 'out of a certain friendly good-will, on account of which a man will sometimes offend God rather than make an enemy of his friends'.[4]

While all these sins, whether major or minor, were eventually destined to be forgiven, the Devil's was irredeemable. Ever since Origen's opinion that Satan would ultimately achieve salvation had been refuted, the Church had held firmly to the view that his fall could never be repaired. In an age so much concerned with justice this belief clearly demanded some explanation. Two were offered. The first was based upon a distinction identical with that made by Alcuin between the Devil, who was the author of his own crime, and Man, who was deceived by a trick. The author of *Cursor Mundi*, for example, justified God's forgiveness of Adam's sin thus:

> For he wit vikeed red was soght;
> þe find was mare worthe to blam
> þat with his suik bi-suak adam.[5]

In a sermon in *Mirk's Festial* Adam excused himself on the same grounds: 'Then prayde Adam sore wepyng to God þat he schuld not set to hard vengens apon hym, but haue mercy apon hym, and haue reward how he synned by ygnorance, and not by males, and was deceyuet by envy of the fende.'[6] To this another medieval sermon added a second possible explanation: 'On skill is for þe feend synned only of ys own schrewdenes in pride with-owte anny temptacion of anny oþur, and þat was for is bewte and is feyrnes. . . . Anoþur skill may be þis, þat mankeend loved hym [God] and preyd hym of grace, but þe dewell wold neuer do so.'[7] It is this second reason

---

[1] *Speculum Historiale*, ii. 42.   [2] *Summa*, II. clxiii. 4.
[3] Loc. cit.   [4] Loc. cit.   [5] *Cursor Mundi*, 816–18.
[6] *Mirk's Festial*, p. 66.   [7] W. O. Ross, op. cit., p. 315.

that Christ uses in Ðe Deuelis Perlament to reject the Devil's attempt to sue for mercy.[1]

The effect of all these comparisons was to minimize the Fall itself, or at least Adam's part in it. Comestor, Vincent, and Aquinas all tended to take a sympathetic attitude towards his sins, and their views were reflected in the literary treatments. The idea, popularized by Comestor, that Eve beguiled her husband with persuasive words received particular attention. The author of Purity, for example, observed that 'þurh þe eggyng of Eve he ete of an apple',[2] and the author of Genesis and Exodus that

> So manie times ghe him scroðt,
> Queðer so him was lef or loðt,
> for to forðen is fendes wil,
> At he ðat fruit, and dede unskil.[3]

Eve's ability to move Adam's feelings was, according to The Fall and Passion, the very reason why the Tempter approached her first:

> whi com he raþer to eue þan he com to adam
> ichul ȝou telle sires by leue. for womman is lef euer to man.
> womman mai turne man-is wille whare ȝho wol pilt hir to:
> þat is þe resun an skille þat þe deuyl com hir first to.[4]

The medieval poets were almost unanimous in their opinion of the form of persuasion Eve actually brought to bear on her husband. In the age of courtly love the Augustinian 'friendly good-will' was inevitably transformed into something much deeper than mere fellow feeling: Adam betrayed God for the same reason as Launcelot betrayed Arthur; for love. In the Chasteau d'Amour it is asserted that Adam lost his inheritance 'fore lufe of hys wyfe';[5] a sermon in Mirk's Festial explained that 'fore Adam loued hyr and wold not wroth hur, he toke an appull';[6] and the author of the Speculum Humanae Salvationis (c. 1309), who usually followed Comestor very closely, went out of his way to emphasize this new point:

> That Adam shuld of the fruyte ete with hir instode Eue
> Whilk ete for hoege luf þt he shuld noght hire greue

. . .

---

[1] Ðe Deuelis Perlament, 305–54. Compare Speculum Historiale, ii. 48. This emphasis on Adam's repentance may have been the result of the popularity of the Vita Adae et Evae, whose subject was the penitence of the fallen pair. See above, Ch. II, pp. 55–56.
[2] Purity, 241.   [3] Genesis and Exodus, 339–42.
[4] Fall and Passion, 27–30.   [5] Chasteau, 150.   [6] Mirk's Festial, p. 66.

And thus Adam for luf ete with dame Eue his wyue.

.   .   .

ffor thogh the Bibles text apertely noght it write
No doubt scho broght him inne with faging wordes white.[1]

In the *Ordinale de Origine Mundi* the process can be seen in action:

> E. Since thou wilt not believe,
> Thou shalt lose my love.
> Ever whilst thou livest,
> Here thou shalt not see me again.

> A. Eve, rather than thou be angry,
> I will do all as thou wishest.
> Bring it me immediately,
> And I will eat it.[2]

The heroic Adam of the *De Mosaicae Historiae Gestis* ate because his wife had insinuated that he was a coward, and the stolid Germanic Adam of *Genesis B* because he had been given the proof he had demanded. To these was now added the romantic Adam, whose motives, no less surely than those of his predecessors, mirrored the values of the literary convention in which he moved.

The assessment of the comparative guilt of Adam and Satan was equally potent in minimizing the former's. Just as in *Genesis B* the contrast between the angelic and human transgressions produced a minimal version of the latter, so in the medieval treatments the continual emphasis on the Devil's trickery and Adam's innocence resulted in a very sympathetic view of Man's first disobedience. It was the desire to stress the Devil's trickery that seems to have determined the distinctively medieval treatment of the serpent, for instance. Patristic commentators had claimed that Satan entered the snake either because it was the only animal he was permitted to use or because its tortuous windings accorded with his devious nature. According to most medieval authors, on the contrary, the Devil chose the serpent because it was peculiarly fitted to deceive Eve by virtue of its appearance, its 'lady visage'.[3] This idea, first put forward by Comestor, was taken up by a large number of later writers. It appears, for instance, in the *Speculum Humanae Salvationis*, the *Chester* play on the Fall, the fifteenth-century *Metrical Paraphrase*

---

[1] See A. H. Huth, *The Miroure of Mans Saluacioune*, 1888, p. 13. This is a fifteenth-century English translation of the *Speculum Humanae Salvationis*.

[2] *Ordinale*, 241–8.   [3] *Piers Plowman*, B passus, xviii. 335.

of the Old Testament, Vincent's *Speculum Naturale* (*c.* 1215), and *Piers Plowman*,[1] besides finding a place in most medieval illustrations of the Fall.[2] Eve, as Bruno Astensis remarked, was not deceived by a palpable Devil; she yielded to the reasoning of an animal whose innocence she had no reason to doubt.[3] Such guile on the part of the Tempter necessarily ameliorated the sin of the tempted. Indeed, in *Piers Plowman*, the Devil himself confesses as much:

> 'That is sothe,' seyde Sathan 'but I me sore drede,
> For thow gete hem with gyle and his gardyne breke,
> And in semblaunce of a serpent sat on the appeltre,
> And eggedest hem to ete Eue by hir-selue,
> And toldest hir a tale of tresoun were the wordes;
> And so thow haddest hem oute and hider atte laste.
> It is nouȝte graythely geten there gyle is the rote.[4]

Satan's fears are seen to be well justified when Christ argues later in the same passus:

> 'For the dede that thei dede thi deceyte it made;
> With gyle thow hem gete agayne al resoun.'[5]

Which brings us to the Redemption itself, where the essentially forensic tenor of medieval thought is perhaps more clearly evident than anywhere else.

The basic issues involved in God's intention to repair the Fall were set out in detail in one of the most popular of all medieval legends, the debate of the four daughters of God. Originally a Jewish *haggadah*, based on Psalm lxxxv. 10, the story was modified to accord with Christian ideas by Hugo of St. Victor and Bernard of Clairvaux, popularized and further adapted by Grosseteste and Bonaventure, and presented in various forms by several other medieval writers.[6] Whereas the Jewish version of the debate concerned the arguments for and against the creation of Adam and was designed to reconcile God's omniscience with His omnipotence, the medieval treatments transferred the debate to some occasion after

---

[1] *Miroure*, p. 12; *Chester*, ii. 193–6; *Metrical Paraphrase*, 183–4; *Piers Plowman*, B passus, xviii. 335.

[2] See J. K. Bonnell, 'The Serpent with a Human Head in Art and Mystery Play', *A.J.A.* xxi (1917), 225 et seq.

[3] *Expos. in Pent.*, In Gen. iii.   [4] B passus, xviii. 283–9.

[5] Ibid. 331–2.

[6] For a detailed discussion see H. Traver, *The Four Daughters of God*, Philadelphia, 1907; S. C. Chew, *The Virtues Reconciled*, Toronto, 1947.

the Fall, changed the subject to the desirability of Man's salvation, and used it to reconcile God's justice and mercy. In this form the discussion could easily develop into an actual trial, and in one or two treatments this happened. According to Pelbartus of Temesvar's *Pomerium Sermonum*, for instance, Mercy pleaded Man's case with recourse to divine, canonical, philosophical, and civil law, arguing that the serpent should not be allowed to benefit from his evil deed.[1] In the *Processus Belial*, the Devil appeared as counsel on his own behalf, the Virgin Mary assuming the Portia-like role of Man's advocate.[2]

When Christ had finally settled the debate by offering to die on Man's behalf, thus satisfying the claims of Justice and implementing the desires of Mercy, He brought the legality of this justification to bear on the Devil. As early as the twelfth century Anselm had objected to this tendency:

> We also commonly say that God was bound to strive with the devil by justice, rather than by force, in order to set man free. On this showing, when the devil killed Him in whom there was no reason for death, and who was God, he would justly lose his power over sinners. Otherwise God would have done unjust violence to him, since he was justly in possession of man; after all, he did not seize man by violence, but man handed himself over to him freely. But I cannot see what force this argument has.[3]

The particular theory to which Anselm was objecting here was the one originally put forward by Origen and popularized by Gregory the Great: that God deceived the Devil by disguising Himself as a man, with the result that the Devil tried unsuccessfully to tempt the God-man and illegally detained Him in Hell, so forfeiting his rights over the rest of mankind. It was this theory that was implicit in this passage from *The Stanzaic Life of Christ*:

> Thenne says the glose that Criste had sette
> a hud hook by his deitie
> to cacche the deuel in mennes dette,
> as to mon bifore did he.[4]

But the forensic tendencies of the Middle Ages were not to be denied. In spite of Anselm's protests most medieval authors portrayed Christ as striving with the Devil 'by justice' in one form

---

[1] H. Traver, op. cit., pp. 25–27.   [2] Ibid., pp. 50–54.
[3] *Cur Deus Homo*, i. 7.
[4] *Stanzaic Life of Christ*, 6349–52. See above, Ch. III, p. 104.

or another, and the harrowing of Hell took the form of a dialectic
victory rather than a military conquest. To the medieval mind the
most satisfying aspect of the Redemption was that it was, as Mercy
says in *Piers Plowman*, 'a good sleighte'.[1] Pseudo-Bonaventure
described it in similar terms as 'a good slei3te and trewe wisdom',[2]
and the author of *Purity* (*c.* 1360–1400) wrote that

> Al in mesure and meþe watz mad þe vengaunce
> And efte amended wyth a mayden þat make had never.[3]

The poetic as well as the legal justice of the Redemption was keenly
appreciated by layman and cleric alike.

The actual nature of the 'sleighte' took many forms. The one
hinted at in *Purity* centred on the miraculous nature of Christ's
birth. In *Đe Deuelis Perlament*, for example, the Devil's claim that
Adam's sin had given him the right to hold mankind in bondage
was countered by Christ's revelation that as He was born of a virgin
He was free of the taint of Adam's guilt and therefore had the right
to free him.[4] The Devil made the same claim in *Piers Plowman*:

> If he reue me my ri3te he robbeth me by maistrye.
> For by ri3t and bi resoun tho renkes that ben here
> Bodye and soule ben myne bothe gode and ille.[5]

Christ's reply, however, was rather different:

> Al-though resoun recorde and ri3t of my-self,
> That if thei ete the apple alle shulde deye,
> I bihy3te hem nou3t here helle for euere.[6]

This somewhat shabby argument He supplemented by explaining
that He would satisfy the old law by offering life for life:

> So leue it nou3te, Lucifer, a3eine the lawe I fecche hem,
> But bi ri3t and bi resoun raunceoun here my lyges.[7]

And on this basis He proceeded to the most important point of all.
Earlier in the same passus Mercy had urged in favour of the Redemption that,

> ri3t as thorw gyle man was bigyled,
> So shall grace that bigan make a good sleighte;
> *Ars ut artem falleret.*[8]

---

[1] B passus, xviii. 160.
[2] See L. F. Powell, *The Mirrour of the Blessed Lyf of Jesu Christ*, 1908, p. 19.
[3] *Purity*, 247–8.   [4] *Đe Deuelis Perlament*, 273–304.
[5] B passus, xviii. 274–6.   [6] Ibid. 328–30.   [7] Ibid. 346–7.
[8] Ibid. 159–60.

The Devil, too, as I have noted, feared that his 'gyle' during the temptation of Eve might vitiate his claim to hold Man in Hell. This is the ground of Christ's third and most powerful answer to the Devil's objections:

> Thow, Lucyfer, in lyknesse of a luther addere,
> Getest by gyle tho that god loued;
> And I, in lyknesse of a leode that lorde am of heuene,
> Graciousliche thi gyle haue quytte go gyle aʒeine gyle!
> And as Adam and alle thorw a tre deyden,
> Adam and alle thorwe a tree shal torne aʒeine to lyue;
> And gyle is bigyled and in his gyle fallen.[1]

Of the all the 'sleighte's this was certainly the most appealing, for it vindicated God's honour as well as His justice. The Devil was not only thwarted; he was outwitted to boot.

I have dwelt on this theory of the Redemption at such length because it is the key to what is in many ways the most characteristically medieval of all the treatments of the Fall story produced in England during the Middle Ages, William of Shoreham's poem *On the Trinity, Creation the Existence of Evil, Devils, and Adam and Eve*. Although medieval authors paid a good deal of attention, as we have seen, to the intricacies of Man's salvation, they were curiously reluctant to explore the corresponding problem of the part God played in the Fall. Comestor, for instance, raised the problem only to dismiss it: 'Again, if it is asked why God permitted man to be tempted, knowing that he would fall . . . we say . . . because He so wished. If it is asked why He so wished, that question is foolish which seeks the cause of the divine will which is itself the first cause of all causes.'[2] The *Speculum Humanae Salvationis* rejected such speculations in similar terms:

> No man for prais of witte presume to seke at alle
> Whi god angels and man made wham he knewe to falle.[3]

And in *Piers Plowman* Langland made the same point even more forcibly, if somewhat less decorously:

> For alle that wilneth to wyte the weyes of god almiʒty,
> I wolde his eye were in his ers and his fynger after,
> That euere wilneth to wite whi that god wolde
> Suffre Sathan his sede to bigile,
> Or Iudas to the Iuwes Iesu bytraye.[4]

---

[1] Ibid. 352–8.
[2] *Hist. Schol.*, Lib. Gen. xxiv.
[3] *Miroure*, p. 14.
[4] B passus, x. 122–6.

William of Shoreham, however, did presume to inquire into God's ways to Man, and his poem is the one large-scale literary attempt in this period to overcome the metaphysical difficulties involved in the Genesis narrative.

After a lengthy discourse on the Trinity and the Creation William notes that everything was necessarily created good, and poses the fundamental question:

> And seþþe god self hyt for-beade,
> Wannes comeþ forþe al þat quead,
> So meche þer hys?[1]

If God so wished, runs the argument, He could abolish evil. Therefore He must permit it for some purpose, namely, to make possible the attainment of virtue. Without conquest there can be no pleasure in victory:

> Nys gryt stryf wyþ-oute queade,
> And þer conqueste hys, stryf hys neade,
> And som yschent:
> þanne nys hyt to god no wrang
> To soffre queade þe gode amang
> To auancement.[2]

This point is very similar to the one Milton was to make in the famous passage in *Areopagitica* denouncing 'a fugitive and cloister'd virtue'. But whereas Milton makes it clear that he is speaking only of the predicament of fallen Man, William applies the principle without any reservations to the events which preceded Adam's disobedience. Thus in his view Satan's rebellion and downfall were a necessary part of the divine plan. God deliberately refrained from creating the angels perfect, because if the Devil had not been free to fall Man would never have been created to take his place in Heaven:

> ȝef hy hade be mad parfyȝt,
> We nedde y-haued ryȝt no profyȝt
> Ine heuene a-boue;
> Nou schal man be in hare loȝ,
> And habbe ioye and blysse ynoȝ,
> And pes and loue.[3]

---

[1] *On the Trinity, Creation, etc.* 313–15. [2] Ibid. 361–6.
[3] Ibid. 433–8.

Satan's fall, in fact, was the first *felix culpa*. But this raises the problem that if God intended that the angel should fall and created him imperfect to that end, then it was unjust to punish him. William's only solution is that Lucifer was glad to do whatever evil he could anyway.[1] The whole argument is then rounded off by an appeal to the extremely unsatisfactory theory of contrast: just as white is set off by black, so the bliss of Heaven would have been incomplete without the misery of Hell beneath it.[2]

No less extreme is William's analysis of the Fall of Man. Stressing again that Adam's creation was the direct result of the Devil's defection, he repeats the argument of glory through conquest and the consequent necessity of original imperfection:

> Ac manne ne mytte nauȝt þe glorye
> Crefte, wyþ-oute victorye,
> My leue broþer;
> For ȝef he nadde hyȝt þorȝ conqueste,
> Folueld ne mytte be hys feste
> Al ase anoþer.
>
> þare-fore god made hym god and wys,
> And mayster ouer al paradys,
> Ac nauȝt parfyt.[3]

The tree of knowledge was forbidden in order to test Adam's virtue, and the Devil was allowed to tempt him for the same purpose. Frightened by the man's resemblance to his Maker but spurred on by his envy, the Tempter decided to use 'gyle'.[4] He assumed the appearance of a serpent, which 'best was of mest schreuhede'.[5] Then in this guise he went to the forbidden tree where, fearing to approach Adam directly, he addressed himself first to Eve, the less steadfast of the two.[6] The ensuing temptation William describes strictly according to the Biblical account, the one addition of any interest being the Augustinian notion that Eve began to feel proud even before she ate the apple.[7]

But although the episode itself is described in unexceptionably orthodox terms, William's subsequent comments on it reveal that his interpretation of the events is far from orthodox. God is not mocked, he claims, for just as the Devil had striven to gain Heaven

[1] Ibid. 469–86.
[2] Ibid. 541–64. Compare Vincent's *Speculum Historiale*, ii. 6.
[3] *On the Trinity, Creation, etc.* 595–603.   [4] Ibid. 619–36.   [5] Ibid. 638.
[6] Ibid. 649–51.   [7] Ibid. 679–84.

by force and by force had been expelled, so his guileful seduction
of Man was amended through guile.[1] God had revealed to Satan
that the forbidden tree contained death; He had not, however, told
him that it also contained life:

> For ine þe trowe deaþ was kene,
> And þat god made wel y-sene,
>   þet hyt for-bead;
> And he [the devil] weste þat hyt sede,
> ȝef man þrof ete he scholde awede,
>   And eke be dead.
>
> And lyf was al-so ine þe trowe,
> Ac þat ne myȝte be nauȝt y-knowe,
>   For god hyt hedde.[2]

It was not called the tree of life for nothing; God knew that His Son
would eventually redeem Man on a tree. Had the Devil known this
he would never have undertaken the temptation of Adam and Eve,
for by doing so he fulfilled the first half of God's plan and made
possible the second.[3]

William's startling conclusion, then, is that God actually intended
that both Adam and Satan should fall. What he has done, in fact,
is to lift the concept of the repayment of guile with guile out of its
context in the theory of the Redemption and transfer it to the other
end of the story, the Fall. The result is this extraordinary version
of the Genesis narrative according to which Adam's disobedience
did not merely become a *felix culpa* by the grace of God; it was

---

[1] *On the Trinity, Creation, etc.* 763-74.

[2] Ibid. 775-83. William thus assumes that the tree of life and the tree of knowledge
were one and the same tree. In itself this combination was not wholly unprecedented
in medieval writings: the *Towneley* play on the Fall designates the forbidden tree as 'the
tree of life' (i. 198-201) as does the *Canticum de Creatione* (MS. Trin., 25-26), while the
York play on the Fall calls it both 'the tree of good and yll' (iv. 56-59) and 'thys tre that
beres the Fruyte of Lyfe' (iv. 83-85). The popular Rood legend may have been ultimately
responsible for this fusion. The typological parallel between the tree of knowledge and
the tree of Calvary had long been a standard feature of Christian interpretations of the
Fall (see above, Ch. III, p. 101; Ch. IV, p. 133). The purpose of the Rood legend, however, was to establish a physical connexion between the two, to show that we were
brought back to life 'þoru Iusus þat us boȝte / Of þe appel treo þat oure vader þe luþer
appel of nom' (*History of the Holy Cross*, 6-8). Reinforced by the allegorical association
of Christ with the tree of life, this legend appeared to imply that the Biblical terms 'tree
of life' and 'tree of knowledge' denoted two aspects of the same tree. William is therefore
able to assume that the two trees were one.

[3] *On the Trinity, Creation, etc.* 799-804.

planned as such from the very outset. Compared with this, Milton's treatment of the theme is delicate indeed, and if some of the critical guns which have recently been levelled at *Paradise Lost* were to be trained instead on the medieval poem they might find it a somewhat easier target to hit. W. Empson, for instance, has written: 'Milton steadily drives home that the inmost counsel of God was the Fortunate Fall of man; however wicked Satan's plan may be, it is God's plan too.'[1] Although this does something less than justice to Milton's poem it is an admirable statement of William of Shoreham's theological position.

William's poem is also of great importance in the wider context of Fall theology, for it demonstrates the grotesque results that could be obtained by pushing certain orthodox ideas to their logical conclusion. The idea that Man was created to take the place of the fallen angels, for example, was a commonplace of Christian speculation, and it appears in several popular medieval works:

> And god of his gudnesse wald make mankynde þrfore
> The falle of lucifere and his, forto restore.[2]

This doctrine, like that of the *felix culpa* to which it is closely related, was all very well so long as it was applied retrospectively. Once it was applied absolutely it soon led to difficulties, as Anselm noted:

> If the angels were created in that perfect number, and men were created purely and simply to replace the lost angels, it is obvious that men would never have risen to blessedness, unless some angels had fallen from it. . . . Then, if anyone says that elect men will rejoice in the loss of the angels as much as in their own exaltation (since unquestionably the latter would not have come about apart from the former), how can they be defended from this perverse joy ?[3]

This is precisely William's position, but, unlike Anselm, he does not attempt to extricate himself from it. He appears to have seen nothing perverse in his joy at the fall of the rebel angels, and his poem is a salutary reminder of the theological pitfalls surrounding the perilous doctrine of Heaven's re-population.[4]

---

[1] *Milton's God*, 1961, p. 39.
[2] *Miroure*, p. 12. See also *York Plays*, i. 138–41; *Towneley Plays*, i. 210–15; *Cursor Mundi*, 514–16; *Fall and Passion*, 18.
[3] *Cur Deus Homo*, i. 18.
[4] Honoré d'Autun is careful to stress that Man would have been created and elevated to Heaven even if the rebel angels had not fallen. See his *Elucidarium*, i. 13–14.

William's justification of the Fall of Man is also built on a thoroughly orthodox basis. The problem of God's tolerance of sin had been posed many times, and had generally been answered along the lines followed by Caxton:

> Whan Our Lord God created the man, he gaf to hym power to doo his fre wille, that is to wete to doo good or euyll, whiche he wolde. Ffor yf God had made the man suche as he myght not haue synned ne to haue don nothing but well, he shold haue take from hym somwhat of his power. . . . Neuertheles it was wel in Our Lordes power, yf it had plesed hym, to haue made man suche that he shold not haue synned ne haue don ony harme ne euyll. But he had not deseruid yet suche merite ne reward as he now doth in no tyme of the world. And therfor God gaf to man playn fre wille to doo weel or euyll to thende that in weel doyng and leuyng the euyll he myght haue more merite; ffor other wise he myght not deserue so moche.[1]

But again the orthodox position is a very precarious one, for in the case of an omniscient and omnipotent being 'to permit' could well be taken to imply 'to intend'. Two centuries later Calvin made just this point: 'It offendeth the eares of some, when it is saide, that God would haue the fall of Adam. But I pray you what is his sufference else, which hath the power to stoppe and stay: yea, who hath the whole matter in his hand, but his will?'[2] The distinction is certainly a fine one, and William was not the only medieval author to blur it. Honoré d'Autun, who had been so careful to avoid William's conclusion concerning the fall of Satan, writes that God permitted the Fall of Man because 'He foresaw how great good He would make from his sin'.[3] And Langland, in spite of his attack upon those who ask why God allowed the Fall to happen, produces a justification which suggests that God intended the Fall all along:

> For-thi god of his goodnesse the fyrste gome Adam,
> Sette hym in solace and in souereigne myrthe;
> And sith he suffred hym synne sorwe to fele,
> To wite what wel was kyndelich to knowe it.[4]

Here the argument of contrast, which William had used to supplement his main thesis, is the crux of the matter. As the Devil himself had said in the *Alethia*, we cannot know good until we have sinned.

William of Shoreham, then, is no isolated eccentric. His poem

---

[1] *Mirrour of the World*, pp. 14–15.   [2] *Commentary on Genesis*, iii. 1.
[3] *Elucidarium*, i. 13–14.   [4] *Piers Plowman*, B passus, xviii. 216–19.

stands in the same relation to the Middle-English writings on the Fall as the *Genesis B* stood to the Anglo-Saxon. The apparent oddities of his treatment, far from being perverse departures from orthodoxy, are simply magnifications of one or two commonplace medieval Christian arguments.

VII

THE DRAMATIC TREATMENTS

UP to this point we have been chiefly concerned with the way in which the poets and theologians of successive cultures attempted to reinvigorate the ancient myth of the Fall by interpreting it in terms relevant to their own social and intellectual environment. The dramatists, whose treatments form the subject of the present chapter, deserve to be studied independently, because in addition to a temporal they also had to contend with a spatial gulf between their audience and the events related in Genesis. As we have seen, the Jahwist's style creates an effect of distance, so that however clearly we may see what happens we cannot always tell why it happens or what its consequences are. Occasional snatches of conversation drift across to us, but for a large part of the time we cannot hear what the characters are saying, and they are too far away for us to guess from the expression on their faces. For example, while we can just make out the details of the creation of the first pair we have no means of knowing what their reaction was either to each other or to the garden in which they found themselves. God's command to abstain from the fruit of the tree of knowledge is audible enough, but Adam's reply is not. When we notice that Eve seems to be alone during the temptation we can only speculate as to how she came to be so. We watch her giving the forbidden fruit to her husband, but we cannot catch the words she is evidently using to prevail on him to eat it. And although we can deduce that they both feel ashamed, from the fact that they clothe themselves with fig-leaves and hide among the trees, we are left to imagine whatever mutual recriminations they might be heaping on each other.

A narrative poet can, when it suits his purposes, preserve this gap between the observer and the action. The nature of his art allows him to focus on those parts of the story that interest him and leave those which do not in the background. The dramatist, however, has no such freedom, for drama is essentially an art of the foreground; the physical proximity of the stage tends to bring the spectator close up to the events he is witnessing. As a result, the Genesis narrative poses a very special problem for the playwright, demanding from him the constant invention of both speech and incident. Every minor inconsistency has to be resolved, every unexplained action or situation accounted for, every unexpressed feeling made explicit. The whole story, in short, must be brought forward until we can see, hear, and understand everything that is taking place immediately in front of us. Questions of continuity and character, questions which I have called narrative and metaphysical, become more crucial than ever.

The dramatist's task is further complicated in this case by the cosmic scope of his material. The rebellion and fall of Lucifer, which by the time the first plays on the Fall began to appear had become an integral part of the legend, would strain the resources of the most elaborate modern theatre, to say nothing of its medieval and Elizabethan forerunners, while the creation of the world would be altogether beyond them. On a smaller scale, though none the less complex for that, there are the problems involved in the presentation of a naked man and woman engaged in conversation with a speaking serpent. And problems of stage-management apart, how is the pre-lapsarian life of Adam and Eve to be treated? Their original innocence was a state rather than an action, and as such, though it could perfectly well be *described* within the framework of a poem, it could hardly be *portrayed* dramatically.

The history of the Fall plays is largely the history of increasingly sophisticated attempts to cope with these difficulties. To begin with the purely technical problems, the authors of the two earliest dramatic treatments of the story, the *Drama de Primi Parentis Lapsu* ascribed to Ignatius Diaconus (*fl. c.* 850) and the twelfth-century French *Mystère d'Adam*, evaded the most serious of them by omitting the supernatural events which preceded the Fall and concentrating exclusively on Adam and Eve's experiences in the garden of Eden. The authors of the English miracle plays, on the other hand, were committed to the dramatization of the whole cycle of sacred history from the Creation to the Redemption. They had, therefore, to begin at the very beginning with the ultimate cause of the ensuing conflict, Lucifer's pre-mundane quarrel with his Maker. Since the limitations imposed by their medium inevitably precluded the staging of a celestial war, they reduced the episode to manageable proportions by presenting it as a verbal encounter or as a single symbolic act consisting of the rebel angel's desecration of God's throne.[1] The motive which impelled him to revolt, they generally agreed, was pride; dazzled by his own beauty he demanded the worship of his peers and claimed to be the equal of God.[2] The one exception is the *York* play on the subject, according to which the Devil fell because he objected to Christ's intention to become incarnate in human rather than angelic form:

> The godhede þat I sawe so cleere,
> And parsayued þat he shuld take kynde,
>   of a degree
> That he had wrought, and I denyed þat aungell kynde
>   shuld it noȝt be;
>
>   .   .   .
>
> The kynde of man he thoght to take,
> And theratt hadde I grete envye.[3]

The related problem of representing the creation of the world was solved somewhat less successfully. In all four cycles the Creator is given a long soliloquy in which He tells the audience exactly what He is doing and leaves it to their imagination to visualize the scene.[4]

Having overcome these initial obstacles, the dramatists were still faced with two further practical difficulties. The first was the embarrassing but Scriptural fact of Adam and Eve's nakedness. A stage direction at the beginning of the *Mystère* suggests at least one way in which they were able to maintain the proprieties: 'Adam indutus sit tunica rubea, Eva vero muliebri vestimento albo, peplo serico albo.'[5] The second was the presence of the serpent and his ability to converse. The most ingenious solution is to be found again in the *Mystère*, where, after the Devil has accosted both Adam and Eve, 'Tunc serpens artificiose compositus ascendet juxta stipitem arboris vetite; cui Eva proprius adhibebit aurem, quasi ipsius ascultans consilium. Dehinc accipiet Eva pomum, porriget Ade.'[6] The Tempter

---

[1] *Chester*, i. 157–92; *Lud. Cov.* i. 53–61; *Towneley*, i. 77–107.   [2] Loc. cit.

[3] *York*, v. 3–13. In essence this is a complete reversal of the Devil's motivation in the Vita Adae et Evae. He objects now not to the creation of Man in the image of God but to God's intention to become incarnate in the image of Man.

[4] *Chester*, ii. 1–80; *Lud. Cov.* ii. 83–101; *Towneley*, i. 162–9; *York*, ii. 13 et seq.

[5] *Mystère*, p. 1. 'Let Adam be dressed in a red tunic, and Eve in a white woman's garment with a white silk wimple.'

[6] Ibid., pp. 15–16. 'Then a serpent, cunningly put together, shall ascend along the trunk of the forbidden tree; unto whom Eve shall approach her ear, as if hearkening to its counsel. Thereafter, Eve shall take the apple, and shall offer it to Adam.'

and his instrument are thus separated, so that Satan can make the necessary speeches in his own person and the stage-prop serpent can appear without actually having to say anything. Moreover, as Auerbach has remarked, the reptile's intervention at this juncture serves a most important dramatic function in that it initiates a completely different approach by Eve. Instead of debating the advisability of dealing with the Devil, as she had been, she turns the conversation round to the forbidden fruit.[1]

The English playwrights were less subtle. To judge from the available evidence they simply dressed up one of the actors in a serpentine costume,[2] thereby accidentally reviving the rabbinic belief that the snake originally walked like a man. This device had far-reaching implications so far as the subsequent temptation of Eve was concerned, for the combination of a human face and form with a serpent's skin created a somewhat ambiguous figure who could have been mistaken for an angel as well as a snake. Consequently in several versions of the episode Eve seems to have been under the impression that the intruder was in fact a messenger from Heaven. In the *Ludus Coventriae*, for instance, she tells Adam that

> A ffayr Aungell þus seyd me tylle
> to Ete þat appyl take nevyr no drede.[3]

And in the two sixteenth-century *Norwich* plays on the theme the Devil introduces himself as such:

> Unto this, angell of lyght, I shew mysylfe to be;
> With hyr for to dyscemble, I fear yt nott at all.[4]

The Tempter's semi-human appearance also made it possible to adapt Comestor's notion that the Devil chose a species of serpent with a maiden's face in order to allay any fears Eve might otherwise have had; and the author of the *Chester* cycle, who seems to have

---

[1] *Mimesis*, ch. vii.

[2] See, for instance, the Norwich account book quoted in M. Rose, *The Wakefield Mystery Plays*, 1961, p. 135. J. K. Bonnell has suggested in 'The Serpent with a Human Head in Art and Mystery Play', *A.J.A.* xxi (1917), 255 et seq., that the artists of the thirteenth and fourteenth centuries were inspired by the miracle plays they saw to represent the serpent as having a human head.

[3] *Lud. Cov.* ii. 238–9.

[4] *Norwich B*, 40–41. See also *Norwich A*, 67–68. As I noted in my article on 'Genesis B and its Background', *R.E.S.* N.S. xiv (1963), 9, it is scarcely conceivable that the authors of these plays were acquainted with *Genesis B*, where the Devil adopted the same disguise. The parallel is more likely to be the accidental result of the exigencies of medieval stagecraft.

been specially well acquainted with the *Historia*,[1] took full advantage of this opportunity. Satan himself outlines his strategy:

> A manner of an Adder is in this place,
> that wynges like a byrd she hase,
> feete as an Adder, a maydens face;
> her kinde will I take.[2]

If the technical problems attendant on the staging of the Fall story came to modify the form of many of its central episodes, so much the more did the narrative and metaphysical difficulties we noticed earlier. The need to find some dramatic correlative for Adam and Eve's unfallen innocence, in particular, gave rise to several extra-Biblical elaborations of the original text. Immediately after their creation, for example, the newly formed couple were given rapturous speeches of thanks for the blessings they had received:

> *A.* A Lord! ful mekill is þy myght,
> And þat is seene in ilke a side,
> Ffor nowe is here a joifull sighte,
> To see this worlde so longe and wide.
>
> . . .
>
> *E.* To swilke a lorde in alle degree
> Be euer-more lastand louynge,
> þat to vs such a dygnyte,
> Has geffynne before all other thynge.[3]

In neither *Towneley*, *Ludus Coventriae*, nor *York*, all of which contain variations of this theme, does anything intervene between the respective creations of the man and the woman. In the fifteenth-century Cornish *Ordinale de Origine Mundi* and the closely related sixteenth-century Cornish *Creation of the World* by William Jordan, on the contrary, the Biblical sequence is strictly preserved and the two events are clearly separated. The space between them is filled up either by Adam's request for a mate or by God's recognition of his desire:

> A mournful thing it is, certainly,
> To see Adam by himself
> Without companionship.[4]

---

[1] See below, pp. 197–8.   [2] *Chester*, ii. 193–6.
[3] *York*, iii. 45–56. See also *Lud. Cov.* ii. 143–68; *Towneley*, i. 226–33.
[4] *Creation*, 381–3. Compare *Ordinale*, 85–92.

This in turn enabled the authors of the *Norwich* plays to supplement Adam's Scriptural reception of his wife with gratitude for her company:

> Oh bone of my bones and flesh of my flesh eke,
> Thow shalte be called Woman, bycaus thow art of me.
> Oh gyfte of God most goodlye, þat hast us made so lyke,
> Most lovynge spowse, I muche do here rejoyce of the.[1]

Whereas the simultaneous creation of the first pair in the three earlier miracle plays circumvented the problem of Eve's knowledge of the prohibition of the tree of knowledge, those dramatists who followed Genesis more closely had to account for the fact that she was aware of God's command even though she could not have heard it herself. Consequently in *Norwich A* God instructs Adam to repeat His words to his wife, while in *Norwich B* He repeats them Himself when He has made Eve.[2] According both to *Norwich A* and to *York* and *Ludus Coventriae*, His warning was greeted with a confident promise to obey:

> *A.* I haue no nede to towche ȝon tre
> Aȝens my lordys wyl to werke now
> I am a good gardenere.
>
> . . .
>
> *E.* oure witte were rakyl and ouyr don bad
> to fforfete Ageyns oure lordys wyll
> in ony wyse.[3]

The authors of *Towneley* and *Chester*, who did not include this feature, turned instead to the *Historia Scholastica* for further material with which to amplify the pre-lapsarian section of the story. Taking up Comestor's suggestion that Adam and Eve received their instructions 'by some other subject creature', the former introduced into the action a cherub, who descends from Heaven to explain to Adam his purpose in the divine scheme and to repeat the command concerning the tree of knowledge.[4] The latter dramatized Comestor's theory that Adam was given a prophetic dream while Eve was being formed from his rib. When he wakes up he asks:

---

[1] *Norwich B*, 25–28. Compare *Norwich A*, 17–23.
[2] *Norwich A*, 34; *Norwich B*, 7; ibid. 17–19.
[3] *Lud. Cov.* ii. 149–64. See also *York*, iv. 70–79; *Norwich A*, 41–44.
[4] *Towneley*, i. 204–25. Compare *Hist. Schol.*, Lib. Gen. xv.

> O lorde, where have I longe bene?
> for, sithe I slepte, much have I seene
> wonders that, withoutten wene,
> hereafter shall be wiste.[1]

Neither Ignatius nor the anonymous French dramatist who wrote the *Mystère* had really come to grips with the question of Eve's isolation at the beginning of the temptation, but several of their English successors did attempt to provide at least a tentative answer. Adam, they assumed, must have left his wife alone while he went off to explore the beauties of their new home:

> *A.* Eue, felow, abide me thore,
>   ffor I will go to viset more,
>   To se what trees that here been; . . .
>
> *E.* Gladly, sir, I will full fayne;
>   When ye haue sene theym, com agane.
>
> *A.* Bot luke well, eue, my wife,
>   that thou negh not the tree of life;
>   ffor if thou do he bese ill paide;
>   then be we tynt, as he has saide.
>
> *E.* Go furth and play the all aboute,
>   I shall not negh it while thou art oute;
>   ffor be thou sekyr I were full loth
>   ffor any thyng that he were wroth.[2]

William Jordan, fearing perhaps that Adam would then be blamed for Eve's vulnerability, reversed the situation so that it is the woman who elects to leave her companion:

> I will go to wander
> Here among the flowers.
> Every pleasure of this world
> In this place see it grown,
> So that it is a comfort to see.[3]

In this as in all the other elaborations of the state of innocence these

---

[1] *Chester*, ii. 137–40. True to his promise, he tells Cain and Abel later in the play that while he slept his soul was transported to Heaven, where the future of mankind was revealed to him (ibid. ii. 441–4). Compare *Hist. Schol.*, Lib. Gen. xvi.

[2] *Towneley*, i. 234–49. See also *Norwich A*, 48–54; *Norwich B*, 32–35.

[3] *Creation*, 538–42. See also *Lud. Cov.* ii. 165–8.

early dramatists anticipated Milton's treatment of the subject in *Paradise Lost*.[1]

The English dramatists were also responsible for the invention of the Tempter's prologue to the temptation. Basing his argument on the assumption that God has created Man to take his place in Heaven,[2] he informs the audience that he intends to prevent his rival from achieving this exalted destiny:

> Shold suche a Caytife, made of claye,
> have suche blisse? nay, be my laye!
> for I shall teache his wife a playe,
> and I maye have a while.[3]

An attentive spectator, however, might well have wondered how the Devil came by this information, for God did not announce His plans until the rebellious angels had been expelled from Heaven. To remedy this fault Jordan subsequently inserted into the story an episode in which God tells the rebel that he is to be not only cast down into Hell but replaced by Adam and his progeny. Satan's reply is characteristic:

> Wouldst thou that the son of man
> When he shall be made of ugly slime,
> Should occupy for certain
> My room, who never had peer
> Here in heaven?[4]

By far the most memorable treatment of the Fall itself is that in the *Mystère*, where it becomes for the first time an essentially domestic tragedy. In His very first speech God warns Adam that no dissent must arise between man and wife, and goes on to order Eve:

> A lui seies tot tens encline
> Nen issir de sa discipline.[5]

Before they are led into the garden Adam is again cautioned:

> Jol di a tei, e voil que Eve l'oie,
> Se ne l'entent, donc a folor s'apoie.[6]

---

[1] See, for instance, A. H. Gilbert, 'Milton and the Mysteries', *S.P.* xvii (1920), 147–69.   [2] *Towneley*, i. 210–15; *York*, i. 138–41.

[3] *Chester*, ii. 177–80. Compare *York*, v. 1–25; *De Mos. Hist.* ii. 89–112.

[4] *Creation*, 254–8.

[5] *Mystère*, 35–36. 'Always submit your heart to him, and do not deviate from his teaching.'

[6] Ibid. 59–60. 'I say to you, and wish that Eve should listen, if she does not hear it then she will turn to folly.'

And when at last they are settled in Eden they receive this last instruction:

> Femme de home nen i avra irur,
> Ne hom de femme verguine ne freur.
> Por engendrer n'i est hom peccheor,
> N'a l'enfanter femme n'i sent dolor.[1]

Clearly the relationship between Adam and Eve is going to be all-important. As in *Genesis B* the Tempter first approaches the man. He begins by trying to undermine his faith in God's omnipotence, and then gradually brings the conversation round to the forbidden tree, which, he claims, will elevate him to divinity. When Adam observes that he already has everything he needs Satan is moved to a fine scornful outburst:

> Ne munteras ja mes plus halt?
> Molt te porras tenir por chier,
> Quant deus t'a fet sun jardenier.
> Deus t'a fait gardein de son ort,
> Ja ne querras altre deport?
> Forma il tei por ventre faire?
> Altre honor te voldra atraire.[2]

But even this fails to shake Adam's resolution, so the Devil retires to consult with his fellow demons.

When he returns, it is to Eve 'leto vultu blandiens'. His opening gambit makes it clear that he realizes he is dealing with the female of the species, for he appeals to her sense of curiosity by offering to tell her a secret. As soon as she has agreed to keep it, however, he abruptly changes the subject:

Diabolus	Tu as esté en bone escole.
	Jo vi Adam, mais trop est fols.
Eva	Un poi est durs.
Diabolus	Il serra mols.
	Il est plus dors que n'est emfers.

---

[1] *Mystère*, 93–96. 'Woman will not incur Man's wrath, nor Man incur shame and trouble from Woman. Man commits no sin by begetting children, nor does Woman feel any pain in bearing them.'

[2] Ibid. 180–6. 'Will you never ascend any higher? Can you esteem yourself very highly when God has made you His gardener? God has made you keeper of His park, and will you not seek a higher position? Did He create you merely to fill your belly? He wished a higher honour to attract you.'

Eva   Il est mult francs.

Diabolus   Ainz est mult sers.
             Cure ne voelt prendre de sei;
             Car la prenge seveals de tei.
             Tu es fieblette e tendre chose,
             E es plus fresche que n'est rose;
             Tu es plus blanche que cristal,
             Que neif que chiet sor glace en val;
             Mal cuple em fist li criator:
             Tu es trop tendre e il trop dur.[1]

Thus Adam's earlier steadfastness is made to appear as self-satisfaction; just as in *Genesis B*, her husband's strength is presented to Eve as a weakness which only she can cure. Having successfully planted this seed of doubt, the Devil finally reveals his secret: the fruit will give Adam power and dominion over all things. But Eve is more interested in the fruit's savour, and on this pretext the Devil returns to his earlier theme:

             A ton bel cors, a ta figure,
             Bien convendreit tel aventure,
             Que tu fusses dame del mond.[2]

By now Eve is almost convinced, yet she still prevaricates, promising that she will eat the fruit later when Adam is at rest. With this the Tempter has to rest content for the moment, so he retires and leaves his seeds to grow.

Adam, who has observed this conversation from a distance, reproaches Eve for talking to the Devil. He is, he reminds her, the enemy of God. Encouraged by the serpent, Eve abruptly breaks off the argument and urges him to eat the forbidden fruit with her:

Adam J'en duit.

Eva   Lai le!

[1] Ibid. 220–32.
'*Satan*: You have been in a good school. I have seen Adam, but he is too foolish.
Eve: He is a little hard.
S: He will be soft. He is harder than iron.
E: He is very noble.
S: On the contrary, he is very ignoble. He will not take care of himself; let him at least take care of you. You are a delicate and tender thing, and fresher than the rose; you are whiter than crystal, whiter than the snow which falls on the ice in the valley. The Creator made an ill-matched couple: you are too tender and he is too hard.'
[2] Ibid. 253–5. 'Such a destiny would well become your beautiful body and countenance, that you should be queen of the world.'

> *Adam*   Ne ferai pas.
>
> *Eva*   Del demorer fais tu que las.
>
> *Adam* E jol prendrai.[1]

Adam succumbs for the same reason as in Avitus's poem, to prove that he is as brave as his wife. The Fall thus proceeds from the inferior-superior relationship of the first pair. This distinction is the point at which they are most vulnerable, for it is the one feature of their life that emphasizes their separateness as two distinct individuals; it is the one gap between them into which the Tempter, who, as J. Crosland has remarked,[2] bears a striking resemblance to the conventional courtly lover, can drive the wedge of his temptations by persuading Eve that she is the traditional *mal mariée*. She falls because she wishes to be not the equal of God but the mistress of her husband; he, because he wishes to prove his innate superiority to his wife. Eve's fall is a denial of their relationship; Adam's, a misconceived attempt to affirm it.

There is nothing in the English plays to match the subtlety of this version of the episode. Indeed, most of them follow the Biblical account more closely here than in any other part of the story. Even in *Ludus Coventriae* and *Norwich B*, in which the Devil masquerades as an angel, Eve's downfall is accomplished merely by the promise of divinity.[3] The one elaboration of any interest occurs in the Cornish plays, where the Tempter actually makes use of his angelic disguise:

> *S.* Take no wonder at all, Goodwife,
>   I have come to help thee
>   Out of heaven with full great haste,
>
> .   .   .
>
> *E.* There is no fear to me of thee,
>   Because thy face is so fair.[4]

Yet in spite of his fair appearance, Eve is still reluctant to disobey

---

[1] *Mystère*, 297–9.
    'Adam: I fear it.
    Eve: Leave it.
    A: I will not.
    E: In delaying you act as a coward does.
    A: I'll take it.'

[2] *Medieval French Literature*, 1956, pp. 230–1.

[3] *Lud. Cov.* ii. 169–207; *Norwich B*, 43–58.

[4] *Creation*, 554–63. Compare *Norwich A*, 55–68; *Ordinale*, 165–6.

the will of God. When she does finally yield it is with the thought of Adam in the forefront of her mind:

> I will not be so greedy
> To keep all myself—
> Adam surely beyond everyone
> I love him—and God forbid
> To keep him without a share.[1]

On hearing this, Satan quickly bends a bough of the forbidden tree down to the ground so that she can reach the fruit.[2]

These Cornish plays are also the only ones to make anything at all of Eve's subsequent temptation of Adam. In *York* and the *Ludus Coventriae*, admittedly, he offers more resistance than the Genesis narrative had implied, but not until the *Ordinale* and the *Creation* does Eve have to do any more than repeat the Tempter's assurances to persuade him to eat the fruit with her.[3] Here, on the contrary, as soon as Eve suggests that he should do so his suspicions are aroused. Is it, he asks, the fruit of the forbidden tree? Eve's contention that an angel gave it to her serves only to reinforce his doubts, and he rebukes her vehemently for listening to the Devil. Confronted by his resolute refusal to fall with her, Eve herself becomes angry:

> *E.* Since thou wilt not believe,
>   Thou shalt lose my love.
>   Ever whilst thou livest,
>   Here thou shalt not see me again,
>
> *A.* Eve, rather than thou be angry,
>   I will do all as thou wishest.
>   Bring it me immediately,
>   And I will eat it.[4]

In the drama as in the narrative treatments the heroic Adam, who ate to prove his valour, ultimately gave way to the chivalric Adam, who ate to prove his love.

---

[1] *Creation*, 682–6. In the *Ordinale*, 199–200, the serpent tells Eve to give it to Adam.

[2] *Creation*, 687–8; *Ordinale*, 201–2. According to the Apocalypsis Mosis, too, the serpent made Eve promise to pass the fruit on to her husband before pulling down a branch for her to pluck. See above, Ch. II, pp. 57–58.

[3] In *Chester*, ii. 261–4, Adam's remarks when he has eaten the fruit suggest that he did not realize that it was from the forbidden tree. A similar account of the incident is to be found in *P.R.E.* xiii: 'When Adam had eaten of the fruit of the tree, he saw that he was naked, and his eyes were opened . . . He said to her: What is this that thou hast given me to eat that my eyes should be opened and my teeth set on edge?'

[4] *Ordinale*, 241–8. See also *Creation*, 830–51.

Between the two temptation scenes, however, the *Norwich* plays had introduced an abbreviated version of the episode first conceived by Avitus, Adam's return, and Jordan followed their example:

> Welcome, Eve, thou art a good wife.
> If the news be good
> Thou shalt be rewarded,
> And my heart also with it
> Thou shalt have ready to thy pleasure.[1]

Again the origins of the corresponding moment in *Paradise Lost* are clearly visible.

Hereafter all the dramatists were more imaginative. In the *Mystère*, for example, Adam bitterly laments the joys he has lost and the misery he has incurred by eating the apple. He is afraid to face his Maker, and only death seems to offer any hope of release from his suffering:

> Oi! mort! por quei me laisses vivre?
> Que n'est li mond de mei delivre?
> Por quei faz encombrier al mond?[2]

He then turns upon Eve in anger:

> Femme desvee!
> Mal fus tu unques de mei nee!
> Car arse fust iceste coste
> Qui m'ad mis en si male poste!
> Car fust la coste en fu brudlee,
> Qui m'ad basti si grand meslee!
> Quant cele coste de mei prist,
> Por quei ne l'arst e mei oscist?[3]

His English successors react in much the same way, either bewailing their loss as in the *Ludus Coventriae*[4] or reproaching their wives as in *Chester* and *York*:

> *A.* Þis werke, Eue, hast þou wrought,
> and made þis bad bargayne.

---

[1] *Creation*, 731–5. Compare *Norwich A*, 72–73; *Norwich B*, 59–60.

[2] *Mystère*, 329–31. 'O death, why do you let me live? That the earth is not rid of me? Why do you make a hindrance to the world?'

[3] Ibid. 357–64. 'Mad woman, it was ill that you were ever born of me. If only the rib, which has brought me to such an evil pass, had been burned. If only the rib had been consumed in fire, which has condemned me to such confusion. When He took the rib from me, why did he not burn it and kill me?'

[4] *Lud. Cov.* ii. 247 et seq.

E. Nay, Adam, wite me nought.

A. Do wey, lefe Eue, whame þan?

E. The worme to wite wele worthy were.
     With tales vntrewe he me be-trayed.[1]

After the interrogation and condemnation, during the course of
which God rectifies his apparent omission in Genesis and puts a
question to the serpent as well as to Adam and Eve,[2] the same theme
is elaborated still more fully. When in *York* an angel has expatiated
at some length on the meaning of the various curses, Adam breaks
into a beautiful formal lament, which is one of the few passages of
real poetic value in the whole corpus of Fall plays:

> Allas! For syte and sorowe sadde,
> Mournynge makis me mased and madde,
> To thynke in herte what helpe y hadde,
>   and nowe has none.
> On grounde mon I neuyr goo gladde,
>   my gamys are gane.
>
> Gone ar my games with-owten glee,
> Allas! in blisse kouthe we noȝt bee,
> For putte we were to grete plente
>   at prime of þe day;
> By tyme of none alle lost had wee,
>   sa welaweye.[3]

In a rather different mood he then rounds on Eve, who replies to his
rebuke in kind, until anger finally gives way to sympathy:

> *A.* Allas! what womans witte was light!
>   þat was wele sene.
>
> *E.* Sethyn it was so me knyth it sore,
>   Bot sythen that woman witteles ware,
>   Mans maistrie shulde haue bene more
>   agayns þe gilte.
>
> *A.* Nay, at my speche wolde þou never spare,
>   þat has vs spilte.

---

[1] *York*, v. 118–23. See also *Chester*, ii. 269–72.
[2] *Lud. Cov.* ii. 309–22; *Norwich B*, 81–82; *Creation*, 903–4.
[3] *York*, vi. 81–92.

E. Iff I hadde spoken youe oughte to spill,
　Ye shulde haue taken gode tent þere tyll,
　　　and turnyd my þought.

A. Do way, woman, and neme it nought,
　For at my biddyng wolde þou not be,
　And therfore my woo wyte y thee,

　　　·　　　·　　　·

　Nowe god late never man aftir me
　　　triste woman tale.

　　　·　　　·　　　·

E. Be stille Adam, and nemen it na mare,
　　　it may not mende.
　For wele I wate I haue done wrange,
　And therefore euere I morne emange,
　Allas! the whille I leue so lange,
　　　dede wolde I be.[1]

Inspired, no doubt, by the medieval translations of the *Vita Adae et Evae*, the author of *Ludus Coventriae* gave Eve a speech in which she suggests that Adam should take his revenge by killing her. Rejecting the idea of harming his own flesh and blood, he proposes instead that they should

　　walke forth in to þe londe
　　with ryth gret labour oure fode to fynde

　　　·　　　·　　　·

　　tyll sum comforth of godys sonde
　　with grace releve uore careful mynde
　　Now come go we hens wyff.[2]

This hint of the possibility of future salvation was taken up in *Norwich B*, where the arrival of the two allegorical figures, Dolor and Myserye, is offset by the intervention of the Holy Ghost, who descends to comfort Adam with the promise of divine help and ultimate redemption. Encouraged by this revelation, Adam advises Eve:

　　Therfor, myne owne swett spous, withouten cavylacion,
　　Together lett us synge, and lett our hertes reioyse,
　　And gloryfye ower God wyth mynde, powre and voyse.[3]

---

[1] *York*, vi. 133–60.　　[2] *Lud. Cov.* ii. 404–12. See above, Ch. II, pp. 55–56.
[3] *Norwich B*, 151–3.

And finally this optimistic ending to the story was expanded in the *Ordinale* to include the medieval legend of Seth's journey to paradise in search of the oil of mercy and his acquisition of the three kernels from which the tree of Calvary was destined to grow.

Such, then, was the raw material which the Biblical playwrights of the Renaissance inherited from their medieval predecessors. The purely internal development of the various episodes was now virtually complete. It only remained to organize them within some more clearly defined dramatic structure, to clarify their outlines and manipulate their sequence rather than enlarge their actual content or multiply their number. This was accomplished in 1601 by Hugo Grotius, who, in his Latin drama *Adamus Exul*, cast the story in the form of a five-act classical tragedy, thereby changing its whole shape and emphasis.

The first act opens with a soliloquy spoken by Satan as he arrives in view of paradise on his mission to pervert Man. Having informed the audience of his purpose, he goes on to describe the distant prospect of Eden in terms which at once look back to the Christian-Latin poets and forward to *Paradise Lost*:

> Hic densa tenuis languidos Zephyri sonos
> Arbusta referunt, silvaque arguto tremens
> Ludit susurro: semper hic placido nitet
> Solare vultu lumen: arridet favor
> Constantis aurae.[1]

He continues with an account of the formation of Adam and Eve, whose mutual happiness he contrasts with his own lonely wretchedness: 'Miserosque non sic esse, quam solos, dolet. / Poenam levabit socius.'[2] Somehow Adam must be prevented from achieving his angelic destiny:

> Hoc, hoc videndum est, regna ne summa occupet,
> Qui jam tenet terrena. tum demum Poli
> Fugisse ab arce pudeat imbellem exulem,
> Si, ut dentur alii, regna deserui mea,
> Locumque generi pulsus humano dedi.[3]

---

[1] *Adamus Exul*, i. 40–44. 'Here the dense thickets carry back the languid sounds of the light breeze, and the trembling wood plays with a melodious whisper; here the sunlight always shines with serene countenance: the grace of a perpetual breeze smiles upon it.'

[2] Ibid. i. 123–4. 'It pains us not to be thus miserable but to be alone. A companion will lighten the punishment.'

[3] Ibid. i. 139–43. 'This, this must be ensured, that he who now holds the earthly

He resolves, therefore, to accost first Adam, in the guise of a friend, and then Eve, whose mind is more fickle, in the guise of a snake. At this point an angelic Chorus appears, bringing the scene to a close with a summary of the Devil's rebellion and a condemnation of his unrepentant hostility to God and Man.[1]

The second act introduces the two human protagonists. In response to Adam's request, 'Narra petenti, quo modo, quoque ordine, / Tam magna numeris machina impleta est suis',[2] an angel tells him of the work of the six days. No sooner has he completed his exposition and left the stage than Eve enters, so Adam now takes over the role of narrator and explains to her the circumstances of her creation. God, he relates, perceiving that he needed a companion, made her from his rib:

> Ubi recreata membra, qui primus fuit,
> Somnus reliquit, ex meis, uxor tua
> Formata membris astitit species mihi,
> Quam cum viderem, languidos artus adhuc
> Stupor occupavit, flamma quem solvit nova,
> Et amoris ignis.[3]

Eve replies in words that might be the theme of Milton's variation in *Paradise Lost*:

> Felicitatis magna pars, aut unica
> Vir est maritae: dulce nunc quicquid mihi est
> Te sine nocebit.[4]

The two of them then join with the Chorus of angels in a hymn of praise devoted to the glories of the Creation.[5]

The third act is comparatively brief. As he had planned, the Tempter approaches Adam, who rejects his overtures of friendship

kingdoms should not occupy the heavenly ones. Then indeed it would shame me to have fled, a conquered exile, from the citadel of Heaven, if I left my realms only that they might be given to another, and in defeat gave over my place to mankind.'

[1] *Adamus Exul*, i. 233–311.

[2] Ibid. ii. 422–3. 'Tell me, I beg, how and in what order so great a system was filled with its numbers.'

[3] Ibid. ii. 670–5. 'When my first sleep left my restored limbs, your form, my wife, made from my limbs, stood before me; when I saw you, amazement seized my still sluggish joints; a new flame and the fire of love melted it.'

[4] Ibid. ii. 682–4. 'Her husband is a great part, or the only part, of a wife's happiness: whatever is sweet to me now, would be painful without you.'

[5] Ibid. ii. 695–841.

no less steadfastly than his predecessors in *Genesis B* and the *Mystère*:

> *Sa.* Oblata ab aliquo quis recusat munera?
> *Ad.* Quemcunque non tam dona, quam donans juvat.[1]

When the Devil has retired with threats of future vengeance the Chorus exhorts Adam to persist in his refusal to eat the forbidden fruit.

In the fourth act Satan puts the second part of his plan into operation. Captured by the beauty of his reptilian disguise, Eve wonders if the mysterious creature can speak.[2] Immediately it does, offering her the loyalty and subjection of all the animals. Although they rejoice in the clemency of their human master, he continues, they are puzzled by the prohibition of the tree of knowledge. Can it be that God envies Man? Eve reminds him that the forbidden fruit will bring death to whoever partakes of it, but he points out that death is only an inevitable part of the natural cycle of birth and decay. God could not, he insists, have created anything evil; the fruit therefore must be good and the prohibition envious. As he urges her to cast off the yoke of servitude and eat the fruit, whose very name is evidence of its goodness, Eve gradually begins to weaken:

> Adeone et alia praeter hominum pectora
> Ratio occupavit? bruta namque haec bestia est,
> At bruta certe verba non visa est loqui.[3]

Her senses respond to the attractiveness of the apple, and she muses aloud over the serpent's arguments until she eventually decides to eat in the name of freedom:

> Non sola tua res agitur: hac hora potes
> Prodesse mille saeculorum posteris.
> Servosne parere an liberos melius putas,
> Homines, Deosne?[4]

Perhaps, after all, God will forgive her, or perhaps He will not even notice what she has done.[5]

[1] Ibid. iii. 935–6. 'Who refuses gifts offered by anyone? He whom the giver pleases less than the gifts.' [2] Ibid. iv. 1050.
[3] Ibid. iv. 1219–21. 'And has reason indeed entered other breasts besides Man's? For this creature is an animal, but certainly did not seem to speak brutish words.'
[4] Ibid. iv. 1289–92. 'It is not only your affair: in this hour you can benefit a thousand ages yet to come. Do you think it better to bear either captives or free men, men or gods?'
[5] Ibid. iv. 1294–5.

As soon as she has eaten the fruit the serpent, observing that Adam is about to return, disappears. Eve excitedly greets her husband with the news that she has disobeyed God's commandment, but succeeds in provoking him only to horror:

> Gelidus per artus vadit excussos tremor,
> Exsanguis asto, crinis erectus riget.
> Vix ipse valido spiritus gemitu viam
> Perrupit.[1]

For a time he resists all her attempts to persuade him to fall with her, but he is finally overcome by her passionate appeal to their love:

> Per conjugalem te precor supplex fidem,
> Tuos per oculos, et per amplexus meos,
> Per, si quid unquam dulce fuit ex me tibi,
> Ne me relinquas: junge te socium mihi,
> Ut nuptialis pacta serves foederis.
>
> .   .   .
>
> Sin juvat amoris candidi ductum sequi,
> Nec hoc vetabo: quid maritali fide
> Prius esse oportet? huc se amor vertat tuus,
> Quo sacra thalami jura, quo foedus vocat.[2]

The issue is presented no less clearly, though a great deal more eloquently, than in the Cornish plays: Adam has to choose between his wife and his God. Overcome by Eve's persuasions, he chooses the former:

> Fallor? an voluit Deus
> Conjugis amores anteferri caeteris
> Etiam parentum? Voluit: huc Pomum mihi.[3]

As he eats, Eve, feeling for the first time the effects of sin, asks that all the punishment should light on her. But her reactions are cut short by the Chorus, which intervenes to lament the Fall and reveal its effects on the future history of mankind.

[1] *Adamus Exul*, iv. 1351–4. 'An icy shiver runs through my shaken limbs, bloodless I stand, my hair stands on end. My very breath barely forced its way out in a mighty sigh.'

[2] Ibid. iv. 1398–1437. 'As a suppliant I beg you by our marriage faith, by your eyes, and my embraces, by whatever in me was sweet to you, do not desert me. Join yourself to me as my companion, that you may preserve the pact of the nuptial bond. . . . If it pleases you to follow the guidance of pure love, I will not forbid that either: what should take precedence over marital faith? Here let your love incline you, to where the sacred vows of the marriage bed and the marriage contract summon you.'

[3] Ibid. iv. 1459–61. 'Do I err? Did God not wish my love for my wife to take precedence over all others, even that for my parents? He wished it; give me the apple.'

At the beginning of the fifth act Satan rejoices over his success and describes the anguish of the fallen pair.[1] When they enter it soon becomes apparent that Eve is the stronger in the face of disaster. Adam merely cries for death:

> Mors quid a tergo mihi
> Crudelis instas? pectus hoc, pectus feri.
> Miseranda coniunx agmen infernum vides?[2]

In spite of Eve's efforts to calm him he grows more and more demented:

> Longas omittam languidae poenae moras,
> Nec aeger ultra funus extendam meum.
> Quodcunque vitae restat, abrumpam manu
> Juste severa.[3]

At last, however, Eve succeeds in consoling him with the hope of expiating their crime through punishment, and averts his suicidal intentions by threatening to kill herself.[4] Their reconciliation is quickly followed by God's summons to the judgement, during the course of which the promise of future salvation is made absolutely explicit.[5] Comforted by this revelation, Adam bids farewell to the garden and leaves with Eve to undergo the sentence God has imposed on them.

Few if any of the major elements in this treatment can be said to be really original. The Devil's opening soliloquy, the intervention of an angelic instructor, the prior temptation of Adam, the serpent's arguments with Eve, Adam's motives for eating the fruit, Satan's speech of triumph, and Adam and Eve's quarrel and reconciliation had all appeared in previous versions of the story. What is original is the classical five-act form and the relatively sophisticated dramatic technique by means of which the traditional material has been adapted to fit it. The Devil's prologue to the temptation, for instance, may have been anticipated by Avitus and the medieval playwrights, and the description of Eden it contains may have been commonplace, but never before had these two standard features been

---

[1] Ibid. v. 1531–89.

[2] Ibid. v. 1594–6. 'O cruel death, why do you stay behind my back? This breast, strike this breast. Pitiable wife, do you see the infernal multitude?'

[3] Ibid. v. 1684–7. 'I shall forego the long delays of slow punishment, nor shall I, wretched man, postpone death any longer. Whatever life remains I will justly cut off with my fell hand.'

[4] Ibid. v. 1780–90. [5] Ibid. v. 1915 et seq.

combined as they are here. Each enriches the meaning of the other, so that the beauty of the garden gains fresh poignancy when seen through the eyes of Satan, while the rebel's misery and depravity stand out all the more clearly in contrast. Again, although the account of the work of the days and Adam's instruction by an angel were both conventional enough, the significance of the Creation is now defined by the presence of its master. The dramatization of these pre-mundane events, moreover, has enabled Grotius to solve the problem of staging the rebellion of Lucifer and the making of the universe by relating them through the mouth of one or other of the protagonists. The clumsy medieval device of making God deliver a running commentary on His own activities thus gives way to a naturalistic conversation between Adam and his angelic teacher. Finally, whereas in the earlier narrative treatments like *Genesis B* and the *De Mosaicae Historiae Gestis* the poet had continually to interrupt the action to express his personal feelings or remind the audience of the implications of Man's disobedience, Grotius is able to make the necessary didactic points through the agency of the Chorus without interrupting the flow of the action.[1] The result is the first genuinely dramatic play on the Fall of Man.

Grotius's adolescent drama, I believe, shaped not only the structure of Vondel's *Adam in Ballingschap* (1664), which is avowedly based upon it,[2] but also that of *Paradise Lost*. In May or June of 1638 Milton visited the great Dutchman in Paris on his way to Italy.[3] Soon after his return to England he began work on the dramatic drafts of *Paradise Lost*, of which the four versions preserved in the Trinity MS. date roughly from 1639 to 1642.[4] While it may be no more than a coincidence that he outlined his plans for a play on the Fall so soon after meeting the author of *Adamus Exul*, the

[1] In the medieval plays the angels had come to take an increasingly large part in the action. Just as Hebrew and Greek transcendentalism removed the Deity from the material sphere, leaving more and more work to be performed by the angels, so the problems of presenting God on the stage evidently had the same effect in the drama. Grotius's angelic chorus may be the product of this tendency.

[2] In his *Milton and Vondel*, 1885, G. Edmundson explored the possible relationship between *Paradise Lost* and the works of Vondel. While it is just possible that one or two details in Milton's treatment may have been derived from *Adam in Ballingschap*, the work appeared too late to have any major influence on the over-all structure of *Paradise Lost*.

[3] The evidence is conveniently summarized in J. M. French's *The Life Records of John Milton*, New Brunswick, 1949, i. 368–9.

[4] I have used the text in the Columbia University Press edition of *The Works of John Milton*, New York, 1938, xviii. 228–32. All subsequent quotations from Milton's works are from this edition also.

growing similarity observable between the successive drafts of
Paradise Lost and the Dutch play can hardly be accidental.

The first two drafts consist only of lists of the dramatis personae,
and it is not until the third draft that any discernible plan emerges.
There, after a prologue spoken by Moses, three allegorical figures,
Justice, Mercy, and Wisdom, debate 'what should become of man
if he fall'. The Chorus brings the first act to a conclusion with a hymn
to the Creation. The second begins with some unspecified action
involving Heavenly Love and the Evening Star and ends with the
Chorus's song in celebration of Adam and Eve's marriage and the
beauties of paradise. In Act III Lucifer appears 'contriving Adams
ruine', after which the Chorus 'feares for Adam and relates Lucifers
rebellion and fall'. The temptation itself is omitted, either because
Milton could not think of a way of coming to terms with Adam and
Eve's nakedness or because he wished to emulate the Greek trage-
dians by reporting the most spectacular action through the mouth of
a messenger, and the fourth act begins with Adam and Eve already
fallen. When Conscience has consigned them to the judgement of
God the Chorus 'bewails and tells the good Adam hath lost'. By Act
V the fallen pair are already exiled from Eden. Having been confronted with various allegorical afflictions, they are finally comforted
by Faith, Hope, and Charity, and the Chorus 'breifly concludes'.

Apart from the five-act form and the use of an angelic Chorus this
has very little in common with Grotius's treatment. Indeed, the
debate between the three daughters of God and the consistent
intervention of allegorical figures suggest that it owes as much to
the medieval as to the classical dramatic tradition. The fourth draft,
on the other hand, is much closer to *Adamus Exul*. For example, the
title, which in draft three had been 'Paradise Lost', has been changed
to 'Adam unparadiz'd', and both this and the cancelled title, 'Adams
Banishment', look very much like translations of 'Adamus Exul'.
The first two acts of draft three are replaced by a conversation
between Gabriel and the Chorus, during the course of which the
former describes paradise and the creation, love, and marriage of
Adam and Eve, while the latter, having explained why it is necessary
to protect Man from the vengeance of Lucifer, sings a hymn to the
Creation. Although it is Gabriel and not Lucifer who describes
Eden, and although it is to the Chorus and not Adam that he discourses on the creation of Man, the actual narrative sequence is substantially the same as it had been in Grotius's play: the description

of paradise, the account of Lucifer's rebellion, the hymn to the Creation, and the relation of the making of Adam and Eve. In comparison the third act is scarcely modified at all. Lucifer laments his fall and expresses his desire to be revenged on Man; the Chorus resists him, and after 'discourse of enmity on either side' he leaves them to sing a song of victory 'as before after the first act was sung a hymn of the creation'. The final acts, however, are expanded by the addition of two vital new features. Before Adam and Eve are arraigned by Conscience, the Devil enters 'relating, & insulting in what he had don to the destruction of man', and after the Chorus has bewailed Adam's fall, 'Adam then & Eve returne accuse one another but especially Adam lays the blame to his wife, is stubborn in his offence'. These innovations, like almost every other, bring the fourth draft still further into line with *Adamus Exul*. If, as Milton instructs us to, we compare the fourth draft with the third, it appears that every major modification he has introduced into the later draft could have been inspired by Grotius's play. Their total effect is to recast the story in a form recognizably similar to that of the Dutch drama.

There is, moreover, some evidence to suggest that Milton went still further in this direction. According to Edward Phillips, Satan's soliloquy at the beginning of the fourth book of *Paradise Lost* was originally the opening speech in a dramatic version of the story.[1] As we have seen, the *Adamus Exul* begins in precisely the same way, so if Phillips's evidence is accepted it would seem that Milton produced a fifth draft which began, like the Dutch play, with Satan's soliloquy as he arrives within sight of Eden at dawn. The increasing number of parallels between the dramatic drafts and *Adamus Exul* may, of course, be no more than accidental, but coincidence cannot be stretched indefinitely. Sooner or later one reaches a point at which the coincidence of the coincidences becomes itself implausible. Such, I submit, is the case here. That Milton should, by the purest chance, have incorporated one or two features analogous to those in Grotius's treatment is quite credible; that he should have incorporated so many so consistently can only be due to his knowledge of the work of his Dutch predecessor.

The ultimate test, however, must be *Paradise Lost* itself. As A. Barker has shown,[2] the 1667 ten-book version of the poem falls

[1] See J. M. French, op. cit. ii. 50–51.
[2] 'Structural Pattern in *Paradise Lost*', *P.Q.* xxviii (1949), 17–30. I follow Barker's

naturally into five acts consisting of two books each. On this basis *Paradise Lost* may be subdivided as follows: Books 1–2 (I–II)—Act I; 3–4 (III–IV)—Act II; 5–6 (V–VI)—Act III; 7–8 (VII, VIII, IX)—Act IV; 9–10 (X, XI, XII)—Act V. Of these 'acts' the first clearly has nothing to do with *Adamus Exul*; its only dramatic analogues are to be found in the medieval cycle plays, which included a scene in Hell immediately after Satan's banishment from Heaven. The second 'act', on the other hand, looks very much like a condensation of the first three acts of drafts three and four. The debate between Justice, Mercy, and Wisdom (draft three) appears as the discussion between the Father and Son.[1] Satan's prologue (drafts three and four), the Chorus's encounter with him, and its consequent song of victory (draft four) remain,[2] and between them are sandwiched Gabriel's description of paradise (draft four), which is taken over by Milton,[3] and the same angel's account of the creation, love, and marriage of Eve (draft four), which is delivered now by the character in question.[4]

The action of 'Acts' III and IV, on the contrary, was never included in any of the dramatic drafts. They conformed to the structure of classical tragedy inasmuch as the crucial events took place off stage and were merely reported either by an angel or by Satan. Act III, perhaps, may be seen as an expansion of the Chorus's relation of Lucifer's rebellion and fall in draft three, but the hymn to the Creation in both drafts can hardly have supplied sufficient material for Act IV. Here, I believe, *Adamus Exul* furnished at least the basic framework around which Milton built Books 7 and 8 (VII, VIII, IX), namely the conversation between Adam and the angel concerning the work of the six days,[5] Adam's narration to Eve, whose place is taken by Raphael, of her creation and his feelings for her,[6] and the temptation of Eve by the serpent and of Adam by Eve.[7] Act V reverts to the plan in draft four. Lucifer's speech of triumph,[8] Adam and Eve's quarrel and reconciliation,[9] their condemnation and expulsion,[10] the masque of the evils of life,[11] Mercy's comforting words and the promise of the Messiah,[12] and Adam's repentance and

---

practice of indicating the books as divided in the 1667 edition with arabic numerals and as divided in the 1674 edition with roman numerals.

[1] *P.L.* iii. 80–343.   [2] Ibid. iv. 32–114, iv. 782–1015.
[3] Ibid. iv. 131–357.   [4] Ibid. iv. 440–91.   [5] Ibid. vii. 70–viii. 178.
[6] Ibid. viii. 250–613.   [7] Ibid. ix. 412–999.   [8] Ibid. x. 460–503.
[9] Ibid. x. 720–1104.   [10] Ibid. xi. 72–262.   [11] Ibid. xi. 423–xii. 110.
[12] Ibid. xii. 324–465.

acceptance of his lot[1] all appear in Books 9–10 (X, XI, XII), and in the same order.

It appears, then, that the influence of Grotius's play did not stop at the putative fifth draft, for the total design of *Paradise Lost* proves to be closer to that of the *Adamus Exul* than any of the previous plans for the work. Unfortunately, Milton's debt to the Dutch drama has been obscured for over two centuries by the activities of the infamous Lauder, whose attempt to manufacture evidence of Milton's alleged plagiarism discredited *Adamus Exul*'s claim as a possible source, before any serious critical attention was paid to Milton's plans for a similar dramatic version outlined in the Trinity MS. As a result, critics like A. H. Gilbert and G. McColley, who have examined the dramatic drafts in some detail, have taken no notice of their increasing similarity to Grotius's work.[2] Indeed, not until W. Kirkconnell's invaluable edition and translation of *Adamus Exul*[3] appeared has an uncorrupted text been readily available to critics of *Paradise Lost*.

In conclusion, I should emphasize that the relationship between *Paradise Lost* and *Adamus Exul* which I have been arguing is primarily a structural one. The ghost of Lauder still walks through the pages of those source critics who have concerned themselves with Milton's possible debt to the Renaissance treatments of the Fall: they may no longer accuse him of plagiarism, but they still concentrate largely on explicit verbal parallels.[4] While these certainly offer the clearest proof of the relationship between any two works, they are not the only or even the most important kind of evidence. The sort of influence we are likely to find may equally well be one of form or concept, and this point holds for most of the dramatic treatments of the Fall story. Their history is one of successive attempts to modify the Genesis narrative to meet the peculiar demands of the drama. The medieval playwrights gradually filled out the more important gaps in the action and amplified the motives and reactions of the characters, Grotius reorganized this material within the limits of a five-act tragedy, and Milton, if I am right, adopted Grotius's new pattern as the skeleton of *Paradise Lost*.

[1] *P.L.* xii. 469–649.

[2] *On the Composition of Paradise Lost*, Chapel Hill, 1947, ch. i; *Paradise Lost*, Chicago, 1940, chs. xi–xii.

[3] *The Celestial Cycle*, pp. 96–220.

[4] See, for instance, M. T. de Maisières, *Les Poèmes inspirés du début de la Genèse à l'époque de la Renaissance*, Louvain, 1931.

PART THREE

Paradise Lost
and the Tradition

VIII

THINGS UNATTEMPTED

WHEN Milton announced that his 'adventrous Song' would pursue 'Things unattempted yet in Prose or Rhime'[1] he could hardly have wanted to convey the impression that he was the first author to take the Fall of Man as his theme. For the exegetical and literary traditions we have already explored were still very much alive in the Renaissance, preserved not only in the standard Biblical commentaries and scholarly editions of the time but also in works like Du Bartas's *Sepmaine*, Joseph Beaumont's *Psyche*, and Samuel Pordage's *Mundorum Explicatio*. What he meant, more probably, was that his epic would outdo all previous treatments of the story in the sheer comprehensiveness of its vision, that it would explore the 'wayes of God to Man' on a scale never before conceived by a Christian poet. In this scarcely more modest claim he was certainly justified; as I hope to show, *Paradise Lost* is in every sense the culmination of the myth's development.

Indeed, the most extraordinary single characteristic of the poem is the immense richness of its intellectual and poetic content. Of the patristic interpretations, for instance, Milton incorporated the allegorical and typological as well as the literal. With them he blended notions derived, directly or indirectly, from rabbinic commentaries, apocryphal documents, Christian-Latin Biblical epics, medieval legends, and recent plays, poems, and tracts on the same subject. What is more, he synthesized all these heterogeneous elements within the framework of a coherent narrative structure modelled partly on the *Aeneid*, partly on *Adamus Exul*. The conceptual control necessary to organize this wealth of ideas would be remarkable in any poet; in a blind one it is little short of miraculous.

The availability of the various facets of the Fall tradition in the seventeenth century has been exhaustively investigated by a number of scholars,[2] and I do not propose to duplicate their researches here. Taking their conclusions as my starting-point, I propose instead to

[1] *P.L.* i. 16. [2] See Bibliography, pp. 303-4.

examine the use to which Milton put the materials he had at hand. If in the process I shall have as much to say about his individuality as about his conventionality I shall be attempting to correct what seems to me to be a false emphasis in many studies of his sources. By concentrating, as they have, on the similarities that exist between *Paradise Lost* and its predecessors they have inevitably tended to stress parallels at the expense of divergences. Thus while one comes away from them with a very clear realization of Milton's possible obligations to earlier writers, one learns little or nothing about his inventiveness. The latter, I would submit, is quite as important as the former; a poet's account, after all, does not consist merely of his debts, and a literary auditor who wishes to produce an accurate balance should also record his client's credits. It may be useful to discover exactly what *Paradise Lost* owes to the works of the Fathers or the Rabbis; it is no less useful to define in what respects it is original, and therefore itself.

To do so involves rather more than the straightforward piece of critical arithmetic implied by the foregoing analogy. It would be convenient, to be sure, if once the derivative passages had been subtracted from the text we were left with an indisputably Miltonic remainder, but in practice the two entities cannot be separated so neatly. They exist simultaneously rather than consecutively, unified by an imagination which was at once both imitative and creative. To take a small but typical example, the Tempter's reasons for concealing himself in a snake had been definitively analysed by Ambrose and Augustine: he chose a shape which, 'being slippery and moving in tortuous windings', conformed to his own devious nature.[1] In Book IX of *Paradise Lost*, on the other hand, Satan

> Consider'd every Creature, which of all
> Most opportune might serve his Wiles, and found
> The serpent suttlest Beast of all the Field.
> Him after long debate, irresolute
> Of thoughts revolv'd, his final sentence chose
> Fit Vessel, fittest Imp of fraud, in whom
> To enter, and his dark suggestions hide
> From sharpest sight: for in the wilie Snake,
> Whatever sleights none would suspicious mark,
> As from his wit and native suttletie

[1] See above, Ch. III, pp. 74, 95.

> Proceeding, which in other Beasts observ'd
> Doubt might beget of Diabolic pow'r
> Active within beyond the sense of brute.[1]

Although the patristic explanation is still the basis of the argument, it has been qualified by strategic considerations that go far beyond the traditional account of the Devil's behaviour at this juncture. What had been an essentially moral extrapolation is now a thoroughly pragmatic manœuvre.

We shall encounter the same fusion of old and new over and over again in the following chapters, for Milton was very rarely content to take an idea or an incident as he found it. Invariably he modified it to meet the particular demands of his own interpretation of the story. Taken out of their immediate context, the constituents which went to the making of *Paradise Lost* may be seen to stem from a wide variety of possible antecedents. Put together again, they form a whole that is unique. In the final analysis Milton's version of the Fall is distinguished not by its indebtedness but by its profound originality.

The treatment of Satan's disguise in Book IX is significant, too, as an example of the kind of transformation which many other commonplace features underwent during the course of the poem's composition. It reveals, that is to say, that however interested Milton may have been in doctrinal questions, the principle which determined his selection from and manipulation of the mass of extra-Biblical amplification at his disposal was essentially literary. In the case in point he subordinated didactic comment on the Devil's corruption to narrative comment on his motivation, and throughout the rest of the story his first concern was always to bring the Biblical myth to life, to portray the characters, circumstances, and events in such a way that they seemed not only fateful but credible. The problems I outlined in Chapter I are solved with such delicacy that we are scarcely aware of them as we read their solutions. They are solved, moreover, in practical as well as theoretical terms. The theological reconciliation of foreknowledge with free will worked out in Book III is, admittedly, unsatisfactory; the poetical reconciliation achieved in Book IX, on the contrary, is a triumph. Milton prepared the ground so carefully that when the crisis comes we do not feel that God's omniscience has had the slightest effect on Adam and Eve's decision to eat the forbidden fruit.

[1] *P.L.* ix. 84–96.

The whole sum of the evidence I shall be presenting suggests that Milton was especially sensitive to difficulties of this sort. The tact with which he handled them hardly bears out Waldock's picture of the naïve blunderer who stumbled unawares into a subject beyond his comprehension. In opposition, therefore, to the still fashionable assumption that Milton did the opposite of what he meant, I shall in the pages following recognize the possibility that he actually wrote the poem he intended to write.

IX

HELLISH HATE AND HEAV'NLY LOVE

Ah wherefore! He deservd no such return
From me, whom he created what I was
In that bright eminence, and with this good
Upbraided none; nor was his service hard.
What could be less then to afford him praise,
The easiest recompence, and pay him thanks,
How due![1]

THIS problem, posed succinctly by Satan himself as he comes within sight of Eden, had never been finally settled by Christian commentators and poets, and as late as the seventeenth century a wide variety of solutions were still being canvassed. The chief difficulty lay in finding a motive for his rebellion which was neither too good nor too bad. If it was too good, God would seem unjust; if it was too bad, the Devil would seem silly. To a poet of Milton's sensibilities the literary implications of the second conclusion must have seemed no less abhorrent than the theological implications of the first, for he took great pains to avoid either.

Early in Book I there is an unmistakable reference to the tradition stemming from Isaiah xiv,[2] that Satan revolted because he was proud:

what time his Pride
Had cast him out from Heav'n, with all his Host
Of Rebel Angels, by whose aid aspiring
To set himself in Glory above his Peers,
He trusted to have equal'd the most High.[3]

But later in the same book it is implied that there was more to the matter than that: the fallen angel confesses that he rebelled 'from

---

[1] *P.L.* iv. 42-48.
[2] See above: Ch. II, pp. 33-34; Ch. III, pp. 87-88; Ch. IV, p. 134; Ch. V, p. 157; Ch. VI, p. 176; Ch. VII, p. 194.
[3] *P.L.* i. 36-40. For the survival of the Isaiah tradition in the Renaissance see C. A. Patrides, *Milton and the Christian Tradition*, 1966, pp. 91-93.

sence of injur'd merit'[1] and cast doubts on God's omnipotence. With these hints of deeper under-currents we have to rest content until Book V, when Raphael tells Adam that Satan objected to the Son's promotion over the angels, who were commanded to worship Him. Envy is thus allied with pride:

> yet fraught
> With envie against the Son of God, that day
> Honourd by his great Father, and proclaimd
> *Messiah* King anointed, could not beare
> Through pride that sight, & thought himself impaird.[2]

Taxed by Abdiel, Satan asserted that as he was self-created he was the equal of the Son, whose elevation over the angels was therefore a gross violation of the celestial order of seniority.

Although very many reasons had been offered for the Satanic revolt, nothing quite like this had ever appeared before. Milton's analysis of it is one of the most genuinely original things in the whole poem. Why, then, did he find it necessary to invent a new version of the episode? Why, in particular, did he reject, or, rather, supplement, the generally accepted theory based on the Isaiah passage? One answer, I would suggest, is that his dramatic sense led him to perceive that the Isaiah story furnished a description of the Devil's rebellion rather than a real explanation. Granted that his sin was pride, something more was needed to account for that pride; a dramatic charge was required to detonate the emotional explosion. Faced by the same problem, the majority of Milton's predecessors had simply followed Origen in adducing Ezekiel xxviii to demonstrate that Lucifer's pride had its origin in his beauty and his pre-eminent position in Heaven.[3] Yet this still did not explain why his pride exploded at one moment rather than another, so the medieval dramatists had concluded that God's temporary absence from Heaven during the creation of the world provided the Devil with an opportunity to challenge His power by attempting to usurp His throne.[4] If Milton knew this crude solution he could not conceivably have used it, for according to his time-table Satan fell before the formation of the universe and according to his theology God was both omniscient and omnipresent.

---

[1] *P.L.* i. 98.   [2] Ibid. v. 661–5.
[3] See above, Ch. III, pp. 87–88; Ch. V, p. 157; Ch. VI, p. 176; Ch. VII, p. 194.
[4] See above, Ch. VI, p. 176.

The *York* play on the subject had proposed a second possible reason for the rebel angel's discontent, namely, that he objected to the fact that Christ intended to become incarnate in human rather than angelic form.[1] As A. Williams has shown,[2] this idea was taken up by several later writers; it was preserved by Zanchius in his *De Operibus Dei* (1597), Andreini in his *L'Adamo* (1613), Vondel in his *Lucifer* (1654), and Thomas Heywood in *The Hierarchie of the Blessed Angels* (1635):

> With Pride and Enuy *Lucifer* now swelling
> Against Mankinde, whom from his heav'nly Dwelling,
> He seemes in supernaturall Gifts t'outshine,
> (Man being but Terrene, and himselfe Diuine)
> Ambitiously his Hate encreasing still,
> Dares to oppose the great Creators Will:
> As holding it against his Iustice done,
> That th'Almighties sole begotten Sonne,
> Mans nature to assume purpos'd and meant,
> And not the Angels, much more excellent.[3]

As Williams has also noted, Calvin dismissed this notion in thoroughly contemptuous terms:

> Certeine curious Sophisters haue feigned, because he foresawe that the sonne of God was to take vpon him humane fleshe, he enuied the same also: but this is a friuolous speculation. For seeing the sonne of God was made man, to deliuer vs whiche were lost, from miserable destruction: how could he foresee that which should not haue come to passe, if man had not sinned?[4]

Consequently, Williams argues, Milton substituted the exaltation of the Son for His incarnation, thus producing the version of the story as we have it in Book V of *Paradise Lost*.

While it is true that this hypothesis is consistent with several of the subsidiary features which characterize Milton's treatment of the episode, a rather more convincing source may be found in a third tradition, that of the Vita Adae et Evae, according to which the Devil fell because he refused to worship the newly created Adam, on the grounds that the angels had been created before him.[5] This

---

[1] See above, Ch. VII, p. 194.

[2] 'The Motivation of Satan's Rebellion in *Paradise Lost*', *S.P.* xlii (1945), 253–68.

[3] Book VI, p. 339 in the 1635 edition.

[4] *Commentary on Genesis*, iii. 1. I quote from Thomas Tymme's translation in *A Commentarie of John Caluine vpon the first booke of Moses*, 1578.

[5] See above, Ch. II, p. 56.

diagnosis of Satan's motives had become very popular during the
Middle Ages in spite of its two obvious drawbacks: first, that the
Devil's objections were perfectly well founded, for he was senior to
Adam, and the Creator was violating the hierarchical order by
commanding the angels to worship a mere man; and second, that
Christian chronology generally placed Adam's creation after rather
than before the fall of Satan. What Milton did, I believe, was to
overcome both these difficulties at one stroke by substituting Christ
for Adam, a substitution made all the easier by the long-standing
association of Christ with the so-called 'heavenly Adam'. There
were, moreover, two positive factors which may have led him to
modify the story in this way. First, in both *Christ and Satan*, which
he may have known,[1] and Lactantius's *Divine Institutes*, with which
he certainly was familiar,[2] the origin of the Devil's rebellion was
traced back to his envy of the Son. After God had begotten Christ,
the latter recorded, He

made another being, in whom the disposition of the divine origin did not
remain. Therefore he was infected with his own envy as with poison, and
passed from good to evil: and at his own will, which had been given to
him by God unfettered, he acquired for himself a contrary name. From
which it appears that the source of all evils is envy. For he cursed his
predecessor, who through his stedfastness is acceptable and dear to God
the Father.[3]

Second, the application of the Vita legend to the divine rather than
the human man emphasized the conflict between Christ and Satan
upon which the supernatural machinery of *Paradise Lost* was
largely founded—it is Christ, for instance, who defeats Satan in the
war in Heaven, Christ who balances Satan's offer to corrupt Man
with His offer to redeem him, and Christ who passes sentence on
Adam, Eve, and the serpent.

Several details in Book V suggest that this theory may be correct.
It accounts, as Williams's does not, for the great stress put on the
worship of the angels, and it explains Satan's very unusual reasons
for refusing to join in that worship. In the Vita he had answered
Michael's demands by stating: 'I am his senior in the Creation,
before he was made I was already made.'[4] In *Paradise Lost* that very
reasonable point is invalidated by the Son's genuine seniority, so

[1] It is contained in the Junius MS.
[2] See K. E. Hartwell, *Lactantius and Milton*, Cambridge, Massachusetts, 1929.
[3] *Div. Inst.* ii. 9.   [4] *Vita*, xiv. 3.

Satan is forced to assert, like his predecessors in *Hamartigenia* and *De Mosaicae Historiae Gestis*, that he too knew no beginning. Again, Abdiel's function in Milton's poem is much the same as Michael's in the Vita—he urges Satan to worship with the other angels and warns him of the consequences of his disobedience—while Satan's objections to submitting to 'one and to his image now proclaim'd' echoes the command in the Vita to worship 'the image of God the Lord'.[1] As in the Vita, too, the Isaiah story is woven into the narrative immediately after the Devil's preliminary outburst, though much more subtly: whereas in the Vita he merely paraphrased his boasts as recorded in the Old Testament passage, in *Paradise Lost* he is called 'Lucifer', associated with the Morning Star by means of a simile,[2] and depicted as setting up his throne in the North. Finally, this alternative theory sheds some fresh light on Milton's ambiguous use of the verb 'beget' in this part of the poem. Quoting Psalm ii, the Father says: 'This day I have begot whom I declare / My onely Son.'[3] A. H. Gilbert has shown that according to most seventeenth-century interpretations of this psalm 'begot' was taken to mean 'exalted',[4] but there is no denying that shortly afterwards the word is used in its normal generative sense when Satan states that he is 'self-begot'.[5] If Milton was indeed attempting to adapt the Vita's account of the Devil's rebellion, then it seems possible that the very ambiguity of the word 'beget' offered a convenient way of incorporating the earlier story into its new context.

Satan's motives for bringing about the downfall of Adam and Eve are far less complicated, though Milton's treatment of them is again somewhat unusual. Once the legend of Lucifer's pre-mundane rebellion and fall was firmly established, the reasons for his hostility to Man presented no great problem: he envied him the delights of his unfallen life.[6] The idea that men were created to take the place of the fallen angels gave this motive still greater urgency, and from Avitus onwards the Devil was usually presented as seducing Adam and Eve in order to prevent them from enjoying the benefits which he himself had lost.[7] Milton, however, made little or no use of this

---

[1] *P.L.* v. 784; Vita, xiv. 1–2. The origin of the phrase, of course, is Gen. i. 26–27.
[2] *P.L.* v. 708–9.   [3] Ibid. v. 603–4.
[4] 'The Theological Basis of Satan's Rebellion and the Function of Abdiel in *Paradise Lost*', *M.P.* xl (1942), 19–42.
[5] *P.L.* v. 860.   [6] See above, Ch. III, pp. 81–82.
[7] See above: Ch. IV, pp. 134–5; Ch. V, pp. 157–8; Ch. VII, pp. 199, 207.

traditional motive until Book IX. Instead he laid all the emphasis on
Satan's desire to be revenged on God, the motive favoured by
Calvin: 'But we ought to content our selues with this reason, that he
being the enemie of God, went to ouerthrowe the order whiche he
had set: because he could not pull God out of his throne, he assailed
man, in whome his image shineth. Man being ouerthrowen, he knew
that the horrible confusion of the whole worlde shoulde followe,
euen as it came to passe.'[1] This is just the possibility to which
Beelzebub draws attention at the end of the diabolic council in
Book II; having mentioned rumours in Heaven concerning the
creation of some new race, he continues:

> Though Heav'n be shut,
> And Heav'ns high Arbitrator sit secure
> In his own strength, this place may lye expos'd
> The utmost border of his Kingdom, left
> To their defence who hold it: here perhaps
> Som advantagious act may be achiev'd
> By sudden onset, either with Hell fire
> To waste his whole Creation, or possess
> All as our own, and drive as we were driven,
> The punie habitants, or if not drive,
> Seduce them to our Party, that thir God
> May prove thir foe, and with repenting hand
> Abolish his own works. This would surpass
> Common revenge, and interrupt his joy
> In our Confusion.[2]

Here, as the poet comments, the prime concern is 'to spite / The
great Creatour'.[3] Later in the same book, admittedly, Satan tells Sin
that mankind may have been created 'to supply / Perhaps our vacant
room',[4] but this is mere conjecture, as he admits. Indeed, it is
difficult to see how the fallen angels could have known God's
purposes in creating Adam and Eve, for it was only after they had
been cast out of Heaven that God declared His purpose of replacing
them with men.[5]

[1] *Commentary on Genesis*, iii. 1.
[2] *P.L.* ii. 358–72. Williams has suggested that this speech and Satan's in *Psyche*, i.
31 et seq., reveal the influence of the Vita story (op. cit.), but in both cases the Devil is
already fallen, and the whole point of the Vita version was the *unfallen* angel's envy.
[3] *P.L.* ii. 384–5.   [4] Ibid. ii. 834–5.
[5] The Cornish *Creation* solves this problem by giving God a speech in which He
declares His intentions to Lucifer just before casting him out of Heaven. See above,
Ch. VII, p. 199.

The effect of abandoning envy as a primary motive is clearly evident in Satan's reaction to his first sight of Adam and Eve. Whereas in every previous treatment of this dramatic moment the Devil had expressed hate and jealousy, Milton's Satan is deeply moved by the beauty and innocence of the newly created pair. He confesses that he is

> no purpos'd foe
> To you whom I could pittie thus forlorne
> Though I unpittied; League with you I seek,
> And mutual amitie so streight, so close,
> That I with you must dwell, or you with me
> Henceforth; . . .
>   if no better place,
> Thank him who puts me loath to this revenge
> On you who wrong me not for him who wrongd.
> And should I at your harmless innocence
> Melt, as I doe, yet public reason just,
> Honour and Empire with revenge enlarg'd,
> By conquering this new World, compels me now
> To do what else though damnd I should abhorre.[1]

The idea that Satan felt the need for companionship in his damnation had first been put forward by Avitus,[2] and it was adopted by several later writers, both poets and theologians. Calvin, for example, observed: 'If we may receiue coniectures, it is more likelie, that he was moued with a certeine outragious madnesse, as commonly the desperate sorte of men are, that he might carrie man with him for companie into euerlasting destruction.'[3] But in its context in *Paradise Lost* Satan's malevolent desire to make Man a partner in his ruin can be presented as 'amitie' without any melodramatic irony, for he does not yet regard him as an upstart creature destined to enjoy the glories he has lost. His speech reveals something infinitely more terrible than the hostility of a disinherited son towards the new heir; like a typical Elizabethan revenger, Satan proposes to kill the son simply to spite the father, recognizing his victim's beauty even at the moment he takes the decision to destroy it.

Pure envy—and the phrase is scarcely paradoxical after what has been expressed in this speech—appears for the first time when

---

[1] *P.L.* iv. 373–92.
[2] See above, Ch. IV, p. 135.
[3] *Commentary on Genesis*, iii. 1.

Satan 'with jealous leer maligne'[1] watches Adam and Eve embrace. While it is possible that both here and in Book IX, when the Devil admires Eve among the flowers, Milton had in mind the Jewish belief that the Tempter lusted after Adam's wife,[2] it hardly seems necessary to invoke a source to explain why the sight of a man and woman making love should excite a being deprived of those pleasures to envy. In any case, there is still no mention of Satan's intention to prevent Man from supplanting him in the celestial hierarchy. This commonplace theme is delayed until the temptation itself is imminent:

> hee to be aveng'd,
> And to repair his numbers thus impair'd,
>
> .   .   .
>
> Determin'd to advance into our room
> A Creature form'd of Earth, and him endow,
> Exalted from so base original,
> With Heav'nly spoils, our spoils: What he decreed
> He effected; Man he made, and for him built
> Magnificent this World, and Earth his seat,
> Him Lord pronounc'd, and, O indignitie!
> Subjected to his service Angel wings,
> And flaming Ministers.[3]

Here at last is the Devil of orthodox Christian tradition, the Devil of the *De Mosaicae Historiae Gestis*, *Genesis B*, the medieval plays, and *Adamus Exul*. What in the earlier books had been no more than a rumour is now stated as a fact, and Man becomes for the first time in the poem the direct object of Satan's hostility.

The Devil's motives, then, undergo a remarkable transformation during the course of the poem. In both cases, the rebellion against God and the temptation of Man, they at first appear to be grounded on essentially heroic values, pride, defiance, and revenge. As such, they accord well with Milton's picture of the fallen angel whose form

> had yet not lost
> All her Original brightness, nor appear'd
> Less then Arch Angel ruind, and th'excess
> Of Glory obscur'd.[4]

---

[1] *P.L.* iv. 503.   [2] See above, Ch. II, pp. 46–47.
[3] *P.L.* ix. 143–56.
[4] *P.L.* i. 591–4. Compare Heywood's *Hierarchie*, vi. 342–3.

But later they are seen to stem from a more ignoble source, envy. What is more, they are organized in such a way that the proud antagonist of God soon gives way to the jealous rival of the Son, and ultimately to the envious tempter of Man. This progressive degeneration, so pungently summarized by C. S. Lewis,[1] may of course be quite accidental, but the kind of manipulation I have described strongly suggests that it was very carefully calculated. In order to achieve it Milton invented a thoroughly unorthodox account of the reasons underlying the heavenly revolt, and suppressed until Book IX the conventional analysis of the motives which inspired the temptation. According to medieval poets and artists, Satan and his followers changed from angels into demons even as they fell. Milton's point seems to be that the floor of Hell does not mark the limit of the Devil's descent; his pictorial and physical fall is followed by a still heavier one in the 'Hell within him'.[2]

Milton's handling of the corresponding theme of 'Heav'nly love' is generally regarded as less successful, and the debate between the Father and Son in Book III, in which the divine benevolence is most thoroughly explored, is perhaps the weakest part of the poem.[3] If we compare it, as Milton clearly intended us to, with the previous council in Hell, the rhetoric of Heaven seems somewhat hollow, and the Son's dramatic offer to save Man pales beside Satan's more adventurous undertaking to corrupt him. God's self-justification, it has often been observed, is both unnecessary and unsympathetic, while the Son's pleas on Man's behalf serve only to emphasize the Father's unyielding severity. The whole scene seems calculated to present God in the worst possible light. That a poet who treated other equally difficult parts of the story with such infinite tact should have been unaware of the perils entailed in this particular episode is hard to believe. Why, then, we may reasonably ask, did he attempt it at all? It was not, after all, essential to the narrative coherence of the story as a whole, and it could have been omitted without serious damage to the dramatic structure underlying the poem.

Two answers may be offered on purely literary grounds. First, Milton may have wished to provide a counterpart to the council of devils in Book II. But the evidence of the dramatic drafts suggests

---

[1] *Preface*, ch. xiii.   [2] *P.L.* iv. 20.
[3] See for instance J. Peter, *A Critique of Paradise Lost*, 1960, pp. 10–14; J. B. Broadbent, *Some Graver Subject*, 1960, pp. 144–57; W. Empson, *Milton's God*, 1961, pp. 115–17.

that the heavenly parliament was conceived before the parallel scene in Hell. The first act of the third draft, in which Justice, Mercy, and Wisdom are shown 'debating what should become of man if he fall', looks very much like the model for the discussion between the Father and Son in Book III of *Paradise Lost*. On the other hand, in none of the four drafts is there anything to suggest that the material of the first two books of the poem formed part of Milton's original conception. It seems more likely, therefore, that the diabolic debate and Satan's offer to risk the journey to earth were inspired by the heavenly conversation and Christ's self-sacrifice rather than vice versa. Second, Milton may have introduced the scene to provide a Christian equivalent to the arguments between the gods character-istic of classical Epic. But again the inclusion of an allegorical version of the debate in the third dramatic draft shows that the episode was an integral part of Milton's scheme long before he decided to cast the story in epic form.

The real key to the episode is to be found, I believe, not in Milton's architectonics or even in his classical antecedents, but in the long-standing tradition of the debate of the four daughters of God. This, as we have seen,[1] had its origin in the rabbinic tractates, where God's foreknowledge of the Fall and its consequences was reconciled with His omnipotence by the invention of a dispute between His four daughters, Love, Truth, Righteousness, and Peace. During the course of their argument, which took place before Adam's creation, Love and Righteousness urged that Man should be created, Truth and Peace that he should not. Later versions of the legend reduced the disputants to two, giving the objections of Truth and Peace to the *Torah* and the counter-arguments of Love and Righteousness to God. In both versions of the legend the dispute was finally settled by God's decision that His love of goodness outweighed His hatred of sin, that His mercy was greater than His vengefulness. The medieval Christian treatments of the subject transferred the debate to some occasion after the Fall and realigned the four contestants so that Peace and Love (Mercy) defended Man while Truth and Righteousness (Justice) accused him. The con-troversy now concerned the advisability not of creating Man but of saving him, and its purpose was to reconcile not God's omnipotence with His omniscience but His justice with His benevolence. Further, it was resolved by the Son's offer to satisfy the claims of Justice by

[1] See above, Ch. II, pp. 38–39.

dying on Man's behalf rather than by an arbitrary decision on the part of the Father.[1]

By the Renaissance this medieval version of the legend had developed along the same lines as the rabbinic, that is, the four conflicting parties were reduced to two, Justice and Mercy. Giles Fletcher's *Christs Victorie and Triumph* (1610), for instance, prefaces the account of Christ's temptation in the wilderness with a detailed description of Mercy's encounter with Justice. The latter accuses Man by rehearsing all his sins, beginning with Adam's disobedience:

> His bodie dust: whear grewe such cause of pride?
> His soule thy Image: what could he enuie?
> Himselfe most happie: if he so would bide:
> Now grow'n most wretched, who can remedie?
> He slewe himselfe, himselfe the enemie.[2]

Justice's eloquence draws enthusiastic approval from the angelic audience:

> She ended, and the heav'nly Hierarchies,
> Burning in zeale, thickly imbranded weare:
> Like to an armie, that allarum cries,
> And every one shakes his ydraded speare.[3]

In reply Mercy points out that the Devil is most deserving of punishment, for it was he who provoked men to sin:

> He was but dust: how could he stand before him?
> And beeing fall'n, why should he feare to die?
> Cannot the hand that made him first, restore him?
> Deprav'd of sinne, should he deprived lie
> Of grace?[4]

---

[1] See H. Traver, *The Four Daughters of God*; S. C. Chew, *The Virtues Reconciled*.
[2] *Christs Victorie in Heaven*, stanza 18.
[3] Ibid. 40. Compare the reaction of the Devils to Satan's speech in *P.L.* i. 663–6:

> He spake: and to confirm his words, out-flew
> Millions of flaming swords, drawn from the thighs
> Of mighty Cherubim; the sudden blaze
> Far round illumin'd hell.

If the analogue is admitted, it may reinforce my suggestion that the devils' council is modelled on the heavenly debate. Again, the image in *P.L.* ii. 488–95 looks very much like an inversion of the image in *Christs Victorie in Heaven*, 41–42. Milton's acquaintance with this work is proved by the prominent verbal echoes in *On the Morning of Christ's Nativity*.
[4] Ibid. 73.

Her pleas finally prevail, and Man's redemption is allowed to proceed. In *The Glasse of Time in the two first Ages* (1620), on the other hand, Thomas Peyton places the debate immediately after the Fall and installs Nature as the arbitrator between the disputants. Eve seeks forgiveness:

> But that hard by stood Iustice in the place,
> And vrg'd him much to prosecute the case:
> When all the reason Mercy well could render,
> Was that her selfe was of the female gender.[1]

In these Renaissance treatments much of the point of the medieval version of the legend was lost. The crux of the problem which the debate was originally designed to solve was that God could not pardon Man without belying His own laws. As Truth put it in the *Ludus Coventriae*:

> Whan Adam had synned þou seydest þore
> þat he xulde deye and go to helle
> And now to blysse hym to resstore
> twey contraryes mow not to-gedyr dwelle.[2]

The incarnation, death, and resurrection of Christ were, in the words of the *Meditationes Vitae Christi*, 'a good sleiȝte and trewe wisdome', because by this means the demands of Justice and the inclinations of Mercy could be satisfied at the same time. In Fletcher's poem, however, these theological subtleties have been totally obscured. All that remains of the original argument is the confrontation of the two dissentients. Rhetoric has taken the place of dialectic, and Mercy overcomes her opponent by sheer force of oratory.

Against this background the distinctive features of the scene in *Paradise Lost* stand out very clearly. As the third dramatic draft reveals, Milton had long intended to introduce the debate into the story, but with two crucial modifications. First, along with Justice and Mercy there appears a third figure, Wisdom, whose presence suggests that the three personifications were to be identified with the three persons of the Trinity. Second, Milton has placed the debate half-way between the positions it occupied in the rabbinic

---

[1] 'The First Age', p. 58. See also Joseph Fletcher's *The Perfect-Cursed-Blessed Man*, 1629, 'Man's Felicitie Consulted-of'.

[2] *Lud. Cov.* xi. 61–64.

and the medieval treatments, after the creation of Adam but before his fall.

Both these modifications bear directly on the presentation of the debate between the Father and Son in Book III of *Paradise Lost*. Here there are only two figures, the reason being that the Son has assumed most of the attributes and functions of the Holy Ghost,[1] but they are now literal rather than allegorical characters. Are we then to equate God with Justice and Christ with Mercy? The idea is certainly tempting, but I believe it would be an over-simplification. Milton evidently went out of his way to avoid just such a direct equation, and for a very obvious reason: it would inevitably direct our sympathies away from the Father and on to the Son. Justice and Mercy are described, rather, as two aspects of the Father Himself. At the conclusion of His first speech, for instance, He says:

> in Mercy and Justice both,
> Through Heav'n and Earth, so shall my glorie excel,
> But Mercy first and last shall brightest shine.[2]

And when the debate has been satisfactorily resolved, the angels address the Father thus:

> He to appease thy wrauth, and end the strife
> Of Mercy and Justice in thy face discern'd,
> . . . offerd himself to die
> For mans offence.[3]

Nevertheless, in spite of Milton's explicit statements to the contrary, the Father and Son do still preserve the characteristics of their allegorical predecessors. The demands of Justice are voiced primarily by the Father:

> Dye hee or Justice must; unless for him
> Som other able, and as willing, pay
> The rigid satisfaction, death for death.[4]

And the arguments of Mercy are given almost exclusively to the Son; the Father may assert that His mercy will eventually triumph

---

[1] The absence of the Holy Ghost is particularly evident in Milton's invocation at the beginning of Book III. Prudentius (*Hamartigenia*, 75–78) and the author of *Cursor Mundi* (271 et seq.) had used the sun to describe the functions and unity of the Trinity; the sun itself was the Father, its heat the Son, and its light or movement the Holy Ghost. Milton used this traditional image, but confined his attention to the first two persons of the Trinity and the two relevant aspects of the sun itself. See also Gervase Babington's *Certaine plaine, briefe, and comfortable Notes, vpon euerie chapter of Genesis*, 1592, sig. B3.

[2] *P.L.* iii. 132–4.   [3] Ibid. iii. 406–10.   [4] Ibid. iii. 210–12.

and that Man will find grace, but it is in His Son that 'Divine compassion visibly appeerd,/ Love without end, and without measure, Grace'.[1]

Herein lies the explanation of the episode's failure, and indeed of the shortcomings of the presentation of God the Father throughout the rest of the poem. For in attempting to 'de-allegorize' the debate of the daughters of God Milton exposed himself to two opposing forces. On the one hand, he was bound to disclaim any specific association of the Father with Justice and the Son with Mercy. On the other, the contrast between the two allegorical figures was so strong that it inevitably came to shape the characters of the divine debaters, with the result that the Father seems far too severe. As J. Peter has remarked, if 'our first impressions of God are strangely unfavourable our first impressions of the Son are unqualifiedly approving'. The contrast is dangerous, he goes on to argue, because the Son's first speech 'is largely, if inadvertently, at his Father's expense, and it tends to confirm our incipient hostility towards God'.[2] The very clear distinction which Milton maintains between the two characters reinforces this reaction, while his assertions that the qualities of Mercy and Justice both reside in the Father serve only to confuse our response still further.

The curiously ambivalent and inconclusive tone of the actual speeches derives from the same contradiction. Milton clearly wanted to present the issues involved in the debate of the daughters of God, but he wanted to do so without the argumentative apparatus through which they had previously been expressed. The Father and Son could not squabble like the younger members of the family; a dignified discussion rather than a vehement controversy was what the situation required. But so long as the overtones of the dispute between Justice and Mercy were present it was impossible to exclude the argumentative tone altogether. Consequently, as Peter has again noted, the Son's speeches shift uneasily between approval and objection. To urge the Father to a decision He has already taken, he writes, 'is to suggest that he is merely volatile, that the Son must firmly remind him of his commitment'. Further, 'when he speaks again we are less relieved to hear his agreement than appalled to realize that the Son should ever have seemed in doubt of it'.[3] Torn

---

[1] *P.L.* iii. 141–2. C. A. Patrides points out (op. cit., p. 157) that according to 'the recurrent Protestant thesis' justice is associated with God, and mercy with Christ.
[2] *Critique*, p. 12.   [3] Loc. cit.

between the rival forces of tradition and expediency the episode has
split open in the middle. The two characters hover between allegory
and theology, and their speeches between debate and discussion.

Yet when this has been admitted, there remain several points to
be made in Milton's favour. If the first of his modifications, the
exposition of the basic arguments by the Father and Son rather than
by Justice and Mercy, was responsible for the episode's faults, the
second modification, the location of the debate before the Fall,
offered at least some corresponding advantages. Milton's declared
purpose was to 'justifie the wayes of God to Men'.[1] What exactly he
meant by that phrase is clarified by a speech of the Chorus in *Samson
Agonistes*. Having maintained that God's ways are just, and therefore justifiable, they go on to comment: 'Yet more there be who
doubt his ways not just, / As to his own edicts, found contradicting.'[2] The debate between the Father and Son in Book III of
Paradise Lost is intended to show that God does not contradict His
own edicts, that His behaviour is wholly consistent with His nature
and His laws. By placing the debate before the Fall and after Man's
creation Milton is thus able to explore both the rabbinic and the
medieval aspects of this question, for the position of the episode
before the Fall allows him to discuss the compatibility of foreknowledge with omnipotence, while its position after the creation
of Adam permits him also to demonstrate the reconciliation of
benevolence with justice.

Each of the Father's first two speeches is devoted to one of these
two problems. His opening one is basically an attempt to show
that His foreknowledge of Adam's disobedience does not conflict
with His omnipotence. He could, He argues, have forced Man to
obey Him, but He deliberately gave him the opportunity to fall:

> Not free, what proof could they have givn sincere
> Of true allegiance, constant Faith or Love,
> Where onely what they needs must do, appeard,
> Not what they would.[3]

Whereas the rabbinic treatments had done no more than pose the
problem, Milton solves it, and along thoroughly orthodox Christian
lines. As we have seen, the patristic view that Adam had to be free
to fall if his deeds were to have any moral value had been reiterated

---

[1] *P.L.* i. 26.   [2] *S.A.* 300–1.   [3] *P.L.* iii. 103–6.

many times,[1] and by the Renaissance it was deeply embedded in the structure of Christian belief. Milton's God is simply giving definitive expression to an idea almost as old as the Church itself.

On this secure foundation the Father then proceeds to an altogether more complex problem: if He could foresee that Adam would sin, then surely Adam sinned not by free choice but by necessity. Ralegh had examined this question in his *History of the World* (1614), and come to the conclusion that 'this prescience of God (as it is prescience only) is not the cause of anything futurely succeeding: neither doth God's foreknowledge impose any necessity, or bind'.[2] Resorting to a very dubious analogue, he pointed out that our foreknowledge that the sun will rise does not mean that we cause the dawn to appear. This is precisely Milton's position:

> if I foreknew,
> Foreknowledge had no influence on their fault,
> Which had no less prov'd certain unforeknown.[3]

The logic of the argument is, admittedly, contestable, but the logic is not Milton's, and to blame him for using it is as foolish as to blame Dante for basing his cosmology on the Ptolemaic system or Homer for believing that the world was flat.

The last lines of the Father's first speech look forward to the subject of His second, the harmonizing of the principles of Justice and Mercy. His initial reason for saving Man is based on the standard medieval contrast between the sins of Adam and those of Satan:

> The first sort by thir own suggestion fell,
> Self-tempted, self-deprav'd: Man falls deceiv'd
> By the other first: Man therefore shall find grace,
> The other none.[4]

To this the Son adds an argument very similar to Gabriel's in the *Meditationes Vitae Christi*, in which the archangel initiated the debate of the four daughters by drawing God's attention to the fact that the adversary appeared to have won the contest for Man:

Oure enemyes hauen the victorie; and of hem [men] oure partye is no3t restored, but the prisoun of helle continuelliche filled. Whereto, lorde, be they borne to so greet meschief? For though it be done after 3oure ri3twisnesse neuerthelesse, lord, it is now tyme of mercye. Haueth in

---

[1] See above, Ch. V, pp. 153-4; Ch. VI, p. 190.   [2] Book I, ch. i, sect. 12.
[3] *P.L.* iii. 117-19.
[4] Ibid. iii. 129-32. See above, Ch. V, p. 153; Ch. VI, p. 179.

mynde that ȝe made hem after ȝoure owne likenesse and though her forme fadres folily and wrecchedly breken ȝoure maundement or heste: neuertheles ȝoure mercye is aboue alle thinges.[1]

The Son's speech, even though its tone is still more studiously respectful, makes much the same points:

> For should Man finally be lost, should Man
> Thy creature late so lov'd, thy youngest Son
> Fall circumvented thus by fraud, though joynd
> With his own folly? that be from thee farr,
> That farr be from thee, Father, who art Judg
> Of all things made, and judgest onely right.
> Or shall the Adversarie thus obtain
> His end, and frustrate thine, shall he fulfill
> His malice, and thy goodness bring to naught,
> Or proud return though to his heavier doom,
> Yet with revenge accomplish't and to Hell
> Draw after him the whole Race of mankind,
> By him corrupted?[2]

The Father readily agrees that at least some of mankind should be redeemed, but He goes on to underline the difficulties entailed in such a plan. Man has broken 'fealtie'[3] and consequently is not in a position to expiate this treason for himself. This is exactly the point at issue in the medieval debate of the four daughters, and it is resolved in exactly the same way; the rival claims of Justice and Mercy can be made to accord only if one innocent life should be offered to pay the 'rigid satisfaction'.[4] Milton thus condensed the essential features of the traditional dispute in one speech of the Father's, with the result that the two sides of the argument appear as a logical progression of thought rather than a real debate. The solution follows hard on the heels of the problem.

When the Father finally asks for volunteers a terrible silence falls on the assembled throng:

> He ask'd, but all the Heav'nly Quire stood mute,
> And silence was in Heav'n: on mans behalf
> Patron or Intercessor none appeerd,
> Much less that durst upon his own head draw
> The deadly forfeiture, and ransom set.[5]

---

[1] *Mirrour*, p. 14. [2] *P.L.* iii. 150–62. [3] Ibid. iii. 204.
[4] Ibid. iii. 212. [5] Ibid. iii. 217–21.

This much commented-on episode was also a common feature of the medieval versions of the debate of the four daughters. The *Meditationes Vitae Christi*, for instance, related that after Christ had suggested that the death of one innocent would settle the controversy, 'In this sentence and dome alle the court of heuen wondring, and commendynge the souereyn wisdam, assenteden wel hereto; but furthermore askeden amonge hem self, where that one myȝte be founden that schulde fulfille and do this dede of charite.'[1] The four daughters go off in search of someone who is both sinless and willing to die for Man, but they fail to find any suitable candidate. Only when they have failed does the Son agree to undertake the task: 'the sone ȝaf gladly his assent thereto: and the holy gost seide he wolde worche therto also. And than fallynge doun alle the holy spirites of heuene and souereynly thonkynge the holy trinite, the foure sustres aforeseide weren kessid and made acorde.'[2] The order of events follows the same course in Book III of *Paradise Lost*. The Son breaks the silence by offering Himself, and the Father accepts His offer, promising to bring about the Redemption through His sacrifice:

> So Man, as is most just,
> Shall satisfie for Man, be judg'd and die,
> And dying rise, and rising with him raise
> His Brethren, ransomd with his own dear life.
> So Heav'nly love shall outdo Hellish hate.
> Giving to death, and dying to redeeme,
> So dearly to redeem what Hellish hate
> So easily destroy'd, and still destroyes
> In those who, when they may, accept not grace.[3]

In response the angels burst into a song of praise, as in the *Meditationes*, in which they thank God that the sisters are at last reconciled:

> He to appease thy wrauth, and end the strife
> Of Mercy and Justice in thy face discern'd
> Regardless of the bliss wherein hee sat
> Second to thee, offerd himself to die
> For mans offence.[4]

---

[1] *Mirrour*, p. 17.   [2] Ibid., p. 19. See also *Lud. Cov.* xi. 153–88.
[3] *P.L.* iii. 294–302. The intensive word-play here is reminiscent not only of Fletcher's rhetorical figures but also of *Piers Plowman*'s elaborate patterning as Christ argues with Lucifer after the debate of the four daughters (see above, Ch. VI, pp. 184–5). The mystery of the Atonement seems to be expressible only through the intricate convolutions of paradox, antithesis, and repetition; a transfigured kind of verbal wit is required to contain the conceptual subtleties involved in the doctrine of the Redemption.
[4] *P.L.* iii. 406–10.

Significantly enough it is not the 'trinite' they thank, but only the Father and Son.

In the light of these correspondences it seems to me very likely that the heavenly parliament in *Paradise Lost* is based upon the legend of the four daughters of God, and, what is more, upon a medieval version of that legend. Milton restored to the debate all the issues which had given the medieval treatments their purpose and meaning, so that what in the Renaissance poems had been little more than a baroque decorative fringe has become once again a functional framework, within which the poet worked out his justification.

X

NATIVE INNOCENCE

ONE of the most extraordinary critical developments in recent years has been the emergence of an interpretation of *Paradise Lost* which inverts the traditional meaning assigned to Milton's version of the Fall and sees in it a great humanist declaration of human liberties. Like the Gnostic and Manichaean readings, with which it has many affinities, this interpretation seems to have originated in the difficulty of believing that any right-minded man could have approved of God's prohibition of the tree of knowledge. Thus B. Willey, having adduced a deal of evidence to show that the seventeenth century in general and Milton in particular regarded knowledge as being essential to Man's spiritual well-being, goes on to observe that Genesis 'represented the Fall as due to, or consisting in, the acquisition by Man of that very knowledge, the knowledge of good and evil, by the possession of which alone Milton the humanist believed that man could be truly virtuous'. Faced by this apparent contradiction, Milton 'dealt most high-handedly with the myth': he was forced, this turns out to mean, to abandon the view that the tree of knowledge actually conferred the ability to distinguish between right and wrong, and to substitute for it 'his own explanation',[1] namely that the only kind of knowledge the tree bestowed was the realization of 'Good lost, and Evil got'.[2] On this basis C. C. Green has constructed an elaborate theory according to which there is a 'paradox' at the heart of the poem. Ignoring the qualifying phrase, 'As therefore the state of Man now is', he assumes that when in *Areopagitica* Milton inquires 'what wisdome can there be to choose, what continence to forbeare without the knowledge of evill?'[3] he is speaking of Adam and Eve's condition before the Fall. The inevitable conclusion is that Eve falls 'in good faith as a Humanist, whose

---

[1] *The Seventeenth Century Background*, 1934, pp. 222–37.

[2] *P.L.* ix. 1072.

[3] *Areopagitica* (Columbia edn., iv. 311). The relevance of this passage to Milton's treatment of the Fall has been discussed by J. S. Diekhoff in 'Eve, the Devil, and *Areopagitica*', *M.L.Q.* v (1944), 429–34.

proper business is to search out knowledge, the prerequisite of true virtue', and that Adam chooses what to his 'really mistaken mind is evil but what to Milton's mind is good'.[1] Reinforced by the older, but still fashionable, concept of Satan as the hero of the poem, Empson's corollary that God is the villain,[2] and Lovejoy's rediscovery of the perilous doctrine of the *felix culpa*,[3] this critical trend has produced an account of *Paradise Lost* of which the Ophites would have thoroughly approved: by releasing Adam and Eve from the sterile confines of ignorance in which their envious and malign Creator had originally imprisoned them the Tempter opened up the way to the 'Paradise within'.[4]

While there is no denying that the problem so clearly defined by Willey is implicit in the Fall story, it was not left to Milton, or even to the humanists of the Renaissance, to notice that the prohibition of the knowledge of good and evil seemed inconsistent with the benevolence of God. From the second century on Christian thinkers had been wrestling with precisely this question, and, as we have already seen, they had evolved some most ingenious answers. The most authoritative was Augustine's. The tree of knowledge, he wrote, was so called 'to signify by this name the consequence of their discovering both what good they would experience if they kept the prohibition, and what evil if they transgressed it'.[5] This explanation was repeated in varying forms by Gregory the Great, Bede, Alcuin, and Raban Maur in the Dark Ages, perpetuated in the *Glossa Ordinaria* and Comestor's *Historia Scholastica*,[6] and, as Arnold Williams has demonstrated, taken over by the vast majority of Biblical commentators in the Renaissance.[7] To take just one example, Andrew Willett asserted in his *Hexapla in Genesin* (1605) that the forbidden tree offered the first pair the knowledge of 'what good they had lost, and what euill they were fallen into' when they ate of it.[8] So what Willey has called 'Milton's own explanation' had been current for at least twelve centuries before *Paradise Lost* was composed, and came down to the poet as part of the theological tradition attaching to the narrative.

---

[1] 'The Paradox of the Fall in *Paradise Lost*', *M.L.N.* liii (1938), 557–71.
[2] *Milton's God*, 1961, *passim*.
[3] 'Milton and the Paradox of the Fortunate Fall', *E.L.H.* iv (1937), 161–79.
[4] See above, Ch. III, pp. 62–69. [5] *De Pecc. Mer.* ii. 35.
[6] See above, Ch. III, p. 96; Ch. V, p. 153, Ch. VI, pp. 169–70.
[7] *The Common Expositor*, Chapel Hill, 1948, pp. 106–7.
[8] *Hexapla*, p. 28. See also Patrides, op. cit., p. 104.

Yet the uneasiness which underlies Willey's criticism of the poem cannot be disposed of so easily, for his case rests on more than a misconception of the tree of knowledge. That Milton's sympathies were totally out of tune with the Genesis narrative is ultimately proved, he claims, by his 'failure to convince us that the prelapsarian life of Adam and Eve in the "happy garden" was genuinely happy'. The poet was, in fact, 'a Promethean, a Renaissance humanist, caught in the toils of a myth of quite contrary import, a myth which yearned, as no Milton could, for the blank innocence and effortlessness of a golden age'.[1] This is a damaging charge, which cannot be refuted merely by a display of patristic texts. It is rooted, I suspect, in the kind of feeling which E. M. W. Tillyard had expressed some four years earlier: 'Reduced to the ridiculous task of working in a garden which produces of its own accord more than they will ever need, Adam and Eve are in the hopeless position of Old Age pensioners enjoying perpetual youth.' If Milton had been stranded in his own paradise, he 'would very soon have eaten the apple on his own responsibility and immediately justified the act in a polemical pamphlet. Any genuine activity would be better than utter stagnation.'[2] This takes us rather more deeply into the problem. What Tillyard is objecting to here is the apparent pointlessness of Adam and Eve's lives before the Fall. The state of perfection in which they are generally held to have been created admitted of no development, no growth, no challenge, nor even any change, except possibly for the worse. If their life consisted simply in cultivating a naturally fertile garden and abstaining from a tree whose fruit would do them no good anyway, then we may be heartily thankful that they preserved their descendants from a similar kind of existence. In Wallace Stevens's words:

> Is there no change of death in paradise?
> Does ripe fruit never fall? Or do the boughs
> Hang always heavy in that perfect sky,
> Unchanging, yet so like our perishing earth,
> With rivers like our own that seek for seas
> They never find, the same receding shores
> That never touch with inarticulate pang?
> Why set the pear upon those river-banks
> Or spice the shores with odors of the plum?[3]

---

[1] Op. cit., pp. 223, 229.   [2] *Milton*, 1930, pp. 282–3.
[3] 'Sunday Morning', 76–84.

The interpretation of the whole poem, then, ultimately hinges on the view taken of Adam and Eve's condition before the Fall, on the significance we give to the word 'perfection' in this context. Willey and Tillyard assume that the first pair already enjoy every possible advantage, physical and intellectual, with the exception of moral exertion, and Lewis agrees with them: 'No useful criticism of the Miltonic Adam is possible until the last trace of the *naif*, simple, childlike Adam has been removed from our imaginations.'[1] Peter, on the other hand, insists on Adam and Eve's youthfulness, inferring that 'being young, they are also in some degree defenceless, inexperienced. There is something fragile about their innocence and their devotion to each other.'[2] These critics are concerned, of course, with Milton's Adam, but their opposing views reflect in a most interesting way the long-standing disagreement over the prelapsarian status of the Biblical Adam. Lewis's opinion is very like that of those poets and commentators who accepted the Priestly writer's estimate of Adam's original perfection,[3] while Peter's might stand for those who inclined, rather, towards the Jahwist's concept of Man's original imperfection.[4] The crucial question here is, to which, if either, of these traditions did Milton himself belong?

The fact that two critics can arrive at two wholly contradictory conclusions on the basis of the same evidence may suggest that Milton's treatment of the state of innocence contains elements drawn from both the minimal and maximal traditions, that, like Augustine, he attempted to find some compromise between them. According to the maximal Fathers, it may be recalled, Man was created the equal of the angels. Besides being immortal and passionless, he fed with the archangels and was designed to procreate in some non-carnal angelic way.[5] This picture Augustine modified by imposing on it the minimal idea of the relativity of Adam's perfection. Adam was a man, not an angel, and although he enjoyed every possible physical benefit his immortality and his virtue were only conditional. Until he had proved himself worthy of further promotion in the celestial hierarchy he would remain human, begetting his children by the normal biological process.[6] This conception of

---

[1] *Preface*, p. 118.   [2] *Critique*, p. 91.
[3] See above, Ch. I, p. 12; Ch. II, pp. 29–32, 39–41; Ch. III, pp. 86–87; Ch. IV, p. 133.   [4] See above, Ch. I, p. 14; Ch. III, pp. 78–80; Ch. IV, p. 129.
[5] See above, Ch. III, pp. 86–87.
[6] See above, Ch. III, p. 94. Lewis, I feel, has over-simplified the Augustinian

Man's first estate is clearly much the closest to Milton's. Indeed, the very idea of hierarchy, which Lewis has shown to be fundamental to the poem,[1] was bound to emphasize Man's intermediate position in the Creation, while the equally potent belief that Adam and his progeny were destined, if they persevered in their obedience, to take the place of the fallen angels further up the scale of being served only to confirm this estimate of his status:

> I can repaire
> That detriment, if such it be to lose
> Self-lost, and in a moment will create
> Another World, out of one man a Race
> Of men innumerable, there to dwell,
> Not here, till by degrees of merit rais'd
> They open to themselves at length the way
> Up hither, under long obedience tri'd,
> And Earth be chang'd to Heavn, & Heav'n to Earth,
> One Kingdom, Joy and Union without end.[2]

Adam is serving a kind of spiritual apprenticeship; he is a novice learning to take his place in the order of perfection, not a member of it already. He has first to undergo the preliminary discipline of 'long obedience'.

The most obvious test imposed on Adam is the command to refrain from eating of the tree of knowledge, and on this most poets and commentators had concentrated their attention. But the meaning of 'obedience' in *Paradise Lost* comprehends far more than the mere abstention from the forbidden tree, which, since Adam and Eve were already aware of their moral duty to leave it untouched, is no more than the 'sign of our obedience'.[3] For, apart from the negative command concerning the tree, Adam was given in Genesis a positive order: to dress the garden and to keep it. Literal commentators had had very little to say about this second precept except to point out that Adam's labour, unlike ours, was in no way tedious or toilsome.[4]

view by laying all the emphasis on his statements regarding Adam's physical perfections and inferring from these that his moral perfections were as great.

[1] *Preface*, ch. xi.

[2] *P.L.* vii. 152–60. Compare above, Ch. III, p. 93; Ch. V, pp. 147–8. H. V. S. Ogden ('The Crisis of *Paradise Lost* Reconsidered', *P.Q.* xxxvi (1957), 1–19) rightly points out that this conception of relative perfection is clearly set forth both in Milton's *De Doctrina*, I. vii (Columbia, xv. 39, 53, and 59) and in his *Doctrine and Discipline of Divorce* (Columbia iii. 441 and 456–7).

[3] Ibid. iv. 428.

[4] See Williams, *The Common Expositor*, pp. 109–11. As he remarks, Adam too

Only the author of the Book of Jubilees paused to wonder what Adam was supposed to guard the garden against. He concluded that Adam had to protect it from the animals,[1] and in the seventeenth century Henry More echoed this opinion in his *Conjectura Cabbalistica* (1653). One of Adam's duties, he stated, was 'to keep things handsome and in order in it, and that it should not be any wise spoil'd or misus'd by incursions or careless ramblings of the heedlesse beasts'.[2] Speculations of this kind were, however, rare, and it is not hard to see why. By common consent, the garden of Eden was ideal. The nature of its ideality varied with the particular advantages each successive age regarded as most desirable—sometimes it was a perfect farm, sometimes a perfect garden, and sometimes a perfect landscape—but it was always perfect. Samuel Pordage, for instance, portrayed Eden thus in his *Mundorum Explicatio* (1661):

> Then was the golden age indeed, Earth gave
> Nor Weeds, nor Thorns, but cloath'd in livr'y brave
> Had a perpetual spring; continual green
> In ev'ry place, on ev'ry tree was seen:
> No dainty Flower, which art makes now to flourish,
> But then the Earth did naturally nourish.
> A constant verdure it retain'd, and then
> With thousand flowers spotted was the green:
> Each tree at one time bore both fruit, and flower;
> Each herb to heal, but not to hurt had power.[3]

In such an environment the climate, the plants, and the animals all behaved in the best possible way, and of their own accord. Adam's supervision, therefore, was scarcely necessary; his appointment as a gardener was a veritable sinecure, and his labour, such as it was, could only be for his own pleasure.

Milton paints a very different picture, which anticipates in many respects the Romantic view of Nature as defined by Lovejoy in his great study of the chain of being: 'The God of the seventeenth century,' he writes, 'like its gardeners, always geometrized; the God of Romanticism was one in whose universe things grew wild and

emphasizes the delight attaching to their labour. The first time Adam mentions the subject, however, he is somewhat guarded. See *P.L.* iv. 437-9:

> our delightful task
> To prune these growing Plants, and tend these Flours,
> Which were it toilsom, yet with thee were sweet.

[1] See above, Ch. II, p. 31.   [2] 'The Literal Cabbala', p. 13.
[3] The First Part, p. 57. Compare Avitus and Victor above, Ch. IV, pp. 115-6, 124.

without trimming and in all the rich diversity of their natural shapes.'[1]
The Eden of *Paradise Lost* clearly belongs in the second category.
When we first see it with Satan it is surrounded with

> a steep wilderness, whose hairie sides
> With thicket overgrown, grottesque and wilde,
> Access deni'd:[2]

and although the poet stresses the beauty of the garden enclosed, we
are never allowed to forget the threat of the encroaching wilderness.
Adam explains to Eve that they must have an early night, because
the next day

> we must be ris'n,
> And at our pleasant labour, to reform
> Yon flourie Arbors, yonder Allies green,
> Our walk at noon, with branches overgrown,
> That mock our scant manuring, and require
> More hands than ours to lop thir wanton growth;
> Those Blossoms also, and those dropping Gumms,
> That lie bestrowne unsightly and unsmooth,
> Ask riddance, if we mean to tread with ease.[3]

The labour is still 'pleasant', but it is also absolutely necessary. In no
previous Eden had there been anything 'overgrown' or 'wanton',
'unsightly' or 'unsmooth', to demand Adam's urgent attention. The
next morning the pair hasten out to their task:

> where any row
> Of Fruit-trees overwoodie reachd too farr
> Thir pamperd boughes, and needed hands to check
> Fruitless imbraces.[4]

And as Raphael approaches them we see him making his way
through

> A Wilderness of sweets; for Nature here
> Wantond as in her prime, and plaid at will
> Her Virgin Fancies, pouring forth more sweet,
> Wilde above Rule or Art.[5]

---

[1] *The Great Chain of Being*, Harvard, 1936, p. 16.   [2] *P.L.* iv. 135–7.

[3] Ibid. iv. 624–32. The crucial words and phrases in this speech are repeated by Eve
in Book IX in her attempt to justify the idea of working apart from Adam. See below,
p. 274.

[4] Ibid. v. 212–15.

[5] Ibid. v. 294–7. In his recent study, *The Paradise Within*, New Haven, 1964, p. 123,
L. L. Martz has glossed the last line, 'That is to say, above ordinary human notions of
rule or art.' This rather strained interpretation may suggest the extent to which the

This very unusual aspect of Eden has not passed unnoticed among critics of *Paradise Lost*,[1] but it has, I believe, been seriously misinterpreted. Tillyard, who was one of the first to stress it, finds in it the theme of Nature's 'bounty', one of the poem's 'unconscious meanings'.[2] But do words like 'bounty' and 'fertility' really cover the impression these passages make on us? What we have here, surely, is not just abundance but over-abundance, a 'wilderness' in which the trees are 'overwoodie' and reach 'too farr' with their 'branches overgrown'. The point Milton is making, and, to judge from the recurrence of these key words, making quite consciously, is that Eden, in all its order and beauty, does not have the stability attributed to it by earlier poets. It does not share the timeless perfection of medieval paintings of it, because the difference between Art and Nature is that Nature grows. The garden will not remain perfect of its own accord, and if Adam and Eve stopped working the wilderness outside would soon engulf it. 'Il faut cultiver notre jardin.' Consequently, to maintain, as Tillyard does, that Adam and Eve's unfallen life is idle and purposeless is to ignore the most strikingly original feature of Milton's treatment. Yet in spite of the poet's repeated statements to the contrary, critics persist in assuming that unfallen Man had nothing to do. Waldock, for instance, has revived the objections made by earlier writers in his pronouncement: 'Milton began his poem with the assumption that the unstruggling innocent life of Eden was good—imagining himself really to believe this. But when it comes to the point he has a great deal of difficulty in persuading us, and perhaps a good deal of difficulty in persuading himself, that such a life would not have meant to any human being normally constituted an eternity of boredom.'[3] In any other Eden but Milton's this might have been true. Whatever else Milton's Adam and Eve may have been in the Eden of *Paradise Lost*, however, they were certainly not bored.

more conventional picture of Eden has been superimposed on Milton's very different conception.

[1] In her study of the transition from the sixteenth to the seventeenth century, *The Breaking of the Circle*, Evanston, Illinois, 1950, p. 164, for instance, M. H. Nicolson suggests that the contrast between the wild luxuriance of the garden and the ordered restraint imposed on it by Adam and Eve reflects two opposing aspects of Milton's personality. Perhaps the most accurate characterization of this aspect of the garden is A. Stein's phrase 'authorized excess' (*Answerable Style*, Minneapolis, 1953, p. 67).

[2] *Milton*, ch. iv.

[3] *Paradise Lost and its Critics*, p. 125. The phrase 'normally constituted', of course, begs the whole question.

In this very unusual treatment of Adam's labour is to be found the key to Milton's equally original handling of the wider issues involved in the state of innocence. We have noted that very early in the course of its development the Fall story was read by Philo as an allegory of Man's moral life. Here the tree of knowledge had little or no part to play, and the main emphasis was placed on the command to keep the garden, which meant that Reason was to control the Passions, protect the Virtues, and generally keep the Soul in good order. This moral interpretation of Genesis had a long and distinguished history, passing down from Philo via Origen, Ambrose, Augustine, Isidore, Bede, Comestor, and the *Glossa Ordinaria* down to the seventeenth century, where, among other places, it is to be found summarized in Ralegh's *History of the World* and expounded at length in More's *Conjectura Cabbalistica*.[1] It was, then, readily available to Milton, and may well have furnished him with the theme of his description of the state of innocence.

For, as J. B. Broadbent has remarked, in paradise 'there is an unusually sustained consonance between the idea and the symbolic expression of innocence'.[2] Adam and Eve's physical relationship to the garden is in fact an image of their psychological relationship both to their own passions and to each other. During the course of their work they

> led the Vine
> To wed her Elm; she spous'd about him twines
> Her mariageable arms, and with her brings
> Her dowr th'adopted Clusters, to adorn
> His barren leaves.[3]

Earlier in the poem Eve's hair was described as hanging

> Dissheveld, but in wanton ringlets wav'd
> As the Vine curles her tendrils, which impli'd
> Subjection, but requir'd with gentle sway,
> And by her yielded, by him best receivd,
> Yielded with coy submission, modest pride,
> And sweet reluctant amorous delay.[4]

The vine simile had been associated with marriage ever since

---

[1] See above, Ch. III, pp. 69–76; Ch. VI, p. 169. Also Ralegh's *History of the World*, I. iii. 2, and More's *Conjectura*, 'The Philosophick Cabbala'.

[2] *Some Graver Subject*, p. 173.

[3] *P.L.* v. 215–19.   [4] Ibid. iv. 306–11.

Catullus's *Epithalamion*,[1] and in the seventeenth century it still carried the same overtones:

> What makes the vine about the elm to dance
> With turnings, windings, and embracements round?
>
> .   .   .
>
> Kind nature first doth cause all things to love;
> Love makes them dance, and in just order move.[2]

The relationship of the vine to the elm thus becomes an image of Eve's relationship to Adam. The equation between the garden and the marriage of the first pair is reinforced by the constant juxtaposition of Eve and the flowers. As she leaves Adam and Raphael to continue their discussion alone we see her for a moment

> among her Fruits and Flours,
> To visit how they prosper'd, bud and bloom,
> Her Nurserie; they at her coming sprung
> And toucht by her fair tendance gladlier grew.[3]

And when, for the second time, she leaves her husband, the Devil first spies her

> Veild in a Cloud of Fragrance, where she stood,
> Half spi'd, so thick the Roses bushing round
> About her glowd, oft stooping to support
> Each Flour of slender stalk, whose head though gay
> Carnation, Purple, Azure, or spect with Gold,
> Hung drooping unsustaind, . . .
> . . . and in her look summs all Delight.[4]

Here Milton may have been half-remembering a passage from William Alexander's *Doomes Day* (1614):

> Through *Edens* garden, stately *Evah* stray'd,
> Where beauteous flowers her beauties backe reglanc'd
> By natures selfe, and not by art array'd,
> Which pure (not blushing) boldly were advanc'd;
> With dangling haires the wanton Zephyres play'd,
> And in rich rings their floting gold enhaunc'd.
> All things concurr'd, which pleasure could incite,
> So that she seem'd the centre of delight.[5]

---

[1] *Opera*, LXI. xxi. See also Virgil's second *Georgic*.
[2] *Orchestra*, stanza 56.   [3] *P.L.* viii. 44–47.
[4] Ibid. ix. 425–54. The difference in the flowers' reaction here immediately suggests that there is also a difference in the circumstances of the two separations.
[5] Book I, stanza lx. That Milton was familiar with it is suggested by other verbal echoes. Raphael's aside, 'such as to set forth / Great things by small' (vi. 310–11), may

But what in Alexander was merely decorative in Milton is also functional, for the unsupported flowers are a metaphor of Eve's moral position:

> Her self, though fairest unsupported Flour,
> From her best prop so farr, and storm so nigh.[1]

Without its elm the vine is going to wanton.

The idea of Eve's dependence on Adam was not, of course, original with Milton. Calvin, for example, had observed that the 'moste sweete melodie should reigne in wedlocke: because the man should haue respect vnto God, and the woman should be a helper of him forward therevnto: . . . and for this cause the woman is giuen to the man to be an helpe, that he may shewe him selfe to be a head and guide'.[2] When the unfallen pair first appear Milton likewise stated explicitly that they are

> Not equal, as thir sex not equal seemd;
> For contemplation hee and valour formd,
> For softness shee and sweet attractive Grace,
> Hee for God only, shee for God in him.[3]

And this inequality is one of the major themes of Book IV, in which our attention and, for the most part, our sympathy are focused on Eve. Indeed, if Raleigh's adjective 'sententious' is to be applied to Adam at all, then it is in this part of the poem, in which Adam's speeches are all admonitory; not until his exchanges with Raphael in Book VIII are we allowed to see very deeply into his character.[4] Eve, on the other hand, reveals a great deal about her thoughts and feelings. As Adam is to Raphael later in the poem, so Eve is to Adam here: she asks questions, relates experiences, confesses misgivings, and, above all, expresses affection. For instance, whereas Adam's first speech is concerned with their duty to abstain from the

---

have been a reminiscence of Alexander's 'If we great things with small things may compare' (I. liv). Likewise Milton's 'No more of talk where God or Angel Guest / With man, as with his Friend, familiar us'd / To sit indulgent' (ix. 1–3) could be derived from Alexander's 'With him whom to content, all did contend, / God walk'd, and talk'd, as a familiar friend' (I. lvii).

[1] *P.L.* ix. 432–3.

[2] *Commentary on Genesis*, ii. 18. See also Williams, *The Common Expositor*, pp. 84–86.

[3] *P.L.* iv. 296–9.

[4] We do, of course, get occasional glimpses of his feelings even before then, as, for example, when he says that his labour, even if it were toilsome, 'yet with thee were weet' (iv. 439).

tree of knowledge, Eve's is taken up with an account of her creation and subsequent union with her husband:

> That day I oft remember, when from sleep
> I first awak't, and found my self repos'd
> Under a shade of flours, much wondring where
> And what I was, whence thither brought, and how.
> Not distant far from thence a murmuring sound
> Of waters issu'd from a Cave and spread
> Into a liquid Plain, then stood unmov'd
> Pure as th'expanse of Heav'n; I thither went
> With unexperienc't thought, and laid me downe
> On the green bank, to look into the cleer
> Smooth Lake, that to me seemd another Skie.
> As I bent down to look, just opposite,
> A Shape within the watry gleam appeerd
> Bending to look on me, I started back,
> It started back, but pleas'd I soon returnd,
> Pleas'd it returnd as soon with answering looks
> Of sympathie and love.[1]

Like Narcissus, mistaking her own reflection for another creature, she was immediately captured by its beauty, but unlike Narcissus she was informed by a mysterious voice that the figure in the water was her own image and that her love should be directed to the man in whose image she herself was created. Yet when she first saw Adam, she confesses, she thought him:

> less faire,
> Less winning soft, less amiablie milde,
> Then that smooth watry image.[2]

Only as a result of Adam's gentle admonitions did she gradually come to see 'How beauty is excelld by manly grace / And wisdom, which alone is truly fair.'[3] The point of this episode, one of Milton's most beautiful and perceptive inventions, is that 'Kind nature' does not on this occasion make the vine embrace the elm, as it does in Davies's *Orchestra*, that Eve's untutored feelings, like the natural growth of the plants around her, do not grow in the right direction spontaneously. They have to be 'reformed', and it is necessary for God to check the 'fruitless embraces' she seeks in her own reflection and lead her to 'wed her Elm'.

[1] *P.L.* iv. 449–65. [2] Ibid. iv. 478–80. [3] Ibid. iv. 490–1.

That she has learned her lesson is evident from the next pair of speeches. Adam again discourses on their duty, emphasizing this time its positive aspect, the supervision of the garden. Eve, in turn, affirms her duty, her submission to and love for her husband:

> Unargu'd I obey; so God ordains,
> God is thy Law, thou mine: to know no more
> Is womans happiest knowledge and her praise.
> With thee conversing I forget all time,
> All seasons and thir change, all please alike.[1]

Here is the criterion by which we are to judge her response to Adam's arguments during the crucial discussion that prefaces the Fall in Book IX.[2]

Up to this point the substance, if not the treatment, of Man's unfallen life resembles that in the medieval plays on the subject. Although it is far more highly developed and richly elaborated, it consists essentially in the exposition of God's commands and Adam and Eve's reaction to them and to each other.[3] What follows, however, has no dramatic precedent, their first experience of night. For an analogue to this we must turn to the Christian-Latin poets, and to Dracontius and Cyprian in particular. The Rabbis, as we have seen, had portrayed Adam's fear of the approaching darkness as a symptom of his fallen ignorance and guilt, and Dracontius had readapted the incident to illustrate unfallen Man's gradual realization of the natural cycle of day and night.[4] Milton follows Dracontius in placing the episode before the Fall, but uses it to reveal not Adam's original innocence but his wisdom. In answer to Eve's queries he explains the function of the stars and their place in the divine scheme. Again, it is Milton's originality rather than his indebtedness which is most striking.

The pair then go to bed, make love, and finally fall asleep, at which point Satan assails Eve with her demonic dream. A wide variety of sources might be adduced to explain this very remarkable feature. To begin with the least likely, Milton may have had in mind the rabbinic idea that the Devil tempted Eve while Adam was deep in a post-coital slumber.[5] Alternatively, he may have known

---

[1] *P.L.* iv. 636–40.   [2] See below, Ch. XI, pp. 274–5.

[3] See above, Ch. VII, pp. 196–8.

[4] See above, Ch. II, p. 54 and Ch. IV, pp. 130–131. Milton may possibly have been acquainted with the rabbinic version of this legend, for like the Rabbis he gave Adam a psalm of praise on the following morning.

[5] See above, Ch. II, p. 48.

Cyprian's version of the temptation, according to which the Tempter approached Eve during the night, promising her that if she ate the fruit the dawn would return.[1] In *Genesis B* this notion had given rise to the belief that when she had eaten the fruit Eve was given a vision of the heavens and earth, which now appeared to her to be far more beautiful than ever before.[2] In *Paradise Lost*, too, Eve has a vision at this juncture, seeing 'The Earth outstretcht immense, a prospect wide / And various'.[3] Either the *Heptateuchos* or the Saxon poem could, then, have provided the details of Eve's dream temptation here.[4] Finally, it is just conceivable that Milton wished to strengthen the standard typological parallel between Eve and Mary[5] by giving Eve an experience analogous to Mary's vision of Gabriel at the Annunciation—he reminds us of this parallel almost immediately afterwards, when Raphael addresses Eve with 'Haile', 'the holy salutation us'd / Long after to blest *Marie*, second *Eve*'.[6]

Of these three explanations I would incline to the second, but there remains the possibility that the episode is to be accounted for in terms of the poem's internal structure. For from the beginning of Book IV onwards the narrative seems to proceed in two clearly differentiated movements, which are related to each other by continual contrasts and parallelisms. The first comprises the opening picture of innocence, with all the emphasis on Eve, her description of her creation and marriage, the dream temptation, and Raphael's relation of the rebellion and fall of Satan and the creation of the world. The second begins with another picture of innocence, with all the emphasis on Adam, and continues with his description of his creation and marriage, the real temptation, and Michael's revelation of the evils which will follow the Fall and the divine plan for their remedy. The sequence of events thus follows the same basic pattern in both movements, and a great part of the poem's meaning lies in

---

[1] See above, Ch. IV, pp. 139–40.   [2] See above, Ch. V, p. 161.

[3] *P.L.* v. 88–89.

[4] This is far the strongest piece of evidence to support the belief that Milton knew the Old Saxon poem, for whereas the similarities between the Satans of the two poems may be due to the influence of Avitus on them both, in this case they are the only two works which contain the idea of Eve's diabolic vision *and* the idea that the Tempter masqueraded as an angel. Unaccountably, J. W. Lever ignores this crucial point in his attempt to establish a link between *Paradise Lost* and *Genesis B* in his article, '*Paradise Lost* and the Anglo-Saxon Tradition', *R.E.S.* xxiii (1947), 97–106.

[5] See above, Ch. III, pp. 100–102.

[6] *P.L.* v. 386–7. See Mother Mary Christopher Pecheux, O.S.U., 'The Concept of the Second Eve in *Paradise Lost*', *P.M.L.A.* lxxv (1960), 359–66.

their relationship to each other, in the differences between, for example, Eve's waking experiences and Adam's, or between the two angelic narratives, each celebrating the transmutation of evil into good. If Eve's dream temptation were omitted, the symmetry would be destroyed.

As this analysis implies, Raphael's lengthy narrative is the bridge between two complementary pictures of the state of innocence. Although its actual content does not come, strictly speaking, within the scope of this study, it is worth pointing out that it had some precedents. These are few but important, for they reveal that the episode is not necessarily to be explained as part of the poem's epic machinery. The idea of the angelic instructor was first mooted by the author of Jubilees, who stated that God deputed His angels to teach Adam the arts of agriculture.[1] In the twelfth century Comestor went still further by suggesting that the command to abstain from the tree of knowledge was given to Adam by some 'subject creature',[2] while in the fourteenth the author of the *Towneley* play on the Fall put this suggestion into practice: an angel descends to tell Adam that he has been created to take the place of the fallen angels and that he must prove himself worthy of that honour by obeying God's precepts.[3] And finally Grotius had included in his *Adamus Exul* a scene in which a divine messenger relates to Adam the creation of the world.[4]

When Raphael has concluded his narrative Adam takes up the story. His account of his experiences from his creation until his union with Eve is one of the finest and most imaginative things in the poem. As a narrative device it serves a number of purposes, the most obvious of which is to balance Raphael's description of the work of the days. I remarked earlier that the Priestly and the Jahwist documents seem to be written from two opposite points of view, the divine and the human respectively,[5] and this is exactly the effect here. Raphael's disquisition has portrayed the Creation from above; Adam's now reveals how it appeared from below. Second, by allowing Adam to assume the role of narrator Milton is able to give an extra dimension to his earlier description of the first pair. In Book IV, where they were seen from the outside, their perfections stood out clearly against the background of Satan's

[1] See above, Ch. II, p. 30.
[2] See above, Ch. VI, p. 170.
[3] See above, Ch. VII, p. 197.
[4] See above, Ch. VII, p. 208.
[5] See above, Ch. I, p. 11.

malevolence. Here, those same perfections are viewed from the inside, so to speak, through Adam's eyes, and they are somewhat modified by the presence of the angel. Third, whereas in Book IV our attention was concentrated on Eve, now that she is off stage we are free to focus on Adam and his relationships.

These are rather more complicated than Eve's because, standing as he does half-way between his wife and his Creator, Adam must learn the right attitude to both. He must learn, moreover, in a different way. To revert to the central image of the garden, Eve's feelings have simply to be guided, like the flowers and the vine, to their 'prop'. Adam's, on the other hand, have to be 'lopped' to prevent them from becoming 'overgrown'. We have already had one example of this process early in Book VIII, when Adam's upward-tending thoughts are 'pruned' by the angel:

> But apt the Mind or Fancie is to roave
> Uncheckt, and of her roaving is no end;
> Till warn'd, or by experience taught, she learne,
> That not to know at large of things remote
> From use, obscure and suttle, but to know
> That which before us lies in daily life,
> Is the prime Wisdom.[1]

From the beginning of Adam's narration on, however, we shall be more concerned with his downward-tending feelings, his relation-ship with Eve.

In the parallel scene in *Adamus Exul*, which may have suggested at least the outlines of Milton's episode, Grotius's Adam simply tells his wife of her creation and his love for her.[2] Milton's Adam is far more informative in his speech to Raphael, and begins with his first waking reactions to his own creation:

> about me round I saw
> Hill, Dale, and shadie Woods, and sunnie Plaines,
> And liquid Lapse of murmuring Streams; by these,
> Creatures that livd, and movd, and walk'd, or flew,
> Birds on the branches warbling; all things smil'd,
> With fragrance and with joy my heart oreflow'd.
> My self I then perus'd, and Limb by Limb
> Survey'd, and sometimes went, and sometimes ran
> With supple joints, and lively vigour led.

---

[1] *P.L.* viii. 188–94. [2] See above, Ch. VII, p. 208.

But who I was, or where, or from what cause,
Knew not; to speak I tri'd, and forthwith spake,
. . . fair Creatures, tell,
Tell, if ye saw, how came I thus, how here?
Not of my self; by some great Maker then,
In goodness and in power præeminent;
Tell me, how may I know him, how adore.[1]

Nothing quite like this had been written since Dracontius's *Carmen de Deo*, where Adam also wakes up, tests his voice, and gazes around him in wonder at the green fields and the creatures grazing in them.[2] In both poems, too, Adam ponders where he came from and why, but only Milton's Adam is able to argue from his own existence to the existence of a Creator. Again, what in the earlier poem had been an illustration of Adam's childlike innocence becomes in *Paradise Lost* a proof of Adam's intelligence. Even more obvious are the similarities between this passage and Eve's account of her creation in Book IV. Like Eve, Adam awakes as from sleep on a flowery bank, asks himself how he came to be there, and lies down on the grass to consider the question. But whereas Eve then had an illusion of herself, Adam has a vision of God; whereas Eve was led to Adam, Adam is led into the garden; and whereas Eve was told to submit herself to her husband, Adam is ordered to keep the garden and to refrain from eating of the tree of knowledge. Set side by side the two passages confirm the moral Milton has been steadily driving home throughout his description of the state of innocence: Adam's destiny lies in the garden and in obedience to God, Eve's in her subjection to Adam.

There follows the episode of the naming of the animals, which, as we have seen, was a source of continual embarrassment to maximal commentators, implying, as it seemed to, that God first looked for Adam's mate among the beasts of the field.[3] If this were really so, then it followed either that Man was akin to the animals or that God made a mistake. Both conclusions were thoroughly unacceptable to orthodox Jew and Christian alike, so the Fathers and the Rabbis went to some trouble to refute them. They argued that the episode was designed to show not Adam's kinship with the animals but his superiority to them, demonstrated primarily by his ability to find

---

[1] *P.L.* viii. 261–80. Compare Adam's reactions in Pordage's *Mundorum Explicatio*, pp. 61–62.
[2] See above, Ch. IV, p. 129.   [3] See above, Ch. I, p. 14.

appropriate names for them.[1] Milton treats the incident along much the same lines—the animals are paraded in order to 'pay thee fealtie'[2]—but he is careful to add the qualification introduced by the Rabbis and confirmed by the Christian-Latin poets that Adam's wisdom derived directly from God:[3]

> I nam'd them, as they pass'd, and understood
> Thir Nature, with such knowledg God endu'd
> My sudden apprehension.[4]

The problem of God's apparent ignorance of Man's real nature was rather more difficult to solve. The author of Jubilees had been forced to 'cheat' by placing God's words, 'It is not good that man should be alone', after rather than before the actual naming,[5] and the Rabbis had maintained God's omniscience only at the expense of His benevolence:

> Then he paraded [the animals] again before him in pairs [male and female]. Said he, 'Every one has a partner, yet I have none'. . . . And Why did He not create her [Eve] for him at the beginning? Because the Holy One, blessed be He, foresaw that he would bring charges against her, therefore He did not create her until he [Adam] expressly demanded her.[6]

By the seventeenth century, however, the difficulty had finally been resolved in a way which preserved both God's good nature and Man's dignity: in *The First Booke of Qvestions and Answers vpon Genesis* (1620) Alexander Ross wrote that Eve's creation was delayed 'That *Adam* liuing a priuate life a while, might the better perceiue the comforts of the married life. Secondly, that hee might loue God the more, who prouided such a comfort to him, when he was alone.'[7] This idea depended in turn on Adam's realization of his loneliness, a notion first put forward by the Rabbis and Dracontius,[8] and expressed in imaginative terms in at least two seventeenth-century

---

[1] See above, ch. II, pp. 39–40; Ch. III, p. 95.

[2] *P.L.* viii. 344. Compare Joshua Sylvester's translation of *Du Bartas his Divine Weekes and Workes*, 'The Sixth Day of the First Week', 992–5.

[3] See above, Ch. IV, pp. 122, 139.

[4] *P.L.* viii. 352–4. Compare Sylvester's *Du Bartas*, 'The Sixth Day of the First Week', 996–1000.

[5] See above, Ch. II, pp. 30–31.   [6] *Gen. Rab.* xvii. 4.

[7] *Questions and Answers*, p. 57. Compare Willett's *Hexapla*, p. 36.

[8] See above, Ch. II, p. 44; Ch. IV, p. 129. E. C. Baldwin has adduced *Jerahmeel* as a possible source in his article 'Some extra-Biblical Semitic Influences upon Milton's Story of the Fall of Man', *J.E.G.P.* xxviii (1929), p. 366.

treatments of the Fall. Joseph Beaumont, for example, suggested of Adam, in his *Psyche* (1648), that

> when their march in loving Pairs he view'd,
> A gentle sigh he fetch'd, to think that He
> Should spend his nobler life in solitude,
> Whilst all Things else injoy'd society.
> What boots it him to reign as *sovereign Lord*,
> If all his World can him no Queen afford.[1]

Out of these two latter elaborations, God's deliberate postponement of Eve's creation and Adam's initial loneliness, Milton constructed the remarkable conversation between Adam and His Maker in *Paradise Lost*. Characteristically, though, he was not content to leave his materials as he found them, and he completely transformed the motives behind God's delay in making Eve. In answer to Adam's expostulation:

> In solitude
> What happiness, who can enjoy alone,
> Or all enjoying, what contentment find ?[2]

God replies that Adam has the animals as company, and when Adam objects that there can be no 'society' among unequals He points out that He Himself has no companion. Again Adam respectfully refutes his Creator's reasoning: just as he is superior to the animals, he argues, so is he inferior to God:

> Thou in thy self art perfet, and in thee
> Is no deficience found; not so is Man,
> But in degree, the cause of his desire
> By conversation with his like to help,
> Or solace his defects.[3]

Only when Adam has made this second point does God relent, revealing that, as He says, 'I, ere thou spak'st, / Knew it not good for Man to be alone'.[4] What Milton has done here is to turn both

---

[1] Canto vi, stanza 192. See also Peyton's *Glasse of Time*, The First Age, p. 27.

[2] *P.L.* viii. 364–6.

[3] Ibid. viii. 415–19. The Rabbis, on the other hand, had given this argument to God. According to them, God created Eve so that the other creatures would not assume that Adam was the Creator on the grounds that he had no mate. See above, Ch. II, p. 43. Willet refuted this belief in his *Hexapla*, p. 35: 'for if man had beene alone, who should haue so thought or spoken ?'

[4] *P.L.* viii. 444–5. By treating the episode dramatically Milton is able to transfer these words from before to after the naming of the animals without contradicting the

criticisms of the naming episode to his own advantage. God actually does appear to be ignorant of Man's real nature, He actually does seem to imply that Adam is the equal of the animals. But, as it turns out, He is only pretending to adopt this position in order to make sure that Adam understands his place in the universal hierarchy. Eve's creation is postponed, not, as in Ross, to make Adam appreciate the delights of married life and love his Maker the more, but to impress upon him that he stands half-way between the animal and the divine orders. What is more, the whole episode re-emphasizes the difference between Adam and his wife: Eve was inclined to fall in love with her own reflection and had to be reconciled to Adam's 'manly grace'; Adam, on the contrary, is dissatisfied with his own company and specifically asks for a companion.

Adam then proceeds to tell Raphael how Eve was made from his rib:

> Mine eyes he clos'd, but op'n left the Cell
> Of Fancie my internal sight, by which
> Abstract as in a transe methought I saw,
> Though sleeping, where I lay, and saw the shape
> Still glorious before whom awake I stood;
> Who stooping op'nd my left side, and took
> From thence a Rib, with cordial spirits warme,
> And Life-blood streaming fresh; wide was the wound,
> But suddenly with flesh fill'd up and heal'd.
> The Rib he formd and fashiond with his hands;
> Under his forming hands a Creature grew,
> Manlike, but different Sex.[1]

On the face of it there is nothing very remarkable about this description, and critics and scholars have paid comparatively little attention to it. The dream, it might well be assumed, is no more than a device invented by Milton to explain how Adam could know all about Eve's creation even though he was asleep at the time. The corresponding passage in Grotius's *Adamus Exul* illustrates clearly enough the kind of problem that could arise when such a precaution was not taken, for there Adam relates to Eve the minutest details of events he could not possibly have observed.[2] Where then, an alert Eve might reasonably be expected to inquire, could her husband have come by

---

Scriptural order of events. God knew that it was not good for man to be alone before He created the animals, but He did not say so until afterwards.

[1] *P.L.* viii. 460–71.   [2] See above, Ch. VII, p. 208.

this lurid information concerning her origins? In Milton's version, Adam's careful account of his 'internal sight' answers the question before it is asked. Yet, crucial though the dream may be to the narrative integrity of the episode as it is recounted in *Paradise Lost*, its presence is not to be explained in terms of narrative considerations only. For Adam's dream is not Milton's invention; behind that brief vision there lies a long and curious history.

In Genesis itself, of course, no mention at all is made of any dream. Adam is merely put to sleep. This divinely imposed slumber was a phenomenon of great interest to rabbinic and patristic commentators alike. The former held that God rendered Adam unconscious to prevent him from witnessing those very details of his wife's creation that Milton took such pains to let him see: if Adam had actually watched Eve being made, they argued, he would have found her thoroughly repulsive.[1] The Fathers, on the other hand, treated the incident far less literally. According to the standard interpretation, the creation of Eve from Adam's rib prefigured the birth of the Church from the wound in Christ's side as He hung on the cross.[2] Of the countless parallels between the Old and the New Testaments none was more popular than this. It appeared in most subsequent commentaries on Genesis, and it found elaborate poetic expression in Avitus's *De Mosaicae Historiae Gestis*.[3] The inevitable corollary of this idea was that Adam's waking words concerning a man's relationship with his wife were in fact a prophecy of Christ's future relationship with His Church. But if Adam's words really were prophetic, an attentive reader might well have wondered how the protoplast could possibly have foreseen the destiny of an institution which was not yet even in existence. By the twelfth century an episode had been invented to solve precisely this problem. Adam's sleep, Comestor pointed out, was no ordinary slumber, but a trance during which God revealed to him the future union of Christ and the Church.[4] This notion became extremely popular during the Middle Ages, and as late as the seventeenth century it was still current. In Joseph Beaumont's *Psyche*, for instance, while Eve is being created Adam has a vision of two trees by means of which the future course of human history is expounded to him allegorically.[5] Here, however, the

---

[1] See above, Ch. II, p. 44.   [2] See above, Ch. III, p. 101.
[3] See above, Ch. IV, p. 133.   [4] See above, Ch. VI, p. 169.
[5] Canto vi, stanzas 206–16. This may have suggested to Milton the idea of Adam's first dream, in which trees also play a prominent part. When he awoke Adam found 'Before mine Eyes all real, as the dream / Had lively shadowed' (*P.L.* viii. 310–11). In

essentially typological character of the incident has been largely obscured. It survives, like another popular medieval legend, the debate of the four daughters of God, merely as a piece of baroque decoration.

But if the typology which had originally given rise to the dream was lost, the dream itself survived. Adam may not, after all, have foreseen the divine destiny of the Church, but he did foresee the impending union of man and woman. This feat, albeit less spectacular, also demanded some rationalistic explanation, and the dream was ideally suited to provide it. Hence Calvin wrote:

> It is demaunded, whence Adam had this knowledge: who at the time that she was formed, was in a deepe sleepe. If we say that his wit was then so quicke and sharpe, that he coulde iudge by coniectures, it shal be but a weake aunswere. But we neede not to doubte, but that God made the truth of the mater knowen vnto him, eyther by secrete reuelation, or else by his worde.[1]

And even when this lower form of prophecy was discarded there was still the problem of accounting for Adam's knowledge that Eve was made from his rib. It is to this end that More uses the dream in his *Conjectura Cabbalistica*:

> as he slept upon the ground, he fell into a dream, how God had put his hand into his side, and pulled out one of his ribs, closing up the flesh in stead therof: And how the rib, which the Lord God had taken from him, was made into a woman, and how God when he had thus made her, took her by the hand, and brought her unto him. And he had no sooner awakened, but he found his dream to be true.[2]

Here, I believe, is the basis of Milton's description in *Paradise Lost*. Taking the most recent and mundane version of the dream, he used it to portray Eve's creation within the context of Adam's first-person narrative.

Although he may have followed this particular version because it was the only one he knew, it is not hard to see why he should have rejected the others, if indeed he was acquainted with them. The

---

Psyche his reaction is much the same: 'And yet the while . . . He thought his wond'rous *Dream* had still possesst him, / And with a gentler Apparition blest him' (vi. 243). In More's *Conjectura*, too, Adam awoke and 'found his dream to be true' ('Literal Cabbala', p. 14). See also Sylvester's *Du Bartas*, 'The First Part of the First Day of the Second Week', 376–7.

[1] *Commentary on Genesis*, ii. 23.
[2] 'The Literal Cabbala', p. 14. See also Willett's *Hexapla*, p. 37.

Jewish view that the process of creation was repugnant would have seemed to him little short of blasphemous, while Comestor's interpretation had the serious disadvantage that it presupposed the Fall before it had actually happened.[1] God's plan for Man's salvation could be fittingly revealed to Adam only after his disobedience had made it necessary, so Milton postponed it until Book XII.[2]

During his premonitory dream, Adam goes on to relate, Eve appeared to him:

> so lovly faire,
> That what seemd fair in all the World, seemd now
> Mean, or in her summd up, in her containd
> And in her looks, which from that time infus'd
> Sweetness into my heart, unfelt before,
> And into all things from her Aire inspir'd
> The spirit of love and amorous delight.
> Shee disappeerd, and left me dark, I wak'd
> To find her, or for ever to deplore
> Her loss.[3]

These initial reactions of delight were by no means original with Milton, though his handling of the episode allowed them to blur over into the dream itself. The Christian-Latin poets in particular had stressed that Eve was made from Adam's own flesh and blood so that he would love her the more,[4] and Victor, the medieval dramatists, and Grotius had all depicted the fulfilment of this intention.[5] In the seventeenth century, too, poets often dwelt at length on the birth of Adam's love for his wife; Peyton, for instance, wrote:

> Though God at first this earth for thee hath made,
> The creatures all at thy command to trade:
> The Sunne and Moone ordaind to be thy light,
> The Stars and all vnto their vtmost might,
> The world it selfe and Paradise the place,
> Where still his loue hath euer giuen thee grace:

---

[1] This is precisely the same objection as that brought by Calvin against the idea that Satan revolted because Christ decided to become incarnate in human rather than angelic form. See above, Ch. IX, p. 225.

[2] See below, Ch. XI, pp. 291–2.

[3] *P.L.* viii. 471–80. The latter lines recall the conclusion of Milton's sonnet 'Methought I saw': 'But O as to embrace me she enclin'd / I wak'd, she fled, and day brought back my night.'

[4] See above, Ch. IV, pp. 120, 124, 130.

[5] See above, Ch. IV, p. 124; Ch. VII, pp. 197, 208.

Yet all of them compar'd in euery part,
Cannot content and satisfie thy heart,
Vntill thy God euen with his sacred Rest,
Had giuen thee this to make thee perfect blest.[1]

If Milton's Adam sounds a little like a seventeenth-century love-poet, he was certainly a far better one than many of his predecessors.
He then proceeds to describe his marriage to Eve:

> the Earth
> Gave sign of gratulation, and each Hill;
> Joyous the Birds; fresh Gales and gentle Aires
> Whisper'd it to the Woods, and from thir wings
> Flung Rose, flung Odours from the spicie Shrub,
> Disporting, till the amorous Bird of Night
> Sung Spousal, and bid haste the Eevning Starr
> On his Hill top, to light the bridal Lamp.[2]

Of all the extra-Biblical elaborations in *Paradise Lost* none has a more varied background than this. The theme of Adam's wedding had first appeared in the writings of the Rabbis, who embellished the incident with all the formalities of a Jewish ceremony.[3] Later, Avitus, inspired either by the rabbinic treatments or by Virgil's account of Dido's union with Aeneas, did very much the same thing, drawing this time on the Roman ceremony,[4] and in the seventeenth century Peyton offered a similar account:

> But now thy God hath perfect made thy state,
> Linck't thee in marriage with so choyce a mate,
> Himselfe the Priest which brought her to thy hand,
> And knit the knot that euer more must stand.[5]

Milton, however, went into far greater detail than any other seventeenth-century author who treated the theme, and it seems likely that he was indebted to Avitus, if to anyone, for his version of the episode.
　Up to this point Raphael's brow has remained uncontracted, but

---

[1] 'The First Age', p. 28. Eve's earlier effusion of love in Book IV of *Paradise Lost* looks as if it may have been a recollection of this passage.
[2] *P.L.* viii. 513–20. This is one of the many passages that connect this second picture of innocence with that in Book IV. Compare *P.L.* iv. 708–13.
[3] See above, Ch. II, p. 45.　　　　　　　　　[4] See above, Ch. IV, p. 133.
[5] 'The First Age', p. 29. Compare *Psyche*, vi. 248. *Purchas his Pilgrimage*, 1613, p. 12.

Adam's subsequent remarks soon bring a frown to the angelic visage:

> here passion first I felt,
> Commotion strange, in all enjoyments else
> Superiour and unmov'd, here onely weake
> Against the charm of Beauties powerful glance.[1]

He realizes that he is Eve's superior 'in the mind / And inward faculties':

> yet when I approach
> Her loveliness, so absolute she seems
> And in her self compleat, so well to know
> Her own, that what she wills to do or say,
> Seems wisest, vertuousest, discreetest, best;
> All higher knowledge in her presence falls
> Degraded, Wisdom in discourse with her
> Looses discount'nanc't, and like folly shewes;
> Authority and Reason on her waite.[2]

Here, critics have been quick to note, are the first signs of the weakness which will eventually lead to Adam's downfall. The whole speech is absolutely central to Milton's presentation of the Fall itself.

Adam's confession appears at first to be one of the most original parts of the poem, for although several poets had remarked on his love for Eve none had gone so far as to suggest that he loved her overmuch or in the wrong way.[3] Nevertheless, the incident was not wholly of Milton's invention, and in its source, I believe, is to be found the final clue to his presentation of the state of innocence. In my account of the background to Adam's earlier dream I omitted to say anything of the allegorical tradition, and, indeed, it has little or nothing to do with that section of the narrative. It does, however, have a great deal to do with this. Philo, as we have seen, interpreted the Fall as consisting in Reason's submission to Sense-perception and found the first instance of this submission in Adam's waking words to Eve: 'For the sake of sense-perception the Mind, when it

---

[1] *P.L.* viii. 530–4.   [2] Ibid. viii. 546–54.

[3] Peyton comes near it in 'The First Age', pp. 27–28:

> So sweete an eye, and pretty pleasing looke,
> Like Adamant and glittring sugred hooke.
> She drawes thy loue to mind her speeches more,
> Then God himselfe that gaue thee her in store.

Here, of course, it is the poet himself who is anticipating the Fall.

has become her slave, abandons both God the Father of the universe, and God's excellence and wisdom, the Mother of all things, and cleaves to and becomes one with sense-perception.'[1] In another work Philo expressed the same idea non-allegorically: 'And woman becomes for him the beginning of blameworthy life. For as long as he was by himself, as accorded with such solitude, he went on growing like to the world and like God.'[2] When Adam first saw Eve, and desired her, 'this desire begat likewise bodily pleasure, that pleasure which is the beginning of wrongs and violation of the law, the pleasure for the sake of which men bring on themselves the life of mortality and wretchedness in lieu of that of immortality and bliss'.[3] During the centuries following, this version of the story was modified at the hands of the Fathers, who gradually succeeded in shifting the Fall back to the violation of the tree of knowledge, while preserving the basic allegorical pattern.[4] But as late as the seventeenth century the original Philonic pattern was available in its purest form in Henry More's *Conjectura Cabbalistica*. Having summarized Philo's equation of Adam with Reason and Eve with Sense, More asserted that when Adam awoke from the sleep into which he had fallen during the creation of his wife,

He straightway acknowledg'd that all the sense and knowledge of any thing he had hitherto, was more lifelesse and evanid, and seemed lesse congruous and grateful unto him, and more estranged from his nature: but this was so agreeable & consentaneous to his soul, that he looked upon it as a necessary part of himself, and called it after his own name. And he thought thus within himself, For this cause will any one leave his over-tedious *aspires* to unite with the *Eternal Intellect, and Universal Soul of the world*, the immensenesse of whose exellencies are too highly rais'd for us to continue long in their embracements, and will cleave to the joyous and chearful *life of his Vehicle*.[5]

---

[1] *Leg. All.* II. xiv.   [2] *De Op. Mun.* liii.   [3] Loc. cit.

[4] See above, Ch. III, pp. 69–77.

[5] 'The Philosophick Cabbala', pp. 42–43. M. H. Nicolson, who first drew attention to this work as a possible source in 'Milton and the *Conjectura Cabbalistica*', *P.Q.* vi (1927), 1–18, assumes that the work is genuinely cabbalistic, and on this basis goes on to discuss the influence of cabbalism on the seventeenth century at large. In fact More's commentary has little or nothing to do with real cabbalism as represented by the *Zohar*. In the seventeenth century the term 'cabbalist' was used very loosely, and could be applied to almost any work of Jewish origin. Writing in 1620, for instance, Peyton says that the Jews are called 'Cabalists and Rabbies' (*Glasse of Time*, p. 35). More's work, or at least that section of it entitled 'The Philosophick Cabbala', is merely a summary of Philo's ideas on the Fall. Nicolson attempts to demonstrate the link between Milton and this source by setting a section of it beside a passage of *Paradise Lost* and italicizing

This, I submit, is a very fair summary of Adam's feelings as expressed in *Paradise Lost*. Committed as he was to a literal treatment of the Fall, Milton simply deallegorized the episode and adapted it to the purposes of his realistic description of the state of innocence.[1] By so doing he modified its meaning in a very important way. In its allegorical context Adam's subjection to Eve at this point virtually constituted the actual Fall; isolated from that context, it becomes no more than a premonition of the Fall. As I remarked earlier, the real originality of Milton's account of Man's pre-lapsarian life lies in his emphasis on the second of Adam's duties, the supervision of the garden, which is presented as being absolutely necessary to the preservation of its perfection. And, as I also remarked, the allegorical exegesis of Adam's appointment as gardener was used by the poet to provide a moral and psychological counterpart to his physical labours. As the vine has to be trained round the elm so Eve's affections have to be trained around Adam. But the elm, too, demands attention. On the one hand, it must be pruned in order to prevent it from overreaching itself, a function which we have seen Raphael performing when he taught Adam that there must be a limit to his intellectual aspirations. On the other, it must not be allowed to yield itself to the vine's entanglements; the prop must be strong enough to support the flower without being pulled to the ground. It is this second lesson that Adam is learning here. Just as he must not seek to inquire too closely into the ways of God, so he must not permit himself to be debased by his passion for his wife.

On the basis of this analysis most of the charges brought against Milton's account of Man's unfallen life can be dismissed. These take two forms, the first of which we have already examined as it appears in the criticism of Willey, Green, and Tillyard. It has more recently been revived by Waldock, who inquires: 'What, after all, has Milton—the Milton of the great famous sayings in the prose works, the Milton who could not praise a fugitive and cloistered virtue unexercised and unbreathed—to do with the effortless innocence, the "blank" virtue of pre-lapsarian Man?'[2] The answer is,

the phrases which show Milton's dependence. In every instance, however, the italicized passage turns out to be an instance of both writers' quoting the text of Genesis. A. Stein (*Answerable Style*, p. 104) relates Adam's speech to a Platonic 'conflict between the soul (Eve) and the intellect (Adam)'.

[1] The same process is to be seen at work in Milton's treatment of the parliament in Heaven. See above, Ch. IX, pp. 231–41.

[2] *Paradise Lost and its Critics*, p. 22.

a great deal. The whole point of Milton's description is that Man's innocence was not 'effortless';[1] Adam and Eve's virtue was neither fugitive nor cloistered, and almost every episode in Books IV, V, and VIII is calculated to show that it was not. Throughout the poem Milton insists that on this earth perfection cannot be a condition of stability. The perfection of Adam and Eve no less than the perfection of the garden they inhabit is nothing if not conditional, for it requires their constant vigilance to preserve the balance of forces on which it depends. These forces, being natural, are always trying to grow, so they must be controlled. The idea of spontaneous self-discipline, so common in previous treatments of Milton's theme, is totally foreign to *Paradise Lost*, and, indeed, to all Milton's thinking: 'And certainly discipline is not only the removall of disorder, but if any visible shape can be given to divine things, the very visible shape and image of vertue.'[2] The Milton of the prose works is, *pace* Waldock, the same Milton who revolutionized the traditional view of Eden and pre-lapsarian Man:

many there be that complain of divin providence for suffering *Adam* to transgresse, foolish tongues! when God gave him reason, he gave him freedom to choose, for reason is but choosing; he had bin else a meer artificiall *Adam*, such an *Adam* as he is in the motions. . . . Wherefore did he creat passions within us, pleasures round about us, but that these rightly temper'd are the very ingredients of vertue ? . . . This justifies the high providence of God, who though he command us temperance, justice, continence, yet powrs out before us ev'n to a profusenes all desirable things, and gives us minds that can wander beyond all limit and satiety.[3]

The widely held belief that there is a discrepancy between Milton's views as expressed in his prose writings and his portrayal of innocence in *Paradise Lost* is, then, the result of emphasizing the idealistic aspects of Adam's life at the expense of the natural ones. Paradoxically, Milton's most eloquent and persuasive advocate, Lewis, has done the poet the greatest disservice by lending his authority to this distortion. The conception of Adam and Eve he outlines is only half of Milton's conception, for he has ignored all those episodes in which the pair are seen as pupils and concentrated on those in which the outward trappings of their life remind us that

---

[1] Both Willey and Waldock use this wholly inappropriate word to describe Adam's unfallen life, and Tillyard comes very near it with 'unstruggling'.

[2] *Reason of Church Government* (Columbia, iii, Part i, p. 185).

[3] *Areopagitica* (Columbia, .iv. 319–20). See also *Tetrachordon* (Columbia, iv. 159).

they are also monarchs.[1] They may, for instance, dine with an archangel, but Milton does not let us forget that angelic digestion is of a higher order than our human one. They may, again, be married with all the formality of kings and queens, but Raphael makes it clear that their love is of a different kind from the celestial. Milton, in fact, goes out of his way to refute the two most popular beliefs of the maximal commentators, that Men fed and procreated like the archangels.[2]

The second charge brought against Milton is based on precisely the opposite kind of distortion. It stems again from Willey, who suggested that 'Milton, in his endeavour to make his epic narrative humanly convincing, certainly has to attribute to them [Adam and Eve] some of the frailties of fallen humanity in order to make their behaviour plausible'.[3] Tillyard, taking up this hint, asserts that both Adam and Eve crossed the line separating innocence from experience long before they ate the apple, Eve during her demonic dream and Adam in his infatuation with his wife.[4] And M. Bell goes even further, finding in Eve's delight in her own reflection a vanity which could only exist in a fallen world, and in Adam's unbridled zest for knowledge a curiosity which a perfect man would never feel. The conclusion of this argument is again the Gnostic one; if Adam and Eve were wicked before they ate the forbidden fruit, then the Fall was the best possible thing that could have happened, for 'it seems to be Milton's thought that only by becoming conscious of these qualities does Man have hope of attaining that inner harmony and the unity with the cosmic purpose which is true Paradise'.[5] Here, as in the former case, one side of Milton's picture has been exaggerated at the expense of the other. The only difference is that now it is Adam's pupillage that has received all the attention and his dignity that has been ignored. One school, as it were, assumes that 'delicious Paradise' adequately defines the nature of Eden, while the other offers the 'steep wilderness' as the sum of Milton's description. The one thing that distinguishes Milton's account from all others, however, is that without this tendency to over-abundance and

---

[1] *Preface*, ch. xvi.   [2] See above, Ch. III, pp. 86–87.
[3] *Seventeenth Century Background*, p. 229.
[4] *Studies in Milton*, 1951, pp. 10–13.
[5] 'The Fallacy of the Fall in *Paradise Lost*', *P.M.L.A.* lxviii (1953), 875–8. See also her exchange with W. Shumaker in *P.M.L.A.* lxx (1955), 1185–1203, during the course of which she insists that any 'unfallen impulses' which are 'potentially dangerous' can be described only by reference to 'fallen qualities'.

wanton growth Man's original condition would have been neither free nor happy. The tendencies Eve exhibits at the sight of her own reflection or in her demonic dream, the forces inside him which Adam reveals in his questions about cosmology and his passion for his wife, these are no more wicked than the upsurging vitality of the plants around them. Hunger, thirst, curiosity, and sexual desire become evil only when they are not properly disciplined, when hunger, whether intellectual or physical, becomes gluttony, and desire lust:

> But Knowledge is as food, and needs no less
> Her Temperance over Appetite, to know
> In measure what the mind may well contain,
> Oppresses else with Surfet, and soon turns
> Wisdom to Folly, as Nourishment to Winde.[1]

Almost every episode in which Adam and Eve are involved before the Fall is designed to illustrate their gradual recognition that control is the chief ingredient of virtue. Consequently it is extremely misleading to talk of 'borders' or 'lines' separating innocence from sin, as if they were two isolated states characterized by completely different kinds of experience. The difference between unfallen and fallen Man is simply the difference between a well and a badly tended garden. It is a difference of degree, not of kind. That is why Paradise can be regained.

[1] *P.L.* vii. 126–30.

XI

FIRST DISOBEDIENCE

ONE of the most intriguing narrative problems posed by the Jahwist document concerned Eve's apparent isolation when the serpent approached her. How did it come about, an attentive reader might ask, that her husband was absent at the critical moment? Jewish sources had offered three possible explanations: Adam may have been deep in a post-coital slumber, God may have taken him off on a tour of his domain, or he and Eve may have been assigned different parts of the garden to supervise.[1] These, if he knew them, Milton was bound to reject, for the first implied that the temptation took place at night,[2] while the latter two made God ultimately responsible for Eve's vulnerability. The medieval dramatists, on the other hand, had effected the separation by inventing an episode in which one or other of the first pair set out to explore the beauties of Eden alone,[3] and in the seventeenth century Peyton pictured the Devil waiting for the time:

> when *Adam* stept aside,
> Euen but a little from his louely Bride,
> To pluck perhaps a Nut vpon the Trees,
> Or get a combe amongst the hony Bees.[4]

This was equally unsatisfactory, though for a different reason. Milton could not afford to admit any suggestion of tragic coincidence into the story at this point; the kind of bad luck that brought about the deaths of Romeo and Juliet could have no place in the unfallen world of Adam and Eve.[5] If they were to part they had to be shown doing so fully aware of the risks they were taking, of the dangers to which they were thereby exposing themselves. Consequently Milton made these risks and dangers the whole crux of the long argument

---

[1] See above, Ch. II, pp 48, 57.   [2] See above, Ch. X, p. 254.

[3] See above, Ch. VII, p. 198.

[4] 'The First Age', p. 32. See also *Psyche*, vi. 271.

[5] In Vondel's *Adam in Ballingschap*, 1460–77, for example, Adam simply goes off to thank God for His gifts, thus exposing his wife to the Tempter. See Peter's comments in *Critique*, pp. 4–6.

between the two protagonists with which he prefaced the temptation in Book IX, thus ensuring that not only the Fall itself but also the conditions which made the Fall possible arose from a decision taken in possession of all the relevant facts.

This decision, moreover, had to be presented as a wrong one *per se*, not merely *ex post facto*, and here the poet was faced with the difficult task of contending with his audience's foreknowledge, which in the present instance could be quite as embarrassing as God's. Knowing the outcome of the discussion, we are naturally predisposed to side with Adam in his attempt to dissuade his wife from leaving him. As a result, we are likely to assume that Eve is wrong without inquiring too closely into the nature of her error. Milton evidently foresaw the possibility of this kind of preconditioned response, and went to some lengths to avert it by giving Eve a very persuasive and superficially cogent case for working apart from Adam. So successful has he been in this respect that a large number of critics have fallen prey to the plausibility of her arguments. Empson, for instance, claims that she simply feels the need to 'flap her wings a bit'; after Raphael's revelation of her future destiny she wants to 'obtain a tiny change in her experience' and she 'could hardly be admired if she had no impulse to react at all'. Adam was quite right to let her go, and those who blame him for doing so 'preach an immoral moral'.[1] Waldock is rather more cautious, but like Tillyard before him he sees in Eve's behaviour nothing more than feminine frivolity. According to his interpretation, her desire to go off on her own is a 'whim' which she follows with a 'pretty obstinacy'; stimulated by Adam's opposition she begins 'to act a little', she 'pretends to be hurt', and 'assumes an air of injured dignity'.[2] Peter, on the contrary, finds nothing whimsical in Eve's remarks. Her proposal is 'entirely natural and clearly dictated by the least frivolous side of her character'; her speeches are full of 'quiet good sense'.[3]

As these conflicting views reveal, the real difficulty here lies in determining what exactly prompted Eve to suggest that she and Adam should divide their labours. Because Milton did not make her motive absolutely explicit almost every critic who has analysed the

---

[1] *Milton's God*, pp. 150–1.

[2] *Paradise Lost and its Critics*, pp. 30–31. A. Stein (op. cit., p. 94) also uses the word 'whim' to describe Eve's desire to work apart from Adam, but he recognizes that there are more sinister undertones to her demand.

[3] *Critique*, pp. 116–19.

episode has found it necessary to make one up, often without the slightest regard for the text. Yet we have been given a clue to Eve's conduct, and in her very first words:

> *Adam*, well may we *labour* still to dress
> This Garden, still to tend Plant, Herb and Flour
> Our *pleasant task* enjoyn'd, but *till more hands*
> Aid us, the work under our *labour* grows,
> Luxurious by restraint; what we by day
> *Lop overgrown*, or prune, or prop, or bind,
> One night or two with *wanton growth* derides
> Tending to wilde.[1]

Like her previous diabolic dream, this speech of Eve's contains 're-semblances. . . . Of our last Eevenings talk';[2] every phrase I have italicized echoes Adam's observations on the same topic in Book IV. What is more, it also contains 'addition strange'.[3] Whereas in Book IV Eve had responded to her husband's admonitions with a clear affirmation of her dependence on him, she is now no longer content either to accept him as her law or to find in her unargued obedience her 'happiest knowledge and her praise'.[4] Instead she proceeds to assume an equality which the whole account of the state of innocence has insisted she does not have. For the first time in the poem she consciously stands on her dignity, resenting any suggestion that she is Adam's inferior. There is more involved here than an innocent and whimsical desire to be alone for a time, more, certainly, than a practical proposal for increasing their efficiency. The vine is trying to disengage itself from the elm.

The symptoms Eve displays during this conversation had been well summarized by Augustine. The woman, he argued, would never have succumbed to the Tempter's wiles if there had not already been in her mind 'a certain love of her own power and a certain proud self-presumption'.[5] Aquinas, realizing the possible implications of this statement, attempted to show that it applied only to the interval between the Tempter's initial inquiry and Eve's final assent: 'This does not mean that pride preceded the promptings of the serpent, but that as soon as the serpent had spoken his words of persuasion, her mind was puffed up, the result being that she believed the demon to have spoken truly.'[6] But there was nothing in

---

[1] *P.L.* ix. 205–12. My italics.   [2] Ibid. v. 114–15.
[3] Ibid. v. 116.   [4] Ibid. iv. 638.   [5] See above, Ch. III, p. 97.
[6] *Summa Theologica*, II. clxiii. 1.

the immediate context to prevent a less scrupulous reader from supposing that Augustine was referring to Eve's feelings before the temptation had even begun, and it may be that Milton found in Augustine's oft-quoted words the theme of her disagreement with Adam at this point of *Paradise Lost*.

It is to Eve's 'love of her own power' that the serpent first appeals in his ensuing conversation with her. Flattering her with a fulsomeness unequalled by those of any earlier Tempter,[1] his words reach 'Into the heart of *Eve*',[2] because after her quarrel with Adam she is in just the frame of mind to listen sympathetically to tributes to her dignity. Her first verbal reaction, however, is amazement:

> What may this mean? Language of Man pronounc't
> By Tongue of Brute, and human sense exprest?
> The first at lest of these I thought deni'd
> To Beasts.[3]

Throughout the poem we have seen her asking questions as she encounters each new phenomenon, but now there is no Adam present to answer them; there is only the Devil himself, who, seeing that she is off her guard, quickly seizes the initiative. His ability to speak, he states, is the result of eating the fruit of a particular tree—which later proves to be the tree of knowledge. In a sense, then, the serpent's seeming command of 'Language of Man' is the key to the whole temptation, for it is upon this proof of the tree's efficacy that he builds his most persuasive arguments for eating of it.

Milton's presentation of this opening gambit is the culmination of a long tradition. Rejecting the fanciful Jewish notion that before the Fall all the animals could talk, the Fathers had gradually evolved the theory that the Devil insinuated himself into the reptile and spoke through his mouth, just as a demon speaks through the mouth of a man possessed.[4] This in turn raised the question of Eve's evident lack of surprise when she met so strange a beast. Avitus castigated her for not suspecting that there was something unnatural about her new-found friend,[5] but little more was said on the subject until Comestor explained that by adopting a species of serpent with a maiden's face the Tempter allayed any suspicions that the woman

---

[1] See above, Ch. IV, p. 135; Ch. VII, pp. 200–1. [2] *P.L.* ix. 550.
[3] Ibid. ix. 553–6.
[4] See above, Ch. II, pp. 31, 47; Ch. III, pp. 88, 95. More and Browne attribute this opinion to Basil.
[5] See above, Ch. IV, p. 136.

might otherwise have had.[1] By the Renaissance, however, the idea of the human-headed serpent had fallen into some disrepute. Browne outlined the case against it most fully:

For first, as Pierius observeth from Barcephas, the assumption of humane shape had proved a disadvantage unto Sathan; affording not only a suspicious amazement in Eve, before the fact, in beholding a third humanity beside her self and Adam; but leaving some excuse unto the woman, which afterward the man took up with lesser reason; that is, to have been deceived by another like her self. . . . Lastly, whereas it might be conceived that an humane shape was fitter for this enterprise; it being more than probable she would be amazed to hear a Serpent speak; some conceive she might not yet be certain that only man was priviledged with speech; and being in the novity of the Creation, and inexperience of all things, might not be affrighted to hear a Serpent speak.[2]

To this several commentators added the possibility that she conversed with it freely because 'during the state of innocency, no creature was loathsome to man',[3] a point which Eve herself makes after the event:

> thou couldst not have discernd
> Fraud in the Serpent, speaking as he spake;
> No ground of enmitie between us known,
> Why hee should mean me ill, or seek to harme.[4]

Yet all these devious speculations were really unnecessary, for, as Calvin observed, there was no reason to believe that Eve was not surprised to hear a snake address her in the language of men: 'And I doubt not, but that Heuah perceiued this to be extraordinarie: and therefore she greedily receiued that, whereat she wondered.'[5] Purchas took the matter still further: 'The woman (whether she had not yet experience in the nature of the creatures, or did admire so strange an accident, and would satisfie her curious mind in the further tryall) entertained discourse.'[6] And Joseph Beaumont incorporated this account of her reactions into his poetical treatment of the confrontation:

---

[1] See above, Ch. VI, p. 170.

[2] *Pseudodoxia Epidemica*, v. 4.

[3] Thomas Adams, *Meditations on the Creed*, 1629. See also Gervase Babington, *Notes vpon Genesis*, sig. C8ᵛ; Henry Holland, *The Historie of Adam*, 1606, sig. B4; Alexander Ross, *Questions and Answers*, pp. 59–60.

[4] *P.L.* ix. 1149–52.

[5] *Commentary on Genesis*, iii. 3.

[6] *Purchas his Pilgrimage*, p. 20. See also Patrides, op. cit., p. 107.

> Admiring *Eve*, who had presum'd till now
> That *Speech* had been Man's privilege alone;
> Thought fair respect to this new *Talker* due,
> And freely join'd communication.[1]

Here, as in *Paradise Lost*, the serpent goes on to assert that it was the fruit of the tree of knowledge that endowed him with this miraculous gift:

> For yesterday, when first I 'gan to taste
> The sprightful *Fruit*, flames kindled in mine eyes:
> My soul awak'd, and from my bosom chas'd
> Those Mists of Ignorance whose thick disguise
>   Muffled my thoughts, and kept me down a beast
>   As dark and dull as any of the rest.[2]

At this stage of its development the temptation scene somewhat resembled the rabbinic elaborations of it, according to which the serpent ate the forbidden fruit himself in order to prove to Eve that it contained no harm,[3] and E. C. Baldwin has suggested that Milton may have been indebted to Jewish sources for his portrayal of the Tempter's strategy.[4] But as the passages quoted above demonstrate, Milton's version has far more in common with Beaumont's than with that of the Rabbis—in neither *Psyche* nor *Paradise Lost* does the serpent actually eat the fruit in front of Eve—and in one vital respect he is wholly original. Whereas in *Psyche* and the rabbinic tractates the Tempter makes it quite clear from the outset that he is referring to the tree of knowledge, in *Paradise Lost* he first arouses Eve's curiosity by leaving the identity of the magical tree in some doubt. He describes it in the vaguest terms as a 'goodly Tree farr distant',[5] and waits until she is thoroughly excited before taking her to see it. Not until they come within sight of it does she realize that it is the one tree forbidden to her. The temptation proper thus begins with Eve already in a mood of frustrated anticipation. By building up her hopes only to demolish them Satan creates in her the very state of mind in which she might be disposed to listen to his arguments with some eagerness. The idea that the Tempter talked with Eve for some time before mentioning the prohibition is not, of

---

[1] *Psyche*, vi. 274.   [2] Ibid. vi. 283. See also *Mundorum Explicatio*, p. 67.
[3] See above, Ch. II, p. 49.
[4] 'Some extra-Biblical Semitic Influences upon Milton's story of the Fall of Man', *J.E.G.P.* xxviii (1929), 366–401.
[5] *P.L.* ix. 576.

course, original with Milton. Willett, for example, wrote that 'the best interpretation is this, that after long communication had with the woman, at length the serpent commeth to that which he intended, to draw from the woman some answer, whereupon he might worke further.'[1] What is original is the way in which Milton combined this idea with Beaumont's description of the episode in order to make Eve's disobedience psychologically convincing.

At this juncture Milton reverted to the account of the Fall given in the third chapter of Genesis. Few verses in either the Old or the New Testament can have been more exhaustively analysed than these, and it is interesting to see just what Milton took from the wealth of interpretations at his disposal. One of the most popular was the theory of the three stages, the lust of the flesh (gluttony, *suggestio*), the lust of the eyes (avarice, *delectatio*), and the pride of life (vainglory, *consentio*), which Heywood used in *The Hierarchie of the Blessed Angels*:

> All sinnes (saith *Iohn*) we may in three diuide,
> *Lust of the Flesh, Lust of the Eye*, and *Pride*.
> She sees the *Tree*, and thought it good for meat;
> The Fleshes lust persuaded her to eat:
> She sees it faire and pleasant to the eye,
> Then the Eyes lust inciteth her to try;
> She apprehends that it will make her wise,
> So through the Pride of heart she eats and dies.[2]

Of these three stages the first two were not always clearly distinguished, with the result that they were sometimes combined as a vague desire to eat the forbidden fruit even before the serpent had proposed doing so:

> *Eve's* longing eye
> Full oft salutes that fatal Tree; desire
> She doth to tast the fruit, approaching nigher
> The subtle Serpent frisking on the Tree
> She spies.[3]

Both Calvin and Luther objected strongly to this analysis. As the latter put it, 'it is stupid to think, as the sophists, the monks think

[1] *Hexapla*, p. 45. See also John Diodati, *Pious and Learned Annotations upon the Holy Bible*, 2nd edn., 1648, p. 4.

[2] Book vi, p. 344. See above, Ch. III, pp. 103-4, and A. Williams, *Common Expositor*, p. 120.

[3] *Mundorum Explicatio*, p. 66. See also William Alexander, *Doomes Day*, I. lxii.

about the temptation, that when Eve looked at the tree, she gradually became inflamed with a desire to pick the fruit, until at last, overcome by her desire, she brought the fruit to her mouth'.[1] Taking up Comestor's comments on Eve's doubt, evidenced by her insertion of 'forte' into the terms of the original threat, they inferred that her first sin was neither gluttony nor even pride, but unbelief: 'Although she has not yet eaten the fruit, she has already sinned against the Word and faith; for she has turned away from the Word to a lie, from faith to unbelief. . . . The outward act of disobedience follows sin, which through unbelief has fully developed in the heart.'[2] By the seventeenth century this interpretation had become a standard feature of Protestant commentaries, and it was often used to refute the Catholic belief that the first sin was pride. Thomas Adams, for instance, wrote in his *Meditations on the Creed* (1629):

The Romish stream is altogether for pride, because Satan said, 'Ye shall be as gods'. . . . But this takes away the difference betwixt the sin of man and of the angels. These fell by their own pride immediately, man by temptation unto pride. There was some fault in man before pride, none before it in the apostate spirits. . . . But we find that Satan's drift was to make man doubt the truth of the commandment and punishment. . . . Therefore the first sin of the world appears to be infidelity.[3]

In his discussion of the various critical views of Eve's fall in *Paradise Lost* Waldock points out that it is almost impossible to find any one formula that will cover all the facets of Milton's presentation of it; Lewis's 'pride', Greenlaw's 'passion', Tillyard's 'levity', and Saurat's 'sensuality' all seem to leave something out of account.[4] The same is true of the theological formulae outlined above. The theory of the three stages could, with a little ingenuity, be applied to Milton's description, but so it could to any version of the story based on the Biblical statement that Eve 'saw that the tree was good for food, and that it was pleasant to the eyes, and a tree to be desired to make one wise.'[5] The opinion that she was first moved by gluttony might find some substantiation in her

---

[1] *Lectures on Genesis*, iii. 1.

[2] Ibid. iii. 5–6. This interpretation lingered on even after the offending word, 'perhaps', had been expunged from the English translations of the Bible. The Geneva Bible, for example, has the following marginal gloss on Gen. iii. 3: 'In douting of God's threatning she yeelded to Satan.'

[3] *Meditations*, pp. 187–8. See also Patrides, op. cit., p. 105.

[4] *Paradise Lost and its Critics*, ch. ii.

[5] Gen. iii. 6.

> eager appetite, rais'd by the smell
> So savorie of that Fruit, which with desire,
> Inclinable now grown to touch or taste,
> Sollicited her longing eye.[1]

But the onset of appetite comes only after the serpent's words have won 'too easie entrance'[2] into her heart. And the distinctively Protestant doctrine of Eve's lack of faith, to which Milton might have been expected to conform, may perhaps be reflected in the speech she makes before eating the apple. Certainly there is little evidence of pride at this juncture—the statement that 'God-head' was in her mind seems to be added almost as an afterthought.[3] On the other hand, doubt is a necessary prelude to disobedience, and the main burden of her speech is not that she disbelieves God but that she has begun to believe the serpent; credulity rather than doubt is what she expresses.[4] It seems to me, therefore, that Waldock is probably right when he suggests that Milton was working very much on an *ad hoc* basis in this part of the poem, that he was more concerned with making Eve's conduct seem plausible than with exemplifying any particular doctrinal interpretation of her actions. She was quite simply 'deceived', as St. Paul had originally stated; her moral defection took place when she decided to leave Adam.

Faced by the necessity of rendering Eve's transgression in convincing human terms, Avitus had taken refuge in a purely visual portrayal of her gradual surrender, using the physical movements of her hand as an image of her mental conflict,[5] and several seventeenth-century poets followed his example:

> On them she (doubtful) earnestly did gaze,
> The Hand oft-times advanc'd, and oft drawn back,
> Whilst Satan cunningly her Parts did praise.[6]

Milton created instead a brilliant verbal impression of her intellectual waverings. As she rehearses the arguments for eating the

---

[1] *P.L.* ix. 740–3. Compare *Psyche*, vi. 290. [2] Ibid. ix. 734.

[3] I think, therefore, that Lewis's 'Pride' is an over-simplified diagnosis of Eve's sin, for in order to maintain it he has to ignore the whole of Eve's speech of consent and place all the emphasis on this parenthesis. See his *Preface*, ch. xviii.

[4] In his analysis of the Fall, in *De Doctrina*, I. xi, Milton gives pride of place to 'distrust in the divine veracity and a proportionate credulity in the assurances of Satan' (Columbia, xv. 181–3).

[5] See above, Ch. IV, p. 136.

[6] William Alexander's *Doomes Day*, I. lxiii. See also *Psyche*, vi. 291; *Mundorum Explicatio*, p. 66.

fruit, her thoughts, like her hand in the earlier poems, reach out
towards the tree, only to recoil when she remembers the prohibition:

> Great are thy Vertues, doubtless, best of Fruits,
> Though kept from Man, and worthy to be admir'd,
> Whose taste, too long forborn, at first assay
> Gave elocution to the mute, and taught
> The Tongue not made for Speech to speak thy praise:
> Thy praise hee also who forbids thy use,
> Conceales not from us, naming thee the Tree
> Of Knowledge, knowledge both of good and evil;
> Forbids us then to taste, but his forbidding
> Commends thee more, while it inferrs the good
> By thee communicated, and our want:
> For good unknown, sure is not had, or had
> And yet unknown, is as not had at all.
> In plain then, what forbids he but to know,
> Forbids us good, forbids us to be wise?
> Such prohibitions binde not. But if Death
> Bind us with after-bands, what profits then
> Our inward freedom?[1]

Each cycle, however, brings her nearer to the deed itself, until
finally 'she pluck'd, she eat'.[2]

The same movement is evident in her next speech. At first she is
carried away by the exhilaration of what she has done—like Grotius's
Eve she even considers the possibility that God has not noticed her
trespass[3]—but the thought of Adam, and it is her first thought of
him,[4] stops her short for a moment. Only for a moment, though.
Her wild speculations fly off on another tangent, until she is again
brought to an abrupt halt by the consideration that she might after
all die:

> then I shall be no more,
> And *Adam* wedded to another *Eve*,
> Shall live with her enjoying, I extinct;
> A death to think. Confirm'd then I resolve,
> *Adam* shall share with me in bliss or woe:
> So dear I love him, that with him all deaths
> I could endure, without him live no life.[5]

---

[1] *P.L.* ix. 745-62.   [2] Ibid. ix. 781.   [3] See above, Ch. VII, p. 209.

[4] Peter's suggestion in his *Critique*, p. 127, that one of the inducements that led Eve
to eat the apple was 'her wish to be an ideal companion' for Adam takes no account of
this fact.

[5] *P.L.* ix. 827-33.

There can be no doubt that this shrewd insight into her character is ultimately of Jewish origin. It has been suggested that Milton found it either in *Jerahmeel*, or the *Zohar*, or in *Pirkê de Rabbi Eliezer*.[1] While it is true that the idea is to be found in all these sources, it seems more likely that Milton came across it in one of the sixteenth- or seventeenth-century Biblical commentaries, in which it was often quoted, if only to be rejected. Willet, for example, insisted: 'Neither did shee giue it to Adam, least, if shee died, he might haue taken vnto him another woman, as some Hebrewes imagine; . . . but shee was desirous to make her husband partaker of her happinesse, as shee thought.'[2] What Milton did was to reconcile these two opposing motives by distinguishing between Eve's real and ostensible reasons for giving the fruit to Adam. Her real reason is revealed in this soliloquy: she would rather destroy her husband than allow him the opportunity of living on with another mate. Her ostensible reason is the one she gives Adam in her next speech:

> For bliss, as thou hast part, to me is bliss,
> Tedious, unshar'd with thee, and odious soon.[3]

Between these two speeches Milton placed his description of Adam's return. Avitus, who had first introduced this beautiful episode into the story, had assumed that he knew nothing of what had happened in his absence, and the medieval dramatists took much the same view.[4] Joseph Beaumont, however, painted a very different picture:

> But absent *Adam's* sympathetic heart
> The sharpest fury of this dint assaild;

---

[1] H. F. Fletcher, 'Milton and Yosippon', *S.P.* xxi (1924), 496–501; D. Saurat, 'Milton and the *Zohar*', *S.P.* xix (1922), 136–49; D. C. Allen, 'Milton and Rabbi Eliezer', *M.L.N.* lxiii (1948), 262–3. The last of these sources seems to have been most popular among Renaissance Biblical expositors. Henry Ainsworth, for example, quotes frequently from *P.R.E.* in his *Annotations upon the first book of Moses*, Amsterdam, 1616. In order to substantiate his claim for *Jerahmeel* as a possible source Fletcher points out that it was translated into Latin in 1541 and subsequently appeared in an English translation by Peter Morwyng in 1558. This evidence would be impressive if it were not for the fact that in neither the Latin nor the English translations was the Genesis story included. They both began at the Book of Maccabees.

[2] *Hexapla*, p. 48. It was the latter reason that the author of the *Cornish Creation* used. See above, Ch. VII, p. 203. Babington, too, suggests that 'Eue meant him no harme, and yet she hurt him because she was wrong her selfe' (*Notes vpon Genesis*, Sig. D 1).

[3] *P.L.* ix. 879–80.

[4] See above, Ch. IV, p. 137; Ch. VII, p. 204.

> Who feeling by this ænigmatic smart
> Himself half-slain, still knew not what he ail'd
> Only he found his yerning bowels drive
> His anxious fear to run and see his *Eve*.[1]

Milton's account synthesizes elements drawn from both conceptions. His Adam, like Avitus's, looks forward with joy to meeting his wife, but, like Beaumont's, he also has forebodings that something has gone amiss:

> Great joy he promis'd to his thoughts, and new
> Solace in her return, so long delay'd;
> Yet oft his heart, divine of somthing ill,
> Misgave him; hee the faultring measure felt;
> And forth to meet her went.[2]

As he did throughout the poem, Milton here smoothed out the sharp angles of the Biblical story while preserving its over-all shape. Avoiding, on the one hand, the over-abrupt transition from joy to grief created by Avitus's description of Adam's happiness, and on the other the sense of anticlimax at the moment of his reunion with Eve produced by Beaumont's emphasis on Adam's fears, he used the scene to illustrate the 'Union of Mind'[3] that existed between the first pair even when they were separated both physically and morally.

Eve greets her husband with 'Countnance blithe'[4] and urges him to eat the forbidden fruit with her so that he too may achieve divinity:

> Thou therefore also taste, that equal Lot
> May joyne us, equal Joy, as equal Love;
> Least thou not tasting, different degree
> Disjoyne us, and I then too late renounce
> Deitie for thee, when Fate will not permit.[5]

The originality of her approach, which has passed unnoticed in most critical discussions of it, is immediately apparent if it is compared with that of any previous Eve. She appeals neither to Adam's love nor to his valour, the two points at which the majority of her predecessors had directed their attacks.[6] Instead, she tells a carefully calculated series of lies designed to arouse his loyalty not to her but to the idea of hierarchy. In her soliloquy she had contemplated

---

[1] *Psyche*, vi. 294.   [2] *P.L.* ix. 843-7.   [3] Ibid. viii. 604.
[4] Ibid. ix. 886.   [5] Ibid. ix. 881-5.
[6] See above, Ch. IV, p. 137; Ch. VI, pp. 180-1; Ch. VII, pp. 203, 210.

keeping 'the odds of Knowledge in my power' in order to be 'som-time Superior' to Adam;[1] now she claims that the reason she is offering him the fruit is to avoid just that possibility. Her real motives are turned inside out, so that the object of her former ambitions, the reversal of the natural order of man and woman, is now presented as a lightly veiled threat. Beneath all her eloquence there lurks the suggestion that if Adam does not follow her example he will lose, not her love, nor even her respect, but his authority over her. Waldock comments on this speech: 'She means this, and who does not feel that she would be capable of it, that if Adam were to be left she would tear herself away from deity, if she could, and go back to him! . . . She is a liar, but who cares?'[2] The answer is: anyone who reads the speech in its context, anyone who is not so carried away by the romantic view of the Fall that he is prepared to ignore everything that has led up to it.

Adam's first reaction is described in purely visual terms:

> From his slack hand the Garland wreath'd for *Eve*
> Down drop'd, and all the faded Roses shed.[3]

Jewish sources had taught that when Eve ate of the tree of knowledge all the other trees shed their leaves,[4] and Luther had used the simile of a garland to illustrate the scholastic view that Man's original righteousness was an adornment rather than a part of his nature, 'as when someone places a wreath on a pretty girl. The wreath is not part of the virgin's nature; it is something apart from her nature.'[5] Milton fused these two ideas together in such a way that the flowers, with which Eve has been associated throughout the poem, become an image of her faded virtue.

Adam's second reaction is expressed in his 'inward' speech, in which, it is important to note, he pays absolutely no attention to Eve's arguments or the premises upon which they were based. He does not even consider the possibility that they will grow 'up to Godhead' and share in 'equal Joy' and 'bliss'. He takes up, rather, the points Eve had debated in her soliloquy, her fears that she might die and he be wedded to another Eve:

> Should God create another *Eve*, and I
> Another Rib afford, yet loss of thee
> Would never from my heart; no no, I feel

---

[1] *P.L.* ix. 820–5.
[2] *Paradise Lost and its Critics*, p. 63.
[3] *P.L.* ix. 892–3.
[4] See above, Ch. II, p. 58.
[5] *Lectures on Genesis*, iii. 7.

The Link of Nature draw me; Flesh of Flesh,
Bone of my Bone thou art, and from thy State
Mine never shall be parted, bliss or woe.[1]

On the basis of this passage Waldock has gone to a deal of trouble to
establish an idea which had been a commonplace since the Middle
Ages, that Adam fell for love.[2] But in the light of Eve's very unusual
form of persuasion her husband's love for her takes on a rather
different colouring. As Milton presented it in *Paradise Lost* it is
a love that is both blind and deaf, stirred not by any such impas-
sioned pleas as those uttered by the Eve of *Adamus Exul*[3] but
by a sly hint that if he does not do something about it he is going
to find himself subservient to his wife. While there is no denying
Adam's nobility when he decides to die with her rather than live
on with a replacement, the knowledge that the very same consideration had already prompted Eve to make sure that he would never
survive to do anything of the kind must surely qualify our response.
The contrast between their respective reactions to the prospect of
'another *Eve*' may heighten the selflessness of Adam's devotion; it
also suggests that 'as the state of Eve now is', to adapt a phrase from
Areopagitica, that devotion is misplaced. One of the fundamental
theses of Milton's portrayal of Man's original innocence was that
nothing is evil in itself; feelings like hunger, curiosity, and sexual
desire become evil only if they are allowed to exceed their proper
limits. The assumption underlying his treatment of the Fall is the
complementary one that Adam's love, no less than Satan's valour and
fortitude, is not good *a priori*; it is good only so long as it is directed
to a good end. Even in Eden life is rather more complicated than the
romantic idealist might suppose.

Adam's second speech, the first one that Eve hears, is delivered
in 'calm mood'.[4] Just as his soliloquy had followed up the conclusions
Eve had reached in hers so here he seems to accept the contradictory arguments of her outward speech at their face value. He
pretends that there is a real possibility of attaining

Proportional ascent, which cannot be
But to be Gods, or Angels Demi-Gods.[5]

---

[1] *P.L.* ix. 911–16. The typological overtones which the concept of the second Eve
had by then acquired serve to reinforce the irony of this passage, for Eve's disobedience
is going to be undone by means of a 'second *Eve*'.

[2] *Paradise Lost and its Critics*, ch. iii. See above, Ch. VI, pp. 180–1

[3] See above, Ch. VII, p. 210.   [4] *P.L.* ix. 920.   [5] Ibid. ix. 936–7.

Assuming the role of the *advocatus diaboli*, he presents the case against death in the authentic Satanic tone:

> so God shall uncreate,
> Be frustrate, do, undo, and labour loose,
> Not well conceav'd of God, who though his Power
> Creation could repeate, yet would be loath
> Us to abolish, least the Adversary
> Triumph and say; Fickle their State whom God
> Most favors, who can please him long; Mee first
> He ruind, now Mankind; whom will he next?[1]

This is yet another example of the way in which Milton successfully harmonized two opposing theories. For by the Renaissance the belief that Adam fell for love or companionship had been challenged by several commentators. Calvin, for instance, noted that 'because Moses simply reporteth that Adam did eate of the fruite which he receiued at his wiues hand, the common opinion is, that he was rather deceiued by her alluring intisements, then persuaded by the deceiuable prouocations of Sathan.'[2] In opposition to this view he urged that 'he did not transgresse the lawe whiche was giuen vnto him onely to obey his wife: but also being drawne by her into pestilent ambition, became a partaker of the same fall and transgression'.[3] Milton was able to use both these interpretations by conducting the entire scene at two levels, the inward and the outward. At the inward level both Adam and Eve recognize the probability that they will die if they eat the forbidden fruit; at the outward, however, they pursue what they both know to be the fiction that they will be raised to god-head.

In what, then, does Adam's sin consist? It seems a little naïve to accept, as Waldock does, Eve's estimate:

> O glorious trial of exceeding Love,
> Illustrious evidence, example high![4]

Adam is captured by the singer, not the song, and in order to account for his surrender our minds turn inevitably to his conversation with Raphael at the end of Book VIII. By omitting the standard feature of Eve's emotional appeal to her husband, Milton created, so to

---

[1] *P.L.* ix. 943–50.

[2] *Commentary on Genesis*, iii. 6. Cf. Willett's *Hexapla*, p. 47.

[3] Loc. cit. See also Patrides, op. cit., p. 174.

[4] *P.L.* ix. 961–2. In his *'Paradise Lost' and the Seventeenth-Century Reader*, 1962, p. 72, B. Rajan rightly describes this speech as a piece of 'frivolity'.

speak, a motivational vacuum which can be filled only by the recollection of Adam's previous revelation of his weakness against 'the charm of Beauties powerful glance'.[1] Thus when Milton concluded that Adam fell 'fondly overcome with Femal charm'[2] he was not, as Waldock would have us believe, falsifying the events we have just witnessed; he was simply indicating the real basis of Adam's decision.

This major reorganization of the episode represents a great improvement on the earlier versions. Ever since St. Paul's famous statement, that 'Adam was not deceived, but the woman being deceived was in the transgression',[3] was applied to the interpretation of the Fall there had been a tendency to minimize Adam's sin at the expense of Eve's. As a result, the whole balance of the story was upset, for it was through the man's disobedience that 'many were made sinners'.[4] Milton overcame this disadvantage by giving dramatic expression to the Augustinian view that Adam was no less culpable than his wife, without resorting to the corollary that he yielded to her persuasions. Although Adam is 'not deceav'd', the fact that he eats 'Against his better knowledge' makes his transgression by far the more serious of the two.[5] As Heywood put it:

> *Eve* sinn'd of *Ignorance*; and so is said,
> Against the God of Wisedome to have made
> Her forfeit (that's the Son:) *Adam* he fell
> Through *Weaknesse*, and 'gainst him that doth excell
> In pow'r (the Father) sinn'd.[6]

Most poets and dramatists who treated the story followed the sequence of events in Genesis, according to which the fallen pair became aware and ashamed of their nakedness as soon as they had eaten of the tree of knowledge. Such a violent transition from innocence to guilt could, however, seem over-melodramatic in the context of a realistic narrative, and Milton's literary tact is nowhere better illustrated than in his handling of this awkward moment. Taking up the rabbinic idea that the tree of knowledge was a vine, he portrayed Eve as 'hight'nd as with Wine, jocond and boon'[7] when she has tasted the fruit. The theme is made still more explicit when Adam has fallen with her:

> As with new Wine intoxicated both
> They swim in mirth.[8]

[1] Ibid. viii. 533.   [2] Ibid. ix. 999.   [3] 1 Tim. ii. 13.
[4] Rom. v. 19.   [5] *P.L.* ix. 998.   [6] *Hierarchie*, Bk. vi, p. 343.
[7] *P.L.* ix. 793. See above, Ch. II, p. 46.   [8] Ibid. ix. 1008–9.

Only when the scene has been set with their inebriated feelings of exhilaration, reflected in their flushed faces and tipsy speeches, does there enter in the Augustinian notion that the immediate result of the Fall was the birth of concupiscence.[1] Consequently their lust does not come as a sudden and totally unexpected change in their experience; it seems, rather, the natural extension of their initial intoxication. This in turn prepares us for their subsequent guilt and shame, which now appear as the inevitable concomitants of the mood of *triste post coitum* combined with a hangover. Thus the crude transformation in Genesis is broken down into a psychologically credible sequence of events by the imaginative use of traditional legend and exegesis.

Jewish and Christian elements also blend in Milton's diagnosis of shame:

> innocence, that as a veile
> Had shadow'd them from knowing ill, was gon,
> Just confidence, and native righteousness
> And honour from about them, naked left
> To guiltie shame.[2]

In order to prove that Adam and Eve were not created blind the Rabbis had been forced to assume that before the Fall the pair had worn some form of clothing,[3] and the Fathers had allegorized this *haggadah* by substituting some such concept as innocence, glory, or contemplation for the rabbinic robes. Gregory the Great, for example, wrote: 'Of the robe of innocence given us aforetime in Paradise, we are stripped naked. . . . For "the first robe" is the robe of innocence, which man being created aright received, but being persuaded wrongly by the serpent forfeited.'[4] In a strictly literal context Milton adapted this allegorical interpretation as a metaphor of Adam and Eve's spiritual condition, so preserving the immediacy of the Biblical account and at the same time invoking the moral associations imposed on the incident by the commentators. By Book X, however, the metaphor has become a fact; when Christ clothes the fallen pair with the skins of the beasts the poet comments:

> Nor hee thir outward onely with the Skins
> Of Beasts, but inward nakedness, much more

---

[1] See above, Ch. III, p. 98.
[2] *P.L.* ix. 1054–8. Compare *Psyche*, vi. 309.
[3] See above, Ch. II, p. 51.   [4] *Mor.* xii. 9. See above, Ch. III, p. 91.

Opprobrious, with his Robe of righteousness,
Araying cover'd from his Fathers sight.[1]

Here, significantly enough, the normal allegorical interpretation of
the skins as the tokens of mortality has been totally discarded. To
take its place the earlier image of Man's spiritual nakedness has been
developed in such a way as to make Christ's action seem more
merciful than punitive. The sentence of mortality is postponed until
after Adam has expressed his fears of eternal sinfulness, with the
result that when it is finally pronounced it appears to be all the more
benevolent.

Like several of his predecessors, Milton dramatized Adam's
ensuing feelings of guilt and shame by giving him an opportunity
to air them in speeches of recrimination and reproach. In cadences
that recall the great hymn to the Creation in Book V Adam cries:

Cover me ye Pines,
Ye Cedars, with innumerable boughs
Hide me, where I may never see them more.[2]

And when he and Eve have covered themselves with fig-leaves they
proceed to conduct an abbreviated but bitter post-mortem, in which
are echoed many of the mutual accusations elaborated in earlier
treatments of the same extra-biblical episode.[3]

It was at this juncture that Joseph Beaumont introduced the
debate of the four daughters of God in *The Perfect-Cursed-Blessed
Man* (1629). Although Milton shifted the main body of this discussion
to its place before the Fall in Book IV, it has left its mark here. As
in the fuller version, the four contestants are reduced to two, both
of which again are presented as being aspects of the Father. God
remarks to the Son:

Easie it might be seen that I intend
Mercie collegue with Justice, sending thee
Mans Friend.[4]

To which the Son replies:

yet I shall temper so
Justice with Mercie, as may illustrate most
Them fully satisfied.[5]

[1] *P.L.* x. 220–3.　　[2] Ibid. ix. 1088–90. See above, Ch. VII, pp. 204, 211.
[3] See above, Ch. VII, pp. 204–6.　　[4] *P.L.* x. 58–60.
[5] Ibid. x. 77–79.

But in spite of these assertions the general effect is precisely the same as it had been in Book IV; the Father, who insists that death must follow the transgression, seems to personify the claims of Justice, while the Son, by reminding us that He has promised to serve whatever sentence He imposes, monopolizes the quality of Mercy.

Seen in the light of this debate, the interrogation and condemnation, which follow immediately, lose a great deal of their apparent ignorance and severity. Christ's questions, posed 'without revile',[1] are no longer the inquiries of an anthropomorphic deity who can neither find his creatures nor understand why they are hiding from him. They are, as the Rabbis and Fathers had insisted, invitations to confession and repentance.[2] What is more, Adam's cowardice and lack of gallantry under cross-examination have also been modified, for he prefaces his accusations against Eve with an anguished statement of his dilemma:

> either to undergo
> My self the total Crime, or to accuse
> My other self, the partner of my life.[3]

Unlike any previous Adam, he has at least some qualms about putting the blame on his wife.

When the curses have finally been pronounced Adam laments to himself 'Through the still Night'.[4] Whether by accident or design, Milton thus created a scene very similar to that in the rabbinic tractates, in which Adam was shown pondering his fate in the darkness, until dawn brought with it the hope of redemption.[5] But whereas in the rabbinic sources it was Adam's first experience of night, in *Paradise Lost* he is already perfectly familiar with the rotation of the sun, so the natural cycle of darkness and light becomes an image rather than the cause of Adam's emotional progression from despair to hope. The actual substance of his speeches, too, had been anticipated in many earlier treatments, particularly in the dramatic ones, though never quite at this stage of the story. His laments and reproaches were usually located either before the condemnation, as in the *Mystère d'Adam* and *Adamus Exul*, or after the expulsion, as in the *York* and *Ludus Coventriae* plays on the Fall.[6] Milton, on the other hand, placed them half-way between

---

[1] *P.L.* x. 118.   [2] See above, Ch. II, p. 52; Ch. III, p. 83.
[3] *P.L.* x. 126–8. Compare above, Ch. II, p. 52; Ch. IV, p. 137.
[4] Ibid. x. 846.   [5] See above, Ch. II, p. 54.
[6] See above, Ch. VII, pp. 204–6, 211.

these two positions, after the condemnation but before the expulsion. While this change may, of course, have been dictated by purely aesthetic considerations—the poet may have wished, for example, to set Adam and Eve's reconciliation against the reactions of Sin, Death, and the devils—there may also have been a more strictly practical reason for it. For the expulsion, as we have seen, had always posed a difficult problem for poets and commentators who were committed to the belief that God was more merciful than the Jahwist's account appeared to suggest. The most widely accepted solution to it was the theory that by depriving Man of the tree of life God saved him from an eternity of sinfulness.[1] By introducing Adam's *Liebestod* at this point of the narrative Milton was able to realize this doctrine in truly dramatic terms. Adam's fears of 'deathless pain',[2] which were provoked by the vague threats of the condemnation, are now relieved by the more precise revelations vouchsafed to him by Michael. As the Father says at the beginning of Book XI:

> I at first with two fair gifts
> Created him endowd, with Happiness
> And Immortalitie: that fondly lost,
> This other serv'd but to eternize woe;
> Till I provided Death; so Death becomes
> His final remedie.[3]

In any other circumstances we might have felt this to be a piece of special pleading; coming to it fresh from Adam's midnight agonies, we are prepared to accept it as a genuine proof of God's 'Eternal Providence'.

Michael's lengthy exposition of the future history of mankind, like Raphael's discourse on the work of the days, falls outside the immediate scope of this study, but it is worth noting, nevertheless, that Adam's vision of the future was a common feature of both Jewish and Christian writings on the Fall. The former located it at various points of the story, before Adam's acquisition of a body, at the moment he ate the apple, or after the expulsion.[4] Christian commentators, on the other hand, almost invariably presented it as a dream which Adam was given during the formation of Eve.[5] Although Milton, for the reasons I have already discussed, post-

---

[1] See above, Ch. III, p. 84.
[2] *P.L.* x. 775.
[3] Ibid. xi. 57–62.
[4] See above, Ch. II, pp. 54, 57.
[5] See above, Ch. VI, p. 169.

poned it until after the Fall, he still linked it with the episode of Adam's sleep:

> let *Eve* (for I have drencht her eyes)
> Here sleep below while thou to foresight wak'st,
> As once thou slepst, while Shee to life was formd.[1]

In setting the scene for the final panoramic vision of human history Milton thus reshaped once more the traditions of which his poem marks the literary and doctrinal culmination.

[1] *P.L.* xi. 367–9.

SELECT BIBLIOGRAPHY

I. GENESIS

Commentaries

BONHOEFFER, D., *Creation and Fall* (trans. J. C. Fletcher), 1959.
CASSUTO, U., *A Commentary on the Book of Genesis* (trans. I. Abrahams), Jerusalem, 1961.
DELITZSCH, F., *A New Commentary on Genesis* (trans. S. Taylor), 1899.
DILLMANN, A., *Genesis* (trans. W. B. Stevenson), 1897.
DRIVER, S. R., *The Book of Genesis*, 14th edn., 1943.
SKINNER, J., *A Critical and Exegetical Commentary on Genesis*, 2nd edn., 1930.
VON RAD, G., *Genesis* (trans. J. H. Marks), 1961.

Analogues

BRANDON, S. G. F., *Creation Legends of the Ancient Near East*, 1963.
HEIDEL, A., *The Gilgamesh Epic*, Chicago, 1946.
—— *The Babylonian Genesis*, 2nd edn., Chicago, 1950.
JAMES, E. O., *Myth and Ritual in the Ancient Near East*, 1958.
JASTROW, M., *The Religion of Babylonia and Assyria*, Boston, 1898.
KRAMER, S. N., *Enki and Ninhursag*, New Haven, 1945.
LANGDON, S., *The Sumerian Epic of Paradise*, 1915.
PINCHES, T. G., *The Old Testament in the Light of the Historical Records and Legends of Assyria and Babylonia*, 1908.
PRITCHARD, J. B., *Ancient Near Eastern Texts*, 2nd edn., Princeton, 1955.
WARDLE, W. L., *Israel and Babylon*, 3rd edn., 1925.

Criticism

CHILDS, B. S., 'Myth and Reality in the Old Testament', *S.B.T.* xxvii (1960), 42–48.
COHEN, S. S., 'Original Sin', *H.U.C.A.* xxi (1948), 275–330.
COPPENS, J., *La Connaissance du bien et du mal et le péché du paradis*, Gembloux, 1948.
FRAZER, J. G., *Folk-Lore in the Old Testament*, vol. i, 1918.
LEWY, I., 'The Two Strata in the Eden Story', *H.U.C.A.* xxvii (1956), 93–99.
OESTERLEY, W. O. E., *Immortality and the Unseen World*, 1921.
TENNANT, F. R., *Sources of the Doctrines of the Fall and Original Sin*, 1903.
WILLIAMS, N. P., *The Ideas of the Fall and of Original Sin*, 1927.

II. THE JEWISH INTERPRETATIONS

Primary Sources

ANON., *Aboth of Rabbi Nathan* (trans. M. L. Rodkinson, *The Babylonian Talmud*, New York, 1901–3, vol. i).
—— Apocalypsis Mosis (trans. R. H. Charles, *Apocrypha and Pseudepigrapha of the Old Testament*, 1913, vol. ii).

ANON., Book of Jubilees (trans. ibid., vol. ii).
—— Book of Sirach (trans. ibid., vol. i).
—— Book of the Secrets of Enoch (trans. ibid., vol. ii).
—— *Chronicles of Jerahmeel* (trans. M. Gaster, 1899).
—— Ethiopic Book of Enoch (trans. R. H. Charles, op. cit., vol. ii).
—— Fourth Book of Ezra (trans. ibid., vol. ii).
—— *Midrash Rabbah* (trans. H. Freedman and M. Simon, 1939).
—— *Pirkê de Rabbi Eliezer* (trans. G. Friedlander, 1916).
—— Syriac Apocalypse of Baruch (trans. R. H. Charles, op. cit., vol. ii).
—— *Talmud* (trans. I. Epstein, *The Babylonian Talmud*, 1935–52).
—— *Targum of Jonathan ben Uzziel* (trans. J. W. Etheridge, 1862).
—— Vita Adae et Evae (trans. R. H. Charles, op. cit., vol. ii).
—— Wisdom of Solomon (trans. ibid., vol. i).
JOSEPHUS, *Jewish Antiquities* (trans. H. St. J. Thackeray, 1930).
MAIMONIDES, *Guide for the Perplexed* (trans. M. Friedlander, 2nd edn., 1904).
PHILO, *De Opificio Mundi* (ed., trans., F. H. Colson and G. H. Whitaker, *Philo*, 1929, vol. i).
Legum Allegoria (ed., trans. ibid., vol. i).
Questions and Answers on Genesis (ed. trans. R. Marcus, *Philo*, Supplement i, 1953).
RASHI, *Commentary on the Pentateuch, Genesis* (trans. J. H. Lowe, 1928).

Secondary Sources

GINZBERG, L., *The Legends of the Jews* (trans. H. Szold), Philadelphia, 1909–25.
HERSHON, P. I., *Genesis with a Talmudical Commentary*, 1883.
MONTEFIORE, C. G., and LOEWE, H., *A Rabbinic Anthology*, 1938.

Criticism

DAVIES, W. D., *Paul and Rabbinic Judaism*, 1948.
GINZBERG, L., 'The Book of Adam', *J.E.* i. 179–80.
GRAY, G. B., *A Critical and Exegetical Commentary on the Book of Isaiah*, 1912.
JUNG, L., 'Fallen Angels in Jewish, Christian, and Mohammedan Literature', *J.Q.R.* N.S. xv (1924), 467–502; N.S. xvi (1925), 45–88, 171–205, 287–336.
KOHLER, K., 'Adam in Apocryphal and Rabbinical Literature', *J.E.* i. 174–7.
MOORE, G. F., *Judaism*, Cambridge, Massachusetts, 1927–30.
STRACK, H. L., *Introduction to the Talmud and Midrash*, Philadelphia, 1945.
WADE, G. W., *The Book of the Prophet Isaiah*, 1911.

III. THE CHRISTIAN INTERPRETATIONS

Primary Sources

ABELARD, *Ethics* (trans. J. R. McCallum), 1935.
—— *Exposition of the Epistle to the Romans* (trans. L.C.C., vol. x, 1956).
—— *Hexaemeron* (edn. *M.P.L.*, vol. clxxviii).
ALCUIN, *Questions and Answers on Genesis* (edn. *M.P.L.*, vol. c).

AMBROSE, *Hexaemeron* (edn. *M.P.L.*, vol. xiv).
—— *Letters* (trans. L.F., vol. xlv).
—— *On Paradise* (edn. *M.P.L.*, vol. xiv).
AMBROSIASTER, *Questions on the Old Testament* (edn. *M.P.L.*, vol. xxxv).
ANON., *Acta Archelai* (trans. A.N.C.L., vol. xx).
—— *Apocryphon of John* (trans. R. M. Grant, *Gnosticism*, 1961).
—— *Clementine Homilies* (trans. A.N.C.L., vol. xvii).
—— *Hermetica* (trans. W. Scott, 1924–36).
ANSELM, *Why God Became Man* (trans. L.C.C., vol. x, 1956).
AQUINAS, *Summa Theologica* (trans. by the Fathers of the English Dominican Province, 1911–1925).
ATHANASIUS, *Against the Heathen* (trans. S.L.N.P.N.F., vol. iv).
AUGUSTINE, *Faith, Hope, and Charity* (trans. A.C.W., vol. iii).
—— *Genesis according to the Letter* (edn. *M.P.L.*, vol. xxxiv).
—— *Genesis against the Manichees* (edn. ibid.).
—— *Homilies on John* (trans. L.F., vol. xxvi).
—— *On Marriage and Concupiscence* (trans. M. Dods, *The Works of Aurelius Augustine*, 1871–, vol. xii).
—— *On Nature and Grace* (trans. ibid., vol. iv).
—— *On the City of God* (trans. ibid., vols. i–ii).
—— *On the Grace of Christ* (trans. ibid., vol. xii).
—— *On the Merits and Forgiveness of Sins* (trans. ibid., vol. iv).
BASIL, *Hexaemeron* (trans. S.L.N.P.N.F., vol. viii).
—— *That God is not the Author of Evil* (edn. *M.P.G.*, vol. xxxi).
BEDE, *Hexaemeron* (edn. *M.P.L.*, vol. xci).
BRUNO ASTENSIS, *Expositions on the Pentateuch* (edn. *M.P.L.*, vol. clxiv).
CASSIAN, *Conferences* (trans. S.L.N.P.N.F., vol. xi).
CHRYSOSTOM, *Homilies on Genesis* (edn. *M.P.G.*, vols. liii–liv).
—— *Homilies on John* (trans. L.F., vol. xxxvii).
—— *Homilies on the Epistles of Paul* (trans. L.F., vol. xii).
CLEMENT OF ALEXANDRIA, *Miscellanies* (trans. A.N.C.L., vols. iv and xii; L.C.C., vol. ii).
COMESTOR, *Historia Scholastica* (edn. *M.P.L.*, vol. cxcviii).
CYPRIAN, *On the Good of Patience* (trans. A.N.C.L., vol. xiii).
CYRIL OF JERUSALEM, *The Catechetical Lectures* (trans. S.L.N.P.N.F., vol. vii).
ERIGENA, *On the Division of Nature* (edn. *M.P.L.*, vol. cxxii).
GREGORY THE GREAT, *Morals on the Book of Job* (trans. L.F., vols. xviii, xxi, xxiii, and xxxi).
—— 'Sermon on the Gospel of Sunday' (trans. M. F. Toal, *The Sunday Sermons of the Great Fathers*, 1958, vol. ii).
GREGORY OF NAZIANZUS, *Orations* (trans. S.L.N.P.N.F., vol. vii).
GREGORY OF NYSSA, *On the Baptism of Christ* (trans. S.L.N.P.N.F., vol. v).
—— *On the Making of Man* (trans. ibid.).
—— *The Great Catechism* (trans. ibid.).
HILARY OF POITIERS, *Homilies on the Psalms* (trans. S.L.N.P.N.F., vol. ix).
HILDEBERT, *Tractatus Theologicus* (trans. G. Boas and A. O. Lovejoy, *Essays in Primitivism*, Baltimore, 1948).
HONORÉ D'AUTUN, *Elucidarium* (trans. ibid.).

HUGH OF ST. VICTOR, *On the Sacraments of the Christian Faith* (trans. L.C.C., vol. x).

IRENAEUS, *Against the Heresies* (trans. A.N.C.L., vols. v and ix).

—— *The Demonstration of the Apostolic Teaching* (trans. A.C.W., vol. xvi).

ISIDORE OF SEVILLE, *Expositions of the Mystic Sacraments* (edn. *M.P.L.*, vol. lxxxiii).

JOHN OF DAMASCUS, *Expositions of the Orthodox Faith* (trans. S.L.N.P.N.F., vol. ix).

JUSTIN MARTYR, *Dialogue of Justin with Trypho* (trans. A.N.C.L., vol. ii).

LACTANTIUS, *The Divine Institutes* (trans. A.N.C.L., vol. xxi).

METHODIUS OF OLYMPUS, *From the Discourse on the Resurrection* (trans. A.N.C.L., vol. xiv).

ORIGEN, *Against Celsus* (trans. A.N.C.L., vol. xxiii).

—— *Homilies on Genesis* (French trans. in L. Doutreleau, *Origène, homélies sur la Genèse*, Lyon, 1943).

—— *On Principles* (trans. A.N.C.L., vol. x).

PELAGIUS, *On Romans* (ed. A. Souter, *Pelagius's Expositions of Thirteen Epistles of St. Paul*, 1922–31, vol. ii).

PSEUDO-BEDE, *Commentaries on the Pentateuch* (edn. *M.P.L.*, vol. xci).

PSEUDO-TERTULLIAN, *Against all the Heresies* (trans. A.N.C.L., vol. xviii).

RABAN MAUR, *Commentary on Genesis* (edn. *M.P.L.*, vol. cvii).

TATIAN, *Address to the Greeks* (trans. A.N.C.L., vol. iii).

TERTULLIAN, *An Answer to the Jews* (trans. A.N.C.L., vol. xviii).

—— *Of Patience* (trans. A.N.C.L., vol. xi).

—— *Prescription against Heretics* (trans. A.N.C.L., vol. xv).

—— *The Flesh of Christ* (trans. ibid.).

—— *Treatise on the Soul* (trans. ibid.).

THEODORE BAR KHONI, *Book of Scholia* (trans. A. V. W. Jackson, *Researches in Manichaeism*, New York, 1932).

THEOPHILUS OF ANTIOCH, *The Three Books of Theophilus to Autolycus* (trans. A.N.C.L., vol. iii).

VINCENT OF BEAUVAIS, *Speculum Historiale* (edn. Jesuit reprint of the *Speculum Majus*, Douai, 1624).

Criticism

ALTANER, B., *Patrology* (trans. H. C. Graef), 1960.

AUERBACH, E., *Scenes from the Drama of European Literature*, New York, 1959.

BATTENHOUSE, R. W., *A Companion to the Study of St. Augustine*, 1955.

BERNARD, J. H., *A Critical and Exegetical Commentary on the Gospel according to St. John*, 1928, vol. ii.

BETT, H., *Johannes Scotus Erigena*, 1925.

BURKITT, F. C., *The Religion of the Manichees*, 1925.

—— *Church and Gnosis*, 1932.

CASEY, R. P., 'The Study of Gnosticism', *J.T.S.* xxxvi (1935), 45–60.

CREED, J. M., 'The Heavenly Man', *J.T.S.* xxvi (1925), 113–33.

CUMONT, F., *Recherches sur le Manichéisme*, Brussels, 1908–12.

DANIÉLOU, J., *Sacramentum Futuri*, Paris, 1950.

DANIÉLOU, J., *Origen* (trans. W. Mitchell), 1955.
DODD, C. H., *The Bible and the Greeks*, 1935.
—— *The Interpretation of the Fourth Gospel*, 1953.
FERGUSON, J., *Pelagius*, 1956.
GRANT, R. M., *Gnosticism and Early Christianity*, 1959.
—— *Gnosticism*, 1961.
HAGENBACH, K. R., *A History of Christian Doctrines* (trans. E. H. Plumptre), 1880.
HANSON, R. P. C., *Allegory and Event*, 1959.
HARNACK, A., *History of Dogma* (trans. J. Millar), 1898.
JACKSON, A. V. W., *Researches in Manichaeism*, New York, 1932.
KELLY, J. N. D., *Early Christian Doctrines*, 1958.
NOCK, A. D., 'A Coptic Library of Gnostic Writings', *J.T.S.* N.S. ix (1958), 314–24.
PLINVAL, G. DE., *Pélage*, Lausanne, 1943.
PLUMMER, A., *A Critical and Exegetical Commentary on the Second Epistle of St. Paul to the Corinthians*, 1915.
PUECH, H. C., *Le Manichéisme*, Paris, 1949.
PUECH, H. C., QUISPEL, G., AND VAN UNNICK, W. C., *The Jung Codex* (ed. F. L. Cross), 1955.
RASHDALL, H., *The Idea of Atonement*, 1919.
ROBBINS, F. E., *The Hexaemeral Literature*, Chicago, 1912.
RUNCIMAN, J. C. S., *The Medieval Manichee*, 1947.
SANDAY, W., AND HEADLAM, A. G., *A Critical and Exegetical Commentary on the Epistle to the Romans*, 1895.
THACKERAY, H. St. J., *The Relation of St. Paul to Contemporary Jewish Thought*, 1900.
TILL, W. C., 'The Gnostic *Apocryphon of John*', *J.E.H.* iii (1952), 14–22.
WILSON, R. McL., *The Gnostic Problem*, 1958.

IV. THE NEO-CLASSICAL TREATMENTS

Primary Sources

AVITUS, *Poematum de Mosaicae Historiae Gestis* (edn. *M.P.L.*, vol. lix).
CYPRIANUS GALLUS, *Heptateuchos* (edn. C.S.E.L., vol. xxiii; trans. A.N.C.L., vol. xviii).
DRACONTIUS, *Carmen de Deo* (edn. *M.P.L.*, vol. lx).
HILARIUS ARELATENSIS, *Metrum in Genesim* (edn. C.S.E.L., vol. xxiii).
LUCRETIUS, *De Rerum Natura* (ed. C. Bailey), 1947.
MINUCIUS FELIX, *Octavius* (trans. A.N.C.L., vol. xiii).
OVID, *Metamorphoses* (ed. A. G. Lee), 1953.
PROBA, *Cento* (edn. C.S.E.L., vol. xvi).
PROSPER OF AQUITAINE (?), *Carmen de Providentia Divina* (edn. *M.P.L.*, vol. li).
PRUDENTIUS, *Hamartigenia* (ed., trans. H. J. Thomson, *Prudentius*, 1949).
—— *Liber Cathemerinon* (ed., trans. ibid.).
VICTOR, CLAUDIUS MARIUS, *Alethia* (edn. C.C., Ser. Lat., vol. cxxviii).
VIRGIL, *Eclogae* (ed., trans. E. V. Rieu), reprint of 1961.

Criticism

CHADWICK, N. K., *Poetry and Letters in Early Christian Gaul*, 1955.
CURTIUS, E. R., *European Literature and the Latin Middle Ages* (trans. W. R. Trask), reprint of 1963.
DUCKETT, E. S., *Latin Writers of the Fifth Century*, New York, 1930.
GAMBER, S., *Le Livre de la 'Genèse' dans la poésie latine au cinquième siècle*, Paris, 1899.
HOVINGH, P. F., *Claudius Marius Victorius Alethia*, Groningen, 1955.
KIRKCONNELL, W., *The Celestial Cycle*, Toronto, 1952.
KUHNMUENCH, O. J., *Early Christian Latin Poets*, Chicago, 1929.
LABRIOLLE, P. C. de., *History and Literature of Christianity* (trans. H. Wilson), 1924.
RABY, F. J. E., *A History of Christian-Latin Poetry*, 2nd edn., 1953.
RAND, E. K., *Founders of the Middle Ages*, New York, reprint of 1957.

V. THE HEROIC TREATMENTS

Primary Sources

ÆLFRIC, 'De Initio Creaturae' (ed., trans. B. Thorpe, *The Homilies of the Anglo-Saxon Church*, 1884, vol. i).
—— *De Veteri et de Novo Testamento* (ed. S. J. Crawford, *The Old-English Version of the Heptateuch*, E.E.T.S., vol. clx, 1922).
—— *Exameron Anglice* (ed., trans. S. J. Crawford, B.A.P., vol. x, Hamburg, 1921).
ANON., *Beowulf* (ed. F. Klaeber), 3rd edn., Boston, 1950.
—— *Blickling Homilies* (ed. R. Morris), E.E.T.S., vols. lviii, lxiii, lxxiii, 1874–80.
—— *Christ and Satan* (ed. G. P. Krapp, *The Junius Manuscript*, New York, 1931).
—— *Genesis A* (ed. ibid.).
—— *Genesis B* (ed. B. J. Timmer), rev. edn., 1954.
—— *Guthlac* (ed. G. P. Krapp and E. V. K. Dobbie, *The Exeter Book*, New York, 1936).
—— *Juliana* (ed. ibid.).
—— *Phoenix* (ed. ibid.).
CYNEWULF, *Crist* (ed. ibid.).
WULFSTAN, *Homilies* (ed. D. Bethurum), 1957.

Criticism

ABBETMEYER, C., *Old English Poetical Motives derived from the Doctrine of Sin*, Minneapolis, 1903.
BECKER, G., *Catalogi Bibliothecarum Antiqui*, Bonn, 1885.
BOSTOCK, J. K., *A Handbook on Old High German Literature*, 1955.
BRADLEY, H., 'The Caedmonian Genesis', *E.S.* vi (1920), 7–29.
EVANS, J. M., '*Genesis B* and its Background', *R.E.S.* N.S. xiv (1963), 1–16, 113–23.
FERRELL, C. C., *Teutonic Antiquities in the Anglo-Saxon Genesis*, Halle, 1893.

GILLESPIE, H., 'The Story of Adam and Eve from Caedmon to Milton', unpublished M.A. thesis, Duke University, 1937.

GURTEEN, S. H., *The Epic of the Fall of Man*, 1896.

IRWIN, R., 'In Saxon England, Studies in the Histories of Libraries', *L.A.R.* lvii (1955), 290–311.

JAMES, M. R., 'Learning and Literature till the death of Bede', *C.M.H.*, vol. iii, ch. xix.

—— 'Learning and Literature till Pope Sylvester II', *C.M.H.*, vol. iii, ch. xx.

KER, W. P., *The Dark Ages*, 1904.

—— *Epic and Romance*, New York, reprint of 1957.

LAISTNER, M. L. W., *Thought and Letters in Western Europe*, 2nd edn., 1957.

—— *The Intellectual Heritage of the Early Middle Ages* (ed. C. G. Starr), New York, 1957.

LEVISON, D., *Studies in the Treatment of Old Testament Themes in the Poems of MS. Junius II, Part I*, unpublished B.Litt. thesis, Oxford, 1956.

LEVISON, W., *England and the Continent in the Eighth Century*, 1946.

McKILLOP, A. D., 'Illustrative Notes on *Genesis B*', *J.E.G.P.* xx (1921), 28–38.

OGILVY, J. D. A., *Books Known to Anglo-Latin Writers from Aldhelm to Alcuin*, Cambridge, Massachusetts, 1936.

ROBINSON, F. N., 'A Note on the Sources of the Old Saxon Genesis', *M.P.* iv (1906), 389–96.

SKEMP, A. R., 'The Transformation of Scriptural Story, Motive, and Conception in Anglo-Saxon Poetry', *M.P.* iv (1907), 423–70.

TALBOT, C. H., *The Anglo-Saxon Missionaries in Germany*, 1954.

THOMPSON, A. H., *Bede, His Life, Times, and Writings*, 1935.

THOMPSON, J. W., *The Medieval Library*, Chicago, 1939.

TIMMER, B. J., 'Heathen and Christian Elements in Old English Poetry', *Neophil.* xxix (1944), 180–5.

WHITELOCK, D., *The Beginnings of English Society*, 1952.

WOOLF, R., 'The Devil in Old English Poetry', *R.E.S.* N.S. iv (1953), 1–12.

WRENN, C. L., *The Poetry of Caedmon*, British Academy, 1946.

VI. THE SCHOLASTIC TREATMENTS

Primary Sources

ANON., *Canticum de Creatione* (ed. C. Horstmann, *Sammlung Altenglischer Legenden*, Heilbronn, 1878).

—— *Cursor Mundi* (ed. R. Morris), E.E.T.S., vol. lvii, 1874.

—— *Deuelis Perlament* (ed. F. J. Furnivall), E.E.T.S., vol. xxiv, 1867.

—— *Fall and Passion* (ed. F. J. Furnivall, *Early English Poems*, Berlin, 1862).

—— *Genesis and Exodus* (ed. R. Morris), E.E.T.S., vol. vii, 1873.

—— *History of the Holy Cross* (ed. C. D'Evelyn), E.E.T.S., vol. ccxxxv, 1956.

—— *Lyff of Adam and Eve* (ed. C. Horstmann, op. cit.).

—— *Metrical Paraphrase of the Old Testament* (ed. H. Kalen), Goteborg, 1923.

—— *Middle English Sermons* (ed. W. O. Ross), E.E.T.S., vol. ccix, 1940.

—— *Mirk's Festial* (ed. T. Erbe), E.E.T.S., E.S., vol. xcvi, 1905.

—— *Purity* (ed. R. J. Menner), New Haven, 1920.

ANON., *Speculum Humanae Salvationis* (ed. A. H. Huth, *The Miroure of Mans Saluacioune*, 1888).
—— *Stanzaic Life of Christ* (ed. F. A. Foster), E.E.T.S., vol. clxvi, 1926.
BOCCACCIO, *Genealogy of the Pagan Gods* (trans. C. Osgood, *Boccaccio on Poetry*, Princeton, 1930).
CAXTON, *Golden Legend* (ed. F. S. Ellis), 1900.
—— *Mirrour of the World* (ed. O. H. Prior), E.E.T.S., E.S., vol. cx, 1913.
GROSSETESTE, *Chasteau d'Amour* (ed. C. Horstmann, *Altenglische Legenden*, Heilbronn, 1881).
LANGLAND, *Piers Plowman* (ed. W. W. Skeat), rev. edn., 1954.
LYDGATE, *The Fall of Princes* (ed. H. Bergen), E.E.T.S., E.S., vol. cxxi, 1924.
PSEUDO-BONAVENTURE, *Meditationes Vitae Christi* (ed. L. F. Powell, *The Mirrour of the Blessed Lyf of Jesu Christ*, 1908).
WILLIAM OF SHOREHAM, *On the Trinity, Creation, the Existence of Evil, Devils, Adam and Eve* (ed. M. Konrath), E.E.T.S., E.S., vol. lxxxvi, 1902.

Criticism

BOAS, G., AND LOVEJOY, A. O., *Essays in Primitivism*, Baltimore, 1948.
BONNARD, J., *Les Traductions de la Bible en vers français au moyen âge*, Paris, 1884.
DUSTOOR, P. E., 'Legends of Lucifer in Early English and in Milton', *Anglia*, N.S. xlii (1930), 213–68.
QUINN, E. C., *The Quest of Seth*, Chicago, 1963.
SMALLEY, B., *The Study of the Bible in the Middle Ages*, 2nd edn., 1952.
TRAVER, H., *The Four Daughters of God*, Philadelphia, 1907.

VII. THE DRAMATIC TREATMENTS

Primary Sources

ANON., *Chester Plays* (ed. H. Deimling), E.E.T.S., E.S., vol. lxii, 1893.
—— *Ludus Coventriae* (ed. A. S. Block), E.E.T.S., E.S., vol. cxx, 1922.
—— *Mystère d'Adam* (ed. P. Studer), 1949.
—— *Norwich Plays* (ed. O. Waterhouse, *The Non-Cycle Mystery Plays*, E.E.T.S., E.S., vol. civ, 1909).
—— *Ordinale de Origine Mundi* (ed., trans. E. Norris, *The Ancient Cornish Drama*, 1869).
—— *Towneley Plays* (ed. G. England and A. W. Pollard), E.E.T.S., E.S., vol. lxxi, 1952.
—— *York Plays* (ed. L. T. Smith), 1885.
GROTIUS, HUGO, *Adamus Exul* (ed., trans. W. Kirkconnell, *The Celestial Cycle*, Toronto, 1952).
IGNATIUS DIACONUS, *Drama de Primi Parentis Lapsu* (edn. *M.P.G.*, vol. cxvii).
JORDAN, WILLIAM, *The Creation of the World* (ed., trans. W. Stokes), 1863–4.

Criticism

AUERBACH, E., *Mimesis* (trans. W. R. Trask), Princeton, 1953.
BONNELL, J. K., 'The Serpent with a Human Head in Art and Mystery Play', *A.J.A.* xxi (1917), 255–91.
CROSLAND, J., *Medieval French Literature*, 1956.

VIII. *PARADISE LOST* AND THE RENAISSANCE TREATMENTS

Primary Sources

ADAMS, THOMAS, *Meditations on the Creed* (edn. Nichol's Series of Standard Divines, *The Works of Thomas Adams*, 1852, vol. iii).

AINSWORTH, HENRY, *Annotations upon the first book of Moses*, Amsterdam, 1616.

ALEXANDER, WILLIAM, *Doomes-Day*, 1614 (ed. L. E. Kastner and H. B. Charlton, *The Poetical Works*, 1929, vol. ii).

BABINGTON, GERVASE, *Certaine plaine, briefe, and comfortable Notes, vpon euerie chapter of Genesis*, 1592.

BEAUMONT, JOSEPH, *Psyche* (ed. A. B. Grosart, *The Complete Poems of Dr. Joseph Beaumont*, 1880, vols. i–ii).

BOEHME, JACOB, *Mysterium Magnum* (trans. J. Sparrow), 1654.

BROWNE, SIR THOMAS, *Pseudodoxia Epidemica* (ed. G. Keynes, *The Works of Sir Thomas Browne*, 1928, vols. ii–iii).

CALVIN, JOHN, *A Commentarie of John Caluine vpon the first booke of Moses* (trans. Thomas Tymme), 1578.

DIODATI, JOHN, *Pious and Learned annotations upon the Holy Bible* (trans. R. G.), 2nd edn., 1648.

FLETCHER, JOSEPH, *The Perfect-Cursed-Blessed Man* (ed. A. B. Grosart, *The Poems of Joseph Fletcher*, 1869).

FLETCHER, GILES, *Christs Victorie and Triumph* (ed. F. S. Boas, *Giles and Phineas Fletcher, Poetical Works*, 1908, vol. i).

FLETCHER, PHINEAS, *The Locusts* (edn. ibid.).

GOODMAN, GODFREY, *The Fall of Man*, 1616.

HEYWOOD, THOMAS, *The Hierarchie of the Blessed Angels*, 1635.

HOLLAND, HENRY, *The Historie of Adam*, 1606.

HUNNIS, WILLIAM, *A Hyve Full of Hunnye*, 1578.

LUTHER, MARTIN, *Lectures on Genesis* (trans. J. Pelikan, *Luther's Works*, 1958, vol. i).

MILTON, JOHN, *Works*, edn. Columbia University Press, New York, 1931.

MORE, HENRY, *Conjectura Cabbalistica*, 1653.

PEYTON, THOMAS, *The Glasse of Time in the two first Ages*, 1620.

PORDAGE, SAMUEL, *Mundorum Explicatio*, 1661.

PURCHAS, SAMUEL, *Purchas his Pilgrimage*, 1613.

RALEGH, SIR WALTER, *History of the World* (edn. *The Works of Sir Walter Ralegh*, 1829, vol. ii).

ROSS, ALEXANDER, *The First Booke of Qvestions and Answers vpon Genesis*, 1620.

SWAN, JOHN, *Speculum Mundi*, 1635.

SYLVESTER, JOSHUA, *Du Bartas his Divine Weekes and Workes* (ed. A. B. Grosart, *The Complete Works of Joshuah Sylvester*, 1880, vol. i).

WILLETT, ANDREW, *Hexapla in Genesin*, 1605.

WOLLEB, JOHN, *The Abridgement of Christian Divinitie* (trans. Alexander Ross), 1650.

Criticism

ADAMS, R. M., *Ikon: John Milton and the Modern Critics*, New York, 1955.
ALLEN, D. C., 'Milton and Rabbi Eliezer', *M.L.N.* lxiii (1948), 262–3.
BALDWIN, E. C., 'Some extra-Biblical Semitic Influences upon Milton's story of the Fall of Man', *J.E.G.P.* xxviii (1929), 366–401.
—— 'Paradise Lost and the Apocalypse of Moses', *J.E.G.P.* xxiv (1925), 383–6.
BARKER, A., 'Structural Pattern in *Paradise Lost*', *P.Q.* xxviii (1949), 17–30.
BELL, M., 'The Fallacy of the Fall in *Paradise Lost*', *P.M.L.A.* lxviii (1953), 863–83.
BELL, M., AND SHUMAKER, W., 'The Fallacy of the Fall in *Paradise Lost*' *P.M.L.A.* lxx (1955), 1185–1203.
BROADBENT, J. B., *Some Graver Subject*, 1960.
BUNDY, M., 'Eve's Dream and the Temptation in *Paradise Lost*', *R.S.S.C.W.* x (1942), 273–91.
—— 'Milton's Prelapsarian Adam', *R.S.S.C.W.* xiii (1945), 163–84.
BUSH, D., *'Paradise Lost' in Our Time*, Cornell, 1945.
CORCORAN, SISTER M. I., *Milton's 'Paradise Lost' with Reference to the Hexaemeral Background*, Washington, 1945.
DIEKHOFF, J. S., 'Eve, the Devil, and *Areopagitica*', *M.L.Q.* v (1944), 429–34.
—— *Milton's 'Paradise Lost'*, 1946.
EMPSON, W., *Milton's God*, 1961.
ERSKINE, J., 'The Theme of Death in *Paradise Lost*', *P.M.L.A.* xxxii (1917), 573–82.
FLETCHER, H. F., 'Milton and Yosippon', *S.P.* xxi (1924), 496–501.
—— *Milton's Semitic Studies*, Chicago, 1926.
—— *Milton's Rabbinical Readings*, Urbana, 1930.
FRENCH, J. M., *The Life Records of John Milton*, New Brunswick, 1949.
GARDNER, H., 'Milton's Satan and the Theme of Damnation in Elizabethan Tragedy', *E.S.* N.S. i (1948), 46–66.
—— *A Reading of Paradise Lost*, 1965.
GILBERT, A. H., 'The Theological Basis of Satan's Rebellion and the Function of Abdiel in *Paradise Lost*', *M.P.* xl (1942), 19–42.
—— 'Milton and the Mysteries', *S.P.* xvii (1920), 147–69.
—— *On the Composition of Paradise Lost*, Chapel Hill, 1947.
GREEN, C. C., 'The Paradox of the Fall in *Paradise Lost*', *M.L.N.* liii (1938), 557–71.
HALLER, W., 'Order and Progress in *Paradise Lost*', *P.M.L.A.* xxxv (1920), 218–25.
HANFORD, J. H., 'The Dramatic Element in *Paradise Lost*', *S.P.* xiv (1917), 178–95.
HARTWELL, K. E., *Lactantius and Milton*, Cambridge, Massachusetts, 1929.
HUNTER, W. B., 'Eve's Demonic Dream', *E.L.H.* xiii (1946), 255–65.
KELLEY, M., *This Great Argument*, Princeton, 1941.
LEVER, J. W., '*Paradise Lost* and the Anglo-Saxon Tradition', *R.E.S.* xxiii (1947), 97–106.
LEWIS, C. S., *A Preface to Paradise Lost*, 1942.
LOVEJOY, A. O., 'Milton and the Paradox of the Fortunate Fall', *E.L.H.* iv (1937), 161–79.

McCOLLEY, G., *Paradise Lost*, Chicago, 1940.

MAHOOD, M., *Poetry and Humanism*, 1950.

MAISIÈRES, M. T. DE, *Les Poèmes inspirés du début de la Genèse à l'époque de la Renaissance*, Louvain, 1931.

NICOLSON, M. H., 'Milton and the *Conjectura Cabbalistica*', *P.Q.* vi (1927), 1–18.

OGDEN, H. V. S., 'The Crisis of *Paradise Lost* Reconsidered', *P.Q.* xxxvi (1957), 1–19.

PATRIDES, C. A., *Milton and the Christian Tradition*, 1966.

PECHEUX, MOTHER M. C., 'The Concept of the Second Eve in *Paradise Lost*', *P.M.L.A.* lxxv (1960), 359–66.

PECK, H. W., 'The Theme of *Paradise Lost*', *P.M.L.A.* xxix (1914), 256–69.

PETER, J., *A Critique of 'Paradise Lost'*, 1960.

RAJAN, B., *'Paradise Lost' and the Seventeenth-Century Reader*, 1947.

RAMSAY, R. L., 'Morality Themes in Milton's Poetry', *S.P.* xv (1918), 123–58.

SAMUEL, I., 'The Dialogue of Heaven: A Reconsideration', *P.M.L.A.* lxxii (1957), 601–11.

SAURAT, D., 'Milton and the Zohar', *S.P.* xix (1922), 136–49.

—— *Milton, Man and Thinker*, rev. edn., 1944.

STEIN, A., *Answerable Style*, Minneapolis, 1953.

STOLL, E. E., 'Was Paradise Well Lost?', *P.M.L.A.* xxxiii (1918), 429–35.

SUMMERS, J. H., *The Muse's Method*, 1962.

TAYLOR, G. C., *Milton's Use of Du Bartas*, Cambridge, Massachusetts, 1934.

THOMPSON, E. N. S., 'The Theme of *Paradise Lost*', *P.M.L.A.* xxviii (1913), 106–20.

TILLYARD, E. M. W., *Milton*, 1930.

—— *The Miltonic Setting*, 1938.

—— *Studies in Milton*, 1951.

WALDOCK, A. J. A., *'Paradise Lost' and its Critics*, 1947.

WHITING, G. W., *Milton's Literary Milieu*, Chapel Hill, 1939.

WILLEY, B., *Seventeenth Century Background*, 1934.

WILLIAMS, A., 'Commentaries on Genesis as a Basis for Hexaemeral Material', *S.P.* xxxiv (1937), 191–208.

—— 'Renaissance Commentaries on Genesis and Some Elements of the Theology of *Paradise Lost*', *P.M.L.A.* lvi (1945), 253–64.

—— 'The Motivation of Satan's Rebellion in *Paradise Lost*', *S.P.* xlii (1945), 253–68.

—— *The Common Expositor*, Chapel Hill, 1948.

WILLIAMSON, G., 'The Education of Adam', *M.P.* lxi (1963), 96–109.

WOODHOUSE, A. S. P., 'Pattern in *Paradise Lost*', *U.T.Q.* xxii (1952), 109–27.

WOODHULL, M., *The Epic of 'Paradise Lost'*, New York, 1907.

INDEX AUCTORUM ET LIBRORUM

INDEX RERUM

Eden: garden of, 15, 18, 27, 28, 43, 64, 79, 81, 84, 87, 89, 103, 123-4, 150-1, 153, 168; creation of, 14; location of, 24, 29, 71, 75; allegorical meaning of, 27 n., 71, 74-77; delights of, 82, 93, 100, 148-9, 157, 174, 207, 247; over-abundance of, 248-9; associated with the Golden Age, 109, 115-18, 247.

Enkidu, 15.

Eve: creation of, 43-44, 70, 120, 124, 130, 138, 148, 169, 208, 215, 261-4; name of, 16, 169; = sense, 72, 74, 76-77, 103, 266-8; type of Mary, 100-2, 255, 285 n.; alone when tempted, 22, 24, 48, 192, 198, 273-5; seduction of, 33, 46-48, 55, 58, 61, 65, 73, 98, 101 n.; temptation and fall of, 13, 49, 57, 72, 118, 125, 131-2, 135-6, 139-40, 154, 160-1, 170-1, 177, 200-3, 209, 275-8; motives for fall, 97, 274-5; motives for tempting Adam, 50, 281-2; vision of, 140, 160-2, 254-5. (Cf. Adam and Eve.)

Expulsion, see Adam and Eve.

Fall, passim, see Adam, Eve, Lucifer, Satan.
felix culpa, 187-9, 243.
Fig-tree, 31, 45, 58, 125.
Finn, 155.
Flood, 121, 169.
Forbidden fruit, 3, 52, 73, 76, 84, 89, 97, 113, 159, 192, 201, 221, 278-9; effect of, 18, 20, 50, 85, 140, 161, 209, 275-7. (Cf. Fig-tree, Tree of knowledge.)
Forbidden tree, see Tree of knowledge.
Free will, 23, 36 n., 76-77, 92, 110-13, 153, 166, 190, 221.

Gabriel, 38, 101, 213, 238, 255.
Gilgamesh, 15, 19.
gnosis, 63, 70.
Gnosticism, 24 n., 35, 62-70, 79-80, 83, 87, 92, 113, 242.
God, passim; nature of, 22, 24-25, 30, 175, 247; benevolence of, 10, 12, 21, 23, 32, 35, 44, 62, 83-85, 89, 92, 112-13, 138, 140-1, 148, 150, 175, 183, 232; omnipotence of, 10, 12, 23, 62, 81, 112-13, 155, 175, 182, 190, 232, 237; omnipresence of, 224; omniscience of, 23, 39, 52, 83, 154, 182, 190, 221, 224, 232, 237; ways to Man, 2, 51, 139,

167, 176, 178, 185-6, 231-41; names of, 11; throne of, 29, 176, 194, 224. (Cf. Trinity.)
Golden Age, 108-9, 114-18, 120-1, 247.
Grace, 60, 110.
Grendel, 155-8, 162.
Guthlac, 145.

Hadrian, 26, 59.
haggadah, 37-38, 49, 52 n., 91, 101 n., 154, 172, 288.
halakhah, 37.
Heaven, 63, 123, 145, 147, 157, 174, 186-7, 189, 197, 199, 215, 224, 228, 231-41.
Hell, 82, 151, 157-9, 162, 166, 183, 187, 199, 215, 231-2.
Heorot, 155-8, 162.
Holy Ghost, see Trinity.
Hrothgar, 156-7.

Ialdabaoth, 64-65, 68 n., 79, 83.
Ingeld, 107, 143, 155.
Interrogation, see Adam and Eve, Serpent.
Iron Age, 121.

Judaism, 12, 26, 30-31, 34, 61.
Justice, 38, 83, 91, 175-9, 183, 185, 213, 215, 232-41, 289-90.

Kingu, 16.

Leo, Pope, 121.
Leviathan, 12.
Lucifer, 174, 187, 227; name of, 34; envy of, 88; pride of, 28, 176, 224; rebellion of, 56, 82, 87, 95, 146, 193-4, 213, 215. (Cf. Satan.)

Man, 62, 68 n., 76-77, 104, 113, 122, 125, 186; depravity of, 36, 63, 121, 141, 166; mortality of, 37-39, 60, 70, 99, 110, 123, 149, 172. (Cf. Adam, Adam and Eve.)
Manichaeism, 62-69, 79, 80, 92, 95, 98, 113, 242.
Marduk, 12.
Mary, The Virgin, 85, 173, 183. (Cf. Eve.)
Mayence, Synod of, 166.
Mercy, 35, 83, 92, 183-4, 213, 215, 232-41, 289-90.
Messiah, 28, 57, 59, 100, 108. (Cf. Christ, Trinity.)
Michael, 38, 56, 227, 291.

PRINTED IN GREAT BRITAIN
AT THE UNIVERSITY PRESS, OXFORD
BY VIVIAN RIDLER
PRINTER TO THE UNIVERSITY